Cultures and Communities: A Series of Monographs

Native Peoples

General Editor: Sally M. Weaver

E99
C6
B57

The Northern Ojibwa And The Fur Trade:

An Historical And Ecological Study

Charles A. Bishop

Holt, Rinehart and Winston of Canada, Limited

Toronto   Montreal

Foreword

The Series

The Native Peoples series is designed to provide the university level audience with scholarly materials presented in an interesting and innovative fashion. Its subject matter is the Canadian Indian, Métis and Eskimo. Its overall aim is to focus the work of authors from various disciplines on the common subject of the Canadian native. Although it emphasizes the contemporary scene, the series includes books which combine ethnohistory with ethnology, and those which present methodological or theoretical arguments illustrated with materials on the Canadian native.

Sally M. Weaver
University of Waterloo
General Editor

The Book

The social and economic life of the Ojibwa Indians has been greatly transformed during the 350 years since first contact with Europeans. This study examines in detail the successive eras of change and adaptation among the Northern Ojibwa through the extensive and critical use of archival materials. These were meshed with observations in the field to produce an ethnohistorical account of change which is unique to Subarctic research to date. The study demonstrates that Northern Ojibwa social organization has switched from a clan-totem system at contact to a flexible bilateral one today. Social and economic changes in Ojibwa culture can be directly related to the fur trade, population movements, and ecological shifts. The historical eras of change were defined by the data in accordance with new and different modes of adaptation under particular contact and ecological conditions.

The Author

Charles A. Bishop attended the University of Toronto where he obtained his B.A. and M.A. in anthropology before receiving his Ph.D. in anthropology from the State University of New York at Buffalo. Before undertaking historical and field research among the Northern Ojibwa, Dr. Bishop conducted a field study of the Six Nations Iroquois. More recently, he has been doing archival research among the Cree Indians of northern Ontario. Dr. Bishop is the author of numerous papers on Northern Algonkians. He has taught at the State University of New York at Buffalo, Florida State University, Eastern New Mexico University, and since 1970, at the State University of New York at Oswego. Dr. Bishop is married to the anthropologist, Dr. M. Estellie Smith.

Preface

Despite the relatively large amount of literature on the Ojibwa, there still exists much confusion and controversy over the exact nature of their culture, particularly as it existed at the time of earliest contacts with Europeans. The fact that a number of major textbooks dealing with North American Indians choose to ignore or treat with brevity the Ojibwa and other Subarctic groups reflects the uncertainty of authors with respect to historical issues. Kroeber's statement (1939:35-36) that the Apache and the Ojibwa are "the least-known" surviving North American groups still seems to characterize the thinking of many American anthropologists. It should be noted that Kroeber, at the time of publication of his *Cultural and Natural Areas of North America*, added a footnote to the effect that the Apache were no longer the least known and by implication this left the Ojibwa.

One reason why the Ojibwa have been ignored in many texts is that field studies by professionally trained anthropologists are relatively recent. Most research has been conducted since the 1930's, long after groups on the Plains or in the Southwestern United States had been studied by Franz Boas and his students. Although the reasons for this omission during the early twentieth century are not clear, it may have been perceived that it was less urgent to study Subarctic peoples than those undergoing more rapid and complete acculturation. The seeming isolation of the boreal forest appears to have been viewed as "protecting" Subarctic Indians from adverse outside effects. Hallowell's studies of the 1930's lend support to this assumption when he defined his "acculturative categories". Hallowell assumed, as did other field workers at this date, that there were still remote, virtually untouched Indians in the hinterland. Had Hallowell had a better understanding of the history of the fur trade, he would not have made such an assumption. Yet we can hardly blame him since the history of the northern interior was poorly known at this date, and never received the attention as did the more southerly regions. When Landes spoke of "aboriginal" Ojibwa culture at Emo Ontario, it reinforced the view that precontact reconstructions could be attained through field work alone.

Another reason for the neglect prior to the '30's may stem from the idea that the culture of Subarctic peoples is (and was) relatively simple. Although Americanists agreed that technologically simple people could have a complex social organization (as witness the Australian aborigines), this did not appear to be the case in the Subarctic. Indeed, it was not until 1930 that Hallowell wrote that the kinship terminology of the Ojibwa reflected cross-cousin marriage, a pattern discovered by Duncan Strong among the Naskapi of Labrador only the previous year.

Finally, when data began to appear, much of it seemed contradictory and inconclusive. Arguments arose over such issues as whether family hunting territories were aboriginal or a result of the fur trade; or whether Northern Algonkians had a precontact high god concept, among others. These problem areas pointed up the necessity for further field research. Yet field studies, while adding much valuable new data on twentieth century Algonkian speakers, were still incapable of answering certain historical questions. Dunning, for example, was unable to determine whether Northern Ojibwa clans were indigenous or adopted from the Southern Ojibwa (1959a:82).

During the 1960's Harold Hickerson, in several publications, analysed historical documents pertaining to the proto historic Ojibwa and some of their descendants who migrated to Wisconsin and Minnesota. He concluded that Ojibwa social organization at the time of earliest contacts with Europeans was predicated upon a corporate patrilineal clan organization. Hickerson stressed the "collective" nature of proto historic Ojibwa culture as opposed to the "atomistic" portrait constructed by others, and showed that atomism, where it existed, was a more recent historical phenomenon. Bernard James arrived at a similar conclusion but without the aid of documentary sources.

In an attempt to offset the shortcomings of earlier works, this monograph uses both field and historical materials and thus is an ethnohistorical study. Ethnohistory is a method which aims at reconstructing former cultural patterns and the processes of change which they have undergone. The importance of early documents to problem solving is emphasized and illustrated, not at the expense of field work, but rather as a method for understanding and interpreting materials gathered in the field.

This is a study of the Northern Ojibwa from the seventeenth century when they first met Europeans, to 1967. The focus is on social and economic change stemming from their altering relationships with fur traders, missionaries, government agents and other Indian tribes; and from shifts in the environment which created new adaptive responses. Institutional metamorphoses, then, are explained historically in terms of both acculturative and ecological pressures. Thus, Ojibwa structures at any moment in time are viewed as a product of existent traditions themselves shaped by past events and the present forces operating to remould them.

Research for this study began in the summer of 1965 and has continued to the present. Historical data were obtained in the Public Archives of Canada and other repositories in Ottawa, notably the Department of Mines Library, the National Museum of Canada, and the Department of Citizenship and Immigration. The Hudson's Bay Company Library in Winnipeg and the Indian Affairs Branch offices in Sioux Lookout were visited in August 1966. In the summer of 1972, the Hudson's Bay Company Archives in London, England, provided data on the period from 1870 to 1905 which was unavailable in the Ottawa archives.

Unquestionably the most valuable historical materials were contained in the Hudson's Bay Company Archives. These documents give detailed continuous accounts of the Indians, the country, and the fur trade kept in the form of day-by-day post journals, district reports, account books and correspondence files. The archives pertaining to the Osnaburgh House Hudson's Bay Company trading post furnished the longest almost unbroken record dating from the founding of the post in 1786. Also of particular value were the documents of the Lac Seul post recorded in great detail between 1822 and 1853. Records kept at other nearby posts and viewed in their totality for the early period included: Cat Lake (1788-95); Sturgeon Lake (1779-80, 1829-37); and Nipigon House (1792-1802, 1827-39). Of less significance in terms of the total history, yet often containing important information, were data taken from Hudson's Bay Company documents recorded at Martin's Falls, Henley House, Gloucester House, Fort Albany, Trout Lake, Berens River, Red

Lake, Rainy Lake, Long Lake, Pic, Fort William (Thunder Bay), Lake Attawapiskat, Fort Severn, York Factory, God's Lake, Island Lake, Lake of the Woods, Michipicoten, and Mattagami (see Map 1 for place locations). Data on the Northern Ojibwa prior to the founding of Osnaburgh House can be found in the Fort Albany, Fort Severn and Henley House journals which also supply detailed information on the James Bay and Hudson Bay Cree.

In order to bring the study up to the present and to crosscheck and verify certain aspects of the historical analysis, several field trips to Northern Ojibwa communities were undertaken. Field work was conducted at Osnaburgh House from October to December, 1965, and from March to June, 1966. During early July, 1966, a ten-day visit was made to Cat Lake, while in August 1969, two weeks were spent at Ogoki.

This study begins with the present and works toward the past, a procedure known as upstreaming. The advantage of presenting an ethnographic account of the recent period is that it provides a basis for interpreting events of the past. In turn, the present situation grows increasingly intelligible as the historical events of the past unfold. As Murphy (1967:34) has stated: "History and ethnography serve each other, and both the present and the past become more understandable from their interplay". In other words, history uses the past to illuminate the present; ethnography uses the present to illuminate the past; ethnohistory uses past and present to illuminate the intricately woven Bayeaux tapestry of Man in Process.

After providing general background data on the geography and history of the Ojibwa, Chapter 2 launches into an analysis of the social and economic conditions of the contemporary Northern Ojibwa of Osnaburgh House. This is followed by an analysis of historical events which led to the present conditions, especially during the late nineteenth and early twentieth centuries. The material for this analysis includes Hudson's Bay Company records, geological surveys, initial government influence, the application of medical treatment, and changing trade and economic patterns.

Chapters 4 to 6 encompass the long time span from the 1820's to the later decades of the nineteenth century. Although in the past some ethnographers have considered the Ojibwa of this era essentially "aboriginal", it will be shown that this is not the case. The conditions of contact through the trading post, and a different ecology both from what followed and what preceded produced an adaptation in the economic arrangement of Ojibwa society which was far from the aboriginal mode. With the aid of historical materials, it is possible to document contact and bring into focus critical relationships among culture, history and environment.

In Chapters 7 and 8, I analyse in detail relations between traders and Indians with respect to general ecological conditions during the period from the 1780's to the early 1820's. The socio-economic organizations of the Ojibwa during this era were quite different from those which followed. Clues to even earlier cultural patterns are in evidence. This modified organization of the late eighteenth century was, in turn, a product of population dispersal and movement into an environment which formerly had only temporary Ojibwa inhabitants. The new arrivals carried with them many norms of collective behaviour which had characterized earlier ancestral, and likely aboriginal groups located farther to the south and east.

Chapter 9 focuses on the conditions which produced permanent groupings in the north and the distribution of such groups. Information on this early contact period from the seventeenth century to the 1770's involving migration and dispersal is by no means as complete as one might hope. Yet, I believe that there is sufficient data, direct and inferential, to warrant conclusive statements.

Chapter 10 comprises summary and conclusions. Here, the loose ends are tied together, and the major theoretical issue of aboriginal Ojibwa social organization discussed.

Charles A. Bishop

Acknowledgements

This study could not have been produced without the help of others. I am especially indebted to the personnel of the Hudson's Bay Company for permission to view their extensive microfilm records in the Public Archives of Canada and the HBC Archives in London, England. At the latter repository, Mrs. Jean Craig, the archivist, was able to locate several manuscripts which otherwise would have gone unnoticed. I wish it was possible to thank those long deceased fur traders whose daily accounts provided the basic source material for a large portion of this study. Of special significance were the documents pertaining to the Osnaburgh House and Lac Seul trading posts. The journal of Charles McKenzie of Lac Seul covering a thirty-one year span (1822-1853) can be singled out as the most outstanding account. McKenzie, an old Northwest Company trader (cf. Masson 1890 1:315-93), typified the very best of these early trader-ethnographers. Unfortunately, space will not permit a discussion of the merits of others. The significance of their insights however, becomes clear in this study.

I wish also to thank the personnel of the Public Archives of Canada in Ottawa, and the Ontario Department of Lands and Forests, Sioux Lookout Branch. I am grateful to John Owens, Superintendent of the Sioux Lookout Indian Agency, for placing valuable documents at my disposal. I remember with gratitude the friendship and cooperation of Father Rodriquez Vezina, Oblate Missionary at Osnaburgh House and later Ogoki, and Mr. and Mrs. William Thordarson who then operated the Osnaburgh House school. I am especially indebted to my Ojibwa and Cree friends, particularly Zach Brown, Jimmy Lawson, Danny Tuckesin, Levius Wesley, Sam Skunk, and Canasia Wesley of Osnaburgh, and Charles and Margaret Gray of Cat Lake.

Special thanks are due Drs. David B. Stout, William W. Stein, Erwin Johnson (Department of Anthropology, State University of New York at Buffalo), and Dr. Edward S. Rogers (Curator of the Ethnology Department, Royal Ontario Museum) for their advice and continued encouragement. To my committee chairman, Dr. Harold Hickerson, I owe much for the many hours of discussion, and for critical comments and helpful suggestions during the many months while I was preparing this manuscript. I wish also to thank Professors Richard Preston of McMaster University and James G. E. Smith of the University of Waterloo for their helpful criticisms and comments while I was preparing the manuscript for publication.

Finally, I owe an immeasurable debt to my wife, Dr. M. Estellie Smith, for her unrelenting encouragement and assistance.

The research on which this study was based was financed by research grants from the National Museums of Canada for the summers of 1966, 1968, 1969, 1970, 1972, and a New York Regent Fellowship (1965-66). I also received grant-in-aid monies from the State University of New York in 1971 and 1972.

Contents

*Truth isn't in accounts but
in account books . . . The
real history is written in
forms not meant as history.*

Chapter One
Introduction

Today, the Ojibwa Indians[1] are widely dispersed throughout the northern United States and Canada, and the particular division known as *Northern Ojibwa* reside in a number of village communities scattered throughout the southern half of northern Ontario and eastern Manitoba (see Map 1). The Osnaburgh House community, which is the focal one in this study, is located in the geographical centre of the Northern Ojibwa area and is generally representative of the region at large.

Like all Indian societies, the Ojibwa have had to adapt to the stresses introduced by traders, missionaries and government agents. Present-day communities like Osnaburgh are a more recent historical development intimately related to the intrusion of the White Man and the history of the fur trade. It was the fur trade, introduced first by the French and later the English Hudson's Bay Company, that precipitated population movements, competition over game resources, and even warfare during the early centuries of contact. Within the past century, change processes have taken new directions with the intervention of missionaries and agents of the Canadian government. This study describes and discusses these social and economic changes in Northern Ojibwa society from the seventeenth century to the present, and is particularly relevant to a fuller understanding of contemporary Indian life and how it came to be.

Although Northern Ojibwa institutions today are very different from those of pre-contact or aboriginal times, they are not carbon copies of rural White ones. Rather, they are the result of an ongoing adaptive response to external pressures and the desire to maintain a sense of social and cultural identity. As we shall see, the Ojibwa have not merely been passive recipients of what the European intruders have had to offer. They were and still are selective in their borrowings. Yet they have had to adapt and modify their behaviour to satisfy new needs arising from such relationships.

1

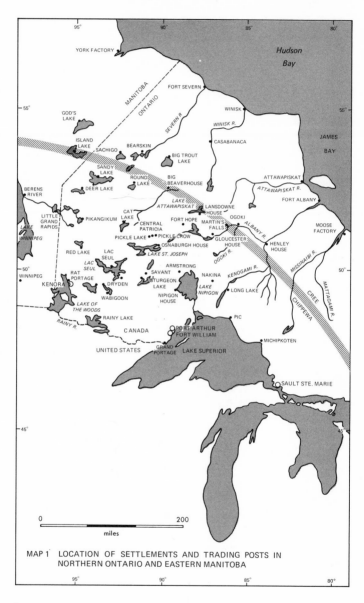

MAP 1 LOCATION OF SETTLEMENTS AND TRADING POSTS IN
NORTHERN ONTARIO AND EASTERN MANITOBA

2

Ojibwa behaviour has also had to alter in conformity with environmental changes. Like all Indians, their pre-contact institutional structures were closely adjusted to the resources upon which they depended for survival. As the environment changed and became depleted of certain key resources, the result of over-hunting or movement into a different geographical zone within the historical period, the Ojibwa were often forced to give up old patterns in order to survive. Ojibwa culture at any moment in time, then, has been the product of multiple pressures. Internal, social, and economic relations have had to adapt to the external environment, both human and natural simultaneously, and always in terms of existent norms of behaviour. Such processes of adjustment involve what anthropologists refer to as *cultural ecological* adaptations.

In order to understand and explain cultural ecological adjustment, it is necessary to examine conditions over time. A study of a group at a given moment in its history can merely provide descriptive data on social behaviour. It cannot account for the manner in which that behaviour has come to be what it is at the moment when the study is conducted.

Before outlining the general trends in Northern Ojibwa culture history, it is first necessary to place the Ojibwa themselves within a broader geographical and cultural context. The Ojibwa language is one of several belonging to the group known as Central Algonkian[2]. The other tribes in this category include: Ottawa, Potawatomi, Cree, Montagnais, Naskapi, Sauk, Fox, Kickapoo, Mascouten, Miami, Illinois, Menomini and Shawnee (see Map 2 for geographical placement). The Ojibwa speak a dialect most closely related to Ottawa and Algonquin (Hockett 1964:240). In some regions of the north today, Ojibwa and Cree are mutually intelligible where the two groups have been in close contact for some time[3].

The Ojibwa at the time of first contact with Europeans were confined to a much smaller area than at present. They resided, during the summer months, along the north shore of Lake Huron and near the east end of Lake Superior. Their Algonkian-speaking neighbours to the east included the Ottawa, Nipissings and Algonquin. To their north and northwest resided the Cree—the *Killistonons* or *Christinaux* of the early Jesuit literature—while to the south were such groups as the Potawatomi and Menomini. Other non-Algonkians inhabiting the adjacent region at contact were the Iroquoian-speaking Hurons of southern Georgian Bay, and the Siouan-speaking Dakota and Assiniboin south and west of Lake Superior. The Hurons had extensive trade relations with Ojibwa and other Algonkians to the east until their dispersal by the New York State Iroquois in 1649, while throughout most of the eighteenth and nineteenth centuries, relations between the Siouan Dakota and Ojibwa were hostile.

By the early nineteenth century, four main divisions of Ojibwa had emerged: the Southeastern Ojibwa, the Southwestern Ojibwa (Chippewa), the Plains Ojibwa (sometimes called Bungi), and the Northern Ojibwa. The four divisions, today occupying an immense area stretching from southern Ontario to eastern Saskatchewan, are the result of an historic process that began in the mid-seventeenth century involving trade, conquest and migration (see Map 3). Ecological and historical factors in each division resulted in variant forms of cultural adaptation. The Plains Ojibwa or Bungi, who vacated the more easterly forests for the prairies of Manitoba at the end of the eighteenth century (Mandelbaum 1940; Hickerson 1956; Howard 1965), adopted many features of Plains tribes such as a bison hunting economy and the Sun Dance. The still inadequately known Southeastern Ojibwa who occupied the lower Michigan peninsula and parts of southern Ontario following the termination of the Iroquois wars (Kinietz 1965:319) took up farming and maple sugar harvesting (Quimby 1962:222, 228). Those groups who came to be designated the Southwestern Chippewa (Hickerson 1962a) gradually pushed into Wisconsin and Minnesota via the south shore of Lake Superior at the expense of their enemies, the Dakota. Their descendants occupy reservations in that area today.

Although there seems to be general agreement on the approximate boundaries of the Ojibwa in eastern, southeastern, and southwestern regions, their occupation of the area north and northwest of Lake Superior, however, has been a controversial subject among recent scholars. The southern extension of the Cree from Hudson Bay, and the eastern extension of the Assiniboin in Ontario at contact is contingent upon the interpretation of the Ojibwa distribution[4]. Some scholars believe that the prehistoric Ojibwa occupied the same general area in northern

4

Ontario as at present, while others have provided data that indicate that a major migration has taken place within the historical period. The historical evidence favours the latter interpretation. There is good evidence, as we shall see, that the Cree occupied most of northern Ontario north and west of Lake Superior during the late seventeenth and early eighteenth centuries. The Assiniboin, at contact, appear to have lived in the region west of Lake Superior from the mouth of the Kamanistiquia River north and west to Lac Seul and Lake of the Woods and beyond (see Map 2). Much of the region inhabited by both Cree and Assiniboin during the late seventeenth century came to be occupied by the westward advancing Ojibwa (see Map 3). It is suggested here, then, that the pre-contact Ojibwa resided little further north and west than the Michipicoten Bay area on the northeast shore of Lake Superior. There are ecological grounds for such a view in addition to the historical evidence. The Michipicoten Bay region is the northern terminus of the mixed deciduous and coniferous forest (see Map 3). South and east of this environmental boundary floral and faunal resources are more varied and numerous. For example, the Virginia deer is very rare to the north of this region but fairly common to the south of it. Also, moose and caribou seem to have existed in sizable numbers near the north shore of Lakes Huron and Superior where the early contact Ojibwa lived. No less than 2,400 moose were killed on Manitoulin Island during the winter of 1670-71 suggesting that the general area was very rich in large game animals (Blair 1911 1:221). The early records indicate that the fisheries of this region, especially those near Sault Ste. Marie, were extremely productive and capable of supplying great quantities of food from May through October. All this evidence suggesting a bountiful food supply near the north shore of Lake Huron and at the east end of Lake Superior lends support to the view that the Ojibwa would have had no need to make extensive migrations either to the north or northwest of Lake Superior into Cree territory in aboriginal times. This, of course, does not mean that occasional excursions into the interior, or perhaps even to the coast of Hudson Bay, did not occur. Indeed they probably did. However, all the evidence suggests that the Ojibwa at contact occupied an area from the east end of Georgian Bay on Lake Huron to Michipicoten Bay on the northeast shore of Lake Superior. It should be clear then, that according to this interpre-

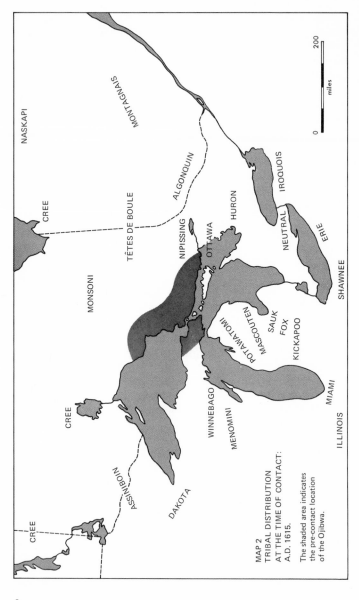

MAP 2
TRIBAL DISTRIBUTION
AT THE TIME OF CONTACT:
A.D. 1615.

The shaded area indicates
the pre-contact location
of the Ojibwa.

NASKAPI

CREE

MONTAGNAIS

ALGONQUIN

TÊTES DE BOULE

MONSONI

CREE

NIPISSING

OTTAWA

HURON

IROQUOIS

NEUTRAL

ERIE

SHAWNEE

POTAWATOMI

MASCOUTEN

SAUK

FOX

KICKAPOO

MIAMI

ILLINOIS

WINNEBAGO

MENOMINI

CREE

ASSINIBOIN

DAKOTA

0   200
miles

6

tation, there were no peoples who could be specifically categorized as "Northern" Ojibwa prior to the arrival of the White Man. The pre-contact geographical parameters outlined here, as we shall see, have important implications for reconstructing aboriginal social organization. It has thus been necessary to go into more detail than is usually required to define them. Data documenting the expansion of Ojibwa north and west of Lake Superior are presented in Chapter 9.

In order to orient the reader, the general trends of culture change are outlined next. However, where the chapters in the text are arranged so that the modern situation is presented first, followed by materials that cover increasingly earlier eras, here we "downstream" from the contact era to the present.

1) Late Prehistoric-Earliest Contact Era (?-1660's)

During this time the Ojibwa occupied the region extending from Michipicoten Bay in the northwest south along the north shore of Lake Huron and also including a tiny portion of northern Michigan. The food resources of the area were relatively abundant and included moose, Virginia deer, Woodland caribou and beaver. Fish of several species were especially bountiful at certain locations, the most famous of which was in the St. Mary's River near Sault Ste. Marie. Although a wide variety of vegetable products were exploited, horticulture—if it existed at all—was of minimal importance. In sum, the Ojibwa of these early times had a rich and varied economy which permitted a semi-sedentary life. During the warmer months of the year, they resided in villages ranging in size from 100 to 300 persons. All totalled, there seem to have been about twenty or more such villages or groupings, suggesting an aboriginal population of perhaps 4,500 persons. These groupings were usually given animal names which to some scholars indicate the existence of clans—in this case patrilineal descent groups with corporate (group) functions[5]. This meant that membership in an animal-named (totemic) group was determined through males. Since it was taboo to marry a member of the same totem group, wives were obtained from neighbouring clan villages. Such groups, it is argued (Hickerson 1962a, 1966, 1970) communally exploited hunting and fishing zones sharing the results of their efforts. To other scholars (Rogers 1963b), the mention of animal named groups in the early historical literature does not necessarily mean that these were descent groups. Rather, they could have been simply bilateral bands of kinsmen with animal names. Even though there is little direct evidence for either position dating to this early period, materials from later times combined with a knowledge of the geographical location of the early contact Ojibwa, lend support to the first hypothesis. Certainly, there is good evidence that these seventeenth century groupings held communal ceremonials, one of which was the Feast of the Dead. During this feast, seemingly held by each group every two or three years, the bones of those who had died during the interim were interred and accompanied by a lavish distribution of foods and other commodities. There seems to be general agreement that cross-cousin marriage existed at contact, a practice which would extend the bonds of kinship to a number of groups especially if they were patrilocal and exogamous.

2) The Era of Population Concentration (1640-1680)

The fur trade and missionary influences had probably reached the Ojibwa by 1610, first indirectly through other intermediate tribes such as the Ottawa and Huron, and by the 1620's directly through Europeans themselves. These early relationships modified somewhat their existent technology and system of trade alliances with other tribes. After 1641, large gatherings of Ojibwa and other tribal groups often numbering 1,500 souls collected near Sault Ste. Marie to exchange fur pelts and material commodities for European items. These were obtained directly from the French or from other Indians who acted as middlemen. The centripetal movement of heterogeneous Algonkian peoples stimulated by the desire for trade wares, also gave rise to more intense social life manifest in more elaborate and complex Feasts of the Dead and other activities. Actually, however, these large gatherings lasted only a few weeks in the summer so that individual group and tribal autonomy was not seriously threatened. For much of the year the Ojibwa groups continued to hunt and fish in their traditional territories.

8

3) The Era of Dispersal and Relocation (1680-1730)

It was during this era that Sault Ste. Marie ceased to be a focal point for many Ojibwa. Following the termination of the wars with the Iroquois, French traders were able to expand the fur trade west of Lakes Michigan and Superior. After 1680 (Hickerson 1962a:85) a major separation of the Ojibwa occurred. Some groups migrated along the north shore of Lake Superior while others penetrated along the south shore. Those to the south established large tribal communities consisting of several animal-named (clan) groupings. Hickerson has argued that these multi-clan villages heralded the doom of the clan as a territorial unit and resulted in the proscription of cross-cousin marriage due to the extension of political and economic ties in these large communities (1962a:84-86). The Midewiwin ceremony itself grounded in earlier shamanistic medical practices replaced the Feast of the Dead as a primary integrating mechanism within a collective village life. To the north of Lake Superior, the Ojibwa acted as middlemen to the Cree and Assiniboin until about 1680. After this date, the newly founded Hudson's Bay Company began attracting the Indians of northern Ontario and beyond to posts on James Bay and Hudson Bay. This competition between the French near the Great Lakes and the English on the Bay grew quite intense and several of the English posts were captured and held briefly by the French at the end of the seventeenth century. The rivalry also created hostilities among the various Indian groups, especially the Cree and Ojibwa. Nevertheless, warfare on a tribal scale was non-existent in the northern forests. Although the Ojibwa, who now had to trap for themselves to obtain trade supplies, made occasional visits to the Hudson's Bay Company posts, there seems to have been no regularized trade pattern, nor was there any permanent residence of Ojibwa groups in the interior north of Lake Superior until after about 1730. The Ojibwa continued to return to sites near Lake Superior during the summer months. The groups which dispersed to the north were quite large suggesting that they were segments of earlier animal-named villages (perhaps lineages) or maybe even whole clans. They continued to maintain their identity and political autonomy.

Until 1736, the Cree and Assiniboin who were located in the area west of Lake Superior were involved in tribal warfare with the Dakota of Minnesota. However, when the Dakota massacred the French traders on Lake of the Woods, their former allies, the Ojibwa, on the pretense of revenge, pushed further west. By this date there were large groups of Indians (Assiniboin, Cree and Ojibwa) near Lake Nipigon and along the International Border west of Lake Superior where French posts had been built. The Hudson's Bay Company posts also were attracting Ojibwa who by the 1730's were beginning to settle near interior waterways; while the Cree and Assiniboin retreated north and west. After the French influence waned during the 1750's, large bands of Ojibwa made regular appearances at the Fort Albany HBC post until the late 1760's. Beginning about 1765, however, traders from Montreal (both Scots and French) infiltrated the region north of Lake Superior and began luring the Ojibwa to their camps. In order to effectively compete, the Hudson's Bay Company was forced to move inland and construct posts in the very area now occupied by the Northern Ojibwa. By the 1770's, the Ojibwa had expanded to their present limits and once interior posts were established the Indian population grew more stabilized geographically. The movement of traders to scattered centres of Indian occupancy was in great measure the result of intense competition among them. The Ojibwa of the interior boreal forests no longer had to make long treks to either the shores of Lake Superior or James Bay. Although trade wares were playing an increasingly important role in their lives as segments of the aboriginal technology were replaced, they were relatively cheap and easy to acquire. Thus, trapping, while important, did not interfere with subsistence activities. The Indians of this era placed heavy dependence on moose and caribou as well as smaller forms of game. The Indian bands remained relatively large during the 1760's and 70's, numbering from twenty to over forty persons. Each band was headed by a chief or "captain" and was referred to by an animal name suggesting that it was a clan remnant. Mass migrations, a changed ecology and the fur trade were opering to disperse segments of former clans and reduce the functional significance of former clan activities.

5) The Era of Large Game Hunting Under Conditions of Competition Among Traders (1780-1821)

The year 1782 marked the founding of the Northwest Company after which rivalry with the Hudson's Bay Company in the interior grew very intense. By the mid-1780's, the upper Albany River drainage region was dotted with numerous competing trading posts. Among the more important Hudson's Bay Company posts established at this time were Osnaburgh House, Martin's Falls, Nipigon House, and Lac Seul. Competition ensured Indians of large quantities of cheap goods which were growing increasingly significant to their survival. However, prior to 1800, both furs and game were plentiful and Indians could obtain enough pelts to supply their trade needs with ease. They, hence, devoted much time to travel between competing stores to obtain extra credit. Only when climatic factors were unfavorable did they suffer from starvation. Clan-named hunting groups numbering about 25 to 30 individuals or more exploited group-owned areas. These large cohesive groups continued to be led by chiefs who inherited their position patrilineally and through primogeniture. These men may have been charged with allocating areas for group members to exploit. Until 1800, at least, they received trade goods on behalf of their band. Group cohesiveness, although modified under the new conditions, was also exhibited in a unified aggressiveness toward traders and other Indian groups, and in the Feast of the Dead ceremony uniting clan-mates upon the death of a leader.

After 1810, a number of changes occurred which gradually led to conditions in the following era. I have called this the period of transition. Its significance to understanding the Ojibwa of later times is paramount. As early as 1805, beaver began to grow scarce in some areas since no conservation measures existed to protect them. By 1821, this deficiency had become widespread throughout the north, and for nearly three decades Indians were forced to rely mainly on substitutes, particularly marten and muskrat, to supply their trade wants. Cervines, which had been the primary support of the large Ojibwa hunting groups, grew scarce in the area south of Osnaburgh by the early 1810's. By the 1820's moose had been totally exterminated, while caribou had grown extremely rare. Following this decimation, Indians were forced to pursue small game, fish and hare, to offset the growing threat of starvation. This meant a great loss of pride to males who had to set snares and fish lines, formerly considered women's work. This change also intensified the reliance of Indians on the trading post, since they now had no trade for moosehide for shoes and snowshoes. European cloth and trapping equipment became increasingly significant.

The coalition of the Northwest Company and Hudson's Bay Company in 1821 ending nearly 40 years of competition, resulted in several policy changes; non-profitable posts were withdrawn; conservation practices were applied to beaver and muskrat; goods were traded directly for furs instead of being given on credit in advance; and the price of materials rose. Needless to say, these changes had a marked effect upon the Ojibwa. It was during the period from 1810 to 1829 that the basis for the "collective" organization of Ojibwa society was largely destroyed and replaced by a more individualistic (if you like, "atomistic") one. Cases of starvation grew more numerous after 1815 as game dwindled. During winter, hunting groups often splintered into family units to more effectively exploit fur and small game. Private ownership was exhibited through the staking of beaver lodges; and most hunters by 1815 were receiving credit as individuals. The withdrawal of many trading centres with cheap goods and the virtual disappearance of large game animals considerably reduced the mobility of Indians who had to rely on a single post, and who were restricted to areas where hare and fish could be found. Often these were not the best places for trapping.

6) The Era of Small Game Hunting and Dependency Upon the Trading Post (1821-1890)

By the late 1820's the transition was over. The Ojibwa by then, totally reliant upon the trading post for survival, were eking out a meagre existence. This condition obtained until late in the century. Survival was precariously balanced between trapping, the primary means of obtaining essential trade supplies, and hunting for food. The transferal of economic ties from within the winter settlement, which had formerly been characterized by sharing patterns involving trade supplies as well as food, to the trading post led to individualism in regard to property, especially fur bearers. By the 1830's, hunters and their families radiated out from central bush settlements to exploit family-possessed tracts of land.

By the mid-nineteenth century, there were six winter settlements (co-residential or hunting groups) averaging 30 individuals each in the immediate vicinity of Osnaburgh House. These groups, although often given clan names, were strictly bilateral. Both clan and hunting group exogamy compelled members to marry distant cross-cousins, if first cousins happened to reside within the same settlement. The large size of these bilateral groups increased the possibility of this occurring. (Cross-cousin marriage was only proscribed south of Lake Superior where large multi-clan villages had existed: to the north where groups had remained smaller marriages with cross-cousins continued.) Sororal polygyny, along with the sororate and levirate were practiced. Frequently a mature hunter had two or three wives (a decline, however, from the previous era when an important trade captain would have double this number). Under the altered environmental conditions members did not reside in a single settlement continuously throughout the year. As noted, families radiated out to exploit fur bearers. Frequently food shortages forced members to disperse. Again, Indians might appear at the post in family units in winter to obtain goods or food donations from traders. However, hunting group members generally travelled and resided together from late April to early autumn. Further south near Lake Superior and the international boundary where the population was somewhat denser, the basic social unit was the extended family. These Ojibwa also tended to be more individualistic than those further north.

7) The Era of Early Government Influence (1890-1945)

Although, in a sense, this too was a transitional period, I have given it separate era status. It also overlaps with the previous era. The Ojibwa continued to live for most of the year in winter bush settlements. However, toward the end of the nineteenth century, the Osnaburgh peoples were experiencing a variety of new contact agents. By the 1870's, Indians at adjacent posts to the south and west had already signed treaties with the Canadian government; while geological surveys were conducted about Lake St. Joseph shortly after. In 1905, the Osnaburgh Indians signed the treaty and a band council was elected. During the next few years reserves were granted. Missionaries had entered the area as early as 1841, but it wasn't until 1900 that the first church was erected at Osnaburgh.

Although the fur trade continued to dominate Indian life, major economic changes were occurring which made existence more secure. After 1865, it became possible to exchange pelts for small quantities of store foods, and by the 1880's, some Indian families were cultivating summer potato gardens, the result of missionary encouragement. Caribou, which may never have totally disappeared in the Osnaburgh area, grew more numerous after 1869 and provided a welcome addition to the diet. After 1895, moose returned and became very significant within a few years. By the turn of the century the variety and quantity of consumer goods was greatly augmented. New varieties of European clothing, matches, canvas tents, and canoes were made available. Some Indians were even building log shacks by 1910!

At the turn of the century there were from eight to ten exogamous bush settlements numbering from 25 to 30 persons each affiliated with the Osnaburgh post. Clan exogamy still regulated marriage although there is evidence that it was weakening. Cross-cousin marriage was still important although most marriages were with distant cousins. Due to improved living conditions following the signing of the treaty, the Osnaburgh band population (which included the Cat Lake Indians) grew slightly from perhaps 300 people in 1895 to over 450 by 1940. Polygynous marriage did not occur after about 1905.

8) The Present Era of Village Ojibwa (1945-1967)

Following World War II, the tempo of culture change and interaction with Euro-Canadian society increased. Even by 1930, white mining settlements had arisen 20 miles north of the Osna-

14

burgh post. By the 1940's Indian trappers were able to hire aeroplanes to transport them to their trapping territories, a practice which destined the use of dog teams to obsolescence. Augmenting this process was the completion of the road in 1954 bisecting the band territory from the railway to the mining communities. After 1949, regular medical service was provided; and the following summer, a school was opened. Such new occupations as commercial fishing, wage-labour in the mines, and guiding tourists supplemented earnings from trapping. Indeed, it was these new sources of earned income, along with new unearned forms (old age pensions, disability pensions, family allowance payments, treaty payments, and both temporary and permanent welfare assistance to needy families) which has led to the stabilization of the population in or near the Osnaburgh village since 1960. The relocation of the village near the road after 1960, and the introduction of permanent day school in 1962 were also significant factors in generating a permanent village population.

The present economy of the Northern Ojibwa is significantly different than it was only three decades ago. Families now live in government-built Indian Affairs houses, while a great variety of new material items such as radios, outboard motors, and automobiles are on hand. Again, the bulk of the food is now obtained from the store. Almost half (in 1965-66) the total band income is derived from unearned sources while trapping is growing increasingly residual. Socially, as yet, the Osnaburgh House community has little overall cohesion. The money economy is actually strengthening the independence of the household at the expense of the hunting group. The kinship terminology is also in a state of flux and will likely emerge as a lineal (Canadian) system within a generation, a type congruent with the increased self-sufficiency of the household and the widening of social relationships within a growing permanent village. Today, community endogamy is preferred while sanctions against intra-clan marriage have weakened. Distant cross-cousin marriages still occur and usually involve people belonging to different bush settlements. Nominal leadership is vested in the band chief and eight councillors who act mainly as liaison officers with Euro-Canadians.

It should be clear now that it was the fur trade which functioned as the catalyst for successive modifications in Northern Ojibwa economy and social organization until very recent times.

As the social life of the Ojibwa became linked to, and ultimately dependent upon, the fur trade, it produced small but cumulative adjustments in the way people related to the natural environment, to each other, and to the trading post. The manner in which these multidimensional relationships were coordinated to fulfil Indian needs is reflected in the dominant themes of the different eras. With this general sketch of Northern Ojibwa culture history in mind, we now proceed to the details of change beginning with Indian life in modern times.

Footnotes

1. Although the etymology of the word "Ojibwa" is uncertain, Jenness (1963:277) indicates that it may mean "people whose moccasins have puckered seams". Hickerson, however, suggests (1970:44) that the term is derived from Ojeejok "plus the suffix /bwa/ connoting 'voice' and referent to the Crane, hence Voice of the Crane". A variant form for Ojibwa is "Chippewa", a term more commonly applied to groups in the United States. Hallowell (1955) and Skinner (1911) generally prefer the name Saulteaux, which is derived from the camping location at the rapids at Sault Ste. Marie (cf. Blair 1911 1:109ff.). They have also been called Bungi from *punki*, meaning "a little" and referring to their practice of begging, by the traders at York Factory and Fort Severn (cf. HBC Arch B123/e/14), and near Lake Winnipeg (Dunning 1959a:3) during the eighteenth and nineteenth centuries. They were also called Nakawawuck by Andrew Graham and other traders on Hudson Bay (Williams 1969:204, 206).

2. Frank Siebert (1967:38-40), on the basis of natural history terms surviving in eastern and central Algonkian languages, states that the original home of all Algonkian-speakers was southern Ontario from whence they dispersed several millenia ago.

3. The Montagnais, or Montagnais-Naskapi, of Quebec and Labrador speak a dialect which is mutually intelligible with the Cree dialect spoken in some areas about James Bay and Hudson Bay. Although closely related to Ojibwa, the Potawatomi language is a separate entity. The Fox, Sauk, and Kickapoo also represent three linguistically close but separate

groups. The Menomini, Miami-Illinois, and Shawnee form separate language groups.

4. Rogers indicates that the Ojibwa inhabited the interior regions of northern Ontario at contact, and that the Ojibwa cultural patterns tended to transform into Cree patterns as one proceeded north (1963b:65-66; 1964a:214-19). Rogers derives his conclusion from informant testimony including genealogical information. Others (Skinner 1911:117; Hallowell 1955:114-15; Warren 1957:59; Dunning 1959a:3-4; Hickerson 1962a:196ff., 1966:4) suggest that the Ojibwa penetrated the boreal forest region of northern Ontario and eastern Manitoba in historical times. The archaeological data, although incomplete seem to conform to the latter interpretation. The area north of Lake Superior and extending westward into Manitoba contain Late Woodland (1150-1600 A.D.) sites producing Selkirk pottery which is generally attributed to the Cree. However, west of Lake Superior in northern Ontario, southern Manitoba and northern Minnesota are a number of sites which produce distinctly different ceramic wares as well as other features which set them apart from Selkirk sites (MacNeish 1958:73). These sites belong to what is known as the Blackduck (Manitoba) Focus. Most archaeologists (Wilford 1945, 1955; Vickers 1948a, 1948b; MacNeish 1958; and Hlady 1964, 1970) agree that Blackduck sites were inhabited by the proto-Assiniboin. In opposition to the Blackduck-Assiniboin hypothesis are James Wright (1963, 1965, 1968c) and Edward Evans (1961). Wright has argued that the heartland area of Blackduck sites was occupied by Ojibwa, while Evans indicates that the Cree were living in the region. Since neither Wright nor Evans has taken the trouble to thoroughly review the early historic accounts that strongly favour an Assiniboin occupancy of the area, the Algonkian hypothesis seems, at present, highly unlikely. Nevertheless, one cannot ignore the possibility that *some* Cree did indeed manufacture Blackduck wares, nor that *some* Assiniboin did produce Selkirk wares. Hlady, for one, (1964:25) suggests that the Cree-Assiniboin cultural alignment actually extended back into the prehistoric period, a hypothesis which would account for the mixture of Selkirk and Blackduck wares on several sites. It is also reasonable to assume that the petroglyphs and rock mosiacs found in the Whiteshell Forest in southwest Manitoba (Hall 1960), and the rock paintings found along rocky shores in northwest Ontario

were the work of Assiniboin. The term *Assiniboin* comes from the Cree: Assina-bwan-uk, meaning *Stone* Sioux. Jenness (1963:306) suggests that this may refer to their practice of cooking with hot stones. However, the similarity between the name of these people and the archaeological remains (petroglyphs, pictographs, and along Lake Superior, pits) in northwest Ontario and southeast Manitoba may be no mere coincidence. It is also interesting to note that James G. E. Smith has recently discovered a group of Cree at Reindeer Lake, Manitoba, known as the *Rocky Cree*. These Indians use the Cree word Assiniboin to refer to themselves. Dewdney and Kidd (1967) who have made an extensive study of Ontario rock paintings state that there is more than one art style present. They ask whether "the earlier indicate the presence of a different people from those who painted the later pictures; different, that is, culturally and possible physically?" (1967:176). They also suggest that a shift in religious attitudes may have occurred. Is it possible, then, that the earlier paintings were the work of the Assiniboin, while the later ones were composed by the early historic Ojibwa who had just entered the area? In sum, the archaeological data, while controversial, would seem to fit with our aboriginal population placement based upon the early records of the seventeenth century. There is no evidence that the Ojibwa were west of Michipicoten Bay and some distinctly contrary evidence that they were west of Lake Superior.

5. The critical question of aboriginal Ojibwa social organization is discussed more thoroughly in Chapter 10 after the reader has been thoroughly immersed in the historical data. Here, I only mention that differences in interpretation exist, although the reader should be clear as to where I stand on this issue. The geographical area inhabited by the pre-contact Ojibwa, which I have outlined, has vital significance to an understanding of their social organization since it can only be understood geographically and ecologically (and, of course, in terms of the suggestive clues in the historic literature).

Chapter Two
The Community Today

Introduction

From the seventeenth century, the history of the Ojibwa of Osnaburgh House, as well as other groups throughout the north, has
been intimately related to the history of the fur trade; and since
1900, these people have also been influenced by missionaries,
government agents, mining concerns and educational and medical
personnel. Despite their comparative isolation in the Ontario
forests, the Ojibwa of today do not manifest the culture of their
precontact forebears. Their culture has altered in the face of
changing conditions of contact and in ecology.

The changes which have occurred can be characterized in
terms of *augmentation, replacement and reinterpretation.* Augmentation refers to the process whereby certain aspects of aboriginal culture are modified to incorporate new elements; while
replacement means that native customs have been lost in favour
of Euro-Canadian ones. Reinterpretation designates the process
whereby a practice takes on a new meaning or function. The
combined effects of these three processes have led to new types of
cultural adaptations. Before turning specifically to these recent
cultural changes, it is first necessary to provide some general
background data on the region inhabited by the Osnaburgh House
Ojibwa.

Environment

Osnaburgh House is only one community of many located in the
Northern Ojibwa area (see Map 1). Although variations exist in
the environment, especially as one advances from south to north,
the mode of adaptation has been generally similar throughout the

19

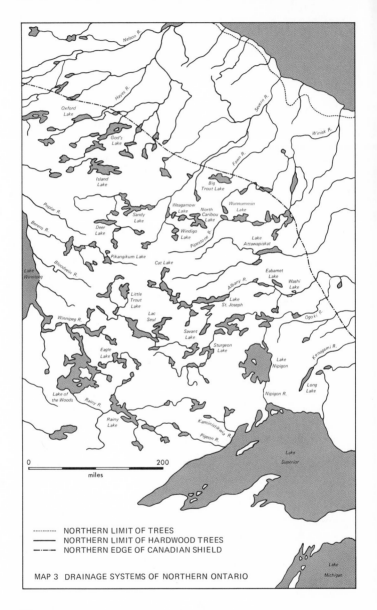

MAP 3 DRAINAGE SYSTEMS OF NORTHERN ONTARIO

---------- NORTHERN LIMIT OF TREES
—————— NORTHERN LIMIT OF HARDWOOD TREES
—·—·—·— NORTHERN EDGE OF CANADIAN SHIELD

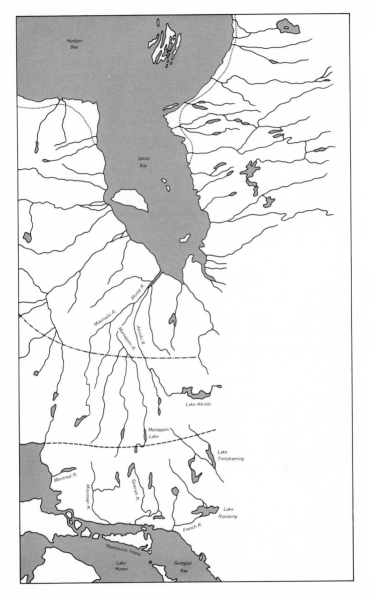

region. Similar subsistence techniques and the fur trade and other policies over three centuries have resulted in the general uniformity in community pattern which presently exists throughout northern Ontario. Most Indians in the north reside in semi-permanent lakeside villages composed of former winter hunting groups. Trapping and commercial fishing partnerships link households belonging to the same settlement, although affinal ties and friendships frequently ally men who, in the past, would have belonged to different groups. Village leadership is poorly developed and there are few activities to integrate these communities.

Today most Osnaburgh Ojibwa reside semi-permanently in, or near, a village located on the east shore of Doghole Lake two miles north of the point where Lake St. Joseph enters the Albany River (see Map 5). The roughly oval Osnaburgh House treaty band territory occupies over 12,000 square miles and is within the pre-Cambrian Shield. A gravel road which by-passes the community bisects the region from Savant on the Canadian National Railway 95 miles to the southwest, to the mixed Indian-White communities of Central Patricia and Pickle Lake 20 miles to the north. Within this area reside about 800 Indians belonging to the Osnaburgh House treaty band.

The area is rocky and flat, the elevation varying from 1,000 to 1,300 feet above sea level. Glaciation has produced a disrupted watershed with numerous lakes, streams, and swamps, most of which are drained by the Albany River system. Lake St. Joseph is the largest body of water within the area and extends from the road just south of the village in a west southwesterly direction for 70 miles to Root Portage leading to Lac Seul. Other major lakes within the region include Cat Lake 120 miles northwest of the Osnaburgh village, and Lake Savant 60 miles due south. A height of land 35 miles north of Osnaburgh separates the Albany drainage system from the Otoskwin River and its tributaries which reach James Bay via the Attawapiskat River. The Pipestone River forms the northwest boundary, while the Canadian National Railway forms the southern boundary. The band territory extends to the east of the village for about 50 miles.

The mean daily January temperature at Rat Rapids located two miles south of the village is -7°F, while the mean daily July temperature is 65°F[1]. By early November most lakes are frozen solid enough to walk upon. The ground remains snow-covered from early November to mid-May, and in midwinter the snow reaches a depth of about three feet. The spring breakup usually occurs in mid-May. From 25 to 30 inches of precipitation fall annually, half of which comes between June and September.

The region about Osnaburgh is typical of most of northern Ontario in that it is enshrouded in a dense coniferous forest, the most common tree being the black spruce. Other conifers include: jack pine, cedar, and balsam. Deciduous trees include: white poplar, mountain ash, and tamarac. In areas swept by forest fires, bushes, alders and poplar spring up.

Large animals include moose, caribou, and bear. Moose seem to have been common throughout northwestern Ontario until the early nineteenth century at which time they disappeared, apparently due to overhunting, only to reappear again about 1900 in the vicinity of Osnaburgh. Caribou have fluctuated in numbers over the last two centuries. From about 1820 until 1870 they seem to have been very scarce. In recent years they have again grown scarce and exist only in a few locations.

Of the smaller animals, the snowshoe hare is the most important to the Indian diet. Animals important to the fur trade include: beaver, muskrat, mink, otter, lynx, marten, fisher, ermine, squirrel, and black bear.

The most important birds in the subsistence are: Canada goose, mallard, spruce grouse, ruffed grouse, sharptailed grouse, and loon. Fish are of importance to Indian economy both as a food and as a means of obtaining cash. Walleye, whitefish, and northern pike are sold commercially. Sturgeon are of high commercial value but few are obtained and they are restricted mainly to certain areas in the Albany River.

Changing Economics

Increased contact with the outside world and a greater quantity and variety of material resources have led to alterations in the economic arrangements of Northern Ojibwa society. At least since the early nineteenth century the Osnaburgh Ojibwa have been integrated into and dependent upon the market system of exchange for some of their needs. Nevertheless, until compara-

23

tively recently these people were only marginal to the total economic system of the Western world. With the introduction of food as a regular trade item toward the end of the last century, the incorporation became more complete. In recent years the introduction of wage labour, government assistance, and educational facilities has further altered the picture. However, this transition in process is not coming to exactly duplicate the Euro-Canadian situation, nor will it in the near future. Although the market is coming to play a larger role than formerly, the economic growth has been hindered by a lack of opportunity, education and/or motivation. Within the past decade growth has been mainly the result of government help while the pseudo-traditional values have remained. The Ojibwa are indeed interested in improving their economic position in accordance with White standards but the means to accomplish this end have proved unsatisfactory. The Ojibwa value system is also quite different from that of the Whites. For example, most forms of wage labour have taken men away from the community and their families into unfamiliar surroundings, while the new institution of school has conflicted with trapping pursuits and bush life. Although Indians in general prefer the easier life in the village and accept its advantages, they have not accepted the means of achieving a stable economic arrangement through production. A lack of understanding of White intentions, the language barrier, and a limited cultural basis for cooperative efforts have been largely responsible for the conflicts.

There are two sources of food for Osnaburgh Indians: those obtained through subsistence pursuits, hunting and fishing; and those obtained from the store. Within the past decade the latter have increased markedly in proportion to the former.

Native Foods

Of the native foods, the moose is the most important and most sought after. Usually about 100 are killed annually. Most of these are killed in the fall or late winter by men on their trapping territories. A few moose are also taken by men at the summer fish camps on Lake St. Joseph. High-powered rifles and 22's are the chief weapons used, although two hunters have employed large

24

snares made of telephone wire within the last few years. A great deal of prestige is accorded a good moose hunter, and to be considered such is a mark of manliness and leadership. When a moose made its appearance on the screen during the showing of a movie in the village, a series of "oohs" and "ahs" accompanied by mild laughter resounded throughout the room. There can be no question that the moose is the king of beasts to the Osnaburgh people. The beaver, although of economic importance, is a distant second.

Table 1 Big Game Killed in the Osnaburgh Vicinity[2]

Year*	Moose	Caribou
1956-57	109	31
1957-58	128	16
1958-59	87	7
1959-60	95	?
1965-66	97	7

*Figures are only given for years when records were reasonably complete (see footnote 2).

The other large member of the deer family, the caribou, is very rare and found only to the north of Osnaburgh. During 1965-66, only eight were killed, but until thirty years ago, they were relatively common and could be found as far south as Lake Savant.

The proportion of large game in the diet depends upon the season of the year, upon the efforts of individual hunters, and upon kinship ties. There are several men who are noted for their hunting ability and who provide the bulk of the meat. Other men who rarely go moose hunting can receive meat as a gift from a hunter who is a close relative, or by purchase. The going rate is one dollar for about five to ten pounds of meat. Moose meat is also frequently exchanged for store foods such as bread, flour, sugar, or potatoes. A moose brought to the village is rapidly distributed, and the hunter and his family rarely retain more than a quarter of the animal. Nevertheless, this is sufficient for a good feast since the hind quarter of a moose will feed a family of six for nearly a week.

Small game includes a great variety of animals of which the

varying (snowshoe) hare is considered to be the most important. Since more time is spent in the village during the winter months than formerly, fewer are now taken. Still, it is common to see the ladies heading for the bush to check their snares, since this task and the preparation of the meat and hide are still considered to be mainly women's work. It is customary for women, and some men, to set a chain of 20 to 30 wire snares within a few miles of the camp which are checked every day or two.

During the fall and spring the meat of some fur animals is eaten, especially the beaver. Other small game animals of lesser importance in the diet include muskrat, squirrel, otter, lynx, marten, mink, and fisher. Within the last decade many of these animals have declined in importance and some are only rarely eaten.

Birds eaten include: geese, ducks, grouse, loons, pelicans, and occasionally smaller types. Of these, waterfowl, ducks and geese are the most important. The most common duck is the mallard. Waterfowl are obtained mainly in the fall and spring. During April and early May they are especially abundant and easy to kill since they are restricted to relatively small areas of open water. They are dispatched with twelve-gauge shotguns by hunters who frequently build blinds of spruce boughs at the mouths of streams. Sometimes they are taken in marshy wooded areas when the weather is somewhat warmer. No decoys are used. Waterfowl are usually consumed immediately by people at the spring bush camps although they are sometimes sold to Indians who remain behind in the village. A large Canada goose brought five dollars during the spring of 1966, while ducks sold for one dollar each. Although the spring waterfowl hunt is restricted to about three weeks, it is anticipated eagerly.

Table 2 Waterfowl Taken in the Osnaburgh Vicinity[3]

Year	Ducks	Canada Geese	Snows and Blues
1956-57	985	75	11
1957-58	1693	299	66
1958-59	1014	129	16
1959-60	1254	240	10
1964-65	621	64	4
1965-66	1109	219	9

Table 3 Waterfowl Taken in the Osnaburgh Vicinity by Season: 1965-66[4]

Season	Ducks	Canada Geese	Snows and Blues
Autumn	301	8	—
Spring	808	211	9

Another bird, the grouse (of which there are three species) is hunted throughout the year. When guns are used, sometimes it is possible to kill several birds in a single tree. The hunter will shoot the lowermost first so that when it falls it doesn't disturb those above, and proceed upwards. Another method is to use a small wire snare attached to the end of a pole. The hunter cautiously slips the noose over the bird's head and gives a sudden jerk snapping the unfortunate creature's neck. Usually about 300 to 500 of these "chickens" (the English term used by the Ojibwa) are killed annually.

Fish are a basic item in the diet of most Osnaburgh Indians, especially during the summer and early fall. The most important fish include the walleye, whitefish, pike, sucker, and sturgeon. The bulk of the fish are taken in gill nets set in the open water or through the ice[5]. Gill nets are obtained from the store or from the commercial fishermen, or are made by women, and vary in length from about 25 to 100 yards. During the summer, great quantities of fish are taken at the fish camps. Although the bulk are sold to the commercial fishermen, many are eaten directly or are preserved by smoking. In the early fall when whitefish begin to spawn, large quantities are preserved for winter use. Since the new village is not situated near good fishing spots, winter fishing for food has declined in importance. Again, fewer families fish commercially in winter than summer. Hence fish as an important element in the diet is restricted to those who fish commercially in winter, and to those who live more or less permanently at the camps on Lake St. Joseph.

The collecting of wild fruits and plants is more important to medicinal practices than to dietary requirements. The most important vegetable product collected is wild rice, most of which is sold commercially. Very little wild rice is consumed by Osnaburgh Indians today because of its high commercial value. Of less significance as food is a variety of wild berries and fruits, gathered during the summer months by women.

At present there are no gardens in the new Osnaburgh village. During the 1950's only two families cultivated small plots in the old village on the shore of Lake St. Joseph. In the past the Indian Affairs Branch encouraged gardening by supplying seed potatoes and other seeds, but the results were meagre. Since about 1940, after commercial fishing began and a variety of other types of wage labour became available, gardening declined in importance and disappeared completely with the move to the new village after 1960. The soil in the vicinity of the new village is extremely poor and would require much effort to be of use.

Native food is preserved by either smoke drying or, in winter, freezing. The preservation and preparation of foods is considered to be women's work. Boiling, roasting, and in recent years, frying are the chief means of preparation. Men are usually served first and often the sexes eat apart.

Store Foods and Changing Consumption Patterns

Today, by far the largest proportion of food consumed by Osnaburgh Indians comes from the store. There are three stores within two miles of the village, two operated by free traders and the Hudson's Bay Company store. Of these, the greatest quantity of foods is procured at the latter. Some Indians who trap north of Osnaburgh obtain foods at Pickle Lake, and some who reside on Lake St. Jospeh obtain food at the store at Slate Falls. Flour, sugar, potatoes, lard, rolled oats, bologna, candy and bread are staples in the diet. A favorite food is bannock made from flour and fried in grease. To make it more appetizing, jam or sugar is added later. The basic drink is tea boiled in a pot. However, if one is in the store, the occasion calls for a bottle of pop and a cigarette (both men and women are addicted to the weed), for a store visit is a highly social event. The men will cluster in one corner or around the entrance to discuss events, while the women browse for their needs.

Dietary changes have occurred concomitantly with the changed relationship of the Indians to the government and other institutions. A number of Indians remarked that it was now

Table 4 Major Foods Sold at the Osnaburgh Hudson's Bay
         Store: 1965

Item	Quantity	Unit
Flour	43,000	lbs
Sugar	22,000	lbs
Potatoes	8,000	lbs
Assorted Candy	6,000	lbs
Lard	6,000	lbs
Rolled Oats	6,000	lbs
Bologna	4,000	lbs
Wieners	1,500	lbs
Tea	1,500	lbs
Bacon	1,500	lbs
Butter	750	lbs
Powder Biscuits	700	lbs
Baking Powder	500	lbs
Macaroni	500	lbs
Salt	280	lbs
Beans	150	lbs
Canned Milk	5,000	tins
Canned Meats	2,000	tins
Pork & Beans	1,000	tins
Canned Fruit	450	tins
Soup Mixes	900	pkts
Kraft Dinners	500	pkts
Pablum	225	pkts
Eggs	600	doz
Bread	6,000	lvs

impossible for them to survive in the bush without store foods. A
man who leaves his family in the village while away at the bush
camps must provide food for his wife and children in his absence.
In former times when families resided in the bush, women set
hare snares and fish nets. They also prepared the meat and pelts
of fur bearers and cervines (moose and caribou) procured by
hunters. Trappers today have little time to devote directly to
food production and must transport most of their foods from the
store to the camps. Again the duration of time actually spent in

the bush has diminished markedly, increasing the dependence on store foods.

The proportion of food sales to the total sales in dollars at the Hudson's Bay post has increased by 10 percent within the last decade. Whereas in 1965, 61 percent of the total sales at the Osnaburgh House Hudson's Bay Company store was spent on food, a decade earlier food constituted only about 50 percent of the total sales. Although the total sales have fluctuated, the actual amount spent on food has steadily increased. During 1965, Osnaburgh Indians living on or near the Reserve spent approximately $100,000 on food, $60,390 of it coming from the HBC store. More than three-quarters of all the food consumed today comes from the store and no family is capable of surviving on native foods alone.

Table 5 Food Sales and Percentages at the Osnaburgh Hudson's Bay Store

Year	Total Sales	Amount Spent on Food	% Food Sales to Total
1962	$63,000.	$35,154.	55.8
1963	56,500.	37,968.	67.2
1964	71,500.	44,902.	62.8
1965	99,000.	60,390.	61.0

Trapping

Although trapping still provides a major source of income for Osnaburgh Indians, it is no longer the most important source. Opportunities for other types of employment, compulsory education for children, improved housing and health conditions, and government subsidies have within recent years altered the importance of trapping from a basic subsistence technique to an increasingly peripheral one.

The decline of trapping as a major economic source of livelihood for Subarctic peoples is well documented in the anthropological literature (cf. Dunning 1959a; McGee 1961; Rogers 1963; VanStone 1965). Although some Indians talk of bush life in ideal terms, they usually do so to contrast it with the conflicts in personal relations and the depressing atmosphere of the village. Few, if any, would admit that village life is more difficult in regard to economic security. Bush life today entails hardships not encountered in the past. With the relocation of the village and the advent of permanent day school in 1962, it has been customary for women and children to remain in the village while trappers go to the bush camps alone. In the past when the whole family lived together at the trapping camp women and children were of great economic assistance. In addition to other chores, they could set and make hare snares, and fish nets; prepare hides for moccasins and snowshoes, and fur pelts for sale; cut wood; and cook and prepare the meat they or the men procured. Today a trapper must do all these things himself upon returning from his trap lines to an empty lonely cabin (cf. VanStone 1965:20). Since much time is now lost by trappers who must perform many of these duties, the duration of time spent at camps has decreased to a few weeks in the late fall and early spring. Many trappers who do not have women to assist them do not take time to hunt for food, and must take greater quantities of store foods to the bush, while the women and children in the village must be fed also. Again, the price of furs has remained relatively constant within the last decade while the cost of living has steadily risen. New types of employment and increased government assistance have made trapping a less desirable occupation. McGee (1961:56-57) has noted a similar pattern for the Montagnais of Northwest River, Labrador where, as at Osnaburgh, people have found means of gaining credit at the Hudson's Bay store other than trapping. School children show little enthusiasm for bush life and are much less knowledgeable about it. Some trapping territories are now overcrowded while others are not trapped at all, especially those at great distances from the village. Again many men are reluctant to leave their wives alone in the village fearing sexual promiscuity in their absence.

After 1947, the Department of Lands and Forests of Ontario took over the responsibility of supervising trapping activities. At that time registered trap lines were established and trappers were required to purchase licenses annually at five dollars. Game quotas were set, and the tagging of furs became mandatory. Each year at treaty time a Lands and Forests official gathers data of fur and game catches. The Indians show resentment of these persons who, it is felt, interfere with the possessory rights of the Indians. Hence, the boundaries of the registered trap lines are frequently ignored, and trappers report fewer animals than they actually take. Complete data on game other than furs is not to be obtained.

The combined Osnaburgh-Pickle Lake area trapped by members of the Osnaburgh band is extensive, covering 12,000 square miles, while the average trapping territory is 235 square miles[6]. From one to eight men occupy a territory. Of a total of 145 men possessing trapping rights in this area, only 78 obtained pelts during the 1964-65 season. From an examination of individual fur returns it is evident that nearly two-thirds of those who obtained furs put little effort into trapping. As noted, many of the less accessible trapping territories are no longer used. Of 48 trapping territories possessed by Osnaburgh band members about 20 were unoccupied during the 1965-66 season.

The length of time spent trapping varies greatly. Some men, particularly those who live more or less permanently on Lake St. Joseph, spend most of the season trapping. A few villagers devote more than a few weeks to trapping activities in the fall and again in the early spring. Today at Osnaburgh, as at Round Lake (cf. Rogers 1963b:76), many men operate directly from their village homes. It appears that those trappers who do exploit territories more remote from the village earn more and devote more time to trapping (cf. Honigmann 1962:121).

Trapping territories modified according to trappers' requests, have less significance than formerly. Although many men trap within the confines of their territories, there is an increasing tendency to ignore boundaries, especially in cases where adjacent territories are not occupied. Also, it is not considered a crime to trap on another's territory if only a few furs are taken. Usually a man will ask permission first and this is rarely refused. Some trappers charge a visitor one dollar for each beaver, otter or mink obtained from the territory, or the visiting trapper may merely give the owner a small proportion of his catch. Requests to trap on another's territory are usually based on the greater accessibility of the territory to transportation lines. Since men are reluctant to trap alone on their own territory, it has become customary to trap with relatives elsewhere. The result is that there are now several camps consisting of a number of related men some of whom actually have more distant lands which they no longer exploit. Also, some territories have been subdivided into smaller sections. It is not land itself which is of value, but rather the rights to the resources. Since these resources have dwindled in economic importance for most village Indians, territorial boundaries have less meaning than in the past. Many villagers either set up camp along the road, or set traps or snares within walking distance of the village ignoring old boundaries. Those Indians who reside on Lake St. Joseph, however, have more precise definitions of boundaries and trespass rules.

The two most important periods for trapping are from mid-October to mid-December and from late March until late May. Very little trapping is done from Christmas until late March due to the intense cold and greater hardships in the bush. Today, more men participate in the spring hunt than in the fall hunt. Conditions in April and early May are somewhat easier and entire families may live together at this time. Spring trapping camps are generally larger.

Trapping activities, if conducted for an entire season, either in fall or spring, require a great amount of preparation and equipment. The expense to outfit a trapping expedition today is much greater than formerly. This has discouraged some men who complain that they cannot afford to support their families in the village while they live in the bush. Basic equipment to outfit trapping expeditions now includes such items as matches, sleeping bags, outboard motors, power saws, transistor radios and large quantities of foods in addition to hunting and trapping requirements (see Table 6 for an inventory of goods required to outfit two trappers). By contrast, prior to 1900, store equipment for a trapping camp consisted of only the following items: clothing, blankets, axes, knives, rifles, cooking pots, traps, twine and files. Small quantities of food, mainly flour, sugar and tea were all that were required until about 1920 when demands for store food increased.

Travel to and from more distant camps is by aeroplane and those who use this method spend more time trapping. Actually within the last decade the aeroplane as a means of conveying people to their winter camps had declined. This has been due mainly to the decreased time spent in the bush which doesn't

Table 6 Fall Trapping Outfit for Two Trappers

Item	Quantity	Item	Quantity
axe—2/camp	10	travel:	
power saw	1	toboggan	2
stove—1/camp	5	sleigh	2
hunting knife	2	snowshoes	4 pair
file—2/camp	10	canoe—18'	2
nails ½" (for pelts)	1 lb	canoe—16'	2
nails 2" (repairs)	4 lbs	outboard—7 HP	1
ambroid (repairs)	1 pkt	outboard—3 HP	1
matches—wooden	12 boxes		
roofing paper	1 roll	clothing:	
cooking utensils		high rubber boots	2 pair
high-powered rifle	2	socks	sev. pr.
high-powered shells	2 boxes	shirts	sev. pr.
22 rifle	2	pants	sev. pr.
22 shells	6 boxes	mitts	4 pair
shotgun	1	parka	2
shotgun shells	2 boxes		
gasoline	40 gal.	food:	
playing cards	1 deck	flour	100 lbs
cribbage board	1	sugar	50 lbs
transistor radio	1	lard	30 lbs
snare wire	4 rolls	rolled oats	20 lbs
brass wire (hare)	10 rolls	rice	10 lbs
twine	2 rolls	jam	8 lbs
traps # 1	60	raisins	5 lbs
traps # 3	30	macaroni	5 lbs
traps # 4	10	butter	4 lbs
sleeping bag or		corn syrup	4 lbs
blanket	2	dry apples	3 lbs
mattress	4	coffee	2 lbs
		canned milk	
		(48 cans)	1 case
		peanut butter	2 jars
		snuff	12 boxes
		tobacco	8 pouches

merit the expense, and to the movement of many camps to locations accessible by car. It usually costs about $50 to transport a family and their equipment to a camp by plane. Today there are only two men who have dog teams, both of whom live permanently on Lake St. Joseph. Dog teams must be fed which means setting nets for fish and few men in the trapping camps wish to spend the extra time and effort to do this.

While at the trapping camp the chief means of travel is by snowshoe. It is usual for men to work in twos and threes, and as one Lake St. Joseph Indian indicated, men who trap together can stay away from the main camp longer and obtain more furs. These main camps are the focal points from which male members of winter settlements radiate to exploit the surrounding territory. Basic equipment while on the trail includes a packsack with food and matches, an axe, a rifle, and traps and snares. Often goods are transported by sled or toboggan. Although men may trap together, they set their traps separately, and each claims only those animals caught with his own devices. Beaver lodges are considered to be the property of the individual; however, foods and equipment are frequently shared. In most cases trapping partners are close relatives. If the trappers plan on staying away overnight, a canvas tent is taken. However, sometimes a simple lean-to of branches and spruce boughs suffices. Traps are usually checked every three to five days. It is explained that traps should not be checked too often since an animal would avoid the location until the human smell grew old.

The most important fur animal is the beaver which is sought in the autumn and early spring. Government regulations regarding beaver are more strict, in that quotas are set which are based upon the number of beaver lodges on trapping territories. Since few men today actually reach the quota registered on their license, it frequently happens that more avid trappers borrow the licenses of others when they reach their own quota. Licenses rather than seals are traded as among the Snowdrift Chipewyan (VanStone 1965:18). The borrower usually gives the lender a small proportion of his catch, or some groceries in exchange for allowing him to register beaver on his license. This practice has tended to distort the figures on individual fur returns.

Views held on the conservation of beaver vary. Some men said that two beaver should be left in each house, while others said that since the animals were given to them by God whenever they were needed, conservation methods were unnecessary. Some said that since the animals moved around, the killing of them all didn't affect game numbers in a territory. Steel traps and wire snares introduced about 30 years ago, are the chief means of acquiring beaver.

Next in economic importance to beaver are mink obtained mainly in the early winter by steel traps (#1½) baited with fish heads and set near small open streams. Marten, fisher and lynx are also captured in a similar fashion in the early winter, although the location of traps is on higher ground. In 1965-66, lynx brought the highest price of any fur bearer but few were obtained. Until 30 years ago lynx were hunted with dogs, a practice that extends back at least to the 1830's. Deadfalls and pen enclosures are only rarely used to catch mink, marten, and fisher today, although these were the chief devices used until late in the nineteenth century. Otter and muskrat rank next to beaver and mink in economic importance. The former are trapped, snared or shot in the fall and spring. One man said that otter were occasionally captured in nets placed in the water near an overhanging bank. Similar nets have been employed to catch beaver at Round Lake (cf. Rogers 1963:C38). Muskrats are almost exclusively sought in the spring after the ice departs. The importance of the spring rat hunt can be traced to the 1820's at a time when other fur bearers had become scarce. Rats are usually caught in traps (#1½) set in shallow water along the shoreline and baited with a fresh poplar stick of castor scent. Sometimes they are shot with 22's. Men, women, and boys set rat traps in the spring. As in the past, changes in the water level affect the number of rats taken. Other fur bearers of lesser importance which are trapped include foxes, weasels, and squirrels. As stated, trapping has declined within the last five years, especially for village Indians.

Although the total Osnaburgh-Pickle Lake area is not as efficiently exploited as in the past, since many remote territories are no longer utilized, a greater proportion of the actual time spent in the bush is devoted to trapping. Whereas in the past Indians spent more time in the bush, much of this was spent on non-trapping activities such as travel, food production and leisure. Today, since larger quantities of food are taken to trapping

Table 7 Osnaburgh-Pickle Lake Fur Returns: 1949-1966

Year	Beaver	Mink	Otter	Muskrat	Lynx	Marten	Fisher
1949-50	3280	1163	118	3558	42	1	1
50-51	3773	1173	235	2746	26		
51-52	5117	1105	240	1690	9	14	1
52-53	6203	1049	280	3822	77	8	3
53-54	4024	1069	275	1999	119	6	10
54-55	3864	984	321	2808	52	18	23
55-56	3638	636	324		35	36	32
56-57	2362	983	237	3206	13	17	11
57-58	3178	1056	340	1786	26	25	49
58-59	3488	1645	330	1683	83	22	26
59-60	2267	1033	162	1939	158	10	27
60-61	2906	1480	270		100	36	35
61-62	3563	1310	314		194	71	24
62-63	3077	875	327		189	91	37
63-64	2087	371	176		79	54	32
64-65	2409*	732	191		33	52	48
65-66	2364*	346	193		20	145	39

*Savant Lake figures were added by the Department of Lands and Forests to the Osnaburgh-Pickle Lake totals. This addition tends to obscure the actual decline somewhat for the last two years. As mentioned, several members of the Trout Lake band resident in Central Patricia now trap within the Pickle Lake region further distorting the picture. Finally, there are more men of trapping age than in 1949 reducing the total number of furs per trapper.

camps, men are able to concentrate their efforts on trapping activities alone. However, I would estimate that the actual average amount of time devoted to trapping per trapper has decreased[7]. The lessening in importance of trapping activities cannot be accounted for by a diminution of the fur bearers. Government officials have indicated that there are actually more fur animals than there were a decade ago, especially since many territories are not exploited.

37

The price paid for a pelt varies, depending on where it is traded (there are now five major stores) and on the quality and size of the animal. Lynx were by far the most valuable animal, a prime pelt bringing up to $40. Beaver varied from about $2 to $20, and muskrats averaged $1.50. Otter were second to lynx, averaging just over $20. Mink and marten brought about $8, while fisher were valued at approximately $10.

The average annual income per trapper was $314 in 1965-66. This figure was averaged from the 78 men who actually trapped, excluding those who had licenses, but did no trapping.

The Osnaburgh Hudson's Bay store is getting an increasingly smaller proportion of the pelts traded. In 1962, the Osnaburgh post paid $24,000 to Indians for pelts. At that date, most Osnaburgh Indians traded with the Hudson's Bay Company and the figure probably represents, within $5,000, the total earnings obtained from furs. This sum was paid to about 80 trappers and if it is assumed that Osnaburgh Indians earned about $28,000, then the average income per trapper that year was about $350. Although this figure is only slightly higher than the 1966 one, it had a greater purchasing value. By 1964, the value paid to Indians at the Hudson's Bay store had dropped to $3,500, and in 1965, to $2,500, a factor indicative of increased competition with other outlets. Comparable data from other stores was unavailable. However, I have estimated that Osnaburgh Indians received about $24,500 from furs in 1965-66, $14,000 of which was paid for beaver[8]. Table 8 gives estimates of the amount received from all the stores from the individual fur return figures.

Table 8 Estimated Amount Received for Furs: 1965-66

Beaver	$14,000
Mink	3,050
Otter	2,950
Muskrat	2,950
Marten	800
Lynx	450
Others	300
	$24,500

One of the most important economic activities of the Osnaburgh House Indians is commercial fishing. Fishing for the Hudson's Bay Company is an activity which occupied several Indians each year from the 1840's until the 1930's. Hence the introduction of commercial fishing on Lake St. Joseph during the 1930's fitted into a well established summer economic pattern.

Today commercial fishing is the most popular and adaptive economic activity at Osnaburgh. It not only allows the people to camp in the bush during the summer months in family and co-residential units, but provides them with a source of income without interfering with the formal education of children. Even those Indians who do not take commercial fishing seriously enjoy escaping from the village to the fish camps. Also, food costs drop during the summer months, as many of the fish caught in the nets are consumed. Fish are eaten at at least one meal almost every day. Commercial fishing at Osnaburgh has, within the last five years, replaced trapping as the chief source of earned income. Most fish are taken from Lake St. Joseph where there are three main camps used each summer by the same families. The camps from east to west have been respectively designated: Smooth Rock, Jackfish Narrows, and Big Narrows (see Map 5).

During the season the price paid for fish fluctuates slightly. Walleye are the most valuable bringing 30 cents per pound in 1965, followed by whitefish at 10 cents per pound and pike at 4 cents. By 1966, the total income from fishing had increased to $43,215, double the amount earned during the late 1950's (Rogers 1972). However, the following year the bottom fell out of the market and earnings dropped to one-fifth what they were before. This certainly must have been a severe blow to Indian economy! While earnings are again (1969-70) increasing they have not yet reached previous highs. Perhaps the recent rise in beef prices during the '70's will increase the value of fish and thus improve the Indian economy. Most lakes do, however, have quotas on the poundage that can be taken set by the government.

In early June the men and their families take their equipment to the camps. Basic equipment includes foodstuffs, nets, tents, and gasoline for outboard motors. Early in the season the commercial fisherman frequently advances Indians credit to cover initial expenses. The commercial fisherman makes three trips a week to the fish camps to collect the boxes of ice-packed fish, and to take families their supplies. On the trip down, empty wooden boxes made by Indians employed at Doghole Bay (the site of the commercial fisherman's warehouse) and other supplies are left at each camp. On the return voyage the fish (packed in crushed ice) are loaded on the boat by the fishermen. On each box is marked the name of the fisherman who caught and packed the fish so that accurate records of individual earnings can be kept. Once back at Doghole Bay the boxes are unloaded by several Indians and immediately taken to the warehouse where the fish are checked for spoilage and repacked according to species. An Indian bookkeeper keeps individual records of the weight and species of fish obtained.

The concept of the fishing territory seems to be developing, although this is still only vaguely defined. Indians have a number of spots where they habitually set nets. On one occasion an Indian complained that the men from another camp were getting too close to the area fished by the Big Narrows men. Men often discuss where they intend to set nets while visiting in the evening so that no conflicts will occur. Usually men work in pairs and nets must be checked daily. Nets are owned individually, and the catch is the personal property of the owner. This also applies in the case of husband and wife teams of which there are three. It is customary to first set one partner's nets, and then the other's nets, using an outboard powered skiff. The cost of the gas used is apportioned according to the approximate distance travelled in setting and checking each partner's nets. Usually one partner owns the boat and motor. The number of nets set by partners varies according to their abilities and to the number owned. Table 9 gives figures on the number of fishermen at each of the three camps and the number of nets set.

There are other Osnaburgh Indians who fish near the west end of Lake St. Joseph. These people sell their fish to the Slate Falls Trading Company which flies the fish directly to Sioux Lookout. Fewer fish are taken than at any one of the three main camps and the price paid for fish is lower due to the higher transportation costs.

Lake St. Joseph is not the only lake in the vicinity where

40

Table 9 Nets Set Per Fisherman: 1965

Fish Camp	No. of Partners	No. of Men Fishing Alone	Total Nets Set	No. of Nets Per Fisherman
Smooth Rock	2	2	24	4.0
Jackfish Narrows	8	2	85	4.7
Big Narrows	4	2	61	6.1
	14	6	170	5.0

commercial fishing is conducted during the summer. Fish from a number of smaller lakes are also bought by the commercial fisherman at Doghole Bay. It is of interest to note that the distinction made by the Indians between Lake St. Joseph Indians and village Indians is clearly evident from the location of families and co-residential units, the time devoted to fishing, and the earnings of individual Indians. Table 10 presents the numbers and percentages of fishermen at different levels of income during the summer of 1965. For comparative purposes, figures for Lake St. Joseph Indians and village Indians have been kept separate.

Table 10 Income Levels in Relation to Time Spent at Fish Camps

	Lake St. Joseph Indians			Village Indians		
	Number	Percent	Time in Weeks	Number	Percent	Time in Weeks
Under $199	4	17.4	2.8	21	70.0	1.2
$200-$499	5	21.7	7.6	7	23.3	3.2
$500-$799	4	17.4	12.8			
$800-$1,399	2	8.7	18.0	2*	6.7	9.0
$1,400-$1,999	4	17.4	18.0			
Over $2,000	4	17.4	17.7			
	23	100.0		30	100.1	

*This figure includes one set of partners (stepson-stepfather) for which only the total earnings were available since they had a joint account.

41

Although a few village Indians may fish on Lake St. Joseph for short periods, not one Lake St. Joseph Indian fishes on any of the other lakes. The earnings of the two groups is directly correlated with the amount of time spent at the fish camps. Village Indians spent only about two weeks at the fish camps compared to about twelve weeks for Lake St. Joseph Indians. The average income of the former was only $211 compared to $975 for the latter (see Table 11). Also the village Indians appear to devote less time to fishing in proportion to the total time spent at the camp, and they set fewer nets. Most villagers consider their stay at the summer camps to be a holiday which offers them the opportunity of earning some cash.

Table 11   Income in Relation to Time

	Lake St. Joseph Indians (23)	Village Indians (31)	Band Totals (54)
Total time in weeks spent at fish camps	279	66	345
Average time per fisherman spent at camps in weeks	12.1	2.1	6.4
Total Income	$22,417.96	$6,544.67	$28,962.63
Average Income per fisherman	$974.69	$211.12	$536.35

Estimates of the total income from fishing activities for 1965-66 are presented in Table 12.

Table 12   Total Income from Fishing Activities: 1965-66

Summer
Fish sold at Doghole Bay $29,000
Income from other activities associated with fishing
    (box making, weighing, packing, bookkeeping) . . .   2,500
Fish sold to trading company   3,000
Winter
Income from fish sold at Pickle Lake   2,500

Total $37,000

42

Today, government assistance to the economies of Subarctic peoples is vital. Without it, many communities could not exist, while the people would be reduced to starvation. Between 1961 and 1967, the total amount of welfare money issued to needy Osnaburgh House families has multiplied by five times (Table 13), a fact closely related to the development of a more permanent village population. Over three-quarters of the welfare assistance was paid to Indians living on the Reserve. The construction of the school in 1962 inhibiting families from travelling to distant trapping camps has been a key factor in increasing their welfare needs. A good test case for the effects of the village school is provided by the Ogoki community located 200 miles east of Osnaburgh. The Ogoki community has no school, rather the children are flown out to schools in Thunder Bay or Sault Ste. Marie. Thus, the adults can devote most of the winter to trapping. Trapping incomes are significantly higher and welfare assistance proportionately lower there than at Osnaburgh. Despite the recent construction of Indian Affairs houses, Ogoki Indians still spend most of the winter trapping. Thus, it is not simply the security of village life that keeps people from economic activities and increases welfare payments. Most of the adults at Osnaburgh indicated that they preferred life at the bush camps. For most communities, the rise in welfare payments has been due to a number of factors: mandatory day schools, improved medical facilities, a growing population no longer capable of supporting itself by trapping and fishing alone, a desire on the part of some young people to avoid the hardships of bush life, and an attitude by others that the government is responsible for them, and in turn, a governmental view that says the Indians are entitled to assistance.

In addition to regular monthly assistance, Osnaburgh Indians received over $800 per month in temporary relief in 1966. This type of assistance is paid to families during certain seasons of the year when they are unable to find employment, or if illness should occur. Although the duration of payment varies, temporary assistance in some cases may change to regular payments. The amount paid to families varies according to the number and age of the dependents. The government rarely ever refuses

Table 13   Estimated Welfare Assistance Paid to Osnaburgh
            Indians

Year	Osnaburgh Reserve & Vicinity	Slate Falls	Central Patricia & Pickle Lake*	Totals
1961-62	$ 6,500	$1,000	$1,500	$ 9,000
1962-63	8,200	1,500	1,500	12,700
1963-64	12,000	2,000	4,500	18,500
1964-65	13,000	3,000	3,000	19,000
1965-66	27,000	4,500	4,500	36,000
1966-67	36,000	5,000	5,000	46,000

*Figures include welfare paid to Trout Lake Indians resident in
Central Patricia.

to assist families, although the Indian agent may threaten to
curtail payments should he feel money is being misappropriated.

Other sources of unearned income include Family Allowance
cheques, old age assistance, pensions and Treaty payments. These
benefits are received regardless of economic needs. Annuity payments began in 1905 when the Indians signed the treaty (Number
9) with the Canadian government providing each person with $4.
In 1945, Family Allowance payments began, providing each
family with an income of from $6 to $8 a month for each child
under the age of 16. Since 1962, when the day school was built,
the Indian Affairs Branch has been able to curtail Family Allowance cheques to families with truant children. Old Age pensions
were extended to the Osnaburgh band about 1950, and in 1965
each person over the age of 70 was receiving a monthly cheque of
$65. The social importance of the aged has been increased by the
introduction of this regular monthly income.

Wage Labour

The importance of wage labour in providing Osnaburgh Indians
with an additional source of income has increased within the last
decade. However, due to the temporary nature of the employment, and to the conditions involved, wage employment has

44

Table 14   Estimated Amount of Unearned Income for
            Osnaburgh Indians: 1966

Source of Income	Osnaburgh Reserve & Vicinity	Slate Falls	Central Patricia & Pickle Lake*	Savant Lake	Totals
Regular Monthly Welfare Assistance	$26,000	$5,000	$5,000	$1,000	$47,000
Temporary Relief	10,000				
Family Allowance	14,000	2,000	2,000	1,000	19,000
Old Age Assistance & Pensions	6,300	780	1,560	2,340	10,980
Annuity Payments	1,480	400	280	160	2,320
Totals	$57,780	$8,180	$8,840	$4,500	$79,300

*Includes welfare paid to Trout Lake Indians living in Central Patricia.

neither economically nor psychologically met the new requirements of semi-permanent village life.

Mining operations in the area terminated in 1966 due to a lack of high-grade ore, and to a lack of labour. Only five Osnaburgh Indians were employed at this date, none of whom resided on the Reserve. The Indian Affairs Branch in recent years has provided employment for Indians through logging operations. Within the past few years the Department of Highways has hired Indians to cut brush along the road during January and February. In summer, several Osnaburgh Indians who live in the Pickle Lake village are employed by the Department of Lands and Forests. There are few other employment opportunities in the vicinity of the Osnaburgh Reserve[9]. Again, the Indians have not adapted to the daily job routine expected by Whites.

Expenditures and Living Standards

Although social and psychological conditions at Osnaburgh House have not improved, and perhaps have actually degenerated, there is little question that the general economic standard of living has improved greatly within the last decade. Both the total amount spent on consumption goods other than foods and the variety and quantity of materials possessed has increased. Where in 1956, Indians spent $33,500 at the Hudson's Bay store, which was then the main source of goods, in 1965 the total sales had risen to $99,000 despite increased competition. Of the latter figure, approximately $38,000 was spent on materials other than foods. If the items purchased at other stores were included, it is likely that over $50,000 was expended during 1965.

The process of augmentation is well illustrated by the number and variety of material items now owned. Almost every household owns at least one canoe and an outboard motor. Several Lake St. Joseph Indians have skiffs and high-powered outboards ranging from 10 HP to 35 HP. Every household owns such items as rifles, crosscut saws and lamps or lanterns. Most households possess a transistor radio, while transistor record players are almost as popular costing between $50 and $80. The sudden recent sale of timepieces (86 watches or clocks in 1965) is indicative of the changing attitude toward time, especially since it has become necessary that children be at school on time. One village Indian owns a tape recorder, while two villagers possess typewriters. One man subscribes to *Time* magazine. Although automobiles are a very new acquisition at Osnaburgh, between 1962 and 1966, no less than 16 vehicles had been purchased by Indians.

Most of the traditional material culture of the Northern Ojibwa has disappeared, sometimes with a replacement, and sometimes without any recognizable one. Of those items that remain, snowshoes, moosehide moccasins, cradle boards, sleds and hare-skin blankets are the most important. Almost every household possesses one pair of snowshoes today, usually laced with twine rather than moosehide. Moosehide moccasins made by women are owned by most trappers, but many wear rubber boots or high leather boots instead. Cradle boards are locally made by men and used by all infants under the age of 18 months. Traditionally manufactured sleds are rapidly being replaced by store-bought toboggans. This applies also to hare-skin blankets which are often, however, covered with quilting or flannel sheets. Birch bark canoes, no longer in use today, were replaced in the 1920's, nor are there any hare-skin parkas or mitts. Bone and wood tools such as awls and needles have virtually vanished. In sum, traditional material possessions have all but disappeared, many of the items noted by Skinner in 1909 (1911:126-32) are no longer in use.

For the Osnaburgh Indians, by far the most important source of income is government subsidies. Indeed, nearly half of the income received is unearned (Table 15). As Dunning indicated (1959a:47), both the length of time which government assistance has been effective and the sudden enormous recent increase have profoundly modified the social and economic arrangement of Ojibwa society. Subsidies along with other forms of labour and the formation of a permanent village have led to a decline in trapping, once a basic subsistence pursuit. These additional sources of income have provided greater economic stability resulting in a higher standard of living, a more sedentary way of life, improved medical facilities and a related population explosion.

Table 15   Estimated Income and Expenditures of Osnaburgh Indians: 1965-66

| | Income | | Expenditure | | |
Source of Income	Amount	% of Total	Source of Expenditure	Amount	% of Total
Subsidies	$79,300	49%	Food	$98,100	61%
Commercial Fishing	37,000	23	Other	62,700	39
Trapping	24,500	15			
Wage Labour	20,000	12			
Totals	$160,800	99%		$160,800	100%

Increased purchasing power through subsidies and other new sources of income have led to the spacial stabilization of the population within a restricted area. While in the past, hunting groups remained dispersed throughout the country during most of the year, the members now reside semi-permanently within or near the village. Although the changed economic situation has been one factor in altering demographic and settlement patterns, there are others, including the advent of a permanent day school,

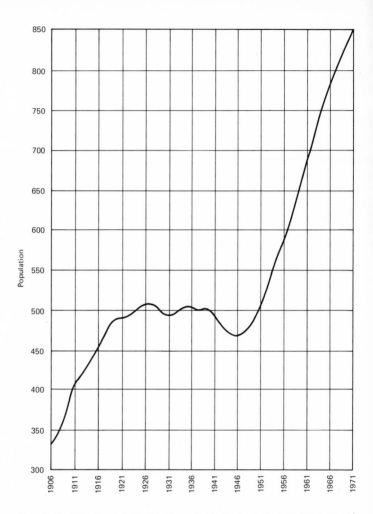

Figure 1: Population Trends in Absolute Figures for the Osnaburgh Band: 1906-1971. Figures for the 1906-1934 period were taken from treaty lists, while later figures were derived from Department of Citizenship and Immigration data. Cat Lake figures were included as it was impossible to separate them from the total. A personal head count made in July 1966 indicated that 154 Indians resided at Cat Lake. There are two sharp increases in population. The first occurred immediately after the treaty was signed and can be accounted for by improved medical conditions and a slightly more reliable food supply. The second increase began in the early 1950's shortly after a medical station was established and when subsidies began to grow. By 1970 there will be an estimated 850 Indians belonging to the Osnaburgh band.

48

improved medical facilities and government-constructed houses. These economic and social changes have re-shaped attitudes both toward Euro-Canadians and toward the traditional way of life. It is to the social effects of these transformations that we now turn.

Changing Social Organization

Demographic Changes

Directly correlated with increased government subsidies and health services is the marked population increase for the Osnaburgh House band as a whole, especially since 1950. Improved medical treatment, better housing facilities, and a more dependable food supply seem to be the more significant factors. There is no indication that attitudes toward birth and family size have altered appreciably. The birth rate seems to have risen slightly within the last decade as life has become more secure, while the death rate is coming to approximate that of the rest of Canada. Where for the thirty-year period from about 1920 to 1950 the band population remained relatively constant, between 1949 (when improved health measures were introduced) and 1972, the population has nearly doubled to over 850 persons (see Figure 1). Today there are over four times the number of Osnaburgh Indians that there were a century ago, a trend that has characterized almost all Northern Ojibwa communities.

Kinship and Marriage

In order to understand more recent changes in the kinship system of the Northern Ojibwa, it is first necessary to present a brief account of the system as it existed throughout the late nineteenth and early twentieth centuries. The Ojibwa of this period, like all people, classified kinsmen by a particular set of terms into a finite number of categories which entailed different modes of inter-action and behavioral expectations. All persons fell into two major categories for purposes of marriage: kinsmen, one's father and his brothers, mother and her sisters and their offspring (parallel cousins); and non-kin, one's father's sisters and mother's

Table 16   Osnaburgh Birth and Death Rates at Three
            Time-Periods

Year	Average* Population	Total Births In Absolute Figures	Total Deaths In Absolute Figures	Birth Rate Per 1000	Death Rate Per 1000
1925-29**	509	92	77	36.1	30.3
1943-47	467	82	88	35.1	37.7
1961-65	726	161	47	48.3	12.9

*This figure includes the Cat Lake Indians since there was no way of separating them.
**Five-year periods were chosen to eliminate the effects of unusual years and to demonstrate general trends.

brothers and their offspring (cross-cousins) (Hallowell 1930; Eggan 1966). Different terms were applied to kinsmen to distinguish them from non-kin while forms of interaction also differed.

A kinship system also, however, includes the way in which people in certain kin categories form groups as well as the relationships between such groups. For the Northern Ojibwa, these groups were not random entities but rather existed to perform certain necessary functions which were closely interrelated with behavioral expectations among the various kinsmen who formed them. The basic social group through most of Northern Ojibwa recent history has been the hunting group consisting of a number (usually fifteen to twenty-five) of "bilaterally" or "patrilaterally" related kinsmen. That is, any individual belonging to a particular hunting group had as co-residents persons of both sexes related to him (or her) either through his mother or father; while the patrilateral emphasis reflects the basic solidarity of males related by blood ties for hunting and social purposes. These hunting groups, as we shall see, were well adapted to the unstable and often harsh conditions prevailing during the last century; for flexibility in structure had adaptive value when game was scarce or when an imbalance occurred in sex ratios. Larger hunting groups could either separate into smaller more viable units during periods of scarcity, or realign themselves to recreate a new balance. Social connections between hunting groups were maintained through marriages since the hunting groups themselves were exogamous. Preferred mates were cross-cousins, although marriages were generally arranged by the parents of a couple.

Another factor regulating marriage among the Ojibwa was membership in a particular totem category[10]. Persons belonging to the same totem or animal-named category, which descended through the male line, were prohibited from marrying even though they might belong to a different hunting group, since they considered themselves to be siblings. In sum, totem exogamy, hunting group exogamy, and cross-cousin marriage established and maintained an extensive alliance system involving a number of hunting groups dispersed over a wide area (Eggan 1966:78-107). Post-marital residence following initial bride service obligations was a matter of choice and expediency.

The kinship system of a century ago has changed greatly, especially within the last thirty years. Not only was it impossible to obtain a consistent set of kin terms agreed upon by everyone, but on occasion the same person alternated in his usage of terms for the same kin categories. This reflects the fact that the way people are coming to classify kinsmen is changing, and changing in the direction of the Canadian system[11]. For example, there is a trend among younger people to merge terminologically collateral relatives of both parents so that there is a single term for father's sister and mother's sister, and for father's brother and mother's brother. The terms for wife's parents are the same as in the recent past (Dunning 1959a:110), but they are different from those applied to cross aunts and uncles. This change is related to the recent decline in importance of marriage with genealogically close cross-cousins. Similarly, in Ego's generation there is a tendency to merge all cousins under a single term regardless of sex, and to distinguish them from siblings. Actually, however, this tendency seemed to apply only in a few cases, since the solidarity and equivalence of siblings, especially brothers, and the generation principle have resulted in a general retention of the *Iroquois* type cousin terminology. While preferred marriage partners still are those in the cross-cousin category, the incest taboo has been extended to first cousins. For those people under the age of 45 years, only one case of first cousin marriage was recorded[12].

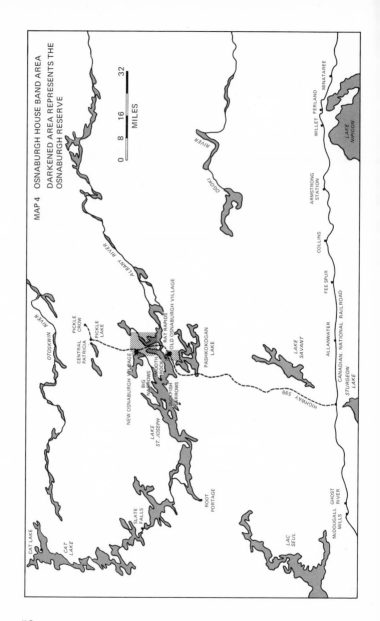

MAP 4 OSNABURGH HOUSE BAND AREA
DARKENED AREA REPRESENTS THE
OSNABURGH RESERVE

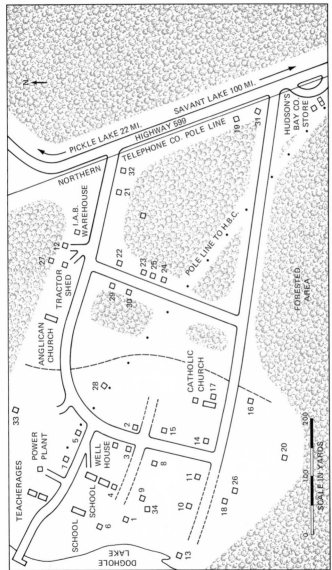

MAP 5 PLAN OF THE NEW OSNABURGH VILLAGE 1966

53

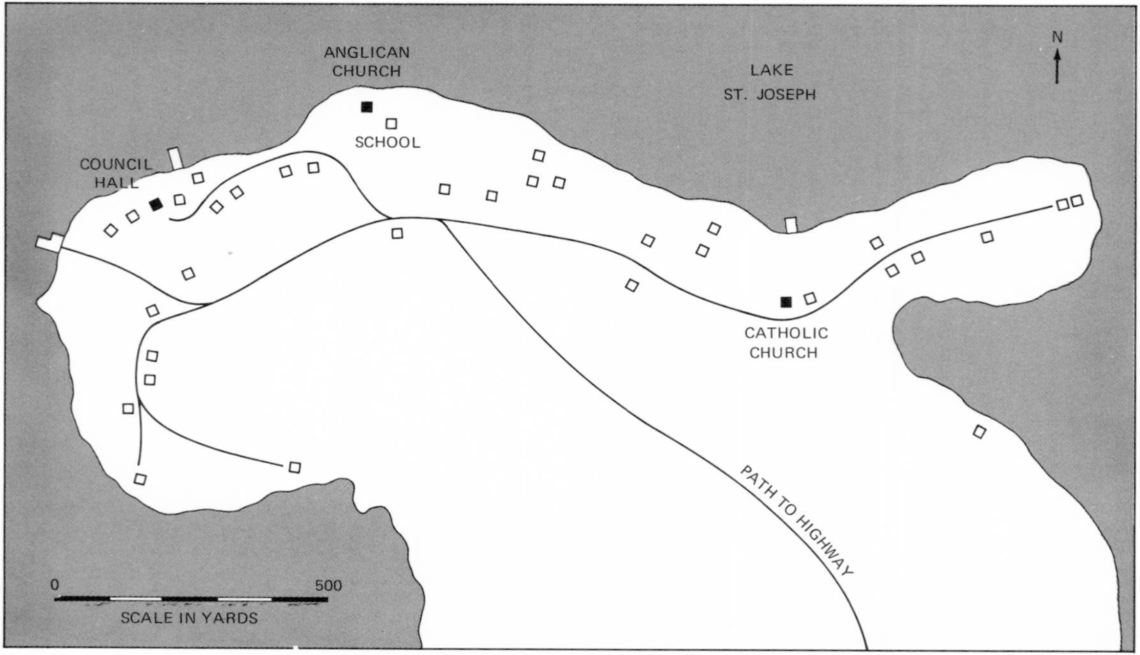

LAKE
ST. JOSEPH

ANGLICAN
CHURCH

SCHOOL

CATHOLIC
CHURCH

COUNCIL
HALL

PATH TO HIGHWAY

N

SCALE IN YARDS

0   500

MAP 6   PLAN OF THE OLD OSNABURGH HOUSE VILLAGE 1959.

Recent missionary activities may be responsible for this low incidence, while the new village life and day school are bringing together unrelated persons, and indeed, persons who in the past would have been prohibited from marrying. Nevertheless, most people still marry outside their hunting group.

It is not the marriage ceremony but rather who one marries that is important. Weddings are very casual affairs of comparatively little social importance. There is no wedding cake, dinner, confetti, nor honeymoon, and couples merely walk to church and home immediately following the ceremony.

Most couples at Osnaburgh have lived together prior to marriage. Several unmarried couples were noted sleeping in the house of one of the parents without any apparent disapproval. If the couple are cross-cousins, adults may refer to them as husband and wife although no marriage ceremony has taken place. In such a case the prospective husband may give his future father-in-law a small gift of tobacco or food. Although romance and love appear to be more important in determining marriage, parents still have much control over arrangements.

Extra-marital sex relations are not condoned and are the cause of much conflict. On occasion they can lead to violence, although this is rare. Since the Canadian version of divorce is unknown, a husband or wife may simply leave. The cause of separation usually involves a third party. In 1966, there were three men in the Reserve area whose wives were living with other men.

There is no prescribed residence norm among the Osnaburgh Ojibwa today. In the past, it appears that residence immediately after marriage was uxorilocal. At present there are seven men in the village living either with their father-in-law, or, as in three cases, with their mother-in-law, the husband being dead. In two cases, the son-in-law is considered to be the owner of the house, so it is questionable whether it is correct to define residence as uxorilocal. In several other cases, sons-in-law are residing in separate houses located near affines. In not a single instance is a married son living with his own parents, although several married males have established residence close to their parents. Trapping and bush life have altered so drastically within recent years that residence outside the village is highly variable from year to year.

Today, the members of a totem group are widely dispersed,

although patrilateral filiation has the effect of bringing and keeping together men of the same group. During the nineteenth century, the hunting group became the primary exogamous unit while totem group membership ceased to have any function other than regulating marriages, largely because members became widely dispersed. Today, marriage within the totem group is frowned on by older people who still consider totem-mates siblings. One middle-aged man said that it was acceptable to marry a totem-mate today, but not when he was young. Preliminary findings indicate that at least five marriages at Osnaburgh involved totem-mates, all of whom are under the age of forty. Totems recorded at Osnaburgh include: Moose, Caribou, Sturgeon, Sucker, Loon and Mallard. Mallard is not an aboriginal totem symbol and was not in existence during the nineteenth century or when Skinner did his research at Osnaburgh in 1909. There is evidence that Mallard has replaced Pelican as a totem symbol. For some Osnaburgh Indians, the sense of totem identity is so unimportant that they do not consider themselves to be members of a named totem!

Units of Social Organization

It is convenient to view the social organization in terms of a series of successively inclusive levels (Sahlins 1962:6). That is, the kin-residential groups are imbedded in increasingly inclusive groupings, each grouping having certain functions within the totality. The units of Ojibwa society are: *household, hunting (co-residential) group, village, community* and *treaty band.*

Household

The basic social unit today is the household or commensal unit (cf. Dunning 1959a:55) whose members reside in a single dwelling. It is the unit exhibiting the greatest solidarity and cooperation. During the summer of 1966, there were 33 occupied houses in the village, 20 of which were Indian Affairs houses constructed by the Canadian government. There were 225 occupants giving an average of 6.82 persons per household (see Tables 17 and 18). Indian Affairs houses which are of superior construction averaged

8.4 people, while the others averaged 4.4 individuals. Of the 20 Indian Affairs houses, 15 are constructed of logs measuring 19 feet by 20 feet. These structures consist, in most cases, of a single room, although originally they were partitioned into three rooms. In all but two houses, the Indians removed the partitions to facilitate uniform heating in winter. Members of one overcrowded dwelling have partitioned the roof space into a small upstairs area allowing greater sleeping room.

The non-Indian Affairs houses were built at the families' expense and are generally smaller. The remaining 5 Indian Affairs houses which have been built since 1965 are of plywood, and are more modern in appearance. The latter have large windows and are partitioned into three rooms. In addition to the above mentioned houses there are 8 dwellings within a half-mile of Doghole Bay, 3 at Jackfish Narrows, and 3 spaced along the road from 30 to 40 miles south of the village. Another family lives permanently at Pedler Path Bay on the south end of the Reserve.

Wood stoves situated in the middle of the dwelling are used both for cooking and heating, wood being obtained near the village. Wood is usually hauled by the one truck owned by an Osnaburgh Indian at a fee. In November Indians stockpile wood for at least part of the winter next to the house. Houses are illuminated by coleman or coal oil lamps, or candles, there being no electricity in any Indian residence. Most homes contain a table and one or two wooden chairs, and a shelf along a wall. Although there is at least one bed in each house, many people, especially children, sleep on mattresses on the floor.

Besides providing a location to eat and sleep, houses have social functions. They are places where people gather to visit, and, indeed, a study of household visiting patterns can provide information on the kinship system. While most people turn out their lights by 9:00 P.M., it is not uncommon to discover a poker or cribbage game with cash at stake in session late at night in some pre-determined household. In summer, square dances are often held in certain houses. During 1965-66, several households cooperatively set up a telephone-radio system by stringing wires between houses which were then attached to the speakers of their battery-operated radios. A record or radio program heard in one household could then be transmitted to all the connecting households. It was even possible to speak with somebody in another house, or to hear a conversation between two other ones. The communication system could be broken if one wished more privacy by simply disconnecting a wire.

Within the village, households are linked through ties of kinship and marriage. With the recent increase in government assistance, and the removal of many functions to outside agencies, which were formerly performed by household and hunting group heads, the household has become increasingly independent despite a more intense social life.

Table 17

House*	Date of 1st Occupancy	Indian Affairs House	No. of Occupants June 1966
1	1959	X	9
2	1959	X	9
3	1960	X	14
4	1960	X	9
5	1961	X	10
6	1961	X	4
7	1961	X	16
8	1961	X	9
9	1962	X	6
10	1962	X	7
11	1962	X	11
12	1962	X	11
13	1962	X	6
14	1962	X	8
15	1962		
16	1962		2
17	1962		3
18a**	1961		8
18b	1963		6
19	1963	X	4
20	1963	X	5
21	1963		4
22	1963		3
23	1964	X	10
24	1964	X	7

House[*]	Date of 1st Occupancy	Indian Affairs House	No. of Occupants June 1966
25	1964	X	7
26	1964		2
27	1964		4
28	1964		
29	1965	X	3
30	1965	X	11
31	1965		4
32	1965		4
33	1965		5
34	1965		4

[*]To locate houses, see Map 6.
[**]House 18a and house 18b are a single building with a wall separating the two households. In the fall of 1966 this building was torn down and replaced by two Indian Affairs houses. In late 1967 seven more Indian Affairs houses were being built.

Table 18

	Number	Number of Occupants	Average per Occupied House
Indian Affairs Houses	20	168	8.40
Others	13	57	4.40
	33	225	6.82

Hunting (co-residential) Group

Until the last two decades, the largest effective economic unit was the hunting (co-residential) unit (cf. Dunning 1959a:55-58), averaging from 20 to 30 individuals at Osnaburgh. Each co-residential unit is composed of several households or commensal units which form the winter bush settlements. In winter, hunting group members occupy a bush settlement in the centre of a communally owned trapping territory. Several males usually form trapping partnerships. Although members of the hunting group cooperate and share food, furs belong to the individual who caught them. In summer, co-residential units form tent clusters at fishing camps. Within the past decade the amount of time spent in the bush has decreased with the consequent decline of the hunting unit in social and economic importance. The weakening of bonds of solidarity can be correlated with a money economy and the relegation of control in many spheres of life to external agencies. As Dunning has noted for Pekangikum, these non-indigenous agencies exercise "considerable control in matters of trapping, fur trade, and credit; illness and hospitalization; schooling, and thus family allowance benefits; and less directly but equally influentially, religion and communal gathering for that purpose" (1959a:185).

Concomitant with these changes has been the decline in authority of the hunting group leader. Where in the past the efficacy of leadership was grounded in magico-religious power attained through the vision quest; missionary influence, improved medical treatment, and education have undermined this basis. Leaders could control the animals necessary for survival and trade, and apply sanctions through the fear of magical power upon wrongdoers. Today, the money economy and subsidies have lessened the importance of subsistence techniques with regard to survival, and the retributive sanctions are no longer feared. In a compact acephalous community composed of formerly dispersed hunting groups, many of whose functions have been taken over by outside sources, social control within such a community is largely restricted to gossip groups (cf. Dunning 1959a:184), and the household tends to emerge as a self-sufficient unit (cf. Rogers 1962:B81). Despite these recent changes, however, there is still the need for economic assistance beyond the household related to bush life at the fish camps and the spring trapping camps.

Village

The Osnaburgh House village is largely the result of government influence involving welfare assistance and services. Until the late 1940's, members of the Osnaburgh House band remained dispersed for most of the year in bush settlements. With the advent of subsidies, improved medical care and new forms of wage labour, the tendency was to reside for longer periods in new log homes on the south shore of Lake St. Joseph across from the HBC store (see Map 7). By 1959, there were 31 completed houses in the village, in addition to a school and two churches. By the late 1950's, several homes were occupied the year round. In this village, house clusters were located about 100 yards apart along the shore for over a mile. These comprised people who generally belonged to the same winter trapping settlement or co-residential group.

After the road was completed between Savant Lake and Central Patricia in 1954, cars and trucks passed within two miles of the Lake St. Joseph village. It thus became possible for Indians to hitch rides to and from the villages to the north, or to camping sites off the road. The road proved to be such an attraction that many Indians began locating their tents near it during the summer, especially near Doghole Bay or Rat Rapids. Thus, after a council meeting in 1959, it was decided that the village should be relocated nearer the road. The Indian Affairs Branch did not encourage the move to a new village site, since as late as 1958 a road was being constructed between the highway and the old village. The chief and councillors, however, chose a spot on the shore of Doghole Lake near the highway which was cleared of trees by the late fall of 1959 after which the first Indian Affairs houses were built. By 1962, most of the Osnaburgh people who had formerly lived in the old village on Lake St. Joseph had been relocated to the new village.

The plan of the new village along with the priority list of who was to get a new house disrupted old residence patterns. In contrast to the old village where house clusters represented hunting groups, houses in the new village are arranged along "streets" according to government specifications. Also, houses were to be separated by about fifty yards to avoid the possibility of fire hazards. Since this was not congruent with the Indian view of things, several people erected non-Indian Affairs houses close to the former in conformity with older patterns. One family even built an Indian Affairs house about thirty feet from another during the absence of the government supervisor in 1964!

Of particular interest is the number of different family units that have occupied each house in the new village. Several of the older Indian Affairs houses have been occupied by as many as four or five different families since their construction. Until the last few years, the concept of usufruct applied to houses in much the same manner as it did to land. During the early 1960's when a family moved out of a house in the new village to go to the bush, another family merely moved in. Upon returning to the village the former residents would look for a vacant house. In the spring of 1966, however, some people locked their doors and boarded their windows upon leaving for bush camps. A certain amount of house trading has also occurred. As one informant stated, people don't like to stay in one spot too long. Some of this shuffling seems to have been an attempt to reestablish the contiguity of hunting group members disrupted by the relocation process since some house clusters approximate hunting groups. However, in a number of cases members of the same group are widely separated in the village.

In addition to the 33 occupied village houses within a quarter-mile-square area, there were several other buildings consisting of the Hudson's Bay Company store and warehouse, a Catholic church, an Anglican church, a four-room school in three buildings, and two teacherages. In late 1966, two houses were added, and in 1967, seven more were built along with a new council hall.

Although the village represents only a minimal amount of cohesion since there are no leaders who are able to organize activities for village welfare, villagers, nevertheless have a sense of identity and are referred to by non-village Indians as the "people of townsite".

Community

The Osnaburgh House community is larger than the village and includes the latter. Community members, although dispersed, tend to reside within a 50-mile radius of the village, or they spend part of the year near the village. Some community members reside at Doghole Bay and Rat Rapids within five miles of the village; while other Indians occupy houses along the shore of Lake St. Joseph, and along the road south of Rat Rapids. What most distinguishes the community today, however, is not primarily the degree of localization, although this is a factor, but rather a conscious distinction between community members and outsiders including local Whites as well as Indians from other communities. The development of a permanent village related to the increase in government subsidies and services has intensified this attitude of separateness. These attitudes toward outsiders, the preference for in-marriage, and a sense of identity as a distinct unit are the criteria upon which the Osnaburgh House community can be distinguished from other such units.

While in theory, the elected chief and councillors represent the band at large, most of their functions pertain to the community only. In the past the men chosen for these positions were heads of their hunting groups. The criteria for choosing a councillor have altered somewhat since a good person for the position is usually one who can effectively exploit the Whites regardless of whether he is a good hunter or not. The councillors are much busier people today, and all formal business matters involving the Indian Affairs Branch are dealt with through the band council. Council meetings are now held about every two months to discuss community problems. The chief and councillors also report illnesses, deaths, crimes, and other emergencies. Where in the past, a councillor might be away trapping or fishing most of the year, so long as he was present at Treaty time when band affairs were discussed for the ensuing year, his position was not jeopardized. Councillors were respected for their bush prowess and generosity, and a knowledge of English was not necessary. Today, a member of the council cannot afford to be away from the village too long. As early as 1958 some Indians were complaining about the absence of the chief and councillors who were away much of the time. In order to communicate community wants effectively, a knowledge of English has become important. Yet while councillors are more involved in community affairs, they still have little authority. Indeed, leadership responsibilities have been weakened by the money economy. Since the advent of the day school and increased welfare, many men's duties have disappeared while women's chores have remained much the same. When White jobs are available, men accept them as individuals. Then again, there appears to be a general distrust between peoples belonging to different hunting groups which becomes manifest only on rare occasions. For these reasons, organized community endeavours have met with little success. Although the Indian Affairs Branch has attempted to allocate greater responsibilities to sanctioned positions, the people involved are often uncertain of the limits of their powers and will either avoid situations demanding the exercise of authority, or will assume their powers are much greater than in fact they are. Most often, however, they are reluctant to make decisions affecting the whole community, and in reality, their rights and obligations are still poorly defined. Whites can and are expected to be bosses, but not Indians.

Due to this general weakening of authority, social control within the community has been delegated mainly to the Euro-Canadian system. Serious crimes are comparatively rare, whereas minor offenses appear to be increasing. The most common acts involve drinking within the Reserve (which is illegal), and juvenile delinquency, both of which are dealt with by the Ontario Provincial Police. In cases involving the former, the person is either fined or sent to jail for a brief period. Juvenile delinquency is a recent phenomenon and has involved acts ranging from window smashing, truancy and drinking, to theft from one of the stores.

In addition to the Canadian forms of legal procedure, the community has means of punishing those who do not conform. In the past expulsion was a traditional means of dealing with undesirable people. Although it is now impossible to expel a band member, and the fear of sorcery has diminished, villagers can ignore the wishes of culprits by applying the sanction of passive resistance. Gossip is another means of social control of considerable importance within the community. However, in cases involving actual violence, the community is inclined to allow the Euro-Canadian system to take action.

A village Indian can go farther than others in antisocial behaviour before action is taken due to the desire to avoid overt conflict between segments of the society. In a crime involving a village Indian, approval of the majority is necessary before action will be taken. In the case of one antisocial act when a villager's support was requested by one of the complainants, the former replied: "We can't do anything. He isn't a relative of ours." In other words the realm of coercive power is limited by the bonds of kinship. Possible trouble was circumvented by allowing the formal exterior Canadian system to pass judgment. Misdemeanours involving villagers are frequently ignored to maintain social

64

equilibrium, whereas it is more probable that action will be taken against non-Osnaburgh people. The expulsion of two Trout Lake Indians from the Osnaburgh Reserve in 1965 is a case in point. Such acts may enhance feelings of solidarity within the community.

Despite individualistic tendencies, contiguity and permanence of residence in conjunction with ties of kinship appear to have produced a feeling of community identity. There is even a general esprit de corps among the villagers at Treaty time, or during council meetings. Nevertheless, there is no overall authority structure, nor economic pursuits requiring the cooperation of all community members. This lack of integration is a product of their history within a restricted ecology where the exploitation of game and furs for trade purposes has been basically a subsistence activity.

Band

In former times the band and the community were identical since, during the nineteenth and early twentieth century, the band was composed of those groups of individuals who habitually traded at the Osnaburgh House post. The boundary between the Osnaburgh band and contiguous bands affiliated with other nearby trading centres was ill-defined, the only criterion of identity being the location where furs were taken and trade goods received. There were always some Indians who shifted from post to post to take advantage of varying trade conditions; or people who alternated according to changes in marital and kin ties. Intermarriage between winter hunting groups resulted in the interlocking of different bands through ties of kinship and marriage throughout the area. In 1905, when the Indians who traded at posts within the Albany River drainage signed the Treaty, the Canadian government designated *treaty* bands whose membership approximated that of the body of Indians affiliated with the trading post. Thus, the Indians trading at Osnaburgh were grouped and classified as the Osnaburgh House treaty band. The arbitrary nature of this superimposed *treaty* "band" is indicated, however, by the fact that the Osnaburgh House treaty band also included those Indians who traded at the Cat Lake Hudson's Bay post. During the 1870's, when the Cat Lake store was reestablished as an outpost of Osnaburgh House, many Indians in the Cat

Lake area began to trade there. The close kinship ties between the Cat Lake and Osnaburgh Indians, and the frequent communication between traders and Indians at the two posts (Cat Lake being supplied from Osnaburgh) led the government to group them as a single treaty band. Indians trading at stores at Bamaji Lake and Savant Lake when the Treaty was signed—but who were on the lists at Osnaburgh because of earlier trade patterns—were also consigned to the latter treaty band. The result is that the members of the "Osnaburgh House Treaty Band" are scattered in settlements as much as 130 miles apart.

At the same time that the Treaty was signed, the government introduced a popular system of elections whereby those Indians recorded as belonging to the Osnaburgh "band" chose a chief and councillors to act as their formal representatives. The chief and councillors were to be elected every two years and the number of formal band officials was to be in the ratio of one per every 100 people. In 1905 there were two councillors but the number has risen to eight at present. Treaty band members, however, do not form a cohesive group and despite the nomination of elected band officials, there is no overall authority structure which operates to integrate society. The band exhibits today a minimal degree of social integration. In all other respects the band operates in much the same manner as the community, the two differing primarily in that:

1. There is a conscious unity of the Osnaburgh House community which is separate from the Cat Lake community and other communities containing Osnaburgh treaty band Indians.
2. Community members, although often dispersed, tend to reside nearer the Osnaburgh House village, or at least they spend a portion of their time in or near it.
3. Community membership does not depend upon treaty band affiliation, (there being several non-Osnaburgh Indians who are members of the community).

Extra Community Relationships

Relations with Other Communities

In theory, Cat Lake Indians are part of the "Osnaburgh Treaty

66

Band", but in practice they are considered to be, and consider themselves to be, a separate band and community. The Indian Affairs Branch has come to accept the two groups as distinct social units and deals with them separately, except in regard to major issues affecting both. The Cat Lake people have expressed their desire to have a separate chief and band account[13]. In turn, Osnaburgh Indians have been reluctant to spend band funds on the Cat Lake Reserve. Ties with Cat Lake have decreased within the past 30 years while only one intercommunity marriage has taken place within the last decade.

Perhaps the closest ties are with some former members of the Fort Hope band. The Hudson's Bay Company did not establish a post at Fort Hope until 1894, although an outpost seems to have preceded it. Hence, until very late in the last century many Indians who eventually became members of the Fort Hope treaty band actually traded at Osnaburgh. The Fort Hope band, however, is as geographically and socially remote as the other treaty bands today.

As mentioned, members of the Osnaburgh band are widely scattered. Those who reside at Slate Falls are most closely affiliated with Lac Seul Indians, with whom several marriages have occurred. However, only one former Lac Seul Indian resides continuously in the Osnaburgh village. This man's son-in-law, a Lac Seul Indian, has recently moved into the father-in-law's house. However, this young man frequently expressed his hostility toward conditions in the Osnaburgh village and the fact that he wasn't wanted. When his father-in-law's position was broached, he replied: "He has lots of relatives here now" indicating the importance of kin ties in determining social acceptance. Lac Seul Indians are feared to some extent for it is believed that they have greater magical powers.

Today, contact with members of the Trout Lake band has increased since a segment of this band was relocated by the government to Central Patricia 20 miles north of the Osnaburgh village during the 1950's. Ties with other bands are weaker. In 1950, a man and his family transferred from the Whitesand band near Lake Nipigon, and in 1952 another man who had married an Osnaburgh woman transferred. These Indians now reside within the village. Connections with Round Lake have been totally severed.

The attitude toward half-castes is similar to that accorded members of other bands; while the caste distinction between Indian and non-Indian is most rigid. Half-breeds and members of foreign bands are outsiders; while interband marriages tend to result in removal from the Reserve and community.

Government

Regular contact with the Canadian government began when the Osnaburgh House Indians signed Treaty 9 in 1905. Through the treaty the government acquired the rights to new territories and a means to administer the native population of the area ceded through the formation of local Indian councils. From the Indians' point of view a treaty guaranteed certain rights and privileges without which they would have no protection. Treaty benefits included annuity payments of four dollars to every person on the treaty list. In addition Indians were to receive Reserve areas (see Map 5), medical assistance, educational facilities, and when needed, welfare assistance.

Contact with the government has increased, especially within the last decade. Until 1950, the Indian agent usually visited Osnaburgh only once a year at treaty time. During his stay the agent made annuity payments and settled the business of the year. After the Osnaburgh village was relocated on Doghole Lake in 1960, the agent or his deputies have made several visits to the village each year, since many new points of contact have resulted in a need for closer communication.

When the treaty was signed, education became a responsibility of the Canadian government. From 1950 to 1961 a schoolhouse which held about 40 pupils was operated during the summer months in the old village by Anglican missionaries. Since September 1962, a permanent day school with resident teachers employed by the Indian Affairs Branch has operated in the new village. In 1967 there were four classrooms and four teachers. In the fall of 1966 there were approximately 95 pupils enrolled, and although three-quarters of them were in the lower grades, several had reached grade six. In 1966 no Osnaburgh Indian was attending high school.

Prior to 1949, medical assistance was largely restricted to the annual visit of the doctor at treaty time and the Hudson's Bay Company manager who dispensed medicines to sick Indians. In 1949, an Indian hospital was built in Sioux Lookout by the Federal Department of Health and Welfare, and a tuberculosis detection program began. Since then, a mobile X-ray apparatus has accompanied the doctor on his visits to Osnaburgh. A nursing station was also opened at Osnaburgh in 1949. This operated continuously until 1959 when the Indian Health Service Branch of the Department of National Health and Welfare opened the Indian Health Centre in Central Patricia. A resident male nurse served Osnaburgh and vicinity. In an emergency Indians are flown directly to Sioux Lookout. In 1969, after the mines in the White towns had closed, the Health Center in Central Patricia was closed and the nursing station was moved to a trailer in the Osnaburgh House village. It is presently staffed by two nurses.

Health conditions in the Osnaburgh village are substandard when compared with White standards in the region. Dietary habits are generally poor, hence people lack adequate nutritional requirements. Houses are poorly insulated, and during the winter, are subject to extremes in temperature depending upon the amount of heat radiated by the wood stove. Again, clothing is frequently inadequate. Almost all Indians frequently suffer from colds and coughs, and due to the proximity of people in the village, diseases may spread to every household. Despite these health deficiencies, conditions are improving rapidly as an awareness of health needs grows.

Government services in the form of family allowance, old age pensions, welfare assistance, including equipment, and improved housing and medical facilities, have operated to reduce some of the uncertainties inherent in the former subsistence economy. Greater dependence upon such benefits has also altered the community organization and enhanced the importance of local liaison officers who represent government agencies. The Indian Affairs Branch is endeavouring to give local people more responsibility in their own affairs in an attempt to break with former paternalistic policies.

At present the position of the government is something of a paradox. At the same time the new services are being provided thereby increasing the dependence of the community, leadership and community initiative are being encouraged. Reliance upon the fur trade and the government in the past, and the newness of the concept of *community* have created a situation common throughout Subarctic Canada. Future success in a planned community development program is contingent upon the economic opportunities of the people near home, and in situations where they have some control. At present these opportunities are too few to maintain the community without welfare assistance.

Missionary Influence

The earliest missionaries to enter the area were Anglicans favoured by the Hudson's Bay Company. About 1900, an Anglican church was built at Osnaburgh and for many years after, missionary contacts were limited to the annual visits of the minister at treaty time. In 1951 a Catholic church was constructed in the old village while in the new village there is an Anglican church and a Catholic church. In 1958 the Northern Evangelical Mission of the Mennonite Church established a mission at Slate Falls on Bamaji Lake and the minister visited Osnaburgh each summer until 1963, when a Mennonite mission was established at Rat Rapids.

The Anglican church has by far the largest congregation and attracts from 35 to 50 people to Sunday services. Services are given partly in English by the minister, and partly in Ojibwa by the Ojibwa catechist. Prayer books in Cree syllabics are used. Although the Catholic church is the most imposing structure in the village, it rarely attracts more than 20 people to services, most of whom are children. However, the resident priest[14] has excellent rapport with the people and speaks fluent Ojibwa. The Mennonite mission which has the smallest following, often holds services in individual households, or transports the handful of followers to Rat Rapids.

Most native religious practices have disappeared, at least within the village itself. The Midewiwin ceremony probably has not been practiced at Osnaburgh since the mid-nineteenth century (cf. Skinner 1911:154). Within the last decade, there have been only two shaking tent ceremonies, the last being held in 1963. In

70

1965, one bear's nose erected on a pole and one medicine bundle and two native drums were noted outside the village. The fact remains, however, that much of the overt behaviour and paraphernalia associated with native religion may be becoming secretive. Again, many have retained a belief in the power of sorcery, while native medicinal cures and ghosts are much feared.

Mining and White Communities

Mining operations began about 20 miles north of Osnaburgh in 1928 and by the early 1930's, there were two major mines in operation: the Central Patricia Gold Mines Limited and the Pickle Crow Gold Mines Limited (LeBourdais 1957:267). Three small White communities sprang up near the mines, they being: Pickle Lake, Central Patricia and Pickle Crow. By 1937, a road joining the mining towns with Doghole Bay was completed. Hydro-electric power was provided to the mines by a power plant constructed at Rat Rapids in 1935, and the Ontario Hydro Electric Power Commission raised the water level of Lake St. Joseph by about eight feet. During the 1960's the Rat Rapids power plant shut down when electric power was supplied to the villages from Ear Falls to the west of Lake St. Joseph. By 1954 a road had been completed from the mining towns to Savant Lake on the Canadian National Railway line.

During the 1940's and 50's, a number of Osnaburgh Indians worked in the mines, and several Indian families moved to one of the White villages. However, it is reported that mine work did not agree with many Indians who were subjected to the prejudices of the miners. Some would work in the mines until the trapping season began at which point they would quit to return to more familiar and relaxed surroundings. The idea of working by a clock was too new to be accepted by many. Again, some were able to buy bootleg wine from miners and after a drinking bout, they would miss work for a few days and were subsequently fired. At the time when the Pickle Crow mine closed in late 1966, there were only four or five Osnaburgh Indians employed. The Central Patricia mine closed down milling operations in 1951.

There is also a small village at Savant Lake on the Canadian National Railway line about 95 miles south of Osnaburgh. The

71

Indian population totalling perhaps 75, consists of people from Osnaburgh, Lac Seul and Nipigon.

Whites and Indians in the towns maintain for the most part a separate existence. The Indians in the villages are definitely the socially and economically subordinate group and over the years have suffered from discrimination and prejudice. There is almost no visiting between the two groups, and although a certain amount of interaction exists, it is limited largely to formal business matters. In effect, the villages consist of two castes, White and Indian.

Traders and Stores

The most important store at Osnaburgh today, as in the past, is the Hudson's Bay Company post. The old Hudson's Bay post on Lake St. Joseph continued to operate until 1963 when a temporary store was established at Doghole Bay nearer the new village. During the winter of 1963-64, a new store was completed near the new village site at Doghole Lake. The new store is well stocked with a wide variety of goods including food, clothing and household equipment. Gear necessary for trapping and bush life is also available. In general, the store stocks to suit the demands and needs of the community which have increased to include a wide selection of materials far beyond those necessary for survival in the bush. Today, the main trade is no longer in furs but in cash received directly, or in credit for consumer goods. Both the social position of the Company employees, and the variety and type of consumer goods available have altered according to the changing position of a marginal people. In effect, the Hudson's Bay post has become a general store.

There are two other stores within 5 miles of the Osnaburgh village: one at Doghole Bay and the other at Rat Rapids[15]. The stock of supplies is smaller than at the Hudson's Bay Company store. There are also three stores in Pickle Lake, one of which is operated by the Hudson's Bay Company.

Attitudes Toward Whites

Within recent years contact with Euro-Canadians has increased markedly. There are resident teachers, missionaries, traders, and also the White villages. Government officials now visit the Osnaburgh village several times during the year, and automobiles pass the village daily. Except for a select few, most Whites are treated with suspicion. The Indians have tended to generalize the status of resident Whites to one of unlimited power, wealth and authority (cf. Dunning 1959a:170-4). The teachers can curtail Family Allowance cheques and strap misbehaving children while the nurse can decide whether an ill person should be sent to the hospital regardless of the person's wishes (cf. Tanner 1971). The government agents can, and have, used the threat of terminating rations payments if Indians do not conform to White expectations. In the White villages, discrimination is prevalent. As Dunning has so aptly stated:

> The Indian members of the society see themselves—in part rightly—as being snubbed, laughed at, or treated sadistically by the upper group (1959a:171).

Conclusions

The effect of White influences on the economy and social organization of the Osnaburgh House people has been significant. It is impossible to evaluate Osnaburgh society except against the external influences which are operating to modify it. Osnaburgh like numerous other Subarctic communities is experiencing a new type of contact situation through multiplex relationships. The impact of these factors is moulding a new type of society, in part constructed upon pre-existing structures, but in no way identical with them. Within the community, endogamy is positively sanctioned producing a deme type society. Subsidies and White influences have tended to weaken the authority of leadership, while households are growing increasingly independent. As Dunning has shown for the Pekangikum Ojibwa (1959a:198), the recent numerical increase and greater density of residence is producing stresses and strains. The same is true at Osnaburgh, only the processes leading to the concentration of people and the permanence of residence have advanced beyond those of Pekangikum. Former kinship obligations are weaker at Osnaburgh

73

today than at Pekangikum during the 1950's. Subsidies paid to individual households are tending to "atomize" community members rather than unite them while at present there are few activities to integrate members of the society which approximate an acephalous agglomeration (Dunning 1959a:200).

The manner in which change is occurring is affected by the institutions of the culture. Within any cultural system, there may be institutions to accommodate or even to encourage change. Those most conducive to change can only be determined by examining the culture in an historical context. Instability or lack of permanency in structure provide clues whereby the focus for change can be determined. For the Northern Ojibwa of Osnaburgh House, the emphasis appears to be on changing economics, since the most notable recent changes, at least, have come as a result of changing subsistence patterns and living standards; while the new social order is more a by-product of these, rather than a catalyst for cultural integration. It is the task now to discuss these recent economic changes and adjustments to the external factors of contact.

Footnotes

1. Records of temperature and precipitation were kept in Toronto, Canada, by the weather station operated by the Meteorological Branch of the Ontario Department of Transport at Rat Rapids from 1934 to 1950. During this period, the extreme minimum was -50°F. and the extreme maximum was 101°F. A weather station has also operated continuously in Pickle Lake 20 miles north of Osnaburgh House.

2. Ontario: Department of Lands and Forests: Sioux Lookout District Annual Fish & Wildlife Management Reports. It should be noted that data on kills obtained by the Department of Lands and Forests are frequently incomplete since Indians deliberately fail to record their kills accurately fearing government interference if they give too high a figure. Also, the Pickle Lake records include large game killed by the Cree from Big Trout Lake residing in Central Patricia.

3. Ontario: Department of Lands and Forests: Sioux Lookout District Annual Fish and Wildlife Management Reports.

4. Ontario: Department of Lands and Forests: Sioux Lookout District Annual Fish and Wildlife Management Reports.

5. Fishing poles are rarely used since fishing for sport is a White Man's luxury. Once, however, after the anthropologist returned one evening with twelve fat pike, several people were seen trying their luck with rod and reel!

6. Dunning (1959a:24) gives a figure of 100 square miles as the average size for Pekangikum, while I have computed from Rogers' figures (1962:C28) that the average Round Lake territory is 278 square miles. Hallowell gives a figure of 93 square miles for Berens River during the 1930's (1949:40). If all 145 men who obtained trapping licences at Osnaburgh in 1964-65 had trapped, the average area per trapper would have been 83 square miles.

7. Further research is needed to support this view. Other forms of labour such as brush clearing along the road, winter commercial fishing, and increased government subsidies have lessened the total man hours devoted to trapping pursuits. The figures in Table 7 do not show positive evidence of these changes except in the case of mink. Mink, which are sought mainly in the early winter, have declined from a high of 1,480 in 1960-61, to a meagre 346 in 1965-66. Since most trapping is done in late April and early May for aquatic fur bearers, beaver, otter and muskrat, the slight drop in numbers does not adequately reflect the actual decline.

8. I have computed this figure and those in Table 8 from the Department of Lands and Forests data on the average price paid for fur bearers in northern Ontario. The figures for the different species have been reduced slightly since it is said that the Osnaburgh House Indians got less for their furs than Indians in other communities because some persons did not prepare the pelts properly.

9. During the late summer of 1966, a number of Osnaburgh and Cat Lake Indians were employed on fruit farms in the Niagara Peninsula. Although they got a good view of the south, living conditions were generally poor. There were few forms of recreation and many persons spent what they earned on

alcohol which would have been prohibited to them on the reserve.

10. While within the past 175 years, totem membership has merely functioned to regulate marriages, largely because members have been widely dispersed, there is good evidence that during the early historic period common membership in a totem group meant common residence and strong cooperative bonds of solidarity, that is, totem members once formed localized patrilineal descent groups with corporate activities and rights.

11. The Osnaburgh House kinship terminology seems to be changing from a *bifurcate collateral* type smaller to that described by Hallowell at Berens River (1937:95-110), and Dunning at Pekangikum (1959a:72-77) to a *lineal* type system. Hallowell, Dunning and Rogers have already presented detailed accounts of the kinship system and changes, while Eggan (1966) has recently summarized the literature on cross-cousin marriage noting the variant manifestations of change processes.

12. Among the Plains Cree of Alberta visited by Hallowell, first cousin marriage is rare while marriage with second cousins is common (Eggan 1966:92). Also, Harold Scheffler has noted that the Plains Ojibwa terminology has remained much the same even though all cousins are now treated like siblings (Eggan 1966:93).

13. About 1970, the Cat Lake people got their wish and formed a new treaty band with a chief and councillor.

14. In 1967, the priest was transferred to Ogoki, and while he was not replaced, a priest visits the village each week to hold services.

15. The store at Doghole Bay was relocated to Rat Rapids about 1968, since it was near a right-of-way on reserve lands.

Chapter Three
History and Conditions at Osnaburgh House: 1890-1945

Introduction[1]

The basis for modern-day Northern Ojibwa life was laid during earlier decades, especially toward the end of the nineteenth century when contact with the outside world intensified. Nevertheless, outside influences were considerably less than in recent years although the major difference between acculturative pressures then and now is primarily one of degree and intensity. Qualitatively, the acculturative process has remained the same in that the Indians of 1900 had comparatively little more control over their destiny than at present. The agents of the outside world thrust themselves upon them, and although the Ojibwa did not necessarily discourage these intrusions, they would have had little power to prevent them. Their culture was now being influenced by such new types as miners, surveyors, geologists, missionaries, and government officials, where prior to the 1880's, contact had occurred mainly through a single type of agent, the fur trader. Thus, the last decades of the nineteenth century marked the beginning of a new era for the Northern Ojibwa with the penetration of Euro-Canadians interested in resources other than furs. Indians attached to trading posts to the south of Osnaburgh were already receiving treaty benefits by the 1870's, while missionary activities, which had begun at Osnaburgh during the 1840's, were intensified during the 1880's. The construction of the Canadian Pacific Railway south of Osnaburgh gave the Indians their first view of the technological complexity of the outside world and resulted in a change in the Hudson's Bay Company supply route to the Osnaburgh House post. Goods were shipped from Dinorwic (Wabigoon Tank) on the CPR line instead of via the older and more difficult route up the Albany River from Fort Albany on James Bay. The change assured a greater quantity and variety of trade supplies and lessened the chance of exhaustion of store goods.

In addition, major ecological changes were occurring toward the end of the nineteenth century. By the late 1860's, it became possible for Osnaburgh House Indians to exchange furs for small quantities of store foods[2], and by the 1880's some people were growing summer gardens to supplement their food resources[3]. After 1870, caribou became more common in the Osnaburgh vicinity[4], and by 1900, moose again entered the region after their disappearance eighty years before. These changes tended to ease the harsh conditions which had prevailed earlier in the century.

We now turn to a closer inspection of these White influences and then to the social and economic life of the Osnaburgh House Ojibwa as it was at the end of the nineteenth century.

Euro-Canadian Influences

Traders and Stores

At the turn of the century, conditions at the Osnaburgh House post were not radically different than during the 1850's. However, there were more trade goods and the food supply at the store was more varied and reliable. The main foods traded to Indians about 1900 were flour, oatmeal, sugar, tea, and small amounts of pork. Between 1900 and 1910, canvas tents and Peterboro canoes began to replace birch bark forms. The first permanent log Indian houses at Osnaburgh were constructed, and were used only during the summer and at Christmas when families came in from their bush settlements. Most Indians, however, continued to live in tents while at the post. Except for parkas of hare hide and mitts and mocassins of moosehide, Indians wore White manufactured clothing.

During the 1890's, the HBC settlement had grown to include about ten buildings surrounded by a garden[5]. Of the crops grown, potatoes were the most important producing about 200 bushels or kegs annually. The only outpost until the end of the century was at Cat Lake where a post had been re-established in 1873 after having been abandoned for nearly 50 years.

At Osnaburgh, there were usually four or five White and half-breed full-time employees with their wives and families. Half-breed employees, while subject to the authority of the manager, had certain privileges about the post by virtue of their employment which bush Indians did not have. Although their work could be both monotonous and often arduous, they were able to live in log houses and eat Euro-Canadian foods. Actually, post chores frequently required the cooperative labour of both the employees and the Indians, and racial prejudices seem to have been relatively rare or, at least, they did not interfere with social relationships. Nevertheless, the traders could and often did apply pressure on Indians who failed to pay their debts when they were capable of doing so. Since making a good catch in furs was highly esteemed by most Indians, a public reprimand by the manager, while humiliating, also reinforced their economic subordination. Managers, for the most part, were benevolent tyrants who generally got along well with the Indians, but who could wield the whip when they had to.

The summer of 1890 marked a turning point for both the Osnaburgh trading post and for the Indians. This was the first year that trade goods were brought in from Wabigoon Tank on the CNR. A warehouse was built at Sandy Lake near the railway from whence the goods were conveyed to Osnaburgh in two boats. Indian freighters did most of the work for which each man was paid sixteen made beaver[6] (one made beaver was worth 46 cents) for a round trip taking twenty-four days. The route to the CNR considerably reduced the effort in getting goods to the post since the old route down the Albany to Martin's Falls and return took some forty days. The Osnaburgh Indians were quick to grasp the significance of the situation, and "objected to going down even as far as Martin's Falls, and the route to Wabigoon had to be adopted . . . " which actually resulted in a considerable saving in pay and provisions[7]. The change in the supply route not only improved freighting conditions, but also allowed for a greater quantity and variety of goods on hand[8]. After 1912 when the Canadian National Railway was completed, the supply route again changed, and goods were shipped from Hudson via Lac Seul and Root Portage. A tugboat towed several York boats each carrying about five tons of supplies down Lake St. Joseph to Osnaburgh House[9]. It is evident from these changes that the summer months had become a very busy time for both the traders and the local Indians who were involved in the freighting activities.

The improved supply route not only allowed the store to keep a better stock of goods on hand, it also provided an access to competitors of the HBC.

By the 1870's, there was a certain amount of competition among the Hudson's Bay Company stores as well as with free traders entering the area from the south. Frequently, the opposition traders visited the Indian encampments so that the Osnaburgh traders had to send men to keep watch over Indians subjected to these temptations. In 1891, R. C. Wilson, the Osnaburgh manager stated that it was necessary to send for and collect furs from Indians regularly or they would be traded with the Lac Seul Indians[10]. According to Wilson:

> The trade is affected by the high prices paid at Lac Seul. Nepigon sends men after the traders opposing us in that district, and these men come among the Osnaburgh Indians and take furs from them. It is to some extent necessary that they should do so in some cases to prevent fur falling into the hands of the traders, but they frequently come too far under this pretext and take away furs which they have no business to touch.

The real threat from opposition traders began in 1901, when the G. A. McLaren Trading Company erected stores near Osnaburgh. In 1901, the McLaren Company built a post on Savant Lake and by July, they were erecting a store twelve miles east of Osnaburgh[11]. That summer, they used a "gram-o-phone" to make speeches to Indians on trade matters to win them over; nevertheless, they procured very few furs the first year. Jabez Williams, the Osnaburgh manager, warned, however, that with a few more supplies and flour, they would make trouble in future. They had hired Lac Seul Indians to do their freighting from Dinorwic. Williams, in order to watch the situation, moved into a small building near the McLaren store for most of the winter:

> I kept close watch of them—and feel sure that they secured very few skins from Osnaburgh Indians—the bulk of what

furs they may have caught coming from among the Nepigon Indians. I judge their whole seasons catch at $500.00.[12]

The next summer saw the construction of several new stores by both the HBC and the McLaren Company[13]. One of the McLaren stores, managed by a man named Edwards, was located directly across the lake at the Pedler's Path[14]. While most of these new posts were actually operated at a loss, the HBC gained the bulk of the trade. Nevertheless, the Ojibwa were able to compare prices and by 1904 the McLaren Company had managed to capture the trade of a number of Osnaburgh Indians despite a drop in the price of the HBC goods. The increased competition was making the Indians more demanding, especially those of Cat Lake who "want everything their own way and ... took a notion to try and find someone else who would use them as they think they should be treated"[15].

The opposition was certainly giving the Osnaburgh HBC post a rough time by 1904. Not only was the HBC losing valuable pelts, but they lost two employees who joined the McLaren Company, while the post at Pedler's Path had to be closed due to high operating costs. That winter the McLaren traders had "two dog teams going all the time, in addition to the little jogs ... placed all over the country in the fall". Although the Bay tried to avoid chasing after Indians lest McLaren capture their furs, the intensive competition now necessitated it even though there was a shortage of sled dogs for travel. At present there is no available data on the outcome of this competition but it seems that by about 1910 the McLaren Company either sold out or was forced out of business.

By the late 1920's, competitors again began to establish stores near Osnaburgh, the first of which was operated by a former Hudson's Bay Company employee on a point two miles west of Osnaburgh House. With the influx of miners during the late 1920's and 30's to the region twenty miles north of Osnaburgh, stores sprang up. By the 1950's, there were three stores in Pickle Lake, one of which was run by the Hudson's Bay Company. Most of the outposts which had been built shortly after the turn of the century were vacated about 1930, largely due to improved transportation facilities. A store at Slate Falls on Bamaji Lake near the west end of Lake St. Joseph, and another store at Savant Lake village (formerly known as Bucke) have operated continuously since the early twentieth century.

During the early twentieth century, Indians kept a record of their balances either on wooden sticks stamped with Hudson's Bay Company seals, or in made beaver coins[16] produced by the Company. Both were useful in ensuring that Indians would trade at the Bay posts, since they were of no value elsewhere. By the 1920's, some Indians were asking for their balances in cash if the value of the furs exceeded their debts. Another method of keeping Indians from competitors at this date was to give them a short supply of matches forcing them to return to the post frequently, since by 1910, Indians could not survive in the winter without matches.

Table 19   Number and Value of Furs Taken at Osnaburgh House: End of May, 1903 and 1904

Species	Number	1904 Value	Number	1903 Value
Bear—black	119	$ 11.55	113	$ 6.00
—brown	2	10.25	1	5.00
Beaver	301	4.45	322	4.40
Castoreum (lb)	10	6.80	11	6.35
Ermine	332	.25 (approx)	281	.73 (approx)
Fisher	189	5.20	116	5.00
Fox				
—silver-grey	9	105.00	5	70.00
—cross	16	7.35	20	5.50
—red	54	5.30	42	4.00
—white	5	4.25		
Lynx	199	6.80	163	5.30
Marten	516	6.25	312	5.10
Mink	1237	2.25	1409	2.15
Musquash (Muskrat)	6745	.07½	5053	.14
Otter	232	9.20	233	10.00
Skunk	28	.68	10	.65
Wenusk (Groundhog)	5	.06	5	.11
Wolf			1	4.10

Prior to the 1940's, the fur trade and associated activities dominated Indian life. Furs were the chief means by which the Northern Ojibwa were able to acquire the trade goods necessary to survival. Indians spent most of the year at bush camps engaged in trapping activities. In spring, and again around Christmas, they would bring their pelts to the post. Table 19 presents the quantities and value of furs obtained at Osnaburgh in 1903 and 1904[17]. Even though the McLaren Fur Trading Company was in the area, the figures probably represent at least 90 percent of the furs obtained by Osnaburgh Indians.

By the 1910's, the price of furs appears to have risen. Indeed, fur prices fluctuated semi-annually and certain species could vary considerably over a two-year period. Table 20 presents fur prices at four different times from October, 1916, to January, 1918[18].

Table 20   Comparative Fur Prices: 1916-1918

Species	Oct. 1916	Apr. 1917	Oct. 1917	Jan. 1918
Bear—black	$ 15.57	$ 12.65	$ 18.25	$ 18.25
—brown	6.08	6.08	7.30	7.30
Beaver	5.96	6.81	11.19	14.84
Ermine (per 40)	20.68	37.60	41.36	41.37
Fisher	26.77	27.98	58.40	46.23
Fox—cross	26.16	27.50	48.67	44.29
—bastard	9.49	11.92	17.03	18.25
—red	9.49	12.65	18.98	15.09
—silver	155.73	131.40	194.67	194.67
—white	20.68	24.33	29.20	31.63
Lynx	6.08	7.30	12.65	13.14
Marten	7.06	10.46	14.11	17.76
Mink	3.77	3.29	4.02	4.50
Musquash	.55	.45	.79	.77
Otter	9.61	12.41	13.14	14.84

As mentioned, the purpose of treaties with the government was to provide a means to govern and protect native people through Indian councils.

In 1850, the Indians residing along the north shore of Lake Huron and Superior relinquished their rights to the land for $16,640, plus a perpetual annuity of $4,400 upon signing the Robinson Treaty[19]. The area extended north of the Great Lakes to the height of land between the Atlantic and Arctic Ocean Drainage systems, and west to the Pigeon River. Three Reserves were established in the Robinson-Superior sector: one near Fort William, the Gros Cap Reserve near Michipicoten and one at Gull River near Lake Nipigon.

On August 3, 1871, parts of southern Manitoba were ceded (Treaty No. 1); and on August 21, 1871, large sections north of this to Berens River were surrendered (Treaty No. 2). Two years later in 1873, the North-West Angle Treaty (also called Treaty No. 3) was signed. The area incorporated included Lac Seul and the extreme west end of Lake St. Joseph. Each person within the area received $12 for relinquishing his claims, and each was to receive an annual payment of $5. Schools were promised, and intoxicating liquors were to be prohibited within the confines of the Reserves. In addition, horticultural practices were encouraged by providing each family that cultivated the soil with gardening equipment. The chief of each band was to receive an annual salary of $25, and each councillor $15. Every three years these officers were to receive a suit of clothes, a medal, and a flag[20].

The provisions of treaty were something the Osnaburgh Indians and those to the north of the Albany River, in what was then the Northwest Territories, were well aware of by 1900. At this date, Osnaburgh lay within the proposed Treaty No. 9 region which included most of the area between the Manitoba and Quebec borders drained by the rivers flowing into James Bay and Hudson Bay. Some Indians in this area as early as 1899 complained that miners, prospectors, and surveyors were becoming so numerous that they were disturbing the game and interfering with the means of livelihood of the Indians[21].

In 1901, the Osnaburgh Indians signed a petition requesting to release the rights to their lands and receive annuity benefits. They complained that explorations for minerals were being conducted on their territories, and Whites were building on their lands. The Osnaburgh House Hudson's Bay Company factor, Jabez Williams, wrote[22] in December, 1901:

> We held a council during October 1901 AD and decided to make formal request as above stated and also discussed the matter of the location of the land which we would like to reserve for the use of ourselves and descendents.

Following another Treaty Council in 1902 provisions to incorporate the bands began. Prior to 1905, many Osnaburgh Indians were travelling to Lac Seul and Nipigon House to receive annuity payments.

The Osnaburgh band officially signed treaty with the Canadian government in 1905. Most of the Indians were present at Osnaburgh when the treaty party arrived except those from Cat Lake who had returned to their hunting territories apparently to avoid signing the treaty. In 1905, the Windigo Lake Cranes[23], who traded their furs at Cat Lake, were led by an old leader who seemed to resent the interference of government officials. Upon the death of the old chief in late 1905, the Cranes agreed to meet the government agents. The Commissioner of the Hudson's Bay Company wrote[24] in October, 1906:

> This is the first time the Cranes have consented to give up their lands, but the death of their old Chief last year has given the chance to settle the matter.

It was not only the Cat Lake Indians who were apprehensive. Those from Osnaburgh had similar qualms, expressed to the treaty party by the old blind leader, Missabay, who

> spoke, expressing the fears of the Indians that, if they signed the treaty, they would be compelled to reside upon the reserve to be set apart from them, and would be deprived of the fishing privileges which they now enjoy[25].

85

The commissioners then explained the conditions of the treaty to the Indians who were to receive $4 per person, but no gardening equipment. The Indians then asked to be given until the following day to give their answer. After considering the matter the Osnaburgh people agreed to sign the treaty and Missabay again made a speech advising his people to listen to those who had brought such benefits. At this time the location of the Reserves was discussed, and the election of a chief and two councillors took place. Missabay became the first elected chief. The ceremonies ended in a feast.

At the time of the first treaty payments, sections of land were promised for Reserves. The size of the Reserves was based upon the number of families, "in proportion of one square mile for each family of five or in the proportion for larger or smaller families"[26]. The Osnaburgh band was granted an area of 20 square miles on the south shore of Lake St. Joseph within the boundary of Ontario, and 53 square miles on the north side of the lake then within the Northwest Territories.

In 1909, when the survey of the proposed Reserves began, it was discovered that the proposed location of the Reserve north of the lake marked at the signing of the treaty was not where the Indians had understood it to have been. The Indians were also unhappy with the section of land on the south shore, as it had been burnt over, and included swampy areas. Due to the confusion the survey was held up until 1912. It was finally decided that the Indians would have to accept the original Reserve area on the south shore of the lake, but they were given permission to change the area on the north side. The new Reserve area north of the Albany River was not officially approved until 1930 when alterations and additions to Treaty No. 9 were made. Mining operations 20 miles north of Osnaburgh and in other regions of the north resulted in the incorporation of Indians north of the Albany River drainage.

The Cat Lake Indians were considered as members of the Osnaburgh band when the treaty was signed. At that date, the Cat Lake Hudson's Bay post was still an outpost of Osnaburgh, and for many years after, the Cat Lake Indians had to travel to Osnaburgh to receive their annuity payments. However, contact between Cat Lake and Osnaburgh Indians was restricted to brief visits at Treaty time. This contact has steadily decreased since about 1920, and for this reason, the Cat Lake Indians did not consider themselves as belonging to the same community as the Osnaburgh people. By 1936 the Cat Lake Indians wrote the Indians Affairs Branch requesting a Reserve on the north shore of Cat Lake adjacent to the Hudson's Bay post in order that they could become a separate band with their own chief and council. They indicated that they "having nothing in common with the Osnaburgh Band at Lake St. Joseph where the Chief and Councillors are elected"[27]. However, in 1938, the Osnaburgh people indicated that they were not willing to split the band even though a proposed Reserve area of 538 acres was surveyed that year. In 1940, negotiations were arranged to purchase the land at $538 ($1 per acre) despite objections by the Osnaburgh people. In 1967, it was discovered that the Cat Lake Reserve had never actually been purchased nor confirmed by the Canadian government, although both the Cat Lake Indians and government officials have been operating unknowingly as if a Reserve *did* exist. Recently the necessary steps were taken to formalize and make official the Cat Lake Reserve.

Contact with the government increased steadily after 1905. Until the early 1920's the treaty party travelled to Osnaburgh by canoe each summer and from about 1924 until the agency headquarters were established in Sioux Lookout about 1939, the group flew directly from Ottawa annually and spent three or four days at Osnaburgh during which time the business of the year was settled. Accompanying the Indian Affairs Branch officials was a doctor, a nurse, and a Royal Canadian Mounted Police officer. Until the 1920's the Indian men would line up along the shore as the treaty party approached firing their guns into the air as a sign of welcome. The following is a description of some of the events that occurred on Treaty Day, July 1st 1929.

At Osnaburgh some 498 Indians were paid treaty money and during the afternoon of Dominion Day a program of sports with suitable prizes was provided. The games consisted amongst others, of running, jumping and stone putting. The unfortunate absence of the movie picture operator lost an opportunity of securing some historic records of the first Dominion Day Celebrations that band had ever experienced. The games were all spiritedly contested and special features such as the Baby Beauty Show, the most successful hunter, and the shot putting contest gave the Indians decided enjoyment[28].

A dance was almost always held in the evening to the music of violins, guitars, and until about 1960, drums. Until about 1954, celebrations were held near the Hudson's Bay Company store.

Before the Osnaburgh Indians signed the treaty in 1905, contact with government agents was minimal. Today, it is difficult to conceive how the members of the Osnaburgh band could survive without government assistance.

Medical Treatment

In 1900, treatment of the ill was left mainly to the curing shamans, although Indians occasionally resorted to the trading post to receive medicine from the Hudson's Bay Company manager, probably only after native remedies failed. This is in marked contrast to the present situation where the Indian Health Service nurses cater to the sick and aged continuously; and where serious cases of illness can be removed to nearby hospitals. Also, most births now occur in hospitals, whereas in 1900, a midwife performed the duty in a remote bush camp.

Although the Osnaburgh Ojibwa were better off economically in 1900 than they had been during the middle of the nineteenth century, starvation and exposure to the elements still took their toll. Disease 70 years ago was a major killer and included severe colds, measles and by 1903, tuberculosis which was spreading throughout northern Ontario causing sickness and death. Although on occasion, a few Osnaburgh Indians received medical treatment at Dinorwic by the late 1890's, Euro-Canadian doctors did not enter the Osnaburgh region until the treaty was signed in 1905. After this date, medical practitioners accompanied the treaty party each year. At the first treaty gathering, Dr. Meindl, the treaty group physician, stated that the Osnaburgh band never "had any medical help, the whole band in a very unhealthy condition. Tuberculosis actively present in 65 percent"[29]. In the winter of 1917-18, a serious influenza epidemic killed at least 13 Osnaburgh Indians in the Lake Savant region[30]. Until 1949, when a nursing station was established at Osnaburgh, disease and exposure resulted in many deaths.

Missionary Activities

Christian churches and missionaries have become an intrinsic part of the social organization among contemporary Ojibwa. All funerals, baptisms and weddings are now performed by missionaries. Although many beliefs connected with the former native religion are still held, the paraphernalia and overt rites have virtually disappeared. Most of these changes can be accounted for by missionary influences over the past 100 years. The shaking-tent ceremony has not been performed since 1963 and native drums and bear ceremonialism are present in the bush, but are becoming increasingly rare. Probably people have not gone on vision quests for nearly 30 years. Missionary and medical influences have largely undermined the influence of the few remaining shamans, although the latter still sell their magic potions. Although all the above forms of native religion were present in 1900, missionary influences had even then produced changes. According to Skinner, in 1909, the Midewiwin

> rites are not practiced north of Lac Seul although there are many Saulteaux living even at Fort Hope who were once members of this society. The head conjuror, or mideo, resided at Lac Seul and it is said appointed one man of each degree at Fort Hope and probably at other posts (1911:154).

It is probable that the Midewiwin disappeared at Osnaburgh during the 1870's about the time that missionary activities were intensified.

Anglican missionaries first entered the Osnaburgh region during the middle of the nineteenth century, but apparently did not make annual visits to the post until after 1870. Nevertheless, by the late nineteenth century, many Indians had become nominal

Christians. Missionaries usually spent about a week at the post each summer during which time they held services and performed marriages and baptisms. In 1891, prayer books and hymn books were sold to several Indians[31] and by 1898 a church was being used for services[32]. Despite Christian influences, however, many old beliefs continued. Table 21 presents the numbers of Indians in different religious categories[33]. Although there was no specific data on those Indians classified as "pagans", these persons may have been those who had not been baptized, or who did not attend church services when the missionary was present.

Table 21   Religious Affiliation of Osnaburgh Indians

Year	Anglican	Catholic	Pagan	No. in Band
1934	430	66		496
1939	314	39	137	490
1944	333	41	97	471
1949	406	29	56	491
1954	505	33	6	544
1959	573	41	39	654

Economic Conditions

The Food Quest

Although cases of death by starvation were very rare after the 1880's, since store foods were available, the food quest took up a considerable portion of the time of Osnaburgh Indians. A scarcity of hare during the winter season frequently caused hardships and interfered with trapping activities. For instance, in 1899, "Indians are bringing poor hunts. They have been starving all spring. Rabbits being scarce."[34] Sometimes, in winter, Indians were forced to fish through the ice or return to the store for a supply of flour or oatmeal.

The return of large game animals toward the end of the century also lessened the threat of starvation. Prior to the 1870's, caribou were very scarce in the region of Osnaburgh but after this date, they appear to have become more numerous providing an important supplement to the Indian diet. Previously, subsistence had been based almost solely on hare, fish, fur bearers and water-fowl except during the summer and early fall when berries and wild rice were collected. Nevertheless, caribou were not always available. Reports indicate that although Indians in one area might kill great numbers, groups in a different quarter obtained none at all.

Moose, which had been exterminated from northern Ontario during the 1820's re-entered the region during the 1890's and early 1900's. Although moose tracks were observed at Cat Lake in 1885[35], the first recorded kill was made near that store in March, 1893. There are a number of reports of moose kills after this date, however, moose do not seem to have been plentiful until after 1905. Skinner, in 1909, underscored the significance of moose to the Indian diet noting that one Osnaburgh hunter killed 32 during the winter of 1908-09 (Skinner 1911:134). The invasion of numerous large animals within a decade appears to have altered subsistence pursuits and the diet. Also, instead of trading for leather at the store as had been the policy, Indians were able to provide their own hides for moccasins, mitts and snowshoes. Smaller game, nevertheless, continued to supplement the larger animals.

During the summer, a variety of foods was eaten of which fish were the most important. Indeed, it would appear that Indian families supplied with nets were overfishing the region near the Osnaburgh post where the traders fished[36].

Although some Osnaburgh Indians tried to farm during the mid-nineteenth century, they failed mainly due to an inadequate knowledge of proper techniques. By the 1880's however, mission-aries at Osnaburgh, and government agents at more southerly posts where Indians had signed treaties, were encouraging garden-ing. In addition to religious instruction, missionaries were teach-ing Indians to grow gardens in order that they become more "civilized". Concerning the Osnaburgh Indians, H. B. Proudfoot, in his survey and exploration report for 1900, stated:

Some years ago the Indians in this district made an attempt at farming on Pushkokon [Pashkokogan] Lake, clearings were made, houses erected, and a short distance down the river from the lake, root houses were built. They have abandoned their farms of late years and now grow their potatoes near Osnaburgh House on Lake St. Joseph[37].

These agricultural efforts are in evidence throughout northern Ontario by the turn of the century. In 1903, the chief of the Cranes was requesting hoes, spades and other garden tools[38]. By 1905, he had built a house at Windigo Lake and was raising potatoes[39]. Despite these gardening endeavours, the Northern Ojibwa were primarily hunters who wintered away from the store.

In addition to native foods and a few potatoes, Indians were able to procure store foods; nevertheless, they could not survive on these alone. In his medical report conducted at the first treaty meeting in 1905, Dr. Meindl stated that except for the

> small amount of provisions obtained from the fur-traders, they are wholly dependent on fish and game as a food-supply. In a territory where both of these are so variable, it is almost a constant state of semi-starvation or over-feeding[40].

Indian Labour for the Post

In addition to trapping, Indians performed several important functions for the Hudson's Bay Company. The most important employment was freighting goods from Dinorwic (and later Root Portage) to the post. Perhaps thirty or more men were involved in this occupation which lasted from early summer to September. While on the supply boats: "The white servants and the natives work together, eat together and associate together on equal terms"[41]. Indians assisted the boats across portages and through rivers and lakes. When they reached their destination, supplies had to be loaded or unloaded. The Indian men were each paid 16 made beaver (about $7.50) in trade goods for each round trip to Dinorwic that they made[42]. Freighting was difficult work and reports of injuries while on voyage are common.

Another occupation for a few Indians involved fishing for the post during the autumn. Usually between 3,500 and 5,000 fish were taken which provided the post with an important food source during the winter. There were from two to four fishing stations on Lake St. Joseph operating during the 1890's and each was manned by two persons from late September to late October. For example, in 1891:

> 4 stations up the Lake. Lawson & Kichence John Skunk & George, Thomas Skunk & Henry Lawson, Moosecheese and his brother, Fanny and his son to North Falls fishing for the Mess[43].

That fall, some 5,760 fish were procured (which was more than usual) of which 2,970 were whitefish. The fish were either salted or smoke dried.

Indians performed a variety of other tasks including cutting and hauling firewood, weeding and digging the potato gardens, and building canoes. Indian women were hired to sew, cook, wash clothes, and keep the buildings clean. Guiding and interpreting for surveyors, missionaries, and government agents was rendered by some Ojibwa, while on occasion native foods such as venison, hare, ducks, geese, and berries were supplied to the post. In addition, a few men were kept in continual employment doing odd jobs about the post. The management of camp trade, which increased in importance with the influx of free traders toward the end of the nineteenth century, was often bestowed upon Indians and half-breeds. Nevertheless, employment in White occupations was of minor importance to the Indian population as a whole who continued to direct their activities toward hunting, fishing, and trapping, albeit under conditions better than those obtaining earlier in the century.

Trapping and Territoriality

Indians of this period (1890-1945) were totally dependent on the trading post for their needs since most of their aboriginal technology had long since been replaced. The chief means of satisfying these needs was through trapping. Mr. Borron, in his report of 1890, summed up[44] the dependence relationship:

> ... flour, **pork**, tallon and woollen clothing and blankets having now become necessaries of life to many of the present generation of natives, and powder, shot, guns, axes and nets, etc. having become equally indispensable to the rudest Indian. . . . The position of the natives of this territory in relation to the Hudson's Bay Company . . . has therefore, been for many years, and still continues to be, a position of absolute subservience and dependence.

Indians dependent on the store for their material wants and on small non-migratory fauna such as hare and fur bearers had developed family hunting territories throughout most of northern Ontario by the middle of the nineteenth century (Bishop 1970). However, by the 1890's the sense of territoriality was growing weaker. In 1909, Skinner reported (1911:151) fully developed trapping territories in the Osnaburgh area, but stated that rules against trespass had grown lax. I have argued (1970) that this weakening was promoted by the return of large game, caribou and moose. Since these migratory animals are not confined by artificially bounded territories, the pursuit of them would convey hunters into the territories of their neighbours where they might also be tempted to trap. Although the return of large game and a modification of subsistence patterns was likely a factor in the decline of territoriality, there were other reasons.

After 1890, there was a certain amount of competition among traders who often travelled about to collect the Indian's furs. This competition, it would seem, was fostering dishonesty among some Indians who may even have been encouraged to poach on the lands of their more scrupulous neighbours. Another factor may have been the population increase toward the end of the nineteenth century which forced Indians to poach in order to acquire enough furs to obtain their necessary trade supplies. I suggest then that it was a combination of these three factors; the change in subsistence emphasis, increased competition in the fur trade, and a population growth which led to a weakening of territoriality toward the end of the last century.

Where trespass is a threat, conservation practices do not work since poachers merely move in and trap areas left fallow. There is evidence that former conservation practices were being ignored at Osnaburgh. According to R. C. Wilson[45], in 1891:

There is not thought to be any permanent increase or decrease in any furs except Beaver which are probably becoming exterminated. The Indians, annually driven further back by the encroachment of hunters from other places, no longer spare a few animals for breeding, even on their own lands, as has hitherto been their custom.

There seems also to have been a fear of White trappers who were encroaching on Indian lands near Lake Nipigon and Sturgeon Lake by this time. As Hallowell has noted (1949:43-44) this would mean that there would be less game available for Indians. There are indications that this threat was perceived by the Osnaburgh Indians who, in 1902, requested that prospectors not disturb their hunting grounds[46].

Although furs themselves were the property of individual trappers, it would seem that most trappers exploited their territories in twos or threes—a practice guaranteeing greater safety and sociability. There is frequent mention of the term "partner" in the journals. For example, in 1888, the Cat Lake trader, Vincent, remarked that

Tooshinan should winter with Whaywhay. But Tooshinan has set off to his Father-in-law's (Shakoquon) but with Wavey's sister as his wife. So left Whaywhay all alone like a crow on a stone, in fact he can't hunt not liking to sleep out by himself[47].

Thus, it would seem that winter camps were occupied by extended families with several trappers. Actually, according to Jabez Williams, in 1902, every girl, woman, and boy trapped a little so that "There are over 200 accounts at Osnaburgh alone—without Cat Lake"[48]. The fact, however, that Williams had to record the name of every person who brought furs to the post regardless of age and sex accentuates the degree to which individualism had permeated certain areas of Ojibwa culture by the late nineteenth century.

Material Changes

Although much of the native technology had already been

replaced in 1900, many items not present today were still in use. Indians then resided in birch bark lodges, although there may have been a few log shacks being constructed. Canoes of birch bark were the only type used until about 1910, and sleds, toboggans, and snowshoes were also locally made. Although the muzzle loader was of far greater significance, the bow and arrow was still occasionally used in hunting. Locally manufactured wooden traps and deadfalls supplemented steel traps and snares obtained from the Hudson's Bay Company. Gill nets made of twine obtained from the store were of considerable importance to native economy to catch fish in the summer and autumn, although native-constructed weirs were important in the spring.

Despite these retentions, many changes had occurred. Not only had many traditional items been replaced, but the inventory of goods possessed by Indians was augmented by guns, hatchets, knives, twine, files, pots, and pans, all of which had become standard equipment. Skinner remarked in 1909, that,

> Almost all clothing, both of the ancient and the transitional period has been discarded, with the exception of occasional rabbitskin costumes which are still worn by invalids, or during winter by healthy persons (Skinner 1911:123).

It is evident from this description that economic conditions were considerably less favourable than they are today. It is also evident that permanent village life was impossible under conditions where the search for furs and food required so much time and energy. To understand the nature of village organization today, it is necessary to examine the effects of the ecology upon the social organization in the past.

Social Organization

The social organization of the Osnaburgh House Ojibwa at the turn of the twentieth century was appreciatively different than today. Then, there was no resident Indian population living permanently near the post and there were few log cabins in use. Sizable numbers of Indians existed about the post only for a short period lasting about a week at Christmas and for perhaps a

96

month during the early summer. Osnaburgh Indians brought their winter catches to the store in early June and departed for fishing localities "not much later than the first week in July"[49].

For most of the year, Indians lived in bush camps or co-residential units of the kind described by Dunning (1959a). According to Skinner, these winter groups were composed of "several related families, though this does not always follow" (1911:149). At the signing of the treaty in 1905, there were 265 Indians listed as having received annuity payments. This figure probably did not encompass all the Osnaburgh Indians since it would appear that some of the people who traded at Cat Lake were omitted. Dr. Meindl, in his medical report that year, stated that the average size of the family was 13[50]. Assuming that these families were actually commensal units which made up larger co-residential groups, there would have been about 20 to 21 commensal units which could be grouped into perhaps 9 to 12 co-residential groups. The number of co-residential groups has been established from informants who located winter campsites dating to 1920. It will be shown in Chapter 5 that there were six co-residential or hunting units averaging 20 to 30 persons each near Osnaburgh during the 1850's. The rather large size of winter camps is supported by Skinner's reference to the two-fire house which, although obsolete in 1909, usually housed four families (1911:120). Winter camps were bilateral and exogamous.

The Osnaburgh clans listed by Skinner were: Sturgeon, Sucker, Loon and Caribou (1911:150). To these I would add Pelican and Moose[51]. Skinner recorded that the clans were matrilineal and exogamous, although informant testimony and comparative materials (cf. Jenness 1935:7-9; Dunning 1959a:79-83; Hickerson 1962a:76-80; 1966) seem to indicate that they were patrilineal. Nevertheless, Hickerson (1962:7) has suggested that the temporary matrilocal residence hinted at during the nineteenth century for more southerly Ojibwa groups, and *Iroquois* cousin terminology may indicate an earlier pre-contact matrilineal organization. Skinner, however, states that post-marital residence was virilocal (1911:151). Informant testimony would indicate that permanent virilocal residence was preceded by a period of uxorilocal residence of an indeterminant time immediately following marriage (cf. also Dunning 1959a:132). Although it is impossible to generalize

97

about residence rules, it seems likely that within the late historic period, the Northern Ojibwa were characterized by exogamous, patrilineal dispersed clans. In 1909, according to Skinner, it was unusual "for more than a few members of the same clan to inhabit the same territory" (1911:150). According to Skinner, the former ideal of clan exogamy had already begun to give way by 1909 (1911:150). This possibly can be accounted for by the fact that the exogamic rule pertaining to clans had been superseded by the rule concerning marriage outside the co-residential unit (cf. Dunning 1959a:115-18). If so, it was considered to have been more incestuous to marry within the winter camp than to marry a clan member belonging to another group. Certainly a weakening of clan exogamy would permit a wider range of selection where the levirate and sororate, along with cases of polygyny, existed. This also might have operated to produce semi-cognatic groups of a non-unilineal sort, especially since the Osnaburgh co-residential groups were fairly large. Again, this might account for the shift from the marriage of first cousins to that of remoter cousins, as it did at Pekangikum (1959a:155), except at an earlier date, and for slightly different reasons for Osnaburgh.

In 1900, polygyny had virtually disappeared, probably due to missionary influence during the preceding three decades. After 1895, Indians were subject to the same penalties as Whites for practicing plural marriage (Dunning 1959a:11). Existent polygynous marriages were allowed, but no more were to occur in the future. There were at least two Osnaburgh Indians who had from three to five wives at treaty time. Skinner's figure of 13 wives for some hunters seems to be a gross exaggeration (1911:151).

Marriage partners were chosen from the cross-cousin category, although the parents of prospective spouses probably made the marriage arrangements. In the case of a girl, Skinner states that her father had the right to give her away, followed by her oldest brother-in-law, and if she had no brother-in-law, her oldest brother had the right (1911:151). Bride price was paid to the girl's father, usually in the form of a gun or steel traps. No further ceremony occurred and the bride went to live with her husband. In 1900, most of these marriages were formalized by the Anglican missionary upon his annual visit.

Leadership was vested in the heads of the co-residential groups who held their position through their hunting abilities and supernatural power as shamans. Shamans had the ability to foresee future events and the ability within certain limits to control them. These men were feared as well as respected and prior to 1900, most leaders were polygynists. Leadership in 1900, was based upon individual initiative and the vision quest and was not inherited, a fact that is congruent with the bilateral structure of Ojibwa society at this date (cf. Helm 1965).

By the late nineteenth century, it would seem that each trading post band had a chief who was elected by popular vote probably as a result of the trader's influence, but not necessarily so. The Osnaburgh chief, after 1876, was the Indian, Missabay, son of Big Blood, a former co-residential group head. Although the chief had little coercive power, he was highly respected both by other Indians and the traders. Each summer at the annual feast he made a speech to the Indians in which he gave them encouragement and instructed them to be honest in their dealings with the Hudson's Bay Company. The chief, in turn, was usually given differential treatment by the traders. Missabay, for example, was sent to a doctor in Dinorwic in 1902, to have his failing eyes examined—all at the expense of the Hudson's Bay Company[52]. Missabay as noted, became the first treaty chief of the Osnaburgh band in 1905.

There was also a chief of the Crane Indians named Kichipenace who hunted to the north of Osnaburgh. Kichipenace had a good deal of influence over the Cranes and like Missabay was treated with deference by the Osnaburgh and Cat Lake traders[53].

When the social organization of the Osnaburgh Ojibwa of 1900 is compared with that of today, notable differences are apparent. At present people reside in permanent houses within the village for most of the year; in 1900, the population remained dispersed in bush camps. Within the last 70 years, the Osnaburgh band population has more than doubled. In 1900 the co-residential units were of much greater social and economic importance although the ideal of clan exogamy was weakening. Today many young people do not even know their clan. Again, the turn of the century marked the end of polygyny. While in 1900, marriage arrangements were largely controlled by parents, today young people tend to select their spouses for themselves. Leaders in the past had supernatural powers and their position was based partly on fear (cf. Dunning 1959a:182), while at present the criteria for leadership are changing, and the few remaining shamans have practically no power. These changes can be directly correlated with external White influences, especially the marked increase in government subsidies and control within the past two decades.

Summary and Conclusions

The Osnaburgh Ojibwa of 1900 were similar to many other Sub-arctic Algonkians and Athapaskans[54] both in terms of the general historical and ecological processes and the resultant cultural "type". There was, however, a certain amount of variation. For example, although all the Northern Ojibwa lived within the Boreal Forest on the Canadian Shield in a generally similar ecology, caribou were more important to Indians north of the Albany drainage while wild rice was a significant food to Indians south and west of Lac Seul. Again, geese were important to the Cree of coastal Hudson and James Bay. The distribution of floral and faunal populations seems to follow a north-south axis in Ontario more than an east-west one.

Different groups also experienced variant historical contacts. Those Ojibwa living along Lake Superior were in contact with greater numbers of Euro-Canadians by 1900 than were interior Algonkians. Several communities were the result of government planning (Rogers 1963b:65). Nevertheless, although a number of Ojibwa groups south and west of the Albany drainage had signed the treaty with the government by 1905, they were not "reservation" Indians in the sense that they were restricted by the boundaries of their government allotted Reserves. They were rather territorial groups who exploited large areas (McFeat 1962:15).

There were also variations in social organization. At Round Lake, located about 140 miles north of Osnaburgh, Rogers (1962:A22) indicates that in 1900 there were four bands of Cranes numbering from 25 to 75 persons each. Although these bands tended to be endogamous, marriages with contiguous ones were frequent (1963b:70). Each band was composed of several *nintipe'ncike'win* literally meaning "those whom I lead" (1962:B82). This term refers to a group of kinsmen for whom the leader (an old male) is responsible and is restricted to three generations of patrikin. Rogers' informants indicate that in the past this group was equivalent to the winter settlement and was exogamous (1962:B85-B86). It appears to have been the largest cooperating unit and operated to control group behaviour and to arrange marriages. I would suggest that this group was once equivalent to Rogers' band of 1900 which by that date had perhaps grown too large to effectively maintain continual residence in the same winter settlement. As I shall show, the people of the Round Lake area (the Cranes) consisted of three winter settlements earlier in the nineteenth century which may be related to Rogers' "bands" of 1900.

The Pekangikum Ojibwa studied by Dunning (1959a) signed the treaty somewhat earlier than the people of Osnaburgh and Round Lake. Hence, there is more precise information in the government records on general sociodemographic features. In 1876 (the year the Pekangikum Indians signed the treaty) there were only 55 Indians belonging to the Pekangikum band composed of 5 or 6 co-residential groups averaging from 9 to 11 persons (Dunning 1959a:57). However, with the introduction of government subsidies and services, the population had expanded to 110 persons by 1906 composed of about 8 co-residential groups. I would suggest that these rather small settlements which were actually closer to households in size may have formed three or four clan-named winter settlements earlier in the nineteenth century. As the population grew, especially after store foods and subsidies were introduced, commensal segments may have split from larger settlements so that by the late nineteenth century six or seven small but separate winter settlements had emerged. These groups were united through patrilateral filiation (Dunning 1959a:77) as at Round Lake, and there was no clear cut rule of residence. Cross-cousin marriage along with group exogamy affiliated the groups.

Clan exogamy was still a strong force at Pekangikum in 1900 although it may have been growing weak at Osnaburgh by this time (Skinner 1911:150). While Rogers could find no evidence of

101

clans at Round Lake (1962:B4), it will be shown that there may have been at least one clan (the Sucker clan) present among the Round Lake people earlier in the nineteenth century. However, with the stress on endogamy and the development of small bilateral hunting groups it seems possible that any memory of such units in some places would disappear. New groupings, perhaps at first modelled on earlier forms but modified in accordance with needs, would soon replace them.

From the foregoing account, it should be clear that the conditions of contact and the nature of the ecology largely determined the nature of Osnaburgh society in 1900. Changes in the contact situation which have been occurring since the 1880's help explain modifications of the social and economic order. However, it must be asked, what was the situation like prior to 1880, when contact occurred mainly through a single agent, the fur trader; and at a time when the ecology was less favourable? The origins of social and economic life at the end of the nineteenth century must be sought in the preceding era, for Ojibwa society was modelled after antecedent forms, the nature of which can only be understood in terms of prior conditions. It is to this era, which began in the 1820's, that I shall now turn.

Footnotes

1. The primary anthropological source on the Northern Ojibwa for this period is Alanson Skinner's *Notes on the Eastern Cree and Northern Saulteaux* (1911). Skinner, who at the age of 23 conducted a survey of Lac Seul, Osnaburgh House and Fort Hope, in addition to Cree groups further down the Albany River, in the summer of 1909, was the first anthropologist to work in the area. Skinner's data were supplemented with Hudson's Bay Company archival materials for the period 1890 to 1905, Canadian government documents and letters relating to Treaty No. 9 signed by the Osnaburgh band in 1905, and geological survey reports made by geologists from the 1880's to the 1910's. An additional source was the abridged journal of the Hudson's Bay Company trader, David Wright, dating from 1906 to 1927, which has been recently published by the Provincial Department of Lands and Forests of Ontario. Wright is said to have kept a diary until his death

about 1961. However, most of the material seems to have been lost in a fire.

2. HBC Arch B155/d/9.

3. Ontario: Department of Crown Lands 1901:175.

4. HBC Arch B155/a/78.

5. In 1891, there were ten Hudson's Bay Company buildings at Osnaburgh House: officer's house, clerk's house, workshop, fish house, provision store, two trading stores, and three men's houses. A picket fence enclosed all the building except the three men's houses (HBC Arch B155/e/14). A warehouse and office were built in 1892 (Ontario: Department of Crown Lands 1901:229). A tamarac flag pole stood in front of the buildings. The area about the post was cleared of trees for about 100 yards for garden space. The country about the post had been swept by forest fires, one of which nearly burned the post in 1892. The only outpost during the 1890's was at Cat Lake which included a dwelling house, men's house, and trading store in 1891. In 1924, the buildings at Osnaburgh House were renewed, while in 1936 some buildings were relocated on higher ground after the level of Lake St. Joseph was raised by the Hydro-electric Power Commission.

6. The "made beaver" was a standard of value by the Hudson's Bay Company during the late seventeenth century. As stated by Captain James Knight of Fort Albany in 1694: "Beaver being the chief Commodity we receive in the trade of these goods we therefore make it the standard whereby we rate all the other Furrs and Commodities We deal for Trading" (HBC Archives). The letters "MB" (sometimes MBr) referred to this standard of value. Although both trade goods and furs of all sorts were evaluated in terms of the made beaver, a beaver pelt was not necessarily worth one made beaver, since the value depended upon the quality and size, in addition to price and demand mechanisms.

7. R. C. Wilson, manager (HBC Arch B155/e/14). Because of the change in the supply route, Osnaburgh House was transferred from the Albany District to the Rainy Lake District in 1893

(HBC Arch B155/a/91) and by 1901, it was included in the Lake Superior District.

8. Where in 1888, the value of goods at the post on June 1st amounted to $1,579, by 1891, the inventory was valued at $4,672 (HBC Arch B155/e/14). By 1901, this figure had doubled since three boats each making two trips conveyed goods to the post. By 1912, when the CNR was completed, a tug boat known as the "Kaytoo" transported supplies from Root Portage on Lake St. Joseph. At this date Osnaburgh was officially known as post K2. The Kaytoo was replaced by another tug, the "Osca", short for Osnaburgh-Cat Lake.

9. By 1926, the Osnaburgh post kept between $65,000 and $70,000 worth of stock to trade and supply outposts.

10. HBC Arch B155/e/14.

11. HBC Arch B155/b/2.

12. HBC Arch B155/b/2.

13. The post on Lake Savant opened in 1901 and was supplied from Sturgeon Lake until 1903 when it became an outpost of Osnaburgh House. The HBC also operated a post down the Albany River in 1902, while the McLaren Company had a post on the Cat River near the west end of Lake St. Joseph.

14. Pedlar's Path Bay received its name during the late eighteenth century when it was the route of the Northwest Company fur brigades to Lake Nipigon. A Northwest post seems to have been located at the mouth of the river during the early 1780's. The "pedlars" were the Northwest Company employees.

15. HBC Arch B155/b/2.

16. See footnote 6. The manufacture of these coins seems to have been the first step toward cash transactions. Yet since only the Company made them, it guaranteed that Indians would not trade with rival traders.

17. HBC Arch B155/b/2.

18. HBC Arch B3/z/4.

19. Canada 1858:57.

20. Canada 1905 2:306.

21. Canada: Letters: Treaty No. 9 Negotiations and Adhesions:n.d.

22. Canada: Letters: Treaty No. 9 Negotiations and Adhesions:n.d.

23. The Crane Indians inhabit the area north and west of Osnaburgh House in the vicinity of Windigo Lake, North Caribou Lake and Round Lake. The majority of them now are affiliated with the Round Lake village. The name "Crane" is derived from the name of the band leader during the 1790's (HBC Arch B155/a/18). The Cranes may not be Ojibwa since there is some historical evidence that they may be actually Algonquins. However, this is uncertain and their relationship with the Cree to the north and their unique history may have blurred their actual origin.

24. Canada: Letters: Treaty No. 9 Negotiations and Adhesions:n.d.

25. Canada 1957:5.

26. Canada 1957:32.

27. Canada: Letters: Pertaining to the Osnaburgh House and Cat Lake Indians:n.d.

28. Canada: Annual Report of the Department of Indian Affairs 1929:22.

29. Canada: Sessional Paper No. 27, 1906:294.

30. Wright n.d. 26-27.

31. HBC Arch B155/d/3.

32. HBC Arch B155/a/92.

33. Canada: Department of Citizenship and Immigration: Census of Indians in Canada. Actually, the table covers the more recent era as well. The number of pagans who were listed, either willingly or unwillingly as such, is indicative of the tenacity of older beliefs despite missionary efforts.

34. R. C. Wilson, Osnaburgh manager (HBC Arch B155/a/92).

35. HBC Arch B30/a/8. During 1894 and 1895, three moose were killed at Cat Lake, while four were reported killed at Osnaburgh House during the summer of 1894 (HBC Arch B155/a/91).

36. According to R. C. Wilson in 1897: "Indians are setting nets all over, confound them" (HBC Arch B155/a/92). Wilson gave them lectures not to do this.

37. Ontario: Department of Crown Lands 1901:175. The gardens were located at Pashkokogan Lake situated about twenty miles south of Osnaburgh House as near as I can discern.

38. HBC Arch B155/b/2.

39. Camsell 1906:144A.

40. Canada: Sessional Paper No. 27, 1906:294.

41. Mr. Borron: Report of 1890 on the Indians of the Southern Department (including Osnaburgh House) (HBC Arch D/26/16).

42. HBC Arch B155/e/14.

43. R. C. Wilson (HBC Arch B155/a/90).

44. Mr. Borron: Report of 1890 on the Indians of the Southern Department (including Osnaburgh House) (HBC Arch D/26/16).

45. HBC Arch B155/e/14.

46. HBC Arch B155/b/2.

47. HBC Arch B30/a/11a.

48. HBC Arch B155/b/2.

49. Canada: Letters: Treaty No. 9 Negotiations and Adhesions:n.d.

50. Canada: Sessional Paper No. 27 1906:294.

51. Skinner also mentions the Snake clan. This is not a clan symbol in northern Ontario. It will be shown in Chapter 8 that there was a hunting group called the Snakes, named after the leader, in the Osnaburgh area during the 1820's.

52. HBC Arch B155/b/2.

53. HBC Arch B155/b/2.

54. cf Lips 1947; Hallowell 1955; Dunning 1959a; Rogers 1962, 1963a for the Algonkians, and Helm 1961; Slobodin 1962; VanStone 1965 for the Athapaskans.

Chapter Four
Trade and Policy: 1821-1890

Introduction

Since the fur trade was of paramount importance to the Northern
Ojibwa, a discussion of trade policies and conditions at interior
posts is presented to provide a background for understanding the
social and economic arrangements of their society.

The period 1821-90, although a lengthy one, is comparatively
uniform in terms of the trade policies implemented, the types of
goods distributed, and the conjunctive relations between traders
and Indians. Nevertheless, there was variation in the trade, and
new policies were tested. The Northern Ojibwa, however, seem to
have been little more dependent upon Euro-Canadian trade goods
during the 1880's than they had been 50 years earlier. That of
course is not to say that they were not dependent: it merely
means that when dependency is evaluated qualitatively, little
change occurred even though there is evidence that by the late
nineteenth century Indians were receiving greater quantities of
supplies. By the 1820's most Indian families could not survive
without guns, hatchets, knives, twine, leather, and clothing
obtained from the store. Few new items of greater significance
were introduced until the last decades of the century. It is most
likely for this reason that recent students[1] have tended to over-
look the tremendous changes wrought by the fur trade prior to
the coalition of the Northwest Company and Hudson's Bay Company in 1821. The illusion is that the social and economic
patterns of the nineteenth-century Ojibwa in relatively remote
areas appear to be essentially aboriginal in character.

Some change did indeed occur during the 70-year period after
1821, representing modifications. But major alterations had taken
place before this date as we shall see; while great transformations
resulting in qualitatively different social and economic arrange-

ments have also occurred during the twentieth century as has already been indicated[2].

Although changes implemented by the Hudson's Bay Company were chiefly of a directed sort (as opposed to non-directed change)[3], such was not always the case, the reason being that Indians had a certain amount of freedom to move from post to post. This freedom of movement existed despite hunting territories, the dependence of most Indians on a single post, and subsistence based largely on small game, hare, and fish. Two factors influenced the amount of mobility: first, the general environmental conditions involving the availability of fur and food resources, especially the latter; and second, the trade policies implemented at Osnaburgh and other nearby posts. During years when food was more abundant, Indians were able to devote more time to travel. Varying trade policies implemented at posts in different districts were also important influences. Since it is the socio-demographic effects of the policies that is of primary anthropological interest, these trade policies will be considered, followed by a general discussion of their effects upon Indian economy and social organization. However, it is first necessary to give a brief background of the fur trade in order to provide a basis for understanding trade relationships during the nineteenth century.

The Fur Trade and the Hudson's Bay Company in Northern Ontario

The fur trade in Canada started in the early 1500's when European fishermen began taking fur bearers in the St. Lawrence drainage area. By the early seventeenth century, the French trade had expanded to the Great Lakes region and involved most of the tribal groups of this region[4]. From the seventeenth century on, the most important fur bearer was the beaver whose pelt was manufactured into robes by the Indians who traded these for European goods, especially iron tools[5]. Even at this early date the native technology was being rapidly replaced by foreign materials. By the 1640's, Indians in the Central Great Lakes region, eager for European wares, had established trade alliances with other tribes[6]. Some tribes who because of

108

differing alliances, or because of attempts to maintain a lucrative middleman position, engaged in open warfare with each other. For instance, during this time the Iroquois raids led to the dispersal of the Hurons and a number of Algonkian groups near Lake Huron. Because such hostilities actually disrupted the fur trade, the French began explorations to the west of the Great Lakes in order to trade directly with more remote groups and to inhibit hostilities. Two of these French traders, Radisson and Groseilliers, subsequently associated themselves with the English leading to the formation of the Hudson's Bay Company in 1670 thereby giving the English a monopoly of the trade in the Hudson Bay Drainage area (Prince Rupert's Land). By the end of the century, a number of key HBC posts were in existence along coastal James Bay and Hudson Bay[7] and were diverting many Indians away from the French to the south. This competition intensified during the early eighteenth century resulting in the collection of huge quantities of furs[8] from Indians who either bartered these directly for European wares, or were given credit based upon the previous year's hunt[9].

After the cession of Canada to the British in 1759, numerous French and British traders supplied from Montreal located north and west of Lake Superior and thus rejuvenated the competition with the Hudson's Bay Company. In 1782, these Montreal traders united to form the Northwest Company at which time opposition grew intense as both companies established numerous trading centres north of Lake Superior[10]. Under conditions of keen competition, vast quantities of goods were distributed to Indians. The most important trade items were: guns, powder, shot, hatchets, files, flints, kettles, knives, cloth, Brazil tobacco, and brandy or rum. The introduction of steel traps led to the virtual extermination of the beaver in some regions shortly after 1800. Large animals, caribou and moose, which were hunted to support both Indians and traders soon grew scarce. By 1805, Northwest Company trade had fallen off in northern Ontario, a process that was repeated in western Canada a decade later.

The Northwest Company was adapted to expanding trade conditions (Innis 1962:262). Once such expansion ended, it was faced with increasing costs and decreasing profits distributed among too many people. Therefore, in March 1821, the Northwest Company amalgamated with the more stable, hence more adaptable, Hudson's Bay Company.

From the seventeenth century on, the fur trade was intimately connected with price and demand mechanisms which determined the value of fur bearers. These values fluctuated in accordance with: 1) changes in fashions in Europe, 2) the number of furs reaching the markets in relation to demand, and 3) the intensity of competition among fur companies, all of which affected back-woods policy concerning their acquisition.

Between the resources and the trading companies who sold their products on the world markets stood the Indian producers. In exchange for furs, traders provided Indians with a variety of goods. In time, many of these goods totally replaced less efficient aboriginal items, so that Indians came to depend upon the trader. However, trade policies were implemented to maximize profits by higher company officals who frequently had little contact with remote interior areas where the furs were taken. These policies were often detrimental to the producers who, because of their dependent, or at least semidependent position, had little control over policy making. This was the situation that characterized northern Ontario after 1821. The coalition of the Hudson's Bay Company and the Northwest Company ended nearly 40 years of competition between the two concerns. Policy decisions after this were less affected by competition, and the Hudson's Bay Company now in control of virtually all of northern Ontario, had greater freedom to experiment and manipulate relations with the Indians who in turn were encouraged to trade at the same store each year.

After the amalgamation, northern Ontario was partitioned into a number of districts each with a central supply depot and chief factor in charge of the area. The districts were set up for the efficient exploitation and transportation of goods to and from trading posts in the area. Price mechanisms and trade policies within each district were generally uniform, however, they could differ markedly from one district to the next. Since the traders of one district had no authority over those of another, posts in adjacent districts often competed for furs. It will be shown that policy differences and competition among districts had a marked effect on Indian mobility. The Albany District included the area

110

drained by the Albany River and its tributaries and was supplied by Fort Albany near the mouth of the major river. Other important posts within this district were, from east to west, Martin's Falls, Osnaburgh House and Lac Seul. The adjacent region to the north drained by the Severn River was included in the Severn District. The focal post was Fort Severn and the major inland post nearest Osnaburgh was at Trout Lake. To the southeast was the Superior District which included posts at Lake Nipigon and Fort William; and to the southwest the Rainy Lake (Lac La Pluie) District to the American border. As we shall see, this was a major trouble spot for the Hudson's Bay Company and the source of much trade loss for the Albany River posts.

General Conditions at the Osnaburgh House Post

By the middle of the nineteenth century, interior Hudson's Bay Company settlements had grown to include a store, warehouse, roothouse, residences for the employees and their families, and an Indian house to shelter visiting Indians. Enclosing these buildings was a palisade originally built for protection against hostile Indians, but continued more as a symbol of colonialism after the 1820's. The area about the post was cleared of timber used for firewood and in the construction of buildings. Usually an acre or more of land was set aside for the potato garden.

In summer, which was the busy season, the resident population usually numbered from 20 to 30 people or more. During the rest of the year, there were from seven to ten male employees. In addition to the factor, there were clerks and labourers who performed a variety of chores. In summer, gardens were cultivated, fishing stations attended, and buildings were constructed or repaired. Furs were graded and packed on the boats for Fort Albany and supplies were unloaded, prepared and stored. In autumn, potatoes, fish, and firewood were stored for winter use, while Indians received their winter supplies. These duties and others kept most adults at the post occupied from May until October.

There appear always to have been several Indian women, wives of the employees and also their offspring, about the post. However, their numbers apparently were growing so great about

111

Hudson's Bay posts that in 1825, it was ordered that no man in the Company's service was to marry an Indian or half-breed woman without the permission of the chief factor in charge of the district[11]. This was partially an attempt to keep the post population down since members lived on store foods, but may also have involved implicit racism. This decree seems to have had little influence on the number of Indian women and their children who resided more or less in the vicinity of the post since Nicol Finlayson reported that in December, 1827, there were 32 people being supported at Osnaburgh "and only 9 of this number in the Mess Book"[12]. Finlayson complained that all these women and children were a nuisance. Although they hunted for themselves, they had killed off all the hare in the immediate vicinity of the post[13].

Lac Seul also had a large resident population, there often being over 35 persons living about the settlement[14]. The manager, Charles McKenzie, was, like most White employees, married to an Indian. She appears to have been a very capable woman who not only set snares for fur bearers and rabbits in winter, but also managed the post in the summer while her husband was away on the supply boats to Fort Albany[15].

Women at the post did a variety of chores such as netting snowshoes, making and mending clothing, washing, and cleaning the yard about the post twice a week, a chore some Indians considered demeaning[16].

McKenzie gave his impressions of the effect on Indian life of living at the post in January, 1849.

No trees can come to grow about place—being peeled of their bark each year by Women & children—"Yea, and by those who don't look upon themselves as "Indian women and children" once in the Company's Service they think they Scoured their Copper—their manners and life is Still Indian as well as their language—as to their occupation it differs little from that of the Indians—except that we live in Log Houses—while the Indians live under Bark Tents[17].

In general, statements by traders would indicate that Indians living at the posts turned out to be less desirable in the traders' eyes than those who lived in the bush. For instance, McKenzie told of a Lac Seul Indian named Donald who had been employed at the post. When this man began drinking to excess and telling other Indians "more than the *Truth* on such occasions", he had to be released as an employee. McKenzie generalized that this type of behaviour had characterized "all the Indians I ever knew to have been brot up at the Forts without a single solitary instance—that when they joined these relations they proved far worse characters than their brothers of the forest"[18].

Osnaburgh appears to have been poorly managed on certain occasions. In 1830, the factor at Osnaburgh had to be removed by Charles McKenzie for drinking all the trade rum intended for the Indians. The new factor, Edward Mowat wrote that it was a pity, "that Osnaburgh had been so poorly managed for some years back—for both the place and the Indians will show how it is been managed for the place is in poor order and the Indians is in no better"[19]. The Indians had not been taught the proper methods of cleaning and stretching the furs, and they had not received their allowance of trade rum. Corcoran wrote Mowat that he was sending 9 gallons of rum to Osnaburgh since "the poor Osnaburgh Indians require a treat of this kind to cheer them—it will be a novel thing to them in the Spring".

Once in the habit, the Osnaburgh Indians appear to have continued to be careless in preparing furs for trade. When, during the 1840's the value of beaver in England dropped considerably so that only the best furs were acceptable, the chief factor at Fort Albany, George Barnston, complained about "the wretched manner in which furs are handled" by the Osnaburgh Indians. The Lac Seul furs were least liable to objection[20]. The manner in which furs were prepared is still a complaint of the traders at Osnaburgh House today.

Services Provided by Indians

Throughout the nineteenth century, traders at interior posts relied upon Indians for a variety of services and goods. At times, these services were vital to the maintenance of the post.

Fish and potatoes were two of the stable foods eaten by Bay employees. Each autumn before ice formed on the lakes,

Hudson's Bay Company servants and several local Indians were employed setting nets to obtain large quantities of whitefish to feed the men at the post and hungry Indians during the winter months. Usually from 30 to 50 nets were set in the fall to catch the spawning whitefish. For example, in the fall of 1842, 13,133 fish were caught in nets with Indian help at Osnaburgh, 8,724 of which were whitefish[21]. That fall there were four fishing stations manned by three Bay servants and four Indians. A prize of one-half a moose skin was offered to the most productive fishery. By the 1860's or perhaps earlier, an Indian was hired to fish for the post during the summer months.

Each fall, Indians at the various Albany posts were employed to assist in taking up the potato crop. The Osnaburgh post produced between 150 and 400 bushels annually, while Lac Seul perhaps averaged 100 bushels more. Although Indian assistance in digging potatoes was a very important service since the crop had to be harvested before the first frosts, the Indians benefited. The Lac Seul Indians never offered to hoe or weed them, but willingly assisted in taking them up, since they were able to steal great quantities which they roasted or boiled: "they hide the choicest in their Blankets & the small children are continually carring away in small Kettles . . . & at night each must get a daily portion"[22]. As estimated three 13-gallon kegs of potatoes were consumed daily by the Indians during the period when they were being taken up. Osnaburgh Indians also took advantage of the situation. In 1873, for example, nearly all the Indians associated with the post were "Knocking about for Potatoes"[23]. By the 1880's, some Indians were growing their own potatoes.

The functions of the Indians at the post were multifarious, ranging from gardening chores[24] to cutting hay for the cattle during the 1850's, to cutting firewood and building planks, as well as supplying the post with birchbark canoes and tenting[25]. Indians also laboured on the supply boats although they disliked this work. Indeed, while Indian labour was necessary to the maintenance of the post, it was not easy to acquire since the wages Indians received were small in proportion to the efforts expended[26]. Two Indians hired in 1847 to work on the boats to Albany quit after eight days since, "they had not *enough to eat* which indeed has ever been a complaint in this River"[27]. Their fare was only a salted wavy, one pound of flour and one-half pound of oatmeal. It will be recalled that the Albany River route was abandoned in 1890, due partially to the complaints of Indians concerning the difficulties in freighting goods on the Albany. In June, 1850, McKenzie remarked:

> True I hired an Indian to assist the only one I could get to become a Slave—(in their thinking) during the Summer—I got him because he is naked but when he & his family are Clothed—'tis most foremible he may take "a French Lieve"[28].

In addition to a variety of services, the Ojibwa supplied the post with food on occasion. Although Indians usually depended more upon the trading post for provisions, they exchanged surplus foods for small trade articles such as ammunition, files and hatchets. In turn, they expected to be fed during periods of scarcity (see Chapter 6). Sahlins (1965:147-48) terms this form of exchange "balanced reciprocity" meaning the recipient of a gift must repay an equivalent amount at a later time.

Fish were probably the most important food exchanged by Indians. Although more fish were supplied to Indians by traders than the reverse, occasionally fish were accepted in times of need —especially if the fall fisheries had failed. For instance, in April 1859, the Osnaburgh factor William Linklater sent one of the servants "to a Indian lodge to see if he can't get us some fish as we are short for provisions"[29]. In 1869, the Indian Mak king wan, caught 2,000 whitefish and traded 1,000 of them to the Company for one and a half made beaver per 100[30]. In May and June Indians supplied the post with sturgeon speared in the Albany River. These fisheries attracted Lac Seul Indians also, there being no sturgeon at the latter place.

Although hares were vital to the Indian economy by the late 1820's, they were seldom accepted by traders in exchange for trade materials. Generally the post servants and their Indian wives were able to procure enough hares to adequately supplement other foods. During the 1850's and '60's, Osnaburgh servants set about 100 hare snares and 30 hooks for fish[31]. Food shortages did, however, occasionally occur at the post as they did in 1827 when the factor accepted 240 hares to keep the employees from starving[32]. In later years, traders accepted "rabbits" to provide variation in their diet, while by the 1860's, some Indians exchanged hares for potatoes for the same reason[33].

Caribou and moose meat was not an important source of food either for Indians or traders at Osnaburgh from the late 1820's until 1870. An Indian named Flint brought the flesh of two moose and a caribou killed beyond Crow Nest Lake[34] to the Lac Seul post in 1829. Except for one stray moose seen in 1833 this is the last mention of a moose killed in the Albany District until 1893. Caribou seem never to have completely disappeared north of the Albany River. For example, in September 1830, two Cranes brought caribou flesh to Osnaburgh[35], but they remained extremely rare for another forty years. By the late 1860's, caribou appear to have been increasing since references to Indians bringing in venison to Osnaburgh become more numerous. In September 1869, for example, T. A. Rae stated that "Big Blood & son arrived & brought me Venison as they are been killing deer"[36]. Several other Indians brought venison to Osnaburgh that year.

Ducks and geese taken in late April and early May were exchanged for powder, shot and tobacco[37].

Wild rice was the most important vegetable product supplied by Indians. Prior to 1840, it was especially important since few European provisions found their way to interior posts. Its compactness and durability made it an ideal food on the supply boats. The Lac Seul post in 1827, according to Charles McKenzie, was to procure "as much wild Rice from the natives as possible in order to bring enough to Osnaburgh and Martin Falls"[38]. Its significance was thus indicated by Nicol Finlayson of Osnaburgh in 1826 who feared that if the Indians brought no rice "we will be under the necessity of killing the Cattle to carry on the business of the Season"[39]. Indians placed a high value on their rice and were not always willing to trade it. When a servant returned to the Lac Seul post in 1832 having been able to obtain only 8 bushels, McKenzie stated that it was a serious event since "we all depend more or less on this Rice & entirely for going to Albany next Spring"[40]. In the fall of 1835, McKenzie stated that "several Indians made a good deal of Rice but they seem to be very fond of it—They were unwilling to part with it Even for Rum"[41]. After 1840, many of the Lac Seul Indians who lived to the south and west of the post in areas where rice was more abundant were lured to the Lac La Pluie (Rainy Lake) and Rat Portage posts. Hence, about this time rice ceased to be an important food commodity in the Albany District traded by Indians.

The Eagle Lake Indians in the region south of Lac Seul occasionally brought corn to the latter post, but placed a great deal of value on it. Small quantities of corn are known to have been traded at Lac Seul by the Eagle Lake Indians in the fall of 1823, 1847 and 1849[42].

Other plant foods traded by Indians included berries of various sorts, especially blueberries[43].

In general, the quantity of food supplied to the post by Indians seems never to have been great, and the Osnaburgh post can be said to have been self-sufficient except on rare occasions. During the 1820's, venison and wild rice were still of some importance in the diet of Hudson's Bay employees. By 1840, these foods had ceased to be significant and during the last three decades of the century, both the variety and quantity of imported Euro-Canadian foods had grown to such an extent that food had become an item to trade out from the post! Nevertheless, the Cat Lake outpost relied fairly heavily on country provisions supplied by Indians for the first decade after it was re-established in 1873. As late as 1886, the trader, Vincent, remarked that: "There is absolutely nothing to eat in the place, that is meat-Kind"[44].

Trade Policies After 1821

The Abandonment of Trading Posts

After the coalition, the Hudson's Bay Company abandoned several outposts which had been costly to maintain, and which had in several cases, been operated at a loss. Among those posts which continued in operation after 1821, for a short period within the range of Osnaburgh Indians were Cat Lake, Red Lake, Sturgeon Lake and Trout Lake (Map 1).

The Cat Lake post which had operated as an outpost for Osnaburgh periodically since 1788 was finally vacated in 1826. It was reopened in 1873 partially to offset competition from traders who were encroaching from the Lac Seul area. It recaptured the trade of a large segment of the Crane Indians after its re-establishment. The Cat Lake outpost remained a small seasonally-occupied store until the 1890's.

The Hudson's Bay post at Red Lake had been established from Osnaburgh during the 1790's to offset Northwest competition. When this ended, it was abandoned. However, when the Red Lake area became the last region where beaver and large game animals could be found, an outpost was again established there from Lac Seul in the winter of 1828-29. By the spring of 1829, these animals had become depleted and the post was once more vacated. The Red Lake Indians subsequently traded at Lac Seul. In 1807, a post was established at Trout Lake about 200 miles north of Osnaburgh and attracted Indians who otherwise would have traded at the latter post. The Indians known as the Cranes, Ojibwa belonging to a group known as the Suckers who were named after the former leader, Crane, frequently traded at both Trout Lake and Osnaburgh. The Trout Lake post was finally deserted in 1829, owing to the paucity of furs in the Severn District. It was again opened in 1844. By the 1850's, the bulk of the Cranes were trading at Trout Lake. As mentioned, some of the Cranes returned to trade at the Cat Lake outpost after 1873.

After the 1790's, the Hudson's Bay store at Sturgeon Lake had been operated first as an outpost of Osnaburgh, then Fort William and finally Lac Seul. When, in June 1837, Roderick McKenzie told the Sturgeon Lake Indians that the post on that lake was to be permanently vacated, they "did not appear to be displeased in the least"[45]. A number seem to have been invariably lost to the Lac La Pluie (Rainy Lake) post, but the bulk continued to trade at Lac Seul thereafter.

The Ready Barter System

With the termination of competition in 1821 the Hudson's Bay Company was able to implement and test a number of policies to further its aims and to improve the drastically reduced trade in beaver, a legacy of the competition and overhunting during previous decades. One such course of action was to introduce what was termed the "Ready Barter System" of trade. This meant that instead of supplying Indians in the summer and early fall with trade items which were to be paid for in furs the following spring, as was formerly the practice on the "Debt System", (*the* widespread trading system prior to the 1820's) the Indians would exchange their furs directly for goods as they brought them to the post. Credit in advance was curtailed except in the case of a few small items. The main reason for the introduction of the ready barter system was to eliminate the accumulation of debts against Indians over several years. Furs brought to the post in the spring frequently did not amount to the same value as supplies obtained in the fall. Once in debt, Indians often became discouraged since their furs were taken to pay old accounts; hence, it became increasingly difficult to get out of debt since a hunter was always at least a year behind in his payments.

The ready barter system was first introduced at Osnaburgh and the other Albany District posts in the winter of 1823-24. It had little effect upon the Indians until the following summer. Furs bartered directly were taken at a higher value than those received in exchange for debts. As stated by John Davis[46], in December 1823:

Goods will in future be Bartered with the Indians you will perceive they will be supplied much cheaper than heretofore. but it is not intended they will be allowed advances in Debt at this rate but only in Trading their Hunts ... after this winter nothing should be given in Debt but actual necessaries to enable them to hunt.

Davis indicated in his district report for 1824, that the new tariff and barter system would be better for the Indians although,

advances on credit in articles of actual necessity for hunting can never be entirely done away with, as from the precarious mode of life the Indians lead, and their improvidence, cases must arise where advances on credit are necessary[47].

Both the Osnaburgh and Lac Seul Indians were apprehensive about the new system, especially the former who visited the post less frequently and who feared that they would be unable to obtain many trade items they formerly received in the fall. The Osnaburgh manager even feared that the Indians would leave to trade at Nipigon and elsewhere where the debt system was still in operation[48].

A few goods considered necessary for survival and trapping had to be advanced to the Ojibwa in the autumn of 1824. They thus were able to trap for a short period. These fall pelts were traded directly for additional goods in the early winter. Indians at Lac Seul were not required to pay their debts until they were able to clothe themselves in caribou hide and hare skins[49]. Thus, the system was flexible and it apparently worked well for those Indians who trapped near the post, and for those who were able and willing to obtain furs. For example, according to Finlayson, the Lac Seul Indians made "excellent hunts in Rats" during the autumn of 1825[50] which they traded directly for their necessary winter supplies. However, the policy failed at Osnaburgh, and tended to drive Indians to posts where they could still get debts. Finlayson stated that "the same system will not do at Osnaburgh as the Muskrats are not so plentiful at the last as at the first mentioned place"[51]. Nevertheless, most Indians were so dissatisfied with these experiments in policy that "the spirits of the Indians are so humbled—they are quite indifferent about hunting". Indeed, they were so exasperated that they would not have brought any furs to the post had they been able to clothe themselves in leather. He went on to point out[52] that the Indians feared

any unexpected change in their affairs, this I knew and therefore endeavoured to explain to them our reasons for adopting this system—they generally acknowledged the justice of my reasoning but at the same time never failed to ask me how they were to live—To enable them to clothe themselves for the winter I advanced from 4 to 15 skins each in ammunition, twine etc.

It was for these reasons that the Hudson's Bay Company re-introduced the old debt system, in the summer of 1825. James Slater of Osnaburgh again gave those Indians who had been faithful in paying their debts, goods in value equal to two-thirds their previous year's hunt "to Enable them to Live and make bitter Hunts than they have ben this 2 years back and they are all much better contented then they was Last fall"[53].

After the coalition of the two companies, many Northern Ojibwa found themselves obligated to a single company owing immense debts accumulated over a number of years and in a country greatly depleted of fur-bearing animals. When the ready barter system was first introduced, traders complained that these old debts should be abolished, as they were only a drawback on an Indian's exertions. An Indian owing a large debt was reluctant to hunt furs, since pelts were taken on old accounts. Finlayson, in 1825, stated that

> the grand cause of the falling off of the trade of OH is that the Indians are entirely dissatisfied with the treatment they receive, and keeping against them numerous balances of 10 or 20 years standing—I am firmly of the opinion that if these balances were given them once clear they would exert themselves to procure clothing for themselves and families[54].

The Ojibwa had been instructed by the traders to acquire hare pelts for clothing rather than hunt caribou for their hide and flesh since caribou had grown very scarce by the 1820's. However, snaring "rabbits" was considered to be a degrading activity for males who formerly had lived by hunting big game. Thus, instead of snaring hare for clothing, they would either try to obtain European apparel which was expensive, or they would frequently cut up their furs for clothing; either way they accumulated debts which they couldn't repay. Thus, some traders believed that if the old accounts were cancelled, Indians would be willing to snare hare if they knew that by so doing they could regain their prestige by paying debts through trapping activities. For this reason, balances against Indians in the Albany District were cancelled in 1827.

Nevertheless, efficient trapping required that Indians receive some of the more expensive goods. This fact, combined with the difficulty in procuring food and certain fur bearers which had

121

grown scarce, meant that many Indians were unable to repay these new debts no matter how hard they tried. Thus, although the debt system was re-introduced in 1825, the ready barter system was again tested at Osnaburgh and Lac Seul in 1834, along with a lower tariff. It was discovered that the policy of debting Indians in the fall often merely resulted in the accumulation of debts again, so that Indians within a few years were back in debt as much as ever. This occurred despite precautions taken to debt Indians in proportion to their previous year's hunt.

Vicissitudes in trade policy between the barter and debt system occurred periodically throughout the nineteenth century. The ready barter system seems to have been affected in the Albany District in 1834, 1845, 1851, 1863, 1868 and 1872[55]. After about two or three years, in each case it seems that the debt system was re-established.

When the barter system was in practice, the Hudson's Bay Company usually allowed the Indians to obtain a few inexpensive articles on credit in the fall to enable them to devote more time to trapping. That these few items obtained on credit were inadequate is indicated by Charles McKenzie of Lac Seul. McKenzie, who among the traders was the one most sympathetic to Indian problems, complained frequently of the hardships Indians experienced in meeting their requirements. For example, he wrote Fort Albany concerning the trading system in 1846:

> They may not indeed pay the very last Skin of their debt—tho' willing enough to pay—I found them almost all in good humour—after getting their *Bare* necessaries or less than their Bare necessaries—if you please—to call things by their names—we do not inquire Religiously what the necessity of an Indian may be—we look what his general Hunt amounts—pass that—and he must stop—whether he has his necessaries or not—we take upon ourselves to be the better judges—an't it So![56]

McKenzie indicated in 1852 that the price of trade goods was too high and the value of furs too low. The Indians could not be "Kept down to 'Small Debts' . . . and large Debts they cannot pay at the price we lay on our goods and allow for furs". For this

122

reason some traders even disregarded formal rules. McKenzie, who devoted 50 years of his life to the fur trade, and over 40 years in the Lac Seul area, often broke orders to ensure that his Indians would be supplied. For example, on occasion, he gave the Lac Seul Indians ammunition for nothing, stating that it was not to the benefit of any post "to be surrounded with poor tenantry who cannot pay their rents"[57].

Although Charles McKenzie termed barter a "most cold calculating system—& not at all times to the mind & disposition of the natives"[58], there were occasions when Indians appeared to benefit from the system. When both furs and food were plentiful, energetic Indians were able to procure more supplies than they could on the debt system, and visited the post more frequently. Indians who normally waited until spring to bring their pelts to the store made visits through the winter to exchange pelts directly for the trade items.

In most cases, however, the barter system operated more to protect the Company than the Indians. When old debts were abolished and the ready barter system was put into effect in 1872 the Osnaburgh manager, T. Harvey, stated upon the arrival of an Indian:

I was obliged to advance the Cock 8 MB to start him per winter, As a *Rule* to *give* No debts, However they will require a few Necessairies to set them a going for this autumn at any rate (I mean to the Indians that is Kept true to this Post — Not to runabouts)[59].

These so-called "runabouts" according to Harvey were usually refused debt of any amount, as was the Indian, Solid Head: "Indeed I would not advance the *vagrant* one roach Knive".

From the Company's point of view, the barter system eliminated the risk involved in giving debts, especially during years when conditions for trapping were unfavourable. It did not, however, provide any means of security for those unable to trap, such as the aged and the crippled. Nor were fluctuations in the local food supply considered. Thus, in times when hare were scarce and Indians needed supplies most, they were unable to acquire them, as efforts had to be directed toward subsistence activities in lieu

123

of trapping. Also, in the early fall before the trapping season, Indians had no pelts to exchange for equipment and clothing necessary for trapping and survival. The result was that they had fewer furs to bring to the post, and hence were unable to acquire the things they needed despite lower costs. Those who trapped a great distance from the post, unable to make frequent visits to obtain their requirements, had to be given extra goods on credit to prevent them from perishing. The ready barter system, along with the availability of rum and cheaper prices in other districts operated to lure Indians in the Albany District to these attractions. Throughout the 70-year period under consideration, a satisfactory balance between the two policies, the debt system and the barter system, seems never to have been made. What worked well at Lac Seul failed at Osnaburgh, or vice versa; and a policy which succeeded one year might fail the next, depending upon the availability of furs, and food, especially hare. In later years when store foods became available, a more successful compromise seems to have been attained. Indians were allowed to receive their necessities, but had to trade directly for what items were considered to be less necessary to surviving and trapping. Invariably these were the more expensive materials.

Conservation Policies

It was not only the trading system and the price differential that drove Indians from the Albany District posts. Conservation policies prohibiting the trade of summer pelts induced Indians to take their furs where they would be accepted.

After 1825, at Osnaburgh House and other Albany River posts, summer furs were no longer accepted by traders, since the pelts were of little value in the London market. Also, a restriction was placed on beaver pelts in all seasons in 1824 to allow beaver to replenish themselves. Such restraints were frequently ignored by Indians. For instance, a Martin's Falls Indian,

> Amitchewaykeeshick . . . did not spare the cub Beaver alive as he was directed last Spring. he said he was hungry at the time and was sorry there were no more of them.[60]

Charles McKenzie stated in 1837 that policies regarding summer pelts were contradictory and hypocritical. Traders complained if Indians brought no furs in summer, and complained if they did for having killed the animals out of season "a pipe of Tobacco and a quarrel is all they can expect—So that the Indians are sure of a lecture whether they bring or bring not". McKenzie added that these lectures actually encouraged Indians to take extraordinary pains to kill the animal they had been told to let alone.

I always thought there is a good deal of Hypocricy in our delivery on this point—we at least expect from the Indians contrary to nature—namely we wish them to hunt during summer—& we do not wish to take nothing but prime furs—which is contrary to reason—true Rats are always in Season—but the Indians cannot make Rats—& we take them only of a certain size—would they bring us their small Rats—& tis only a repeatition of a former Lecture they can expect & their small Rats left on their hands—we praise them who bring us the greatest number of Large Rats—whereas that these are the greatest destroyers of furs for every two Large—they destroy a dozen small ones at the most moderate calculation[61].

Once the large rats were killed the young would die if left alone[62]. In the summer of 1843, fall rat hunting was discouraged since muskrats in the London market were of little value and by September 1844, a definite prohibition on the acquisition of fall rats was introduced. And by April 1847 they were not accepted at any season[63]. The effects of this edict upon the Indians of Osnaburgh and Lac Seul was disastrous as it came at a time when the ready barter system was in operation. In addition, the Lac Seul Indians had experienced a serious epidemic which had killed many Indians the two previous summers. Rat hunting, then, provided demoralized or disabled families with the only means that they had of fulfilling their trade needs. The trading post also suffered since small debts had been promised in exchange for rats. McKenzie justifiably feared that this prohibition would drive Indians to the Rainy Lake post where they could trade rats and get debts and also rum[64].

The above mentioned edict affected the trade at Lac Seul more than at Osnaburgh where rats were of less significance although of greater value. In 1840, McKenzie related that muskrats valued at 20 per made beaver at Lac Seul were worth 10 per made beaver at Osnaburgh[65]. Indians at both posts continued to bring in rats despite the prohibition, and traders frequently were forced to accept them in exchange for goods or drive the Indians to other posts. By the early 1850's winter muskrat pelts were again traded although summer pelts remained unacceptable.

One means of controlling the number of fur bearers taken which were restricted by conservation policies was to prohibit the use of steel traps. Steel traps, although in use prior to 1821, were outlawed in the Albany District from the 1820's until the summer of 1848, when they were re-introduced and sold for three made beaver each[66]. However, Indians at posts in surrounding districts, Lac La Pluie (Rainy Lake) and Lake Superior, continued to receive them during this period. In the spring of 1834, Osnaburgh and Lac Seul Indians had a great deal of difficulty acquiring muskrats and beaver owing to the high water. Had the Indians been permitted to use steel traps, "let the water be high or low, the winter severe or mild, with Traps the Rats cannot Escape them"[67]. In August, 1834 McKenzie broke orders and gave out the 60 steel traps in the store stating: "what is 60 Rat Traps among as many Indians while their neighbours of the N. Department have from 10 to 12 each"[68]. Indeed, a constant complaint of Osnaburgh and Lac Seul Indians during the years when steel traps were prohibited involved Nipigon and Lac La Pluie Indians who ravaged the hunting territories of the Albany District Indians with their steel traps (see Chapter 5).

Prohibitions placed on the acquisition of beaver had even less effect. In 1845 when Charles McKenzie told the Lac Seul Indians not to hunt beaver for a five-year period in order to allow them to recover, these Indians exchanged beaver pelts with Osnaburgh Indians for powder and shot. Beaver being more numerous in the Osnaburgh area were not subject to the same restriction. Lac La Pluie Indians with steel traps, and Osnaburgh Indians without them, moved into the hunting territories of Lac Seul Indians to kill beaver restricted to the latter. In addition, Lac Seul Indians continued to kill beaver for food and clothing: "every one finds as plausible an excuse in their own Sight—'tis either—'a feast for the dead of Sunged Beaver' or 'did you give me Deer Skins for snow Shoes last fall!"[69] By 1848, the value of beaver in the London market fell so low that the Osnaburgh Indians were also prohibited from taking them[70]—paradoxically the same year that steel traps became available! So displeased were the Osnaburgh Indians that one even threatened to take the post.

As a compromise measure, Indians were encouraged to hunt small animals—hares, squirrels, skunks, and marten. However, since in 1850 it took 30 hare skins to make one made beaver at Lac Seul and 20 per made beaver at Osnaburgh, McKenzie reported that Indian women were reluctant to take the time to clean and prepare them[71]. In addition, hare were not traded at the Albany posts for the more valuable items such as guns and blankets. Thus, the supply of guns, traps and heavy articles in the store remained uncirculated. As McKenzie noted: "The Inds get powder & shot which are useless without guns. Keeping guns & traps doesn't help the Inds live & get furs"[72]. Hence, the lure of heavy articles unobtainable at Osnaburgh and Lac Seul in exchange for small furs continued to attract Indians to the more southerly posts.

In 1851, hare were very scarce and only 207 were traded at Lac Seul[73]. The following year, however, 13,000 were obtained, and in the spring of 1853, 25,000 pelts were shipped from Lac Seul[74]. Osnaburgh produced 6,000 hare pelts in 1856, the last year they were accepted in trade. Where in 1847, the Osnaburgh post had a surplus of trade goods since many Indians had traded at other posts, in the spring of 1854 George McPherson stated that so many small furs—hare, squirrels, and skunks—were traded that "I am out of Goods of every sort"[75]. By that date castoreum, and hence beaver were in demand again. In 1856, "Skunks and Skunkfat are in demand". Two whole skunks were worth one made beaver[76]. This was a substantial increase over the value of four per made beaver in 1848. In 1852, 24 squirrel pelts were equal to one made beaver at Osnaburgh[77].

The trade in small furs was to the benefit of the Indians although traders reported that old beaver hunters were ashamed to bring in "rabbits" themselves. Instead they would send their wives and children to the post with them[78]. During the early 1850's when other types of furs were extremely scarce, McKenzie of Lac Seul wrote that "Rabbits and other trash are a 'Godsend' to the poor Indians in such a year as this"[79]. Small furs were the only means by which the Indians could obtain their necessities.

These policies seem also to have influenced property concepts regarding fur resources. Conservation policies introduced by the Company may have encouraged Indians to consciously "farm" their beaver. This would have been especially true after 1848 when steel traps were traded permitting Indians in the Albany District to compete for furs on an equal basis with Indians in adjacent districts.

Decrees banning the trade in the more valuable furs occurred from time to time, and were usually the product of price and demand in the London market, or local scarcity and hence conservation measures. It mattered little to the Ojibwa what the reasons were so long as they received their supplies. If they could find no outlet for their furs at their own post they went elsewhere until they found a buyer or at least somebody who would assist them with goods. Conservation policies never worked well in the Osnaburgh area since Indians would take their furs to Nipigon in another district. The traders at the posts adjacent to the American border discovered that they could not afford to practice conservation policies for fear of losing the trade. Again, when the Albany posts attempted to practice conservation prior to 1848, Indians from other posts moved into the temporarily vacated territories and ravaged them with steel traps. When this occurred, as it did during the early 1840's at Osnaburgh and Lac Seul, there was no preventing local Indians from killing every beaver or muskrat they could find. For this reason, the Hudson's Bay Company tried to direct Indians to hunting smaller furs by increasing their value. Marten in particular became valuable after the 1850's and by the 1860's an annual prize of 20 made beaver was offered at Osnaburgh for the "King of the Martin hunters" (the Indian who obtained the most marten pelts)[80].

The Attraction of Liquor

Of considerable importance to Indian trade from the seventeenth century was liquor. Prior to 1821, vast quantities had been distributed to Indians, and at that time a trade chief often received an entire 13-gallon keg of watered rum which he distributed to members of his group. After 1821, the amount of liquor that Indians received was reduced to cut expenses and each adult hunter obtained on his own a quantity in proportion to his hunt. Most drinking took place during the summer when Indians would gather near the post. Drinking was a social phenomenon that was frequently associated with feasts and ceremonials.

Since drunken Indians often created problems for traders and became involved in fights among themselves, some traders appear to have been against the distribution of liquor. Nicol Finlayson of Osnaburgh indicated in 1828 that if it was prohibited, Indians "would live more socially among themselves and would get more honest in paying for any advances they might get from the Company's Stores"[81]. Despite the partial restriction of liquor at Osnaburgh that year, which was not adequate according to Finlayson, Indians made equally good beaver hunts as they had when liquor was distributed more freely. Control of the quantity of liquor distributed after 1821 ended "the scenes of debauchery which had formerly marked trade-time at the posts"[82].

Nevertheless, Indians in the Albany District continued to receive liquor in trade until 1839. Often during the summer Indians would exchange their furs for liquor instead of provisions necessary to survival and to trapping. For example, the Lac Seul Indians were reported "drinking some of their Rats"[83]. Traders, thus frequently had to supply Indians with their needs at a later date which created added expenses. In addition, violence often occurred among Indians during drinking bouts. To prevent aggression, some traders such as Donald McIntosh of Nipigon in 1829,

gave the different bands their rum separately, and sent them to drink it at some distance from the Fort, in different directions, by taking this precaution they gave us no trouble nor did we hear of any quarrels amongst themselves[84].

Liquor was banned as a trade item in the Lake Superior District in 1836. At the Nipigon post, which was included within this district, the factor John Swanton reported that the Indians were very disappointed, and many had left or intended to leave for the Albany and Lac La Pluie Districts, and the American posts where it was still available. Posts in the vicinity still distributing rum included Martin's Falls, Osnaburgh, Lac Seul, Sturgeon Lake, Lac La Pluie, and the American posts at Grand Portage and Rainy Lake. That year a whole band consisting, in part, of 9 hunting men, vacated Nipigon for Sturgeon Lake[85].

By 1839, a proclamation was issued by Governor George Simpson prohibiting the sale and distribution of "spirituous liquors" to Indians in the Albany District[86]. McKenzie reported that at Lac Seul the news

came upon the Indians like a Thunder Ball—they received it with the same welcome as they would a message from death—in truth they are chop fallen—They have been gathering here these ten days starving—but patiently waiting the Arrival of the Boats—merely for a Bouse before going to look for Rice.

At Osnaburgh, the Indians appear to have been equally disappointed. John Vincent stated that Indians "have threatened to put an end to my existence with medicines"[87]. To console them he gave each a glass of rum. Indians both at Osnaburgh and Lac Seul noting the numerous kegs of rum on hand at these two posts "pressed hard for spirits". They demanded why it was not being distributed and threatened not to trap unless "encouraged with a little liquor". The Osnaburgh Indians became so aggressive and demanding according to Vincent, that he had to take a knife and blanket away from one belligerent person "to make an example of him". Those Osnaburgh Indians who were employed to assist the Hudson's Bay Company servants with the fall fishery refused to work without receiving liquor and hence Vincent was forced to deviate from the rule

Otherwise I will subject the Establishment to starvation and besides if the Indians takes it into their Heads after I send off all my men to the fisheries they are able to Plunder the Establishment. Neither have I the means of preventing them consequently with the greatest respect to the governor's Command I have consented to distribute a few drams and at the same time give some liquor when they are going off to the fisheries.

The reaction of the Lac Seul Indians was almost as violent. For example, one Lac Seul Indian

spoke Treason against the Queen—irreverendly—against prest-craft—provanity 'gainst Religion and disrespectful toward the Governor & Indian Traders for Abolishing the use of Liquor to the Indians[88].

One Lac Seul Indian known as the Lobster, threatened to go to Albany

to see our "*kuge-okimas*" or Superintendent-in-chief—to have Rum once more in the Albany District—I told him he might, but that none in this Country had that power— except he who abolished the Liquor—The Governor—Sir George Simpson—so the Lobster is to keep a sharp lookout for Sir George the first time he will pass River Winnipic and tell him his mind—"a bit" and faith he is the very man to tell his mind—provided he had a couple of good Glasses of Rum on his Stomach first![89]

By 1846, the Lobster was the "ring leader and master of this Rum project". McKenzie related that the Lobster's strategy was to make each Indian at Lac Seul save one made beaver which the latter would take to Rat Portage the following summer where he intended to meet Governor Simpson. He would then make the governor

"walk upon furs from his landing place to the door of the House" where Captain Lobster will have a "Talk" cut and dry to Edify all hearers—The Indians can do all this and Should it succeed Indians of other posts can do the Same—I would sooner part with Captain Lobster & Co than see Rum introduced once more to Lac Seul[90].

As it turned out, the Lobster's plan failed, according to

McKenzie, owing to the Indian's own selfishness. Lac Seul, however, was closer to the Lac La Pluie District and the American traders who continued to trade rum for furs. In ensuing years, many Lac Seul Indians were lost to the more southerly posts where liquor was available and prices were generally lower.

Aware of the "rum project" the Osnaburgh Indians were "speaking hard why they cannot get Rum" and "threatening that they will leave this post should none be sent up this summer and go where they have Rum"[91]. Despite these complaints, the Osnaburgh post remained dry for several decades. Nevertheless, the attraction of liquor at other posts and later in the century brought in by free traders continued to lure Indians away. After 1870, traders were chasing "untrustworthy" Indians and obtaining furs from their tents in much the same manner as they had been forced to do prior to 1821.

Competition and Mobility

It is evident that trade policies of the Company were not always a success, since Indians disappointed at the Albany River posts left to trade in other districts when environmental conditions were favourable. In addition to measures regulating the means by which Indians obtained certain materials, the Hudson's Bay Company frequently withheld some items from the Albany District posts; or provided cheap substitutes in order to economize. One tactic not previously mentioned involved promises concerning trade items kept back. Traders were urged to promise new trade materials requested by Indians the following year to encourage them to trap, and to prevent them from trading at other posts. For example, when Lac Seul Indians asked for steel traps in 1837, Charles McKenzie stated:

> I promised them Traps & many other things ie. "Next Year"—I was indeed told demi-officially—to satisfy the demands of Indians by a promise of every thing "next year"—whatever good quality these promises may have[92].

These economizing measures by the Company frequently resulted in a deficiency of supplies at the Albany posts. However, not only was there often a shortage of materials, but also the quality of many items was inferior. The effect was neither beneficial to the Indians nor to the fur trade. As stated by Charles McKenzie in his 1838 annual report:

> they complain most bitterly—that their Coats, Blankets, Cloth & Guns do not last out over half the year—The truth of this is evident—The Blankets are thin & in holes from the hands of the Manufacturer—Care must be taken in cutting the Cloth lest it should tear the wrong way . . .
>
> The Gun Locks are as brittle as Common Brass and seldom a Gun lock stands a month without some part giving way—Nay 'tis not unfrequently they break in their hands before they are out of the store with them—This is a great hardship to the Indians . . .
>
> That if the Country was rich instead of being wretchedly poor—the more they consumed the better—But the Company is obliged to support them—and by giving them bad Articles no party is benefited except the Manufacturer & the contractor who devide the profit between them to the prejudice of all concerned[93].

Such a policy often resulted in much mobility among Indians when better or cheaper goods were available elsewhere. Variation in trade policies in different districts lured Osnaburgh and Lac Seul Indians to stores near the American border where competition with American fur traders continued. For example, when the ready barter system was introduced in 1845, George McPherson wrote that some Indians

> went off immediately in the sulks for other posts. By the advice of Mr. MacKenzie I was obliged to supply some of them with Twine and Ammunition Tobacco etc to the Amount of 10 Made Beaver skins to each[94].

Another reason for going to the border posts was that even on the debt system, prices were lower than at Osnaburgh due to competition with the nearby American Fur Trade Company posts. At Rainy Lake the Indians received "4 skeins Twine for a

Single Beaver Skin—here it would cost a Beaver Per Skein—Let us not blame the Indians for going to the Best Market with their furs"[95]. Indians had no trouble recognizing differences in prices. Their ability to calculate values accurately is indicated by the fact that they would often bring to the post pieces of birch bark on which the value of their furs was marked[96]; or they would send bundles of small sticks indicating the total made beaver in furs[97].

When the Trout Lake post was again established from Fort Severn in 1844 by William McKay, George McPherson of Osnaburgh was instructed "to be extremely careful in giving Debts to Some Indians that hunt about Cat Lake and the Cranes"[98]. Some of the Cranes were lured back to the Trout Lake post that year and by the 1850's, the bulk of the Cranes traded at the Trout Lake post and at the Cat Lake outpost when it was re-established during the 1870's.

In 1845, no less than 22 Osnaburgh Indians went elsewhere to trade; Nipigon House, Lac La Pluie, Trout Lake, and Martin's Falls being the posts visited. And this despite the fact that the barter system was accompanied by the abolition of old debts! In 1847, a number of Osnaburgh and Lac Seul Indians were intercepted by Lac Seul traders on their way to Rat Portage who were not willing to give up their furs hoping to trade them for rum. During the 1846-47 season, 18 Indians debted at Lac Seul took their furs elsewhere: 10 to Rat Portage, 3 to Fort Francis, 3 to Nipigon, and 2 to Berens River[99]. Of 30 former Lac Seul Indians who hunted to the south of that post in 1848, only about half a dozen still traded at Lac Seul and these were doubtful cases. The rest had all been lured to the south by trade policies and the availability of rum[100]. Traders by this time were actually moving north with rum, according to McKenzie, to entice Indians from the Albany posts. So strong was the lure of liquor in 1849, that two kegs of rum were to be sent to Osnaburgh to "Draw those Indians who have gone to other Posts in search of this Article back to Osnaburgh and of improving thereby the trade"[101]. Rum was not to be traded for furs, but rather it was to be distributed to "worthy" Indians gratis. However, an error in shipping had been made and no rum was to reach Osnaburgh that year.

Although the old debt system was re-installed in August 1847, many Osnaburgh Indians had become aware of better prices elsewhere, and indeed, traders in the Lake Superior District were complaining about Osnaburgh and Lac Seul Indians who wished to trade there, since the difference in tariff for Osnaburgh, and both the Lake Superior and Rainy Lake Districts, was "so great that it is quite enough to induce all the Indians to leave us"[102].

Despite the liberal treatment of some traders, Indians continued to take advantage of better bargains elsewhere. For example, in 1850, 9 Osnaburgh Indians traded at Martin's Falls who had been debted at the Osnaburgh post. In 1849, 97 Indians were debted at Lac Seul to the amount of 3,752 made beaver[103]. The following year, 76 Indians received 1,976 made beaver, and in 1851, 68 got 1,578 made beaver in goods. As fewer supplies were given in trade, fewer Indians remained to trade. The attrition of Indians trading at Lac Seul was due to the availability of rum at the more southerly posts, the higher price placed on trade goods, and an edict prohibiting the purchase of muskrats in the Albany District[104].

It is evident that there was a considerable amount of competition between the Hudson's Bay posts in the different districts. By the 1850's Indians in the Osnaburgh-Lac Seul area, unhappy with their plight often had the option of trading where bargains were best, as had been the case while the old Northwest Company was in operation. Lac Seul, situated closer to the Lake Superior and Lac La Pluie Districts seems always to have had trouble in maintaining its Indian population. Differences in trade policy stimulated the competition which at times grew as intense as it had been 50 years earlier. The Rat Portage post was particularly detested by the traders at Osnaburgh and Lac Seul. In June 1849, at a time when the trade policies of the Albany District were unfavourable to most Indians, Charles McKenzie remarked upon the arrival of the Indian, Little Boy and his band.

> They pride themselves much—that they did not like others go to Rat Portage, or the Yankees—notwithstanding all Temptations . . . no white men could withstand these Temptations—so very near and ready for them[105].

McKenzie indicates the growing independence of the Indians due to the competition and variation in trade policies:

> But the time is gone by, when Indians "must come around"

—and they know it—'tis us who must come around—we must yield to them—we fear them—and have to fear them—whilst we advance them—the very best can Scarcely be trusted.

According to McKenzie "this is one of the worst oppositions ever started in this country. Each HB post an Enemy to its Neighbouring HB post". In 1855, a good number of Osnaburgh Indians had left to trade at Nipigon having been invited by the factor there. McPherson was told that more would go next year if summer muskrats were not accepted at Osnaburgh. Also, Indians received more for their pelts at Nipigon and goods were cheaper there[106]. It was also reported that Nipigon traded items not obtainable at Osnaburgh[107]. The loss of Indians to other posts had a marked effect upon fur returns.

In the summer of 1847, there were so many trade goods left at the Osnaburgh post, many Indians having traded elsewhere, that it "is almost enough to prevent Goods being sent to that place"[108]. Hence, by 1851, the barter system was to be re-introduced and the value of trade goods reduced, to stimulate the Osnaburgh Indians "to exertion in fur hunting and of preventing them from going to other places hereafter with their furs", and since the system of giving debts "has been found injurious to the Indians and to the Concern we should endeavor to abolish it as Speedily as possible"[109]. In 1852, George McPherson was instructed to restrict his advances to Indians "to such articles as are absolutely indispensable to enable the Indians to hunt"[110].

The lure of rum, cheaper prices elsewhere, and variations in trade policy continued to attract Osnaburgh Indians throughout the century. For example, in December 1868, two servants were sent "up the Lake to visit our Indians who hunts in that direction in case the Lac Seul men is coming amongst them with their Rum or fire water"[111], while the next year some Osnaburgh Indians arrived at the post with furs and requested that the factor send men to their tents to get the furs lest "the Nipigon or Fort William men" get them first[112]. One Osnaburgh Indian and four Martin's Falls Indians arrived that same spring unable to get goods at the Martin's Falls post owing to the ready barter system in practice there. The Osnaburgh factor was forced to debt them, otherwise they would have taken their furs to Trout Lake. By January 1870, traders from Red River were penetrating the area west of Osnaburgh, and in April it was reported that a Lac Seul Indian, having been given a keg of rum, was visiting the Cat Lake Indians to acquire their furs. The following winter, traders from Lake Nipigon and Lac Seul were travelling about in the vicinity of Osnaburgh to get furs.

By the 1860's Osnaburgh employees were again travelling to Indians' encampments to protect and acquire their furs. In addition, Indians considered to be honest by traders, were sent to procure the furs of others, or were given extra supplies "to trade with the Cranes . . . I don't think it will be a loosing spree as they are both good trusty Indians"[113]. In order to prevent future losses in the Cat Lake area, Thomas Lawson and the Indian, Shinna-wash, were sent in March 1873, with trade goods to spend the remainder of the winter there; and for these reasons, permanent winter camp trade was inaugurated at Cat Lake[114]. Nevertheless, competition with traders from other posts continued, as for example, in 1876, when Lac Seul Indians supplied with store foods were

going amongst our Indians trading. I must say that is a Strange way of doing business one Comp'ys Post defrauding the other[115].

The Osnaburgh post, however, took advantage of the situation also as witness James Vincent's report of 1879:

I believe the Officer in charge of Nepigon is furious in consequence of his Indians trading here . . . That is not my fault . . . "Every one for himself & the Deuce take the hind-most" is my motto[116].

Despite this competition, it would seem that the majority of Indians were "honest" in paying their debts by this date. However, the very nature of the fur trade actually encouraged a certain amount of competition. Not only were prices different at different posts, but managers received additional monies according to the quantity and value of the furs traded. Then, too, the quality and quantity of trade items, including flour and other foods, had made existence less precarious and allowed Indians a greater latitude of movement from post to post. The increase in the caribou population around Lake St. Joseph about the same time may also have augmented this process. The value of furs seems also to have risen by the 1880's[117].

Conclusions

During the nineteenth century, the Northern Ojibwa were reliant upon a regular supply of Euro-Canadian trade materials which they acquired primarily through trapping activities. The means by which these goods were distributed were strictly regulated by the Hudson's Bay Company to maximize profits. Paradoxically however, variations in policies from post to post helped to foster inter-post movements, environmental conditions permitting, since Indians seized any opportunity for bargaining that would improve their precarious situation. It is clear, then, that the network of posts, hunting group settlements, and trade relations formed an intricate web of sociocultural affect and effect.

Footnotes

1. E. S. Rogers (1963b:67-69), for example, makes this assumption although he is not alone in this belief. The new historical evidence which has been forthcoming since the mid-1960's is changing older views.

2. E. S. Rogers (1962:A26-A27; 1963b:69).

3. E. Spicer (1961:521).

4. See Phillips 1961, chapter 1; Innis 1961, chapters 1-4, and Rich 1967, chapters 1-3.

5. Beaver pelts were taken in winter, cut, scraped on the inside, and sewn into robes which were worn by the Indians fur-side-in so that after a year's wear the fur had become soft and greasy. These *castor gras d'hiver* became significant to European hat-makers (Innis 1962:14).

6. The Nipissings and Ottawa acted as middlemen to the western tribes (Phillips 1961:54-55) until the raids of the Iroquois led to the westward dispersals. However, by the 1660's, the trade had expanded to incorporate the Algonkian-speaking Ojibwa, Fox, Sauk, Potawatomi, Miami, and Cree, and the Siouan-speaking Dakota, Winnebago, and Assiniboin. Often over 1,000 Indians gathered at such key locations as Michilimackinac and Sault Ste. Marie.

7. These key posts included Port Nelson, York Factory, Fort Severn, Fort Albany, Moose Factory and Rupert's House (recently renamed Fort Rupert). A good many Indians, especially the Cree and Assiniboin who formerly had to trade through Dakota and Ojibwa middlemen were lured to these posts which were well stocked with relatively cheap goods. To avert these trips to the English, the French established trading centers at Lake Nipigon and at the mouth of the Kaministikwia River (Innis 1962:49). After 1686, the French captured and temporarily held several Hudson's Bay Company posts until the Treaty of Utrecht in 1713 when they were returned to the English. However, by the 1720's, the French trade had expanded to the west of Lake Superior with the explorations of La Véréndrye and others.

8. In 1750, for instance, the French trade north of Lake Superior produced approximately 500 packs of furs (Innis 1962:100). A fur pack usually contained about 90 pelts. Between 1739 and 1752 from eight to twenty-seven French canoes loaded with trade goods were sent north of Lake Superior annually.

9. After 1713, the Hudson's Bay Company trade grew rapidly and involved large quantities of goods and men. The large well-stocked Bay posts often contained over 30 men who were employed to manufacture goods for the post and for the Indians. Inventories for the following year were kept and estimates made. To reduce overhead costs, post personnel were encouraged to live off country produce supplied by the Indians. Furs were packed and marked with the post insignia. Beaver were graded according to size, color, and quality.

10. Grand Portage near the west end of Lake Superior became an important rendezvous spot to interior regions. After 1790, two sloops conveyed supplies to Grand Portage, and

from there, Northwest Company traders established numerous and shifting outposts throughout the country north of Lake Superior. The Hudson's Bay Company, to compete, built Gloucester House (1777), Osnaburgh House (1786), Nipigon House (1792), Martin's Falls (1794), Trout Lake (1807), Berens River (1814), in addition to numerous outposts. Prior to the 1770's, the HBC had confined its activities to the coast, the only inland post being Henley House 120 miles inland from Fort Albany which was built in 1743. Henley House had an intermittent history disrupted by Indian attacks until the late 1760's and did not trade furs at this time, but only "country provisions" (venison, fish, hare and geese). Indians still had to go to Fort Albany for their trade goods (see Map 1 for post locations).

11. Thomas Vincent, chief factor at Fort Albany (HBC Arch B107/a/4).

12. HBC Arch B155/a/39.

13. Despite his complaints, Finlayson himself appears to have been married to an Indian as he stated in 1828 that he "got 70 rabbits and a Cat from my Mother-in-law" (HBC Arch B155/a/39).

14. HBC Arch B107/a/3.

15. Charles McKenzie was very proud of his Indian wife who he was constantly praising for her efforts and abilities. He claimed that she was the only woman who would set traps and snares and that the other women were too lazy. McKenzie raised a family of three children two of whom settled in Winnipeg and the third in Kingston, Ontario. He and his wife retired to Winnipeg in 1853.

16. HBC Arch B107/a/5; B155/a/39.

17. HBC Arch B107/a/27.

18. HBC Arch B107/a/6.

19. HBC Arch B123/a/28.

20. HBC Arch B155/a/55.

21. HBC Arch B155/a/54.

22. HBC Arch B107/a/14. In 1842, McKenzie wrote:

> 'twere as easy to guard a Band of Apes in a Garden of fruit—as these old Indian women 'gainst stealing the

finest potatoes—To detect them is nothing—they have neither shame nor honour. When every hole and corner about their body that can hide a potato is full—they go into the woods & discharge their burden—and repeat the same over again—but the men are more honorable (HBC Arch B107/a/21).

23. HBC Arch B155/a/81.

24. These gardening chores included digging the soil, weeding and hoeing the potatoes, and supplying moss for them. After the 1870's boiled fish were used as fertilizer at Osnaburgh.

25. Birchbark canoes were time consuming to make and few Indians wished to trade them. For example, Charles McKenzie bought two canoes from the Indian, Tripie: "The Dearest Canoes ever bought at this place, certainly but Tripie is the only Indian that would take the trouble to make them" (HBC Arch B107/a/6).

26. Summer labor on the supply boats not only took men away from their families and subsistence activities, but they also suffered from discrimination. They received the worst of the food available and often were not allowed to sleep in the tents at night.

27. HBC Arch B107/a/26. Although the Ojibwa of the interior were reluctant to work for the small wages paid for odd jobs, the Cree who resided along coastal James Bay reacted differently. According to Charles McKenzie, in 1847, the coastal Cree

are kept as Summer Labourers—fed & paid as laborers —Nay they offer their Services—while the inland Indians— can hardly be got for a summer trip. They will tell plainly—"We are poor 'tis true but we shall not be Slaves" (HBC Arch B107/a/25).

28. HBC Arch B107/a/29.

29. HBC Arch B155/a/71.

30. HBC Arch B155/a/78.

31. HBC Arch B155/a/71.

32. Nicol Finlayson that year wrote that "were it not for that we were starving I would take no rabbits from any Indian" (HBC Arch B155/a/38).

33. In 1869, an Indian traded 120 hares for potatoes (HBC Arch

B155/a/78).

34. Location unknown. It appears to have been near Cat Lake since Flint hunted northeast of Lac Seul (see James Sutherland's map—HBC Arch B78/a/14).

35. HBC Arch B155/a/54.

36. HBC Arch B155/a/78.

37. HBC Arch B155/a/71.

38. HBC Arch B107/a/6.

39. HBC Arch B155/a/38.

40. HBC Arch B107/a/11.

41. HBC Arch B107/a/14.

42. HBC Arch B107/a/3; B107/a/26; B107/a/28.

43. HBC Arch B155/a/77.

44. HBC Arch B30/a/9.

45. HBC Arch B211/a/9.

46. Letter: John Davis factor of Lac Seul to James Slater factor of Osnaburgh House (HBC Arch B155/a/35).

47. HBC Arch B107/e/1.

48. For example, James Slater remarked in September 1824 that:

> they seem all to be discontended as they cannot get debts as usual but that can't be helped . . . In place of the Indians from Lac Nipigon and Sturgeon Lake coming here I am afraid the Indians of this place will a great many of them go there as they cannot get debts here (HBC Arch B107/a/4).

49. Nicol Finlayson (HBC Arch B107/a/4).

50. HBC Arch B107/a/4.

51. HBC Arch B107/a/4.

52. HBC Arch B107/a/4.

53. HBC Arch B155/a/37.

54. The letters "OH" refer to Osnaburgh House. Traders frequently abbreviated: for example. LS-Lac Seul, MF-Martin's Falls, and LLP-Lac La Pluie, etc. (HBC Arch B107/a/4).

55. HBC Arch B107/a/13; B107/a/24; B155/a/65; B155/a/78; B155/a/80; B155/c/1.

56. HBC Arch B107/z/2.

57. HBC Arch B107/e/4. McKenzie again wrote in 1834: "I will not distress a good Indian—I rather break the 'letter of the Law' than distress an Indian & chase him from the place in disgust—Advanced the Flint 20 MB" (HBC Arch B107/a/13). When an Indian known as the Kingfisher arrived that year who hunted far to the north of Lac Seul, McKenzie advanced him 40 made beaver in goods, since "Indians at so great a distance cannot take advantage of a *Cheap* Barter—erroneously so called" (HBC Arch B107/a/12). Nevertheless, often an Indian "would rather trade at a disadvantage than deliver his hear's hunt to pay for the Goods that are in Rags on his back" (Ibid).

58. HBC Arch B107/a/13.

59. HBC Arch B155/a/80.

60. John Davis. Martin's Falls district report for 1824 (HBC Arch B123/e/8).

61. HBC Arch B107/a/16.

62. HBC Arch B107/a/21.

63. HBC Arch B155/a/53; B107/a/23.

64. McKenzie's sympathy to the Indian cause is again illustrated by the following quote:

> There was nothing remaining to finish the ruin of the Trade than the prohibition of taking Rats at this Season!—We almost overcome so far death and disease —and made up the loss of those Indians inticed to other posts—by the Temptation of Rum—having got the better share of their hunts—but to overcome the loss of Rats is impossible—what else can the poor Indians get at this season—after being promised all winter that we would take their Rats. In the Spring— and even giving out debts on the faith of Rats ... Indians come in ... but with what will they pay—that is the Question—This prohibition or interdict upon Rats comes more heavy upon our Indians here—than the abolition of the Corn Law in England but they seem indifferent what sort of furs we prohibit, provided they get goods—and will pay "if they can" but if

refused they certainly will try other posts—who seem ready to receive them (HBC Arch B107/a/25).

65. HBC Arch B107/a/18.

66. HBC Arch B155/a/60.

67. Charles McKenzie (HBC Arch B107/a/5).

68. HBC Arch B107/a/13.

69. Charles McKenzie (HBC Arch B107/a/23).

70. HBC Arch B155/a/60.

71. HBC Arch B107/a/30.

72. HBC Arch B107/z/2.

73. HBC Arch B107/z/2.

74. HBC Arch B107/a/31.

75. HBC Arch B155/a/60.

76. HBC Arch B155/z/1.

77. HBC Arch B155/a/65.

78. HBC Arch B107/a/31.

79. HBC Arch B107/a/31. Traders were as contemptuous of small furs as were the Indians. When Lac Seul Indians brought squirrels and hare to the post to trade in 1852, McKenzie remarked:

> Which I cannot call furs not any one who entered the Trade in the "Beaver Age" as I did—Rabbits and Squirrels may satisfy those who entered the trade in this "pen & paper Age"—they have seen no better things—nor is there any reasonable apperance that they will see better (HBC Arch B107/a/30).

80. HBC Arch B155/a/77.

81. HBC Arch B155/a/39.

82. Rich 1961 3:477.

83. Charles McKenzie (HBC Arch B107/a/13).

84. HBC Arch B149/a/11.

85. HBC Arch B149/a/19.

86. HBC Arch B107/a/18.

87. HBC Arch B155/a/51.

88. HBC Arch B107/a/18.

89. HBC Arch B107/a/20.

90. HBC Arch B107/a/24.

91. HBC Arch B155/a/59.

92. HBC Arch B107/a/16.

93. HBC Arch B107/a/16.

94. HBC Arch B155/a/57.

95. HBC Arch B107/a/24. Again, in 1847, McKenzie stated that a coat that cost 12 marten skins at Lac Seul could be got at Rainy Lake for four (HBC Arch B107/z/2). Marten pelts at Nipigon were worth one made beaver each, but only half that at Osnaburgh; while two otters were valued at 10 made beaver at Lac Seul compared to 15 at Fort Francis in 1850.

96. HBC Arch B107/a/13.

97. HBC Arch B107/a/29.

98. HBC Arch B155/a/55.

99. HBC Arch B107/z/1.

100. HBC Arch B107/a/26.

101. HBC Arch B155/a/61.

102. HBC Arch B155/a/60.

103. HBC Arch B107/z/2.

104. HBC Arch B107/a/29.

105. HBC Arch B107/a/27.

106. HBC Arch B155/a/67.

107. HBC Arch B155/a/69.

108. HBC Arch B155/a/59.

109. Thomas Corcaoran (HBC Arch B155/a/63).

110. HBC Arch B155/a/65.

111. T. A. Rae (HBC Arch B155/a/77).

112. HBC Arch B155/a/78.

113. HBC Arch B155/a/78.

114. T. A. RAE (HBC Arch B155/a/81).

115. Alexander Harvey (HBC Arch B155/a/84).

116. HBC Arch B155/a/84.

117. HBC Arch B3/z/4. Table 22 gives the tariff price of furs from 1888 to 1891.

Table 22   Value in Dollars of Furs 1888-1891

Furs	1888	1889	1890	1891
Bears—black	$11.68	$17.42	$10.90	$14.75
—brown	11.68		12.26	16.00
Beaver	4.87	5.89	5.55	6.60
Castoreum (per lb)	6.82	7.69	5.84	6.25
Ermine (per 40)		4.09	2.34	2.40
Fisher	4.48	8.19	5.89	6.00
Fox—silver	50.62	75.24	44.77	76.50
—cross	8.56	9.54	7.54	10.30
—red	1.95	2.43	1.80	1.85
—white	2.53	1.36	2.48	1.75
Isinglass (per lb)	.78	.49	.39	.40
Lynx	2.14	3.78	2.68	2.75
Marten	1.63	1.96	1.17	1.40
Mink	.39	1.06	.73	.95
Musquash	.08	.16	.15	.15
Otter	6.42	8.62	7.35	8.10
Rabbits (per doz)	.19		.13	.20
Skunk	.68	.63	.58	.95
Squirrels (per 100)	.97	.78	.97	.75
Weenusk	.05	.08	.03	.03
Wolves	6.62	1.60	1.31	8.75
Wolverines	3.90	4.48	3.80	2.65

Chapter Five
Community and Social Organization During the Mid-nineteenth Century

The purpose of this chapter is to examine the social organization of the Northern Ojibwa as it functioned during the middle of the nineteenth century. Attention is given to the role of the trader and missionary, especially the former, since these persons formed part of the total social network. Because Indians were economically dependent upon traders, the nature of social relationships with them tended to structure Ojibwa behaviour. Demographic and ecological factors are also discussed, since these operated to set limits on the size and structure of hunting groups, and also affected inter-group relationships. By the nineteenth century, both the habitat and the economic arrangements of Ojibwa society had undergone considerable modification over a 200-year period. Thus, special emphasis is given to analysing social and cultural features in relation to contact and ecological variables as a baseline for gauging the amount and direction of change both in earlier times and with the present. Hunting groups and marriage patterns are examined in detail since they provide clues to understanding earlier and aboriginal patterns.

The Osnaburgh House Community

The Osnaburgh House Hudson's Bay Company store was one of several foci in northern Ontario where Indians resorted to exchange their furs for trade supplies. During the summer the post was a beehive of activity. The furs procured during the past winter season were packed and loaded on the boats for Fort Albany, and trade supplies for the ensuing year were unloaded and stored in the warehouse. Boatloads of traders and goods travelling to and from other posts stopped at Osnaburgh. Often 100 or more Indians living off fish and dried foods congregated near the post in June or July to await the summer shipment of trade supplies. It was at this time also, that the Midewiwin, the shaking tent ceremony, drum dances, and marriage festivities occurred.

By autumn most Indians had returned to their winter settlements scattered over a wide area within 120 miles radius of the post. The precarious nature of the food quest and trapping activities prevented the possibility of a permanent Indian population at the trading post. Even in summer when fish were taken in gill nets, food was not plentiful and there are numerous references in the journals to Indians starving while awaiting the supply boats.

The community was too unstable to have a church, and missionary endeavours were restricted to the summer months. On occasion traders performed Sunday religious services and funerals when Indians brought their dead to be buried.

The Trader: Contact Consequences

By the early nineteenth century, the Northern Ojibwa were dependent upon the trading post and the good will of the factor. Hence, a picture of the total social organization in the north would be incomplete without a discussion of the type of social relations between traders and Indians. Some aspects of this relationship have already been touched upon although the focus was upon trade policy. In this and the following section the focus is upon how the linked roles of trader and missionary and Indian were enacted, involving the cultural backgrounds of each.

The Indian traders of interior posts, isolated from the outside world, developed a unique relationship with Indians. In addition to their daily interaction with the other servants at the post and their Indians wives and offspring, they frequently became intimate with the Indians of the area. Fluent in the native tongue, true friendships often developed between trader and Indian. The Lac Seul trader, Charles McKenzie, for example, has recorded numerous friendly conversations with Indians and it is from such amiable relationships that a knowledge of Indian culture developed which has been recorded by more literate factors. Many of the Hudson's Bay Company factors appear to have had a liberal education and by the middle of the nineteenth century most interior posts contained a small library.

The attitudes and personality of the post manager were important in determining the content of social relationships with Indians. McKenzie, highly influenced by his Indian wife and his many years in the bush, exhibited cultural relativism both in word and deed. For example, in his Christmas Day prayer for 1838 he wrote: " . . . and what is the difference betwixt us & these natives—but that we are better provided with materials for taking fish and less improvident when caught"[1].

Not all traders displayed such liberal views. Some appear to have disliked the rugged life in the bush and considered Indians as inferiors to be exploited in whatever way possible. For example, J. D. Cameron of Lac La Pluie, in 1826, wrote: "The great leading traits in the character of Indians, particularly Oat-che-buoys are Treachery, Insolence, Superstition & Drunkenness"[2]. Hostility was greeted by hostility: There are a number of recorded instances of provocations at Osnaburgh, usually by individual Indians. When hostilities did occur, they happened mainly in the summer months when large groups of Indians had congregated at the post to await trade supplies and to receive their debts.

During the year following the abolition of liquor in the Albany District (1839), a number of threats were made by Osnaburgh Indians. In May 1840, James Heron was told by some Ojibwa "to be upon our guard as its likely some of their relations will muster a Party of Strange Indians to give us some trouble about Liquor"[3]. These strange Indians, whoever they may have been, were often a menace to the known Osnaburgh Ojibwa. For example, an Indian, was shot at and wounded by them in July 1840[4]. In October that year some unknown Indians broke the fishing canoes and fishing basket of the Bay employees at Dog-hole Bay on Lake St. Joseph and the next night unknown people tried to get over the stockades but were driven off by gunshots. The following October, Heron stated:

Big Blood and his followers came in armed today suprising that I would be intimidated into their views but I told them frankly that I neither solicited their friendship or dreaded their enmity. We kept a sharp look out, neither did we visit the nets[5].

Strange Indians and personalized threats of violence (often the result of policy changes undesirable to Indians, but over which the factor had little control), continued to be reported throughout the nineteenth century at the Albany posts[6]. The palisades were maintained around a number of Hudson's Bay posts until the twentieth century. The palisades at Osnaburgh appear to have been torn down during the 1880's.

Although the views and values of traders influenced their relationship with Indians, an important aspect of this relationship was subject to the whims of the manager's superiors. Thus, it may have been expedient to maintain a degree of social distance. No matter how sympathetic traders might feel toward suffering Indians, they were forced to operate in terms of the Company's welfare. This accounts for the numerous complaints of sympathetic traders concerning Indian misfortunes.

One of the small ways Indians had of expressing friendship and gratitude for services rendered was through gift giving. Although gratuities were more frequently given by traders, often due to Company policy, but not always so, Indians on occasion would bring presents to the factor, especially if he was liked. Charles McKenzie of Lac Seul recorded that the Indian, Little Boy, made a present of ten prime beaver pelts and an otter. Such a gift was enough to "give rise to the most charitable feelings which exist within the bosom of an Indian Trader—if not that trader must be callous & far gone indeed"[7]. That year, Young Tripie presented McKenzie with a large beaver when the post was depleted of food although the former was starving: "yet he did not forget that he owed his life to this house the greatest part of the winter". A more sophisticated reciprocity was instituted by the Indian, Kingfisher, who trapped far to the north of Lac Seul. Upon bestowing a gift of 10 prime beaver, the canny Indian made a speech to get a post established at Red Lake. McKenzie then gave the Kingfisher what he thought was a generous gift. However, the Indian thought differently: "he knew well the value of the present he made & the furs he traded—& was not a little suprized that 'so great a man as me' (these were his words) did not know the Etiquette of these things better".

Often traders provided needy Indians with goods on charity with no hope or desire that the gifts be returned. In 1832, for example, Charles McKenzie gave the Indian Niconice "his most

150

necessary articles for his family to live . . . all for nothing—promising at the same time that I would not be hard upon him should he make a good hunt"[8]. Again, when the Indian, Assiniboine, died during the influenza epidemic at Lac Seul in 1845, leaving two widows and four children, his sons arrived with the father's last request to McKenzie:

"to come and find me in hopes that I would not see his children go naked—that I would do them charity"—The dying man must not be disappointed[9].

Sometimes the personal involvement of traders in Indian miseries led them to be more generous than was Company policy. In 1891, it was recommended that the Fort Hope manager, a Mr. Baxter, be removed from his post, the reason being:

he is liked very much by the Indians, I am told, on account of his careless generosity. His one great failing is that he permits his kind-hearted generosity to run away with his better judgment regarding the Profits of the place[10].

In addition to gifts of food and other materials, traders fulfilled a number of rather unusual role obligations. When an Indian shot his wife, the other members of the hunting group requested the Osnaburgh factor's opinion on a suitable punishment[11]. In the spring of 1839, James Heron of Osnaburgh "inoculated the Indians"[12]. That same spring, George Barnston of Martin's Falls wrote:

every soul who has come to the Establishment (with the exception of one Girl who went off without my knowledge) has been vaccinated and I have instructed the heads of families, how to inoculate their children & relatives with a fluid at their own wigwams[13].

This is the first evidence that general health measures were being introduced to entire Indian groups as a preventative against disease. Sick Indians who arrived at the post were often provided with medicines[14], and indeed, they appear to have resorted to the

151

post to receive medicinal aid perhaps when their own cures failed. If Indians died while at the post, traders frequently dug graves and made coffins for them. Indians on the verge of death were often brought to the post to die and be taken care of by traders.

In conclusion, Indians depended upon the post for goods while traders depended upon Indians for furs. There was one difference however. Traders could survive without pelts, but Indians could not live without assistance from the post. Hence, the Indians were, in part, subject to the sanctions of Euro-Canadian traders as well as to sanctions within their own system. Trade policies disliked by Indians were, perhaps blamed directly on traders who remained more aloof from Indian life and who were less able to make predictions due to personal prejudices. Although Indian groups throughout the north were directed partly for humanitarian reasons, and partly for exploitation and control, the success of regulations depended to a very large degree upon the trader's behaviour since he was the medium through which change flowed during most of the century. The trader was not a free agent in his role of liaison between the Company and the Ojibwa but his personality could influence the behaviour of Indians.

The Missionary: Contact Consequences

Many Ojibwa religious practices appear to have experienced the effects of missionary influences by the middle of the nineteenth century. For example, the Midewiwin ceremony, itself a response to post-contact socio-political arrangements (Hickerson 1962b), seems to have disappeared at Osnaburgh by the late nineteenth century perhaps due to missionary influences.

Although the ancestors of the Osnaburgh Ojibwa may have encountered French Jesuits during the seventeenth and early eighteenth centuries, their effects upon later generations appears to have been minimal. After the migration of Ojibwa groups to interior northern Ontario during the early mid-eighteenth century contact with missionaries occurred only rarely for the next 100 years.

While at the post Indians, on occasion, had the opportunity of observing traders perform Sunday services and rituals pertaining to funerals, in addition to the annual Christmas and Easter ceremonies. However, trained missionaries did not enter the area until the summer of 1841. The Osnaburgh factor, James Heron, noted the arrival on June 26th of the Reverend William Mason of the Wesleyan Missionary Society, and his interpreter from Lac Seul; "of course we had prayers, a new circumstance at Osnaburgh"[15]. The children of the Bay servants were baptized, and two marriages took place. Four days later, Reverend Mason returned to Lac Seul and preached to the Indians in the yard in front of the store. More than 100 people were present "all bending the Knee with Great reverence—as if they were old disciples of some years"[16].

Not all Indians accepted the new missionaries that summer. Some of the Indians who trapped to the westward of Lac Seul were acquainted with the Winnipeg River and Lac La Pluie missionaries. They asked McKenzie:

"what those Black Robes came here for? did they come to destroy the Indians & their Children?—'We are resolved not to hear them" . . . yet Some of them said—had they been here at the time they would have their children Baptized— as to ourselves we are too foolish & old to learn—but our Children said they—may learn more wisdom.

In May 1842, Reverend Mason again visited Lac Seul, arriving from Lac La Pluie. On this visit, he performed a number of marriages as well as baptisms[17]. In August that year, the Indian known as the Lobster arrived from the Winnipeg River at Lac Seul claiming he had embraced the Roman Catholic faith. A mission house known as the White Dog had been built by some priests on the Winnipeg River that summer. The Lobster, according to McKenzie told the other Lac Seul Indians "that what our Ministers tell them is no Religion at all 'they only cheat the Indians' "[18]. The Lobster then told McKenzie that the priests had taught him everything about religion. McKenzie asked the Lobster if the priests told him to be honest in paying his debts. The Indian paused and replied, "He is not a Trader to tell us that".

The Catholic mission appears to have had considerable success in converting Indians since McKenzie reported that by the summer of 1848 all the westward Indians were at the White Dog Portage "learning to be Bon Catholique Romain"[19]. In 1844, the Lobster informed McKenzie how the priest Bellcour had told him "how the Trader cheated the Indians". McKenzie continued:

'Tis very evident that these priests have more influence over these Indians than the Company's missionaries, and that they can get the Indians to do work for them for nothing—which they would not do for us by payments.

This was a frequent complaint of Protestant traders, and one which often extended to all missionaries (cf. Hickerson 1965b:20).

In the winter of 1843, Charles McKenzie received word that a church was proposed at Osnaburgh[20], however, the plan did not materialize until late in the century. There is no mention of a missionary visiting either Osnaburgh or Lac Seul again until the summer of 1845 when a Reverend Pater Jacobs visited both posts. At Lac Seul, he intended to build a mission in place of the one at Lac La Pluie established several years earlier. McKenzie was cool to the idea. "Missions are good things but they require Zeal to be of use—Here they have proved abortive so far"[21]. Jacobs gathered the Indians to build a church a mile from the post that summer, but an epidemic struck and Jacobs, apparently discouraged with the situation, left. McKenzie's comment, although not without sarcasm, is informative:

As to the Sick Indians, they may go to Heaven the best way they can—indeed when he (Jacobs) did visit the Indians they tormented him for something to Eat—"Give us something to Eat & we will listen to what you have to Say"[22].

There is no mention of Jacobs ever returning to either Osnaburgh or Lac Seul. When, in 1852, the Lac Seul Indians heard that a missionary was on his way there, they all dispersed from the point: "They do not wish to see the Bishop—being afraid of 'Black mantles' "[23].

There is some evidence that these early missionary activities were having effects upon the Indians. In 1845, at Lac Seul one Indian sent his dying child to the post since the child had been baptized and the father indicated that McKenzie should bury him[24]. At Osnaburgh, in 1855, George McPherson reported that some Cranes "put up lodges near the fort waiting for the arrival of the boats as well as the Bishop"[25]. The following year the "Cranes came in to see the Rev. John Horden"[26]. Mission work began at Big Trout Lake about this time and seems to have attracted a number of the Cranes.

By 1871, a priest from Fort William was making an annual visit to the nearby Nipigon House post[27]. As at Lac Seul, there appears to have been a certain amount of friction between the priest and the Bay manager. On one occasion, the priest, according to the factor, preached to the Indians against the Protestants:

> To say the least it was very bad taste as we all know that he would take a long time to make the congregation understand the difference between Roman Catholic and Protestant.

Until late in the nineteenth century the most important effects of missionaries were not in the religious sphere. The most notable results of their instruction seems to have been to persuade Indians to cultivate gardens, and toward the end of the century, to write in Cree syllabics. Missionary influences on native religion seem to have been greater at Osnaburgh than at Lac Seul, since the overt ceremonials, notably the Midewiwin, disappeared at the former post perhaps by 1880 while it seems to have continued at Lac Seul into the early twentieth century. For the most part, however, it would appear that Indians in northwestern Ontario retained many of their former beliefs and practices throughout the century.

Social Organization

According to Hickerson (1962a, 1970), the early contact Ojibwa of the seventeenth century were characterized by corporate patrilineal descent groups devolving around clan-possessed fisheries near the north shore of Lake Huron and east end of Lake Superior. It would seem, then, that considerable changes had taken place by the nineteenth century at which time the Ojibwa were residing in small bilateral kindreds scattered throughout the southern half of northern Ontario and eastern Manitoba. These changes occurred as the Ojibwa expanded westward. The original migrant groups consisted of lineage segments of parent clans (Hickerson 1966:12) or perhaps even whole clans. The members of the segments at first named themselves after the parent clan, but under new ecological and contact conditions gradually ceased to be corporate descent groups. Certainly, as we shall see, the concept of descent expressed in membership in totem groups did little more than to regulate marriages by the mid-nineteenth century. Although persons having the same totem could not intermarry, they did not form cooperating or residential groups; rather, the largest effective residential group was composed of males belonging, in most cases, to two or more totem groups.

The task here is to reconstruct from historical data the structural and functional nature of Ojibwa social organization during the mid-nineteenth century as a first step in tracing changes backward in time to test Hickerson's hypothesis. There is, at present, a dearth of information on the acculturative stages of change in Northern Ojibwa social organization from a proposed early clan-based society to that of the twentieth century.

Ecology and Demography

In 1830, the Osnaburgh population numbered 279 Indians[28]. In general, the population appears to have increased gradually between 1830 and the end of the nineteenth century (Table 23).

At first glance at Table 23, it appears that there was a considerable decline in the population between 1830 and 1858. There is considerable evidence that this was not the case. First, the figures only indicate the number of Indians who received their debts and traded at Osnaburgh. By the late 1840's, as mentioned, many Indians were trading at nearby posts instead of Osnaburgh, driven elsewhere by unfavourable trading policies. The bulk of the Cranes were trading at the Big Trout Lake post, re-established in

Table 23   Population Changes for the Osnaburgh Band

Year	Total
1830	279
1858	181
1881	474
1890	440
1905	265

1844 and numerous other families had left for Lac La Pluie, Nipigon, Lac Seul and Martin's Falls. During the 1820's, the furs procured by the Cranes comprised a large proportion of the total brought to Osnaburgh, but by the 1840's, few Cranes resorted to Osnaburgh. For these reasons, it appears that the overall population remained more or less constant between 1830 and 1860. Although epidemics occurred periodically, often resulting in several deaths, there is no mention of a major catastrophe which would have reduced the population by one third. It is more likely that Indians continued to hunt and trap in the same general region and merely took their furs to other posts.

The population increase from 181 persons in 1858 to 474 in 1881 can be accounted for by an improvement in the standard of living following the introduction of store foods beginning in the late 1860's and by the inclusion of a large segment of the Crane Indians who began trading at the Cat Lake outpost during the late 1870's. In 1885, there were 150 Cranes trading at Albany District posts[29].

The figure of 265 persons in 1905 was taken from the annuity payment list at the time of the first treaty payments. It would seem that this figure was too low. The government agent probably missed a number of persons, especially the Cat Lake Indians who were included in later lists. Nevertheless, during the 1890's, a number of Indians who hunted to the east of Osnaburgh affiliated themselves with the Fort Hope store located 100 miles down the Albany River. Hence, the area trapped by those Indians trading at Osnaburgh was considerably less than it was in 1830 since the descendants of many persons who once traded at Osnaburgh were trading at other stores by 1905. The 1905 figure actually represents an increase in population since the early mid-nineteenth

157

century, especially after 1870. As stated by R. C. Wilson in 1891: "The Indians are fairly well off and are increasing in numbers"[30]. Store-bought food, the return of large game, summer gardens and a general overall improvement in the conditions of existence would seem to support this view provided that the birth rate did not change, and there is no evidence that it did.

Assuming that the territory exploited by Osnaburgh Indians was somewhat larger in 1858 (circa 15,000 square miles) than at present since there were fewer trading posts, the population density would have been about one person per 83 square miles[31]. By 1885, the population density of Indians trading at Osnaburgh House and Cat Lake had increased to about one person per 40 square miles. However, it appears that the area south of Lake St. Joseph and the Albany River was more densely populated than regions to the north of the post.

Despite an increase in the population between 1830 and 1905, especially after the 1870's, the composition of the population appears to have remained much the same. The risk of starvation had been reduced by the end of the century, but disease and the rigors of a harsh life in the bush may have maintained a similar demographic composition. Table 24 gives a very rough breakdown by sex and age near the beginning and end of the period. It may be that the criteria separating the age categories in 1830 and 1905 were different. If the 1830 figures were altered so that some males under 18 were considered to be "adults" and some females over 14 were considered to be "girls", then the general composition would be the same in 1830 as it was in 1905. The total number of females was the same for both years, while there were 14 more males in 1830 than in 1905.

Table 24   Osnaburgh Population in 1830 and 1905

	1830	1905
males from about 18 years upward	56	53. . . . . . men
males under 18 years of age	82	71. . . . . . boys
females from about 14 years upward	77	71. . . . women
females under 14 years of age	64	70. . . . . . girls

The only complete band population breakdown by age which I

158

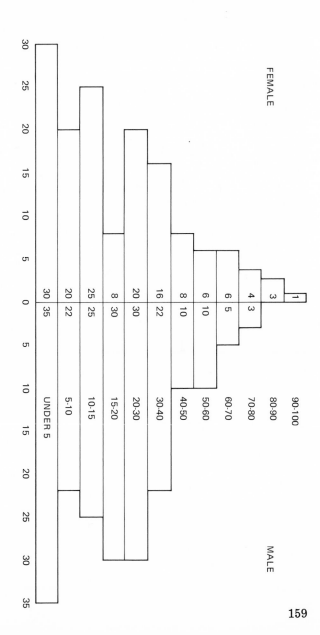

Figure 2: Lac Seul Population Polygon: 1838.

was able to locate for the mid-nineteenth century was made by the Lac Seul factor, Charles McKenzie for 1838. McKenzie reported that the Lac Seul population had increased considerably between 1820 and 1838. A serious measles epidemic had reduced the Lac Seul population in 1819. Figure 2 is the Lac Seul band population polygon for 1838. It may or may not be representative of the general population in the north. The total population numbered 339 of which 192 were males and 147 were females. McKenzie stated that, "This Census is correct in regard to number—there being more births than deaths since—but allowances must be made in regard to Ages"[32].

It is difficult to account for the discrepancy between the number of males and females in the 15 to 20 age group; disease of a differential potency (due, for example, to greater care being given to sick male babies), females of that age group marrying out, or even female infanticide may be the causal factor. (I suggest the latter since the people in that age group were born about the time of the switch from large game hunting to small game hunting or when large animals were getting very difficult to find.) It may have been that females were sacrificed since men were the primary food hunters. The number of males and females in the next younger category were born at a time when small game was increasing in importance and this may account in part for the more equal sex ratio.

The Lac Seul population in 1829 numbered 218 people consisting of 107 males and 111 females. Hence, the sudden population increase within the next decade and the marked difference in the sex ratio are rather startling. Parallel data exists for Martin's Falls for the same period. In 1829 the total population there was 167 made up of 89 males and 78 females. By 1839, the Martin's Falls populations had grown to 265 consisting of 143 males and 122 females[33]. In 1838, of the 339 Lac Seul Indians, 82 were receiving debt and hence were categorized as hunting Indians. Due largely to unfavourable trade policies only 76 and 68 Indians traded at Lac Seul in 1850 and 1851 respectively[34]; however, by 1859, 97 Ojibwa got debt; and in 1868, 95 received debt. Table 25 lists the number of Indians who traded furs at Osnaburgh from 1847 to 1864 during the years for which totals were available[35].

The figures only indicate the actual number of Indians who traded each year, not the total number of names on the debt

160

book. For example, in 1847, 70 Indians actually traded at Osnaburgh but approximately 25 others were noted that traded at other posts; Lac Seul, Nipigon, and Trout Lake. These figures can also be correlated with the fur returns presented in Chapter 6. The figures also included Indians who properly belonged to other posts. Assuming that the ratio of hunters to non-hunters is approximately one to three (Hallowell gives a figure of one to 3.5 at Berens River for the 1930's) (1949:40), which is congruent with figures from Lac Seul and Martin's Falls, then the figure of 181 people given as the Osnaburgh population in 1858 may be slightly low. Perhaps the factor only included those Indians who traded regularly at Osnaburgh in his census. The low figure of 65 in 1864 may indicate that more Indians were trading with free traders entering the area. Also, there is some evidence that the 1858 figure included people belonging to the co-residential units which resided near Osnaburgh and whose male trappers generally traded regularly at the Osnaburgh post. Marginal co-residential units may have been omitted from the population figures.

Table 25   Number of Indians Trading at Osnaburgh House by Year

Year	Number	Year	Number
1847	70	1855	86
1848	83	1856	92
1850	84	1857	92
1851	76	1861	83
1852	82	1863	71
1853	87	1864	65
1854	92		

The Osnaburgh House population of 1821 had almost doubled by 1905, although by the latter time, many Indians were affiliated with other posts. Nevertheless, high infant mortality, and death by starvation and disease resulted in a relatively slow growth until after the 1870's. Periodic epidemics struck the Ojibwa reducing the population. The diseases listed were influenza, measles, smallpox, chicken pox, scarlet fever, jaundice, whooping cough and severe colds[36]. In the summer of 1845, a severe illness struck the Lac Seul post killing several people and causing McKenzie to write "This House is more an Hospital than a Kitchen"[37]. The summer of 1846 was no better since a measles epidemic hit all the Albany River posts killing several Indians at

161

every one. Perhaps as many as 40 Indians died in the Osnaburgh-Lac Seul area. Thus, disease appears to have been a greater leveling factor than cold or starvation—and although no data exist on the infant mortality rate, it is reasonable to assume it was much higher than at present. The gradual population increase toward the end of the nineteenth century probably can be accounted for by improved living conditions rather than a change in the birth rate. While the overall population increased gradually throughout the century, hunting groups, however, tended to remain about the same size.

Hunting Groups

A reading of the historical documents relating to the Osnaburgh Ojibwa indicates that hunting groups were considerably larger than extended families or groupings of two nuclear families. The territory exploited by each winter hunting group was fairly extensive.

In 1858, the Osnaburgh factor, William Linklater, took a census of the population, including group size and composition. Here I will merely note group size, and the structure of the units will be discussed later.

Table 26   Osnaburgh Hunting Groups: 1858

Co-residential Group	Number of People per Group
1	20
2	26
3	29
4	32
5	34
6	40
	181

As noted in Table 26, there were six groups having a total population of 181 persons[38]. The average size of the groups is a rather startling 30.2 persons. The average size in 1828 was 29.3 people[39]. Hallowell has given an average figure of 14.9 persons per hunting group for the Berens River Ojibwa during the 1930's (1949:40), although he indicates that groups may have been larger in the past (1942:28). Near Round Lake to the north of

Osnaburgh, Rogers states that there were at least four bands about 75 years ago consisting of from 25 to 75 people (1962:A22). In 1828, there were three bands of Cranes averaging 26.3 persons each[40]. Dunning's figure of 9 to 11 people per co-residential unit at Pekangikum in 1876 (1959a:57), appears to be unusually low. However, the east side of Lake Winnipeg was the last area to be occupied by Ojibwa, and the historic records of the late eighteenth century indicate that very few Indians were in this region following the mass migrations of Cree to the westward. The Pekangikum and Berens River hunting groups of the mid-nineteenth century bore animal (totem) names and remained independent entities despite their small size—a fact related to their earlier history rather than to specific ecological determinants.

During most of the nineteenth century, the structure and size of winter hunting groups remained relatively constant throughout the area inhabited by the Osnaburgh House Ojibwa. From the 1820's until late in the century, subsistence was based primarily upon hare and fish. Throughout most of the year, the Ojibwa remained in bilateral co-residential groups. The co-residential (hunting) group, within which there was continual cooperation, was

in every sense a unit adapted to the specific requirements of the fur trade in an inhospitable environment: directly adapted when the hunting group was concerned with trapping; indirect when it existed as a subsistence hunting or fishing unit (Hickerson 1966:18).

It is impossible to understand either the size or the structure of winter co-residential units during the nineteenth century apart from the ecology. The abundance of food and furs would set limits on the size of the hunting group as well as the extent of the territory exploited. Hare, of primary importance to survival, were subject to cyclical fluctuations approximately every seven years producing starvation and even cannibalism at the nadir of the cycle. Thus, perhaps more than any other food resource, it was the hare under minimal conditions, which set the approximate limits of population features. That is not to say that Indians didn't exploit whatever they could in times of scarcity. Actually during the annual cycle, Ojibwa relied on a series of foods. Yet, hare, as we shall see, were critical to both survival and trapping activities.

It should not be understood that the members of co-residential units remained together continuously throughout the year during the nineteenth century. There is considerable evidence that they did not or could not when food became scarce[41]. In addition, some Indians came to live at the post for brief periods while others, for various reasons, held back. Charles McKenzie wrote in January 1831 (when hare were extremely scarce) that the Indians were coming to the post for food[42]. When hare were scarce it seems that larger co-residential units were "atomized" into commensal units which sometimes had to abandon hunting territories for larger lakes to fish[43]. For example, George McPherson of Osnaburgh related in January 1851 that,

> the Indians are Starving everywhere as far as I have heard of them, No Rabbits, less than last year, fur bearing Animals are as Scarce as the Rabbits ... It is not only food that the Suffers. It is for want of Warm Clothing also, there being no rabbits from which they used to Depend upon for their Winter Clothes. I fear Many of them will perish[44].

So long as food was obtained almost solely from subsistence pursuits, it appears that two ecological factors of prime importance tended to set the limits on hunting group size: population density and the abundance of food. Where food was a scarce commodity, and where the population was dense, the available territory exploitable to each group would be comparatively smaller than in areas less densely populated. For this reason a smaller territory might not be capable of supporting large winter co-residential units. Food could best be exploited by smaller groups, perhaps extended family units, or groups consisting of two or three related families evenly dispersed throughout the country. Rogers' statement that "hunting group size is relatively constant throughout the entire eastern subarctic" (1963a:88) is not borne out by the documentary evidence.

Not all Indians near Lac Seul lived in large winter units, and indeed some groups actually approximated nuclear families. Groups at Lac Seul generally appear to be smaller than at Osnaburgh, and fission was a more frequent phenomenon. The Lac

Seul population was slightly larger than that of Osnaburgh, numbering 339 persons in 1838[45]. Also, the area exploited was slightly smaller. In these respects Lac Seul fell about halfway between Osnaburgh and the area to the north, and the Rainy Lake-border region during the mid-nineteenth century. Indians residing to the north of Lac Seul were able to maintain larger more cohesive groups for longer time spans. For example, in 1853, McKenzie stated,

> Greean and his tribe of Pelicans 10 men in number came in from the Cat Lake quarter—with their wives and children—but not all, or the House would not hold them—These brought the best haul of Furs that came in for many years . . . —I gave him a white cloth capot 4 Ells and a shirt—as a present which he is well deserving—by keeping his band together[46].

It is evident that this large co-residential group, perhaps numbering 40 individuals, had plenty of territory to exploit after 1851, since "no other Indians are now in that quarter—The very last of that large Gang of 'Cotton Shirts' died last winter of Starvation"[47]. The Archives contain evidence of other large hunting groups near Red Lake and to the east near Sturgeon Lake[48].

The Osnaburgh Indians, fewer in number, were able to remain in larger groups for longer periods of time than those to the south. Also, the winter settlements appear to have been separated by greater distances allowing families and hunters to radiate out from these camps in order to exploit a greater area. Nevertheless, large numbers of Indians related through kinship bonds often hunted in the same area when possible. For example, Big Blood, who hunted to the east of Osnaburgh, was starving in 1839 since "there was no less than 8 Families of Indians that were hunting in the Same Quarter"[49]. Again, in 1869, T. A. Rae sent two men to the Osnaburgh chief's lodge "to visit the Little Hunters or say 8 heads of families . . . " who hunted near Cat Lake[50]. It is evident that the Little Hunters formed a hunting group consisting of perhaps eight nuclear families totalling about 35 persons. Although the data are by no means clear it is possible that the groups resided in a single settlement even though it was midwinter. Evidence does exist showing that groups involving such numbers could reside together when food was plentiful[51].

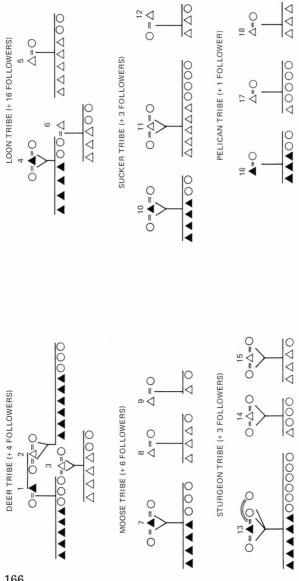

Figure 3: Osnaburgh House Co-Residential Units: 1857-58. Males of the same clan as the family head have been darkened. Where a man has two or more wives, the children are shown as belonging to both.

166

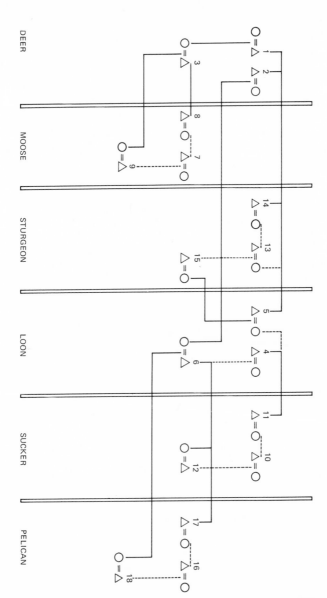

Figure 4: Tentative reconstruction of kinship ties. The broken line indicates assumed relationships.

167

It has been noted that there were six co-residential groups averaging about 30 persons affiliated with the Osnaburgh post in 1858. Their structural composition is now discussed. The Osnaburgh factor William Linklater produced a chart which is presented as he compiled it in 1858 (Table 27)[52]. It should be noted that although Linklater refers to the Deer "Tribe", etcetera, this in reality refers to *clan*-named groupings.

Table 27   Census of the Indian Population Attached to the Osnaburgh Trading Post: 1857-1858

No.	Name of Tribe	Relationship or Connection	Wives	Sons	Daughters	Followers or Relatives	Total
1	Attick or Deer Tribe	head of family	1	5	2	2	10
2		brother of 1	2	6	3	1	12
3		son-in-law of 1	2	4	2	1	9
4	Mang or Loon Tribe	head of family	2	4	1	4	11
5		brother of 2	1	5	2	2	10
6		son-in-law of 2	1	3	2	10	16
7	Moose-uack or Moose Tribe	head of family	2	4	3	5	14
8		brother of 3	1	3	1	1	6
9		son-in-law of 3	1	1	1		3
10	Moanu-pen or Sucker Tribe	head of family	2	4	2	1	9
11		brother of 4	2	5	4	1	12
12		son-in-law of 4	1	2	1	1	5
13	Namau or Sturgeon Tribe	head of family	3	5	6	2	16
14		brother of 5	2	1	3		6
15		son-in-law of 5	2	3	1	1	7
16	Shickey or Pelican Tribe	head of family	1	3	2	1	7
17		brother of 6	1	1	4		6
18		son-in-law of 6	1	3			4
			28	62	40	33	163

From Table 27 and other documentary evidence a reconstruction of general features of Ojibwa social organization is attempted. The reconstruction (see Figure 4) should not be construed as conclusive in any sense since a number of assumptions have had to be made. Nor should the generalized model be taken as typical for the area inhabited by all Northern Ojibwa groups. It is more likely that under variant ecological and historical conditions a number of types or subtypes of social organization had emerged by the nineteenth century. However, verification of these awaits further research.

Linklater appears to have chosen three hunters in each group and arranged all others about them. It should be noted, however, that the three chosen were not randomly picked and were identical for the last five "tribes" in the table. This will be discussed shortly. Since all the relationships were not given, it is impossible to completely ascertain how the groups were related. For the sake of simplicity the genealogical relationships for each group are diagrammed separately excluding those people listed as followers or relatives for which no affinities were given (see Figure 3).

Each group termed by Linklater a "tribe" is assumed to have been a single co-residential unit. The bilateral structure of the groups is evident, and Linklater would have no reason to lump the people into these units unless, in fact, they actually were winter settlements.

If it is assumed that the three leading men in each co-residential unit are related in some way, in addition to being related to members of other co-residential units as noted in Table 27, the structure of the groups would make more sense in terms of what is presently known about Ojibwa society. Ideally, a cross-cousin was the preferred mate (Hallowell 1930). Assuming this to have been the case in the Osnaburgh region during the middle of the nineteenth century, the data can be adjusted accordingly. The tentative reconstruction is presented in Figure 4.

In all, I have only had to reconstruct three types of relationships for each unit except the Deer group for which the relationships were given. First, in each unit I have assumed that the person termed "son-in-law" in Table 27 was, in fact, the actual son of the family head. This assumption is based upon the knowledge that an elder son should inherit the rank, titles, and property of his father. This will be discussed in more detail shortly. In addition, all the men termed son-in-law were married with large

169

families and would most likely be living virilocally, especially if they were to inherit from the group leader. If this assumption is true, our reconstruction is consistent for every group except the Deer unit. It is thus not too far-fetched that the factor, Linklater, familiar with Ojibwa culture, was well aware of it and would assume others would understand when he ordered his data. Omitting the Deer group again, evidence in support of the reconstruction is presented in statistics on wives and children. It should be noted that the family heads in all cases except for the Pelican Tribe have at least two wives, whereas the persons termed son-in-law have only one wife except for the Sturgeon group where this individual has two. The leaders have a total of 34 children compared to the sons-in-law who have only 17 as one would expect, they being younger. The son-in-law in the Loon group having five children and ten followers may well have been a mature male and probably was able to support a larger commensal unit.

The second type of relationship which I have reconstructed is the affinal tie between the group leader and the second individual in each group. Again Linklater's rank ordering would support this relationship. Thus, in all cases except for the Deer unit, the second individual would be a brother-in-law of the leader who would probably be approximately the same age. Dunning has stressed the institutionalized joking relationship between brothers-in-law (1959a:124-28), while Rogers has noted the brotherly attitude between them (1962:B33-B34). At Round Lake today, brothers-in-law advise, care for, and aid each other; and frequently trap together.

It is probable that under the exigencies of the environment in the nineteenth century, the ideal of virilocal residence had given way almost completely so that permanent uxorilocal residences became frequent. The bilateral structure of groups is evident without making any reconstructions. There seems to have been, however, a tendency for a co-residential group leader to choose a single son as his heir who would reside virilocally while other sons might have had an alternative in where they chose to reside after having fulfilled bride service obligations. Again, where a man had no sons, this would mean sons-in-law would have to be brought in if the group was to maintain its existence. In sum, there was likely much variation in residence depending upon circumstances.

170

My reason for assuming the second man in each group was a brother-in-law of the leader, rather than a brother is based on the assumption that children of brothers were considered siblings, whereas those of opposite-sex siblings would be considered eligible marriage partners. Morgan's kinship schedules (1871), and after him the data gathered by Hallowell, and Dunning all support the view that cross-cousins were once desirable mates. In my reconstruction, if for example, one assumed that individual No. 4 was a brother of individual No. 5, and also individual No. 2 then No. 4's son would be marrying his parallel cousin, if of course he was No. 4's son.

If, in contrast, we assume that the leader and the second man are brothers-in-law, then the son-in-law would have married his FaSiHuBrDa, or by extension, his second cross-cousin producing patrilateral cross-cousin marriage. This would be true in every case except in one where I have made an adjustment so that first cross-cousins have married, i.e., I have assumed that No. 5's sister was the mother of No. 15. This may not have been the case, although it fits with what we might expect. It does not alter the reconstructions.

If the reconstruction is correct, then the residence patterns favour a virolocal tendency. Of the 18 marriages 12 are virilocal while 6 are uxorilocal. The impression created, however, may be false, since there are no data on the residence patterns of other married people. The category entitled "Followers or Relatives" in Table 27 quite probably included married peoples, and also widows and widowers. Also, it is possible that those in the categories "Sons, and Daughters" may have been married to persons in the category Followers or Relatives. Except for the three males listed for each group, an affine of any one of these would be forced into this slot.

Despite a virilocal tendency, it would seem that the rigours of a harsh environment, I suggest, led to the disintegration of a regularized residence pattern producing co-residential groups of mixed clan affiliation. The statistics show a total of 62 sons and 40 daughters. The discrepancy may be accounted for in part by the earlier marriage of women. Nevertheless, as Dunning has noted:

There is both a maximum and minimum limit to the size of

the local settlement; the former controlled by the nature of the economy, and the latter by the need for a socially viable unit. In short, in societies with a "poor" natural habitat and hence a limited economy, the range of numerical variation in each settlement is indeed critical. With such narrow population limits on each trapping camp it follows that any asymmetrical sex/age/birth ratio will prove to be a major difficulty in the adjustment of the group to its habitat (1959a:67).

It appears that marriage partners were generally always sought in other co-residential units, or in units attached to other posts. Thus, contiguous groups, and not so contiguous ones, were likely united in a huge web of kinship through northwestern Ontario during the nineteenth century.

There is considerable evidence for the exogamic structure of co-residential units. It is, moreover, extremely important to note the contrast between the exogamic structure of the nineteenth century units and the endogamous marriages of present-day Ojibwa. No longer would an Ojibwa from Lac Seul or Sturgeon Lake go to a place such as Osnaburgh "for a wife only"[53].

The above citation also supports Dunning's more recent findings at Pekangikum where group structure is to a large degree based upon the solidarity and co-operation of brothers.

In 1836 the Lac Seul Indian, Stump, was murdered by his son-in-law who split his skull with an axe and set off immediately for his home, Sturgeon Lake. The death of the Stump meant that his wife and five children were left "almost naked to the mercy of a most rugged season without a relation in this quarter—Except the Fly or Ougi"[54]. It appears that Stump's wife came from another winter camp, whereas the son-in-law from Sturgeon Lake may have been fulfilling bride service obligations.

In every single case recorded marriage partners belong to different co-residential units; however, there seems to have been little pattern in regard to post-marital residence[55]. The Lac Seul Indian, Quiesance, who headed a large family consisting of two sons-in-law and four sons, and whose wife was a "Stout old woman—a Siouxess by descent and nature", "Keeps his sons together—and makes them keep to this post in spite of their

172

wives—who are from different quarters—and (he) . . . is the only Indian . . . respected".

In another case, an Indian who belonged to the Whitefish Lake post arrived at Lac Seul. His wife was apparently from Lac Seul, for when McKenzie tried to encourage the Indian to return to his own post, he added that "The Indian himself was willing to go back—but his wife & her relations were unwilling"[56].

The preferred form of plural marriage was with sisters. These arrangements did not always prove agreeable. For instance, in 1830 McKenzie reported the arrival of Two Hearts who had hunted poorly all winter as a result of a family squabble.

> A misunderstanding between himself & his two young wives is the cause of his flight in this manner . . . the two lovely sisters . . . each would have the young man for herself & would not allow him to share his affections between them—so he was obliged to send one of them back to their father for a time, in hopes of them getting into a more sisterly temper . . . "[57].

McKenzie also tells how Shawanness, a Sturgeon Lake Indian, had made no hunt because:

> his wives—the three sisters—Keep him ever in 'hot water'—A Battle almost every day—among the Sisters—& when he interferes—they'll fell upon him—as the common Enemy— he comes off the worst in these general 'Sprees'[58].

Polygyny seems to have functioned to ensure greater economic productivity when game was plentiful[59]; and abundant children likely enhanced a man's status.

There appears to have been a certain amount of feuding between co-residential groups who traded at different posts despite intermarriage. The Indians of Sturgeon Lake were intermarried with those of Nipigon, yet there was a certain amount of fear and hostility between them, and Nipigon Indians frequently encroached on the lands of Sturgeon Lake peoples. John Swanton, factor of Nipigon in 1835 wrote that the Indian, La Choitte, and his band "originally belonged to this place . . . indeed I should be glad if they were to receive their wants at Nipigon as the Indians of Sturgeon Lake do not like those of Nipigon"[60]. McKenzie of Lac Seul said in 1843 that prices were so good at Nipigon that "all the Sturgeon Lake Indians would go there were they not afraid of the Nipigon Indians"[61].

Animosity also existed between Osnaburgh Indians and those belonging to other regions, McKenzie wrote in 1834 that,

> These Osnaburgh wretches keeps all the west ward Indians in great terror—because say they—"We do not wish to shed Blood" which Emboldens the other Rascals—who committed half dozen murders before now—their wives 'tis true —and a few orphan children which they do not think a Crime[62].

In 1842, some unknown Indians killed some dogs belonging to the Crane Indians while several Cranes were killed by Cree at Trout Lake during the 1840's. T. A. Rae, factor of Osnaburgh, wrote in 1871 that there were "more rows between some Crane Indians or other & some Indians belonging here"[63]. Most of the Cranes were trading at Trout Lake at this date.

Co-residential units then appear to have been politically and economically autonomous. It has also been noted that a wife living with her husband's group could hope for little or no help from her affinal relatives should anything happen to her husband. Again, it appears that a husband who resided uxorilocally could never achieve high status and would remain subordinate to his father-in-law or brothers-in-law. Dissatisfaction of this sort appears to have led the Indian of Sturgeon Lake to transfer his trading account and residence from Osnaburgh to Lac Seul where his brothers resided. In some cases, the animosity between affines even resulted in murder as was the case when the Stump was dispatched by his son-in-law who fled to his consanguinal relatives. McKenzie has provided another excellent example. A wife brought her dying husband to the post in 1848 to be cared for and although the factor gave him medicine.

> the poor man Died . . . under the most excruciating torment with his breast and throat . . . and no doubt he was poisoned by his father-in-law & sent here to die . . . as the

Indians say.

All the Indians here about came to his Burial—To whom I gave 12 plugs Tobacco and 2 Galns Rice—"Festin des morts"—Feast for the Dead—and altho' there was some crying—his young wife who was present did not shed a Tear or Cut a Lock of her Hair—as mournful widows do on Such occasions—and had no wish or desire to be *Burnt or Buried alive with Her Husband.*[64]

There are other similar examples in the Archival records[65].

If my interpretation of the data in Table 27 is correct, then it indicates the diverse origin of the males in each Osnaburgh co-residential unit. It also suggests that a rather high proportion of men were living uxorilocally. If a man's FaSiHu resided in his own co-residential group, hypothetically the FaSiDa, being a cross-cousin, would be an eligible marriage partner. However, where group exogamy was desirable, such a marriage might not be permitted, and thus cross-cousins in other groups would be sought if available. This might eliminate a large proportion of first cousins who otherwise would be available. In my reconstruction, if accurate, it should be noted that most marriages that were recorded actually occurred between second cousins allying different camps[66].

The hypothesis again is dependent upon the accuracy of the reconstruction. If, in fact, it is reasonably accurate and representative of the total Osnaburgh population, it possibly indicates the greater intensity of the rule of exogamy within groups over a preferential marriage pattern. I would suggest that when cross-cousins resided within the same co-residential unit, behaviour stereotypes may have developed where these persons would come to consider themselves kin as opposed to non-kin, hence extending the incest taboo and forcing a person to seek a spouse elsewhere. Among the contemporary Ojibwa of Red Lake, Minnesota, Elizabeth Bott (Eggan 1966:91) discovered that the patrilineal/partilocal clan system was still in operation, and although the kinship terminology still reflected cross-cousin marriage, the behavioural expectations had changed so that cross-cousins were treated like siblings.

It should also be noted that the co-residential units at Osnaburgh in 1858 were quite large (30.2 per group). This might mean that a large number of male affines would be residing with the core members of any group. Hence, marriages with more distant cousins might possibly be more frequent where the rule of incest prevailed, than in cases where co-residential groups were smaller, as for example, at Pekangikum in 1876 where group size averaged from 9 to 11 persons. If such was actually the case, then this would account for the apparent earlier disintegration of a first cousin marriage pattern at Osnaburgh than at Pekangikum, and the extension of the incest taboo to incorporate a large group of persons forbidden to marriage.

The apparent high incidence of uxorilocal residence may have been, in part, responsible for leading Skinner to state that the Northern Ojibwa clans were matrilineal (1911:149-51). Skinner, however, stated in regard to marriage that a woman "went to live in her husband's lodge". Both the historical documents and the field data which I gathered seem to indicate that clans were patrilineal rather than matrilineal.

The co-residential units in Table 27 were given clan names, although their structure was bilateral producing groups of mixed clan affiliation. The group in each case is named after the clan affiliation of the leader. During the nineteenth century, clans remained largely exogamous although members were dispersed. Charles McKenzie recorded an unusual marriage at Lac Seul in 1847 when an Indian wed,

> the Daughter of his own Sister—which he took by his "bow & Spear"—from another Indian—this Autumn—seldom so close relations marry among Indians—They Regard their "Totem" more than relationship on the women's Side[67].

In general, then, clans regulated marriage and appear to have been "concerned with the levirate, sororate, and ensuring of the widow(er)'s mourning period of indebtedness" (Landes 1937:31-37). Landes states that consistent with gens (clan) exogamy: "after-death mourning by the spouse and arrangements for remarriage are phrased in gens terms" among the Emo Ojibwa (1937:44). Outside of regulating marriage, this function appears to have been one of the last clan rituals to have disappeared, but by the middle of the nineteenth century it too had all but become extinct. McKenzie of Lac Seul mentioned in September 1845 one of the last clan mourning ceremonies:

> Assiniboine died at a Small Lake—in the forest—but his Tribe—Eagle Tribe came in a Body and took the Corps to Lac La Glaize and Buried it among his fathers—The only instance of the Kind I have known for many years[68].

Assiniboine's relations came to Lac Seul in deep mourning for their clan member reporting that the Indian's mother died two days after him. Assiniboine never came to the post "either Summer or winter without her—to carry his Bundle".

Co-residential units appear to have been named after the clan affiliation of the leader who passed the title to his eldest son who ideally resided virilocally after marriage. McKenzie, in 1831, mentioned an Indian who

> has some ideas of taking his late father's Title & honours to which he is entitled by birth—being the Eldest son of the late old Nabagache—a chieftain of former days[69].

It would appear that the tendency of the eldest son to inherit his father's titles and reside virilocally was all that remained of a pattern which had insured the corporateness of the clan.

It is of interest to note that the co-residential units at Pekangikum recorded by Dunning for 1889 bear clan names (1959a:56). The Osnaburgh factor, William Linklater, was still referring to the Indians to the "Moose Tribe" during the late 1850's[70]; while T. Rae, in 1872, reported the arrival of "another band . . . the 'Sturgeon Family' "[71].

In sum, the Osnaburgh House Ojibwa during the nineteenth century seem to have been living in winter co-residential units averaging about 30 people each, distributed approximately at equal distances from each other within 100 miles of the post. The members of each group resided together except when food scarcity forced splintering and when hunters radiated out from the base camp to exploit their trapping territories in family units. Group exogamy and clan membership regulated marriage. Winter

177

groups tended to be bilateral being composed of affines, consanguines and agnates. Residence was bi-local although there appears to have been a tendency for the eldest son of the leader to inherit from him and to continue to reside in the same group after marriage. Although there is evidence that brothers preferred to hunt together, the groups were bilateral and membership was based on filiation, not primarily descent. Exogamy within these rather large mixed groups may have meant that second cross-cousins became desired over first cross-cousins as they would likely be more numerous and dispersed among other co-residential units.

Footnotes

1. HBC Arch B107/a/17.

2. HBC Arch B105/e/6.

3. HBC Arch B155/a/51.

4. HBC Arch B155/a/52.

5. HBC Arch B155/a/53. I was only able to discover one well-documented instance after the 1820's when the Osnaburgh House post was in real danger of being seized. That occurred during June 1848 when a large number of Indians had congregated at the post to await the boats with trade goods. Anxious for supplies and evidently in a bad mood, one group known as the Macimmies, five in number, "dashed into the House with bludgeons and knives" (HBC Arch B155/a/60). The factor, George McPherson, recorded the incident and events leading up to the attack in detail:

   > one of them came into my Room where I was sitting in a very bad way his knife at his side. Said he give me a piece of tobacco I want to smoke, which he got, and he said, I suppose you are satisfied with the little furs you get, by no means, said I, the more I get the more I want, then he said, It is for this reason I ask for Tobacco, the more I Smoke the more I wish to Smoke, then I told him he had got a piece, he had better go and take a smoke, then he stood a while, had his knife in his hands and soon after went out, and found the others

that were sitted out side of the Fort and then ten or twelve came in to the Kitchen, the only passage from the Room where I live in and watched my Coming out, which I had occasion to go out soon, and as I was passing to go out, they all surrounded me with their Knives, where I had nothing to defend myself with, to make the story short they demanded goods or my life would go for, but by good chance the boats Came a sight (HBC Arch B155/a/60).

Again in 1848, Big Sturgeon threatened to take the post, and his sons repeated the threat the following summer. After almost murdering another Indian, "they threatened to Murder us too which they can easily do should they wish" (HBC Arch B155/a/61).

6. HBC Arch B155/a/74; B155/a/75; B155/a/79.

7. HBC Arch B107/a/9.

8. HBC Arch B107/a/11.

9. HBC Arch B107/a/24.

10. HBC Arch A12/125.

11. HBC Arch B155/a/53.

12. HBC Arch B155/a/50.

13. HBC Arch B123/e/14.

14. HBC Arch B107/a/7.

15. HBC Arch B155/a/53.

16. HBC Arch B107/a/20.

17. HBC Arch B107/a/20.

18. HBC Arch B107/a/21.

19. HBC Arch B107/a/22.

20. HBC Arch B107/a/21.

21. HBC Arch B107/a/24.

22. HBC Arch B107/a/24. cf. also, Hickerson 1965b:14-24.

23. HBC Arch B107/a/30.

24. HBC Arch B107/a/23.

25. HBC Arch B155/a/68.

26. HBC Arch B155/a/69.

27. HBC Arch B149/a/23.

28. HBC Arch B155/e/13.

29. HBC Arch B3/e/26.

30. HBC Arch B155/e/14.

31. This figure is congruent with Dunning's estimate (1959a: 48-49) for 1875 of one individual per 87 square miles in the Lake Pekangikum region. However, it is considerably below Hickerson's estimate (1967a:54) of one person per 32 square miles near Rainy Lake during the early 1820's. The Rainy Lake area had a denser population in the early nineteenth century than did regions to the north half a century later.

32. HBC Arch B107/a/16.

33. HBC Arch B123/e/14.

34. HBC Arch B107/z/2. See Chapter 4.

35. HBC Arch B155/z/1.

36. For example, in 1832, the whooping cough killed several Lac Seul Indians (HBC Arch B107/a/11). In 1834, the Nipigon House post experienced a smallpox epidemic and the following year an influenza epidemic raged for two months among the Lac Seul and Osnaburgh Indians (HBC Arch B107/a/13). In 1871, and again in 1879, measles was reported among the Osnaburgh Indians, while in 1882, the whooping cough killed several persons (HBC Arch B155/a/80; B155/a/84; B155/a/86).

37. HBC Arch B107/a/24.

38. HBC Arch B155/z/1.

39. HBC Arch B155/a/39.

40. HBC Arch B155/a/39.

41. HBC Arch B107/a/13.

42. HBC Arch B107/a/9.

43. HBC Arch B107/a/13.

44. HBC Arch B155/a/62.

45. HBC Arch B107/a/16.

46. HBC Arch B107/a/31.

47. HBC Arch B107/a/30.

48. In May 1834, the Red Lake Indians arrived at Lac Seul in a group. The hunters included: "The Little Boy, Squirrel, Marten, Fish Hawk, Donald, Baptist Vincent's Son, White Head, Wawkyish" in addition to a "swarm of women & children" (HBC Arch B107/a/12). The Little Boy was the leader, and it was reported that he was always able to maintain a large winter group.

   The Sturgeon Lake Indians, in 1834, consisted of sixteen hunting Indians "Men & Boys" (HBC Arch B107/a/13). There may have been two separate hunting groups, since one group, at least consisted of seven hunters plus the leader Maquimotte (HBC Arch B211/a/6). After the Sturgeon Lake post was abandoned in 1837, Maquimotte "the Great Sturgeon Lake Chief & his band of 8 Indians" (hunters only) traded at Lac Seul and encroached on the territories of Lac Seul Indians (HBC Arch B107/a/16).

49. HBC Arch B155/a/49.

50. HBC Arch B155/a/78.

51. When in January, 1874, Musquaweyea, Mukquanoo, Oocheechalk, "The Barrel's Tribe", and Wabanoo's family arrived at the post with few furs, the manager, Alexander Harvey, remarked:

   No Wonder, as they are all been stopping together Since Winter Set in
   And
   The fact is the Indians is not trying for furs, only for their Greedy Bellies, as Rabbits is plentiful (HBC Arch B155/a/81).

52. HBC Arch B155/z/1.

53. HBC Arch B107/a/24.

54. HBC Arch B107/a/14.

55. HBC Arch B107/a/24; B107/a/25.

56. HBC Arch B107/a/12.

57. HBC Arch B107/a/8.

58. HBC Arch B107/a/17.

59. HBC Arch B107/a/22.

60. HBC Arch B211/a/7.

61. HBC Arch B107/a/22.

62. HBC Arch B107/a/21.

63. HBC Arch B155/a/78.

64. HBC Arch B107/a/27.

65. HBC Arch B107/a/24.

66. Among the contemporary Pekangikum Ojibwa, Dunning has recorded a case where cross-cousins lived within the same hunting group. The man came to think of this mother's brothers as patrikin and although sexual liaisons occurred with his cross-cousins, he eventually married outside the unit (1959a:117-18).

67. HBC Arch B107/a/26.

68. HBC Arch B107/a/24.

69. HBC Arch B107/a/10. Jenness notes a similar pattern among the Parry Island Ojibwa during the 1930's (1935:2).

70. HBC Arch B155/a/67.

71. HBC Arch B155/a/80.

Chapter Six
Ecology and Economy During the
Mid-nineteenth Century

This chapter discusses the economic and ecological basis for Northern Ojibwa society. The subsistence struggle, involving the quest for food and furs, and Indian dependency upon the trading post are related to environmental conditions. As we shall see, both food and pelts were necessary to survival although often difficult to obtain. In order to survive, Indians had to adjust their exploitative patterns, especially those relating to land tenure and property concepts. Adaptation meant giving up old patterns and replacing or reinterpreting them within the changed environmental and trade context.

The Subsistence Struggle

There is no question that subsistence activities frequently interfered with the fur quest throughout the entire period under consideration. For instance, in 1831, the Osnaburgh factor, Edward Mowat wrote:

> all of the Indians have med pour hunts the whole of them have starved all the winter and have prevented them from maken to good hunts as they would have don. ther ar no martens on this quarter and no dear nor Rabits for the Indians to live on to enable them to pay ther debts or to Enable them to hunt other furs[1].

Hare were particularly scarce near Osnaburgh in 1850 and on this account "the Indians will do very little . . . for want of them the Indians will pass away their time in hunting for food"[2]. They suffered so much from starvation that "not an Indian is Making any hunt in furs". The fur returns were reported to have been extraordinarily low, although fur bearers were not scarce. "The

Indians, as they say, they did nothing else but Angle Jackfish from day to day to Save their lives". Hare did not increase enough to allow Indians sufficient time to trap until 1853.

During the late 1860's, when some food was available as a trade item at Osnaburgh, subsistence activities still prevailed over trapping. When "rabbits" were scarce Indians "were obligated to leave their lands and proceed where they would catch fish for a subsistence"[3]. The lack of food meant that Indians often shifted

about every now and again not looking for furs . . . never comes in their minds but hunting for the belly[4].

In order to trap fur bearing animals, the Ojibwa needed certain trade goods as well as an ample supply of food. Often trade policies that prohibited them from obtaining these necessary goods created the paradoxical situation which prevented them from trapping. Thus, such policies had to be changed, as they were in 1847:

As it is found that you Cannot make anything of the Osnaburgh Indians without giving them Debts you may give them moderate advances this Season[5].

Yet while sufficient quantities of food and trade materials were necessary if Indians were to devote their time to trapping, sometimes when food was abundant, they might spend their time "hunting for the belly" instead of trapping.

After the coalition of the Hudson's Bay Company and the Northwest Company in 1821, the Northern Ojibwa were forced out of necessity to deal with a single trading company. By the latter date certain trade items had become essential to survival and trapping, since much of their aboriginal material culture had been replaced gradually by attrition during the previous 200 years. Subsistence patterns involving the food quest had also altered from the preceding era. Competition and overhunting had decimated both the fur bearers and game animals. Subsistence activities took up valuable time, and trade items became more difficult to obtain, although their value in terms of survival increased after the disappearance of large animals. The result was that trapping had become an important subsistence activity, for it was only through the trade in furs that the Ojibwa could obtain items necessary for survival, and in turn, for trapping itself. Throughout most of the nineteenth century survival was balanced precariously between subsistence pursuits and trapping. Although both were necessary, it frequently happened that the immediacy of starvation necessitated the search for food over furs. The food quest, then, influenced the type and quantity of furs traded at the post, which in turn, defined the limits of an Indian's purchasing power. It is for this reason that a discussion of subsistence activities must include data on hunting and trapping as well as types of equipment necessary to both.

Native Foods

Prior to 1895 there were no moose in the Osnaburgh region, and before 1870, caribou were very rare. Earlier in the century large game animals had become virtually extinct throughout much of northern Ontario. Moose had disappeared completely by the 1820's, while caribou had grown so rare that they provided a very minor element in the diet of the Ojibwa. Hence, the quest for large animals was abandoned in favour of smaller game, since the law of diminishing returns in regard to the amount of time spent in searching for large animals had exceeded the limits of survival. Several Crane Indians starved to death in trying to hunt caribou during the late 1820's. Thus, the killing of caribou became infrequent and most likely occurred upon the accidental discovery of this animal in the region of an Ojibwa winter camp.

The area to the north of Osnaburgh where the Cranes resided appears to have continued to maintain a few straggling caribou. The Indian population density seems to have been less than to the south of the Osnaburgh post and it may have been for this reason that caribou never became totally extinct there. Again, it was the Crane band, of all of Osnaburgh Indians, that was most reluctant to give up the big game hunting pattern. For instance, in May, 1830, two Cranes came to the post with some leather and 60 pounds of venison[6] to trade. Later in September of the same year, two Cranes "brought some deers meat" to the post[7]. During the next three decades, there is virtually no mention of Indians bringing venison to Osnaburgh and it can safely be assumed that this omission in the records indicates that the caribou was a rare animal.

By the late 1860's, it appears that caribou were again increasing in number and the Ojibwa were once more hunting them. In April, 1869, the Osnaburgh factor, T. A. Rae, wrote:

Chief arrived brought 13½ MBr and some *venison* the first I have seen ever since I arrived at this romantic spot[8].

After 1870, caribou are mentioned by traders fairly frequently. There is some evidence that small caribou herds may have infiltrated the Osnaburgh area from the north. For instance, Alexander Harvey, feared that since so much snow had fallen, the Indians would "not endeavour to Hunt Furs, as their attention will be drawn to Deer Hunting"[9]. When Thomas Lawson arrived back from the Cat Lake outpost in April 1876 he reported to Harvey that the Indians there were "Killing Deer by Hundreds" and that some persons had slain as many as thirty caribou. During the 1880's, the Hudson's Bay Company employees often went on hunting expeditions to supply the post with venison, especially during March and April when conditions were most suitable.

Moose, as noted (see Chapter 3) were of little significance until after 1900. Informant testimony indicates that by the end of the century caribou could be found as far south as the Canadian National Railway tracks south of Lake Savant and perhaps even around Sturgeon Lake. As noted, moose did not re-enter the area about Lake St. Joseph until 1900.

After 1821, fish and hare provided the basis for subsistence. Even during the closing decades of the nineteenth century there is strong evidence that caribou were not numerous enough to have been a major factor in the diet, although they must certainly have been a welcome arrival. Dependence upon small animals appears always to have been precarious and cases of starvation and the scarcity of hare are frequent entries in traders' journals. Numerically, hare fluctuated approximately every seven years producing periods of famine and hence poor years for the fur trade.

In addition, the Osnaburgh Ojibwa were reported to have been fond of such furred animals as beaver, muskrats, otter, bear, skunk, lynx and other small animals. Skinner has stated that they even ate snakes and turtles during the summer (1911:134).

Next in importance to hare in the diet were fish. When hare were scarce, Indians relied heavily upon fish taken through the ice on the larger lakes with lines and, in later times, with nets. In the warmer months of the year, fish were the principal food source. By the middle of the nineteenth century, nets became a regular trade item at Osnaburgh. Also, Indians made their own nets from twine supplied by the post. In addition to nets and hooks, Indians employed weirs in rivers during the spring and fall when fish spawned. Spears were also employed, especially for sturgeon.

During the spring and autumn, waterfowl, ducks and geese, were hunted. Indians, in general, appear to have looked forward to the spring goose hunt, especially after a difficult winter when food was deficient and invariable. For example, at Lac Seul when the first geese were sighted, Charles McKenzie, wrote, "If these strangers will not sent in the Indians nothing will!"[10]. So long as the geese were migrating, Indians would not trap fur bearers.

During the harsh winter months, in addition to hare and fish, Indians were reported to have obtained a few partridge and other nonmigratory birds.

In summer, vegetable products were of some importance. In August, 1842, McKenzie stated:

> The Indians are Starving every where as there are no Berries this year—which is generally their main support at this Season . . . the Summer Frost destroyed them all[11].

In early September, wild rice was harvested by some Indians. However, it was never as important in the Osnaburgh region as it was further south near the American border since it seems never to have grown in abundance north of the Albany River drainage system.

When game of all sorts was scarce during the winter, Indians occasionally ate vegetables. Sometimes the bark of the jackpine was removed to get at the pulpy matter beneath for food[12]. On occasion, Indians were forced to dig through the snow to obtain roots and tubers. In the winter of 1851, a Lac Seul Indian was in an extremely weak state

Sitting in a hole in the Snow—breaking the frozen earth with an Ax—In search of a certain Root called by the Indians *As-ki-bois*—which in good soil are as large & long as the middle finger. This Root is not bad to the taste & is eaten Raw—'tis crisp & waterish—On these Roots he fed or rather existed his wife & 4 children the two last days & nights[13].

The cultivation of vegetables by Indians did not occur on a regular basis at Osnaburgh until late in the century. Early attempts at gardening proved abortive largely due to an insufficient knowledge about plant husbandry. However, the Indians at Eagle Lake and at Lake of the Woods were reported to have grown small quantities of Indian corn[14]. McKenzie of Lac Seul related an incident in November, 1832, when the Indian Tripie and his wife arrived to take up some potatoes they had planted.

I gave 2 kegs of seed to the old man last spring with tools to plant the potatoes. They eat the half of the seed while they were breaking up the ground for the other half—They gave a kind of Hoeing to them in the Summer & now they come to collect the harvest—Old Tripie lost all his crop of potatoes—The potatoes had frozen and thawn twenty times perhaps since the first frost[15].

Although the influence of traders and general observations made by Indians on occasions induced Indians to attempt cultivating gardens, the greatest encouragement may have come from missionaries. After a missionary visited the Osnaburgh and Lac Seul posts during the summer of 1841, Charles McKenzie of the latter post made the following statement in the spring of 1842:

This Farming Mania of our Indians is the only part of the precips & moral discourse of our last Summer "Missionary" that they seem to Remember ... Our missionary promised them Seeds to Sow. I promised to give potatoes and they are sown—but in Soil, the most part that will not yield the Seed[16].

Missionaries probably encouraged Osnaburgh Indians to cultivate the soil also and by the 1890's, at least some Osnaburgh Indians were cultivating gardens annually. In 1882, James Vincent, the Osnaburgh manager, remarked:

> Arrival Mikingwan & son. They brought 4 kegs potatoes for sale, the first I presume ever bought by the Company here from an Indian, of his own growing[17].

Indian Dependency Upon the Post

After 1821, new trade policies, in conjunction with a changed subsistence pattern and fewer fur animals, now meant that Indians actually received fewer goods which had become increasingly significant to survival than they were formerly. Despite these changes, a few Indians attempted to remain independent of the trading post even after 1821, but they were exceptions and even the most independent had to resort to the post at least every three years[18]. More often, Indians were forced to make trips to the post at least once a year to obtain supplies necessary for survival.

Because the food quest took up time and the valuable furs were difficult to obtain, Indians had increasing difficulty in procuring certain trade materials which had become necessities. Certain trade items, formerly of little or no significance, now became important, for example, twine, European clothing and leather. Charles McKenzie summed up the dependent relationship of the Ojibwa on the trading post in 1851:

> The Indians also must be provided with their most necessaries . . . the natives stand in the same yearly necessity. having nothing within themselves to cover their nakedness —save a few miserable Rabbit Skins when kind providence sends that most necessary Supply—both for their Sustenance and Covering—yet so very simple a thing as a *Rabbit Snare*—must come out of the Trading Shop—They not even wherewithall to Sew their Shoes—without recourse to the Shop[19].

When large animals became depleted, Indians became dependent upon substitutes. In the subsistence cycle, hare and fish replaced cervines. However, the former animal was subject to cyclical fluctuations creating periods of starvation every few years. Hare pelts, although useful for parkas and blankets, were not adequate as clothing at all times of the year. Shoes or snow-shoe netting could not be produced from their thin hides. For instance, one Lac Seul Indian, "was for four months in the same tenting place for want of shoes to leave it"[20]. Snare twine, formerly of little importance, became an important item of trade.

Nets had become an important item necessary to the Indians of Lac Seul by the 1830's, " ... whatever other articles is refused—they are never refused nets"[21]. So that by the 1840's McKenzie could write that nets "they must get as they can hardly live without nets in the Summer"[22].

The gun was an important trade item in Ojibwa culture as early as the late seventeenth century. However, there seems never to have been enough guns to supply all the hunting Indians at Osnaburgh and Lac Seul until late in the nineteenth century. If all were to have guns, Charles McKenzie said, "Every second Indian would require a Gun yearly"[23]. McKenzie illustrated the significance of the gun to Indian culture:

> There is another heavy article in the trade—that traders seldom consider as a *First Necessary* is—Guns—but what is an Indian without a Gun?—He can make shift for other Articles—but his Bow & Arrows are a lame substitute for a Gun unless he was a Horse back in the Plains[24].

Despite the importance of guns McKenzie tells how in 1851 he gave the Indians fish hooks when hare were scarce as "hooks are more value to them than Guns—with Hooks they will not die—but they will do nothing else"[25].

As noted (Chapter 4), steel traps were prohibited in the Albany District from the 1820's until 1848. This proscription added to the hardships Indians had in procuring furs, especially foxes and muskrats.

There is little doubt, then, that the Northern Ojibwa were dependent upon the store by the mid-nineteenth century. As we shall see, this was not the case 50 years earlier. Charles McKenzie, in his Lac Seul correspondence book for 1852, commented upon this dependency:

'Tis certain if we wish the Indians to work, that we must supply their necessaries—now in the olden times when the country was rich "Necessaries" were understood to go no farther than putting *Tools* into their hands. But now comes the word Necessities which has a Greater latitude—I should like to ask you Gentlemen—when you tell us to give the Indians no more than their *Real necessaries* I should like to know what you mean by real necessaries—That after putting Tools into their hands does not Clothing come under the head of necessaries—or is clothing as necessary to a naked Indian as tools? Is not a Gun absolutely necessary for an Indian—or what is an Indian without a gun—he can kill Squirrels only—with his Bow & Arrows. One thing clear the Lac Seul Indians did not get their Real Necessities this season.

And,

You'll say d—n them let them cover themselves with Rabbit Skins—Aye let them—as they must—and God help them should Rabbits fail them—both for covering and food and I often Shudder at the thought ... and that would be ruinous to you also—being as you are Gentlemen Responsible for their lives[26].

There is some evidence that conditions had improved by 1860 after which Indians were receiving greater quantities and varieties of goods in exchange for their furs than they ever had before. Although many items were of little significance to survival, the necessary articles were in greater abundance and probably of a better quality. In 1869, during September (the month when most Indians received their fall debts), Osnaburgh Indians received such items as: 43 rolls (varied widths) of cloth, 163 skeins of twine, 54 boxes of matches, 32 assorted kettles and pans, 25 blankets, over 1600 pounds of gunpowder, shot and shot ball, not to mention 85 pounds of tobacco and 18 Jews harps! In Table 28, I have presented the goods Osnaburgh Indians received during the year of 1884-85 (Outfit 1884)[27]. The variety and quantity of materials that Indians were receiving is strong evidence that they could not survive without post assistance. The itinerary also indicates the shift in trade goods dependency from the 1840's to the 1880's.

Table 28   Goods Received by Osnaburgh House Indians in Debt, Gratuities and Game Trade, Outfit 1884

Item		Unit	Quantity
Awls		No.	48
Balsam, Turlington		No.	1
Basins & Saucers	(2 types)	No.	7
Beads, white enamel		lbs	3/4
Bells, dog		No.	2
Belts, worsted	(4 types)	No.	8
Blankets	(8 types)	No.	89
Buttons		No.	48
Caps, men's cloth		No.	1
Capots	(11 types)	No.	65
Cloth		yds	2-1/6
Combs	(2 types)	No.	34
Cotton	(2 types)	yds	266
Coburg, assorted		yds	10
Druggets	(2 types)	yds	220-3/4
Duffle, white		yds	1/2
Essence, peppermint		No.	2
Ferrets, silk		yds	10
Flannel	(3 types)	yds	18-1/2
Files		No.	84
Frocks, Yarmouth		No.	3
Garters	(3 types)	No.	144
Gimlets, snowshoe		No.	11
Gauze, cotton		yds	1
Guns, common flint		No.	3
Guns, common percussion		No.	6
Guns, fine-style brass		No.	2
Guns, fine-style steel		No.	1
Guns, double brass		No.	1
Guncaps, percussion		No.	3325
Gunflints		No.	60
Gunworms, wire		No.	48
Handkerchiefs	(3 types)	No.	54
Hats, common felt		No.	10
Hooks and Eyes		No.	36

Hooks	(2 types)	No.	1700
Horns, powder	(2 types)	No.	7
Kettles, 11 sizes		No.	58
Knives	(6 types)	No.	104
Lines, cod single		No.	1
Moleskin, drab		yds	2
Mufflers, woollen		No.	2
Mugs		No.	3
Needles	(3 types)	No.	400
Pans	(7 types)	No.	22
Pipes, clay	(2 types)	No.	135
Plates		No.	9
Ribbon	(2 types)	pce	1-2/3
Rings, finger brass		No.	13
Scissors	(2 types)	No.	4
Shawls	(6 types)	No.	11
Shirts, 8 sizes & types		No.	31
Shot, assorted		lbs	418
Soap		bar	7-1/3
Spectacles		No.	2
Spoons, iron table		No.	6
Steels		No.	20
Strouds	(3 types)	yds	101-1/2
Tartan	(2 types)	yds	78
Tents, sheeting		yds	1
Thimbles, women's		No.	9
Thread, Linen		lbs	12
Thread, reels		No.	9
Tobacco	(2 types)	lbs	152-1/2
Trousers	(3 types)	No.	43
Twine, 6 sizes		Skn	494-1/2
Vests, men's		No.	5
Wincey		yds	8
Provisions			
Flour		lbs	979
Oatmeal		lbs	74
Suet		lbs	37
Tea		lbs	151
Sugar		lbs	60

Canada Goods			
Axes		No.	4
Belts	(2 types)	No.	4
Matches, telegraph		No.	96
Painkiller		No.	4
Traps, No. 1		No.	7
Traps, No. 1-1/2		No.	14
Traps, No. 2		No.	17
Traps, No. 3		No.	3
Traps, No. 4		No.	2
Country-Made Goods			
Axes	(2 types)	No.	35
Chisels		No.	4
Shagganappee		lbs	10-1/2
Skins, dressed moose		lbs	1-1/4
Skins, dressed reindeer		lbs	48-1/4
Skins, parchment		lbs	45-1/4
Skins, dressed buffalo		lbs	40

After about 1865, Indians were able to obtain small quantities of foods at the Osnaburgh post in exchange for furs. However, prior to this date, and for several decades after, during times when hare and other foods were scarce, hungry Indians who arrived at the post usually received a meal of fish and potatoes, in addition to a good supply of these foods to haul back to their camps. Although fish and potatoes were the most common foods distributed to Indians, on occasion, they received other foods such as wild rice, flour and tea. At the Albany posts during the autumn, additional fish above post requirements were caught by traders and Indian helpers to feed starving Indians in winter[28]. When native foods were scarce, Indians often resided in the vicinity of the post, even during winter months, living off post victuals for a week or more. The quantities eaten were frequently quite large[29]. The reliance on fish and potatoes supplied by traders during harsh winters acted as a form of insurance that obligated Indians to the trading post (see Chapter 7).

Although food freighted from Fort Albany was introduced as a trade item at the Osnaburgh post during the 1860's, the quantities of store-bought foods was small[30]. The quantity of flour indicated, in Table 29, 1010 pounds, amounted to approximately four pounds per capita.

Table 29   Foods Traded by Month at Osnaburgh House
             In Pounds: June 1869-May 1870

Month	Flour	Oatmeal	Beef Suet	Sugar	Tea
June, July Combined	171			8	½
August	48		6	1	1
September	148	3	1	36	3½
October	24		1	4	½
November	33			8	1
December	105		3	10	2
January	93	6	2	4	1
February	54				
March	88		2	12	
April	117		1	10	½
May	129		2		1
Totals	1010	9	12	88	11

By 1886, the quantity of store foods obtained by Indians had increased somewhat, but there was still little variety. In Table 30, I have presented a breakdown of the quantities of various foods and the means by which they were obtained[31]. It would seem that although the amount of flour actually decreased slightly between 1870 and 1886, other types of foods became more significant in the diet. I have excluded the food consumed on "voyaging" expeditions to assist the boats to and from Osnaburgh House. Since most voyaging was undertaken by Indians accompanied by two or three traders, these figures represent a substantial amount. During the summer of 1886, some 650 pounds of flour, 85 pounds of oatmeal and 240 pounds of pork were consumed in assisting the boats, most of it by Indian labourers. It is evident that by the late nineteenth century Indians in the north relied, in part, on store bought foods.

Mr. Borron in his report of the district remarked in 1890 that

There are few Indian families, however, in the territory,

that do not consume more or less flour, oatmeal, lard, and pork, flour more particularly, of which some families will, notwithstanding its high price, use as much as four or five bags yearly[32].

At Osnaburgh in February, 1868, four Indians carried off 300 fish at one time—one-third of the total amount distributed annually at Lac Seul 20 years earlier! On New Year's Day, 1872, Indians at Nipigon House received a dinner of cake, soup, tea and tobacco.

Table 30   Store Foods Consumed by Indians In Pounds: 1886-87

Source	Flour	Oatmeal	Beef Suet	Sugar	Tea	Raisins	Pork
Indian Debts and Trade	342	177	4	27½	58¾	6	
Indian Labour	235½	64¾	30⁵/₈				
Gratuities	114	52	12¾	1¾	1⅛		
Game Trade	87	12½	2¼	7	6¾		
Misc. Expenses	120	28½	19	21½	4	3	3
	898½	334¾	68⁵/₈	57¾	70⁵/₈	9	3

Fur Animals and Trapping Techniques

After 1821, the trapping of fur bearers cannot be considered a subsidiary activity in the lives of the Northern Ojibwa. Trapping became the basic subsistence pattern, for it was only through the acquisition of furs that the Ojibwa were able to obtain the materials from the post upon which they had come to depend for survival. For these reasons then, a discussion of hunting techniques, and of ecological factors effecting the fur bearers is necessary to a full understanding of subsistence conditions.

The capture of fur bearers involved a variety of techniques including snares, deadfalls, traps, nets, and guns or bows and arrows depending upon the species and weather conditions. Indians tended to focus on certain species at certain times during the trapping season. The aquatic fur bearers (beaver, muskrat, and otter) were obtained mainly in the spring and fall since hunting them in midwinter through thick ice proved somewhat difficult. During the cold winter months, the Ojibwa focused on lynx, marten, mink and fox. However, climatic conditions and the scarcity of certain species often forced trappers to change their plans. Some general data from the archival sources on each of the major species of fur bearer is given.

Beaver

There are little data on how beaver were obtained; they were probably shot, or their houses were broken open. The quantity of steel traps obtained in the Osnaburgh region prior to 1848, was likely small and other hunting techniques were probably more commonly employed. Spring seems to have been the most important hunting season for beaver as well as the other aquatic fur bearers (otter and muskrat).

The beaver had been the most important fur bearer obtained by the Northern Ojibwa until the 1810's when it grew very rare. After 1830, there was a slight increase as conservation policies and attempts at establishing hunting territories were made. During the 1870's and '80's, the fur returns suggest that beaver were relatively common. By the 1890's, however, Indians were again overtrapping their territories at which time beaver declined numerically.

Otter

This animal appears to have been generally of high value to the fur trade and was highly esteemed by Indians. After 1848, steel traps were employed along shores of lakes and streams. Ecological factors frequently influenced hunting conditions. For instance, changes in water level affected an Indian's catch. When the water dropped considerably leaving a space "of some feet of hollow ice—where the Otters made their winter habitations . . . (they) have no occasion to come out"[33]. However, if the water rose too suddenly it would destroy all the Indian traps[34].

Muskrat

Muskrats were of considerable importance to Indian economy

when other fur bearers were scarce. Prior to 1848, the main means of obtaining rats was by shooting them during the spring. In May 1834, six Cat Lake Indians had run out of ammunition, the result being that "they brought very few rats although they say that the Muskrats are very numerous on their lands"[35]. During the 1830's some Lac La Pluie Indians with steel traps were hunting on the lands of Lac Seul Indians, which McKenzie feared would soon deplete the muskrat population since Indians were already obliged "to shoot the small as well as the Large"[36].

McKenzie has provided an excellent account of the effect of ecological conditions upon the muskrat population:

> The Rat is the most prolific animal in this country save the Rabbit—brings forth three times in a Season—and have each time from seven to fifteen—some instances of twenty have been seen. But like the Rabbit they have many enemies— The Pike or Jackfish the greatest & next the mink who enters their houses & will not come out until the whole family is destroyed—but a severe winter is the great destroyer of Rats—worse than all their other enemies & Indians together[37].

Should the water level rise in the fall, the muskrats would disperse to higher ground in the woods where they would become prey to other animals, or if they remained they would freeze during the winter lacking protection. Although prey to other animals, once in the woods Indians found them impossible to hunt. In the fall of 1828, the Indian Tripie told McKenzie that the water rose nine inches in 48 hours in some lakes, the result being that, "The Rats keep in the woods where the Indian Eye can hardly see them & they are off at the least noise they hear"[38]. Again, if the water rose too suddenly in the spring, the rats would drown[39]. However, such prolific breeders could also recover rapidly from these population depletions[40].

Marten

Marten appear to have been taken in wooden traps made from a series of closely placed sticks covered with brush. At the entrance a log was placed on a slender twig attached to a string at one end, and to a fish head placed inside the enclosure. When the marten took the bait, he would pull the string releasing the log which would crush him. Since these traps were usually built in the snow, the best season was late winter.

Weather conditions had to be suitable. Even when they were numerous they would not take the bait if it was too cold[41]. If the weather became too mild the snow would melt and the traps would fall down. In 1830, there was a great deficiency of marten in the Osnaburgh store due to the general scarcity and to "the warm weather having set in so early—the Indians were obliged to abandon their traps nearly two weeks sooner than usual in the very best time for Marten hunting"[42]. According to McKenzie: "tis an infallable custom with them never to set up Traps after they are fallen down by Rain"[43].

The marten population in a region varied according to the availability of the food upon which it subsisted[44]. Yet, marten were rarely found on rabbit ground because, although they could chase a rabbit down in open country, "they have not the patience to watch them like a Cat—& Bounce on them in passing as the Cats do"[45]. Thus, since Indians depended mainly upon hare for food, the abundance of this animal affected their ability to acquire marten. When hare were scarce, Indians were not able to travel to areas where marten might be found.

Mink

Little data exist on mink. It is likely that they were taken in wooden traps and snares. Mink may have been less subject to numerical fluctuation than were marten or lynx. Charles McKenzie reported that:

> The Mink is not subject to migration as his food is in great plenty at all seasons . . . wherever there is a spring or open source there this mink is—feeding upon his muckworm and delicate snail shells[46].

The worst enemy of the mink apparently was disease. Indians stated that mink died after having eaten dead fish at the edge of pools.

Lynx

Lynx appear to have been quite important to the fur trade in the Albany District, especially during the 1830's and 1840's. Lynx were not only caught in wooden traps as were marten, but were also hunted with dogs. In 1844 McKenzie reported that all the Lac Seul Indian dogs were dying from some disease and added:

> The greatest drawback that can befall an Indian 'tis worse than an Indian without a gun—A good Dog is invaluable to an Indian—his dog can run a Cat,—fisher—Marten & even a Wolverine up a Tree—he can take them down with Bow and Arrows—His dog may also find a Bear in his winter "wigwam" . . . but without a dog all these can laugh at him[47].

Lynx could only by pursued by dogs under certain climatic conditions. If there was no snow, dogs would not track them[48]. However, the condition of the snow was important[49], and too much snow could also prevent hunting[50].

The primary food for lynx was hare. When hare were scarce so were lynx. However, an overabundance of hare might mean that wooden traps and snares would be of little use since the lynx need not go near the traps for food[51]. Snares were perhaps even less effective than wooden traps since informants testify that a lynx is one of the few animals which will back out of a snare rather than press forward and choke itself. This of course does not apply to the spring snare which lifts the animal off the ground by the neck.

Fox

The fox became extremely important to the fur trade during the 1840's and was valued at from two to five made beaver each, depending upon whether it was a red, cross, or silver fox. Like lynx, foxes lived primarily upon hare, and hence varied as did the latter animal.

Foxes were reported to have been an extremely wary animal, "too shy and not hungry enough for wooden Traps"[52]. They were sometimes pursued with dogs but their speed and cunning made them difficult objects to catch. Steel traps were the most efficient means of catching foxes. However:

> Every Kind of Steel Traps are prohibited in this District above Albany—while our very next neighbours of the Northern Department have Traps for both Beaver & Foxes or Rats. "Tis not for Beaver or Rats our Indians want Traps—but for Foxes purely. If there are a chanced Beaver Hill on lands—they know well how to take them without Traps—and should they leave them alive—their neighbours will soon take them up—There are many ways of killing Beaver—but few of catching Foxes without Traps[53].

After 1848 when steel traps were available, both foxes and hare became very scarce. It was not until the late 1850's when foxes and hare again became numerous in the Osnaburgh region, that the number taken annually was of any great significance.

Bear

The number of bear taken in trade was never numerous although a pelt was worth about two or three made beaver. Bears were shot, hunted with dogs, or killed by wooden deadfalls. They were killed in summer or in winter if a den was discovered. The principal food of the bear was fruit, particularly berries. If berries failed bears frequently starved during the winter:

> Several Dams were killed—who had had young ones in the winter but none of these are alive 'tis well known they were eaten by their Mother—So miserably lean are the Bears this Spring that few or none of the Indians eat there flesh—The want of Summer Fruit is the Cause of all this evil to the Trade[54].

The Lac Seul Indians found several bears one summer lying dead upon the remains of others which they had eaten[55]. During a harsh winter bears might freeze to death in their dens.

Other Animals

Among those animals not previously mentioned, the fisher

appears to have been the most important, but the number procured annually was never great.

Hare and squirrels were accepted at Osnaburgh during the early 1850's, and skunks and skunk fat were taken after that date until 1870 at least (see Chapter 4). Of the three animals, skunks appear to have been the most valuable but few were taken annually.

Fur Returns and Subsistence Pursuits

Trade policies and ecological factors affecting the fur bearers and the availability of food for Indians have been discussed to provide a basis for an understanding of fur returns. As we have seen, the fur trade was connected with price and demand mechanisms in the World Market which determined trade policies concerning fur bearers. No doubt social and religious factors also played a role in determining the quantities of furs secured. For instance, if a member of a hunting group died, the hunters would cease trapping for the remainder of the season. It is thus possible to correlate these factors with totals where they exist, with a certain amount of assurance. Table 31 presents the total furs valued in terms of made beaver taken at Osnaburgh for the years that this information was recorded[56]. Table 31, it should be noted, records the total value in made beaver which changed slightly from year to year, so that the same number of furs might have been worth differing values. Allowing for this fact certain correlations can be made.

During the early 1820's the ready barter system of trade was in practice and many Indians had not completely adjusted to subsisting on small game. Numerous cases of starvation were reported. Also, attempts were made to conserve the beaver, which was virtually extinct in some areas. By the late 1820's beaver trapping was allowed, Indians were receiving debt and conditions had improved slightly. This is reflected in the jump from 1,600 made beaver to 2,500 made beaver within a year from 1826 to 1827.

The extremely low figure in 1847 can be partly explained by the trade policy. As noted in Chapter 4, Indians were unable to get debts at Osnaburgh and this fact, coupled with the difference

Table 31 Total Furs in Made Beaver by Year Taken at Osnaburgh House

Year	Total Made Beaver
1825	1600-1700
1826	1600
1827	2500
1828	2498
1847	1975-3/4
1848	2545-3/4
1850	1994-3/4
1851	1685-1/4
1852	2093
1854	2670
1855	2646-3/4
1856	3313
1857	3876-1/2
1861	2434-1/2
1863	2660-3/4
1864	3037-1/4

in prices at Nipigon and Trout Lake, had lured many Indians away. That year both marten and mink were reported to have been scarce. The following year Indians were able to get debt.

Hare were reported to have been extremely rare in the Osnaburgh area from 1850 to 1852. Thus, Indians had to devote most of their time to subsistence activities. Furs were stated to have been as uncommon as hares. By 1854, hares were again numerous although fur bearers were still reported to be rare. In 1855, both hare and furred animals had increased but many Osnaburgh Indians, unhappy with trading conditions, had taken their furs elsewhere. In 1856 and 1857, both trade and ecological conditions appear to have been at their optimum; however by 1861 hares were again scarce and Indians had to devote their time to the food quest. Although furred animals were relatively numerous that winter, the Indians

say that they cannot hunt furs for want of Rabbits for they

say that ther is a few Martens on thir Lands but they cannot Make Traps for want of Provisions to live on[57].

Table 32 gives a breakdown of the species procured at Osnaburgh for the years when figures were available[58]. Beaver became increasingly important to the trade after the mid-1850's. However, I am unable to account for the low figure in 1858. The drop to only 588 beaver in 1887 appears to be due to the decline of beaver as a result of trespass and overtrapping. Otter were reported to have been scarce during the early 1850's and hence the low figures.

By the late 1850's and early 1860's, marten were numerous and apparently of high value. Lynx were of high value during the early 1840's, but varied numerically with hares which were very scarce in 1850 and 1851. By the late 1850's, both hares and lynx were again abundant. Mink also varied with the Indian food supply. Fox were of high value during the 1840's and 50's. Fluctuations in the muskrat take were due mainly to alterations in climatic conditions. However, the quantity of both foxes and muskrats obtained was affected by the availability of steel traps. For example, although the Lac Seul post produced 49 fur packs in 1833-34, Charles McKenzie estimated 60 could have been gotten had the Indians been allowed to employ steel traps.

Table 33   Number of Pelts Procured at Osnaburgh House and Lac Seul by Year

Species	1851		1856		1857		1858	
	OH	LS	OH	LS	OH	LS	OH	LS
Beaver	427	143	538	867	800	1154	348	1088
Otter	223	184	446	279	383	264	329	247
Mink	399	513	2793	2464	2301	2123	1423	1756
Marten	923	359	1818	1343	1687	793	1381	662
Lynx	73	331	207	942	535	1463	821	1209
Muskrat	3659	6000	4118	9000	3228	6900	2267	3043

Table 33 compares fur returns at Osnaburgh and Lac Seul for the years when data were available[59]. The most notable thing is the remarkable increase of beaver at Lac Seul while the beaver

Table 32   Number of Pelts Procured at Osnaburgh House
by Year

Animal Species	1840	1850	1851	1856	1857	1858	1868	1870	1875	1887
Bear	56	15	62	47	25	33	22	76	33	38
Beaver	388	376	427	538	800	348	1011	976	1248	588
Castoreum (lb)	15¾	22½	23	32½	45	22	70	55	50	
Ermine			55	61	75	7	22		136	147
Fisher	42	107	120	97	140	218	50	109	53	105
Fox	18	69	68	43	155	202	122	59	106	107
Hare		134	7410	6248						
Lynx	1405	190	73	207	535	821	575	370	206	543
Marten	478	531	928	1818	1697	1381	1112	617	962	443
Mink	1006	267	399	2793	2301	1423	946	851	1505	1310
Muskrat	1008	1328	3659	4118	3228	2267	3240	4350	4600	7727
Otter	463	201	223	446	318	329	216	380	368	308
Skunk			8	135	132	88	11	19	4	51
Squirrel			708							

count remains fairly constant at Osnaburgh. Either beaver increased rapidly in the Lac Seul area, or Indians from other posts were taking their beaver pelts to that post. Unfortunately, post journal records are not available at Lac Seul after 1853 which might help explain the returns at that post. Otter appear to have been always slightly more numerous in the Osnaburgh area, whereas the figures indicate that approximately the same number of mink were obtained at both stores. On a number of occasions traders reported that Osnaburgh was a better marten country than Lac Seul. The rise in the number of marten and mink taken at both posts during the mid-1850's can be correlated with the availability of hares at that time as well as trade policies. Marten were of high value during the 1850's. The Lac Seul Indians relied heavily upon dogs to hunt lynx which may account for the higher figures. Again, lynx may have been more numerous at Lac Seul. Since lynx feed primarily on hares, there is a direct correlation between the high figures and the supply of the latter animal during the mid-1850's. Finally, Lac Seul seems to have been a better muskrat country and the Indians there appear to have devoted more time to their acquisition. Muskrat, however, were more valuable at Osnaburgh.

After 1850 both Osnaburgh and Lac Seul produced fur returns of approximately the same value. However, during the 1830's and 1840's when the Lac Seul post was managed by Charles McKenzie, it consistently outdid Osnaburgh. For example, in 1838, Osnaburgh produced 31½ packs of furs, while Lac Seul made 41½ packs[60]. The following year 100 Osnaburgh trappers made only 30 packs, yet 83 Lac Seul Indians produced 55½ packs. Again in 1840 Lac Seul outproduced Osnaburgh by 23 packs. It should be pointed out, however, that a valid comparison would involve the types of furs taken.

Land Tenure

Land tenure among northern Algonkians has been a topic of controversy for several decades. Speck (1915; 1923; 1928), Speck and Eiseley (1939; 1942), Cooper (1939), and Hallowell (1949) have argued that small patrilocal unit tenure—the family hunting territory system—was pre-contact; while Jenness (1935), Leacock

(1954), Rogers (1963a), Hickerson (1962a; 1967a) and Bishop (1970) have presented evidence that it was a product of trade, contact, and environmental changes. Although the latter view has gained general acceptance, there are still little data on the processes leading to the family hunting territory system, and on the conditions under which it emerges.

In the family hunting territory system among northern Algonkians, which was first described by Speck (1915; 1923), the hunting group habitually returns to a well demarcated tract of land bounded by natural landmarks. Within this area the group, presumed by Speck to be the extended family, possesses exclusive rights to the resources. Trespass involving the acquisition of fur bearers by other families, unless for food purposes or in cases of starvation (Lips 1947:433), is strictly forbidden and is punished by supernatural sanctions (Landes 1937:87; Lips 1947:476-84; Hallowell 1955:227-280). The right to fur resources within the area tends to be passed to male consanguines preferably an eldest son (Lips 1947:435). Views concerning rights to food vary. Lips (1947:432) and Burgesse (1945:12) state that food resources for the Montagnais were free goods; while Landes (1961) for the Emo Ojibwa and Cooper (1939) for the Tête de Boule have indicated that food within the territory is individually possessed. Cooper and Landes stress extreme individualism in property concepts. Kohl, in writing about the Ojibwa south of Lake Superior in 1859, indicates that beaver lodges, sugar bushes, and berry patches were owned by family units (1957:421). Actually there appears to be much variability in land tenure forms which Leacock (1954) and Hickerson (1967a) indicate represents a wide departure from aboriginal forms. According to Hickerson (1967a: 42) there has been a "shaping and reshaping to meet specific microecological and microhistorical variations".

Speck and Eiseley reject the view that family hunting territory systems are a product of the fur trade (1942:241). They state that small non-migratory fauna, especially beaver, could best be exploited by individual family units. They assume that small game constituted the primary food source for the aboriginal Montagnais, and that larger units would have starved on such a subsistence basis (cf. also Cooper 1939:81-82; Landes 1961:87-88). Related to well demarcated territories with rules against trespass were conservation policies regarding fur resources

(Speck 1915:293-94). Only where well defined boundaries exist and where game is nonmigratory are such practices possible.

The forms of property concepts described by Speck, Cooper and Lips and assumed by them to have been aboriginal first came under extensive scrutiny by Leacock (1954). She demonstrated that private ownership of resources and individually inherited rights to land developed in response to the fur trade. Leacock states that there is no ethnohistorical data which would tend to support the existence of the family hunting territory during the seventeenth century. Indeed there is much evidence against it. The primary food sources for the seventeenth-century Montagnais seems to have been large game, moose and caribou, (1954:3) which require the cooperation of several hunters (Rogers 1963a: 80). Also there was no population pressure on resources, nor were there any attempts at conservation. Speck and Eiseley do note the nomadism of groups in northern Quebec who pursue migratory caribou (1942:219). However, they account for the difference in property concepts in the north solely in terms of ecological factors ignoring historical ones. An allotment system of tenure where each group leader announces annually his group's intended hunting area appears to have existed in northern Quebec during the late nineteenth century (Turner 1894:276).

The factors responsible for the emergence of the family hunting territory system according to Leacock are as follows: the weakening of cooperative bonds between group members as economic ties are transferred from within the group to the trader; the increasing self-sufficiency of family units supplied with store foods who can best exploit nonmigratory fur bearers separately; the increasing scarcity of game, both large animals and fur bearers, forcing larger groups to splinter into family units; the preference of traders to deal with individuals rather than groups; and the increasing dependence on a single trading post thus hindering mobility (Leacock 1954:7-9).

As I understand Leacock's contention, individual family hunting territories are incompatible with subsistence activities (1954:6-7; 24-26). She maintains that it is only when food hunting does not compete with trapping, and when furs are deemed more important than food, that true family hunting territories can emerge. This, according to Leacock, apparently can only occur when store foods reduced the Indians' "dependence upon meat ... to the point where hunting need not seriously compete with trapping" (1954:26). Leacock has also noted a definite correlation "between early centers of trade and the oldest and most complete development of the hunting territory" (1954:12). It is probably not coincidental that these early centres of trade were located in areas aboriginally inhabited by Algonkian groups including the Ojibwa. It will be shown (see Chapter 9) that later interior posts in northern Ontario were built as roving groups of Ojibwa moved into areas occupied only a few decades prior to their construction. Thus, Leacock would argue that well-defined territories would be less likely to exist in regions surrounding the latter posts. So long as Indians were wandering in a random fashion after furs and large migratory game animals, conservation policies would be impossible. As we shall see, the family hunting territory system did not emerge until the late 1820's or early 1830's in northern Ontario. Although store foods may hasten the development of tenure in severalty and intensify individualism as seems to have been the case in southwestern Labrador, the other causal factors may also produce "true" family hunting territories. Although the Osnaburgh Ojibwa were not obtaining the bulk of their food from the store until the last few decades, they did indeed have trapping territories by the middle of the last century. Yet the boundaries in the Osnaburgh region, and to the north of it, were not as rigidly defined as were those in regions slightly to the south of that post. The task now is to present data on the conditions at Osnaburgh.

One factor that seems to account, in part, for the formation of hunting territories, is the form of food pursued. The subsistence basis for the Montagnais of southeastern Labrador where territories are not fully developed seems to have been migratory caribou (Leacock 1954:24-25). This in itself would produce a more nomadic existence mitigating the formation of well-defined territories since caribou migrations are not restricted by any artificially bounded regions. The Osnaburgh people, from the 1820's until late in the century, however, subsisted primarily on small nonmigratory game, hare and fish. Hence, since hare snares required constant daily observation, Indians would be less likely to rove over large areas than if they were pursuing large animals. When subsistence patterns changed from large game to small during the 1820's, the Archival documents indicate a marked decrease in both the amount of mobility and the distances traversed by Indians. Their mobility restricted to a more precisely delineated region, members of hunting bands might also come to view the furs within the area as the property of group members.

It has also been shown that store foods merely supplemented native foods at the end of the century.

There is some evidence that cooperation under harsh environmental conditions was a more important value, especially in regard to food-sharing, than was competition. There is good evidence for this even in regard to fur bearers prior to 1821, as will be demonstrated (Chapter 8).

The cultural practice of not hunting fur bearers when a close relative died may have been an additional factor mitigating the formation of stable territories. For example, in 1844, six Cranes arrived at Osnaburgh 105 made beaver short of their debts. "Death among them. the Chiefs Wife & one of his Sons died which stopped them from hunting"[61]. Further examples of the same practice come to light at the Lac Seul post in 1845 and at Osnaburgh in 1875.

Trading policies also influenced the formation of hunting territories (cf. Leacock 1854:6-9). For example, George Simpson, Governor of the Hudson's Bay Company, had been instructing traders to encourage individualism:

On the subject of nursing the country . . . my Despatch from Moose of alloting certain tracts of country to the different bands can only be carried into full effect in extended Districts such as Albany, where the population is very thin; but in small Districts frequented by Rein Deer and where the Fisheries are not numerous the Indians are under the necessity of going sometimes from one extremity thereof to the other, in search of the means of living, on these journies which are usually performed during the season of open water, they discover Beaver, which they were in the habit of destroying out of season, until by entreaties and threats we succeeded, in prevailing on them to discontinue their summer hunts; but in the winter they retrade their steps to where they discovered vestiges of Beaver in order to make their Hunts. We are endeavoring to confine the natives throughout the country now by families to seperate and distinct hunting grounds this system seems to take among them by degrees, and in a few years I hope it will become general, but it is a very difficult matter to change the habits of Indians, altho they may see the ultimate benefit thereof to themselves and families[62].

If Indians had been able to maintain an existence primarily upon large migratory fauna, it is doubtful whether the instructions issued by George Simpson would have been followed. Mobility in the quest of caribou which could supply many Indian needs would render a concept of rigidly-defined territoriality impractical. The furs procured, however, could still be considered the private property of individual trappers without the land necessarily being viewed as such even where big game constituted a primary food source. This latter situation seems to have been the case in some regions during the 1820's.

While traders dealt with Indians individually, encouraging private ownership of fur resources within bounded areas by family units, competition between Hudson's Bay posts in different districts operated to reduce the importance of fur resources, and indirectly the need for hunting territories. Indians were able to travel to nearby posts unrestricted to take advantage of better trade bargains. In some cases, Indians delivered only a part of their furs to the post while threatening to trade elsewhere if their demands were not satisfied[63]. Nevertheless, the evacuation of many trading locales after 1821 reduced the mobility of Indians considerably.

Another factor that might account for the early formation of hunting territories in some areas is population pressure both on furs and food. For example, the areas closer to Lake Superior and the American border seem to have been overpopulated. The factor at Fort William, in 1829, reported that the native population there was "By far too many for the District and the furs"[64]. There is additional evidence from Nipigon House, Lac Seul and Rainy Lake that the population had grown far too large to effectively exploit the fur resources by the middle of the nineteenth century[65]. All of these posts lay to the south of Osnaburgh House. However, there is evidence that by the late nineteenth century, the Osnaburgh population was increasing. It is significant to remember that trespass and overtrapping were noted by the 1880's.

Under conditions where a population is great and furs scarce, it is probable that family territories would emerge due to the pressure on resources although ideas of conservation might not arise where all available resources are needed. Population pressure might necessitate the partitioning of lands to maximize the exploitation of game and furs. Such seems to have been the case south of Osnaburgh.

Contrary to Rogers' view (1963a:77) that there is no functional relationship between the hunting group and the hunting territory, historical evidence indicates that the two are, in fact, intimately connected. To support this hypothesis, data are presented on two areas where the population was dense, and where food shortages were frequent. These will then be compared with Osnaburgh materials. The areas chosen are Mattagami situated about 240 miles southwest of James Bay and Lac La Pluie west of Lake Superior near the American border.

Alexander Christie, wrote in his Mattagami district report for 1826:

> The Indians who are from the West, to the North ward and Eastward of the house possess a much more valuable Fur country, and from the circumstances of each Indian having a certain allotement of land for himself and family, a portion of which he hunts annually, which gives the remainder a little time to recruit, but from the great population and the small space which falls to each family, they generally go over the extent of their hunting grounds, once in two years[66].

In addition to fully developed hunting territories, Christie has emphasized population pressures and the small size of winter hunting units. In 1829, at the same post, Hugh Faries, related the endemic shortage of food and rather frequent occurrence of cannibalism:

> My Report regarding the occurences of this quarter differ very little from that of last year, the same dismal tale to

212

relate of the distressful situation & disasters of the Natives, they suffered still more this last winter then the proceeding —several have died through want of food—actually starved to death—& what is most painful to relate, destroying one another to save themselves, a Father & Mother having subsisted some time on their children three in number & the Mother at last dispatched the Father for the same purpose & subsisted on his flesh . . . this is not the only instance of the Kind this winter, several similar *Catastrophes* occurred[67].

Again, in the Lac La Pluie region, the population numbered 563 Indians in 1830[68]. This was more than double the population for Osnaburgh about the same time, yet the total area inhabited by Lac La Pluie Indians appears to have been somewhat smaller. Food at Lac La Pluie was a constant problem and family hunting territories may have emerged relatively early there (cf. Hickerson 1967a)[69]. Ruth Landes, who did field work among the Ojibwa of the same general region during the 1930's has described conditions as they may have existed during the late nineteenth century:

All accounts of old Ojibwa life are shadowed by fear of starvation, and each man hunts for himself, alone on his trails, the hunters scattering as widely as possible in order to make the most of the thin supply of game. The household of wife and children who depend upon the man's hunting lives in complete isolation during the winter season (1961:87).

And,

On his isolated estate, the husband hunts as though he were alone in the world . . . Surrounding him at accessible distances are fellow Ojibwa all trying to keep off starvation (1961:88).

Although individual families may have possessed trapping territories, it is doubtful whether the winter co-residential unit was equal to the conjugal family. Landes herself modifies this view when she says,

Bilateral relatives tend to hunt together. This means that small domestic families hunt in contiguous areas, each couple having its own grounds (1937:90).

The evidence seems to indicate the "atomizing" effect of large populations in restricted areas where the acquisition of food was a constant problem. Certainly the dependence upon the trading post and upon small nonmigratory game for survival were instrumental in leading to the development of the family hunting territory system.

It appears that territorial boundaries were by no means well defined in the Osnaburgh-Lac Seul area during the middle of the nineteenth century. For example, Tripie and his two sons-in-law, Two Hearts and Dick Crow, with whom the former hunted, arrived at Lac Seul in January 1830, to acquire some fish and potatoes from McKenzie "in order to change or shift quarters"[70]. In January 1834, two Indians came from Cedar Lake to tell McKenzie to send men for their furs "as they are to leave that quarter & go more to the west"[71]. In September 1842, McKenzie wrote that the Lac Seul

Indians are roving about—uncertain where to go to pass the winter—their old haunts being exhausted of fur bearing Animals[72].

There are a few statements in the historical materials that would indicate land was possessed by families or slightly larger units. At Lac Seul in 1828, McKenzie wrote that Baptist Vincent was "to winter on his own lands, Trout Lake"[73]. In 1831, an Indian traded at Lac Seul rather than at the Windy Lake post "which he finds too far from his father's land & his friends"[74]. Although goods received on credit were limited to small articles in 1834, the Flint received heavier goods as "his lands are too far to profit by trade"[75]. There are numerous additional examples both in the Osnaburgh House and Lac Seul journals[76].

There is also some evidence that attempts at conservation were being made during the 1830's and '40's. However, it is difficult to determine to what extent they were successful. In most cases mentioned, attempts failed since other Indians moved into the temporarily vacated areas. Where individuals moved around a great deal, and preferred to remain in larger groupings, conservation practices would be impractical.

There is evidence that former cooperative patterns continued well into the nineteenth century. It appears that although hunting territories were in existence by 1850, they were by no means as clear-cut as those further to the south, and to the southeast, where the population was denser. Furthermore, when possible, Indians appear to have preferred to reside in social groupings larger than family units. For example, Charles McKenzie wrote in 1831, that the Indian, Assiniboine, brought only 15 made beaver to Lac Seul in the spring of 1831, having starved most of the winter, the reason being that he

> had his father & his brother on his hands both of whom are as helpless as small children & of far more trouble Yet he did not abandoned the one or the other, as several of the Indians were expecting, he would be under a necessity of doing to save his own life & the lives of his children[77].

An interesting reaction to individualism is supplied by Charles McKenzie of Lac Seul in 1837. The Indian, Little Boy, received a very large debt that year,

> particularly when considered that Indian is *impotent* in both feet—But he has three strapping sons—for whom he takes debt in his own name—tho' one of these has a family of his own—makes this young man hunt for the whole family—He is the only Indian in this quarter who possess any authority over their children—he is also greatly esteemed (not feared) by all other Indians—All widows, orphans, those in distress—gather around the Little Boys tent & he relieves them all—even in his poverty—for he is always poor—I have not said too much of him—He will not make as good a hunt this winter as he did last year—he almost ruined his lands—& winters this year in a different quarter—to let his Beaver recover . . . Consequently all the western Indians followed him[78].

It is evident from the above statement that most Indians able to trap accepted debt from the store on their own, even though they might trap with their fathers. In addition, it appears that the scarcity of beaver and overtrapping was forcing some Indians even in large social groupings, to practice conservation policies. Eight years later, in 1845, Little Boy was still making his sons "take Debts together"[79].

Although in 1838, McKenzie wrote that "Beaver are scarce because they are not allowed to increase"[80], by 1845 Little Boy had adopted a conservation policy. However, conservation appears definitely to have been impractical during the 1840's and 1850's despite the scarcity of beaver. The shortage of food was one reason. Trespass was another.

> The Little Boy had one River which he left for 3 years— with many beaver in it—but when he went there this winter he found that they were all destroyed by River Winnipic Indians. He therefore determined to Kill his Beaver himself and not leave them for Strange Indians—who can blame him[81].

There are numerous references to Indians trespassing on the lands of others. At Martin's Falls, to the east of Osnaburgh, in 1836, the Indians,

> One and all of them complain very much of the trespass of Osnaburgh Indians that hunt on their lands every winter these four years past . . . They also complain of the trespasses of Lake Nipigon Indians . . . and as they are well provided with Beaver and Rat Traps articles of trade not allowed to the Indians of this District they destroy all the Beaver and rats in every quarter that they go through[82].

There was no reason for trespassers to spare beaver, and those whose lands were violated were forced in self-defence to "kill all the beaver in a house"[83]. The Martin's Falls Indians urgently begged for steel traps to compete with Nipigon and Long Lake Indians[84].

The lands of the Sturgeon Lake Indians were also being overrun by Nipigon Indians during the 1830's and 1840's. McKenzie of Lac Seul has reported on these encroachments:

216

The best & richest part of Sturgeon Lake was always to the SE and SWest of it & would have been so to this day were it not that the Lac Nipigon Indians have overran all that ground of late years—Either from fear of doing mischief themselves or that vengeance should be the consequences & some there have taken possession of all that part of the Country so rather their Name has been proclaimed over it which is True enough to deliver all other Indians from going that way—some go by stilth as to an Enemy's country—who make well out while they remain—but few likely to pass the winter—when such Visitors are duly expected[85].

In consequence, the Sturgeon Lake Indians, forced out of their own territories, encroached upon the lands of the Lac Seul Indians.

Two Hearts & Wecose ... came from old Tripies tent—they complain much of the Sturgeon Lake Indians having over-run their lands—there are no less than 5 of these within a short days march of this house—The Sturgeon Lake Indians Keep on our lands both Summer & Winter of late years—not that these lands are better than their own—but they are dubious of Nipigon Indians who are encroaching on their lands[86].

Osnaburgh Indians encroached on the hunting territories of Lac Seul Indians as well as those belonging to Indians of Martin's Falls[87]. By 1839, there were no less than ten Osnaburgh Indians poaching on Lac Seul territories[88].

By 1845 Lac Seul Indians were being crowded from both sides. That year "their lands are over run by Lac La Pluie Indians"[89]. Twelve families well supplied with steel traps had moved into lands possessed by Lac Seul Indians. In 1847, McKenzie wrote that the Sturgeon Lake Indians

are confined to a narrow Circuit of their land—being Surrounded as usual by Strange Indians both of St Ann and Lac La Pluie—who have Ruined their lands of the very last Beaver—while they were prohibited Killing Beaver—There is indeed too much truth in all this—I am also sorry to see so many of the Osnaburgh Indians coming this way—we do not want them[90].

Do these statements then, imply that no hunting territories were in existence? The data suggest that, in fact, territories did exist. There can be no trespass without boundaries, and no resentment if ideas concerning rights were not present.

The Osnaburgh Ojibwa of the mid-nineteenth century and later, appear then, definitely to have had hunting territories despite the fact that subsistence pursuits took up valuable trapping time. As noted, the subsistence pursuits may even have led to the stabilization of groups and families in certain areas provided that hare were available. Leacock's view that territories are incompatible with subsistence activities would only apply when large migratory animals were the chief food sought. This fact might account, in part, for the late development, and poor definition of territories among Northern Athapaskans (Jenness 1963:124). Among the Ojibwa of Osnaburgh, territories were in existence prior to the return of large game animals toward the end of the century which may have weakened sanctions on trespass. Sanctions against trespass in 1909 when Skinner gathered his data had become "lax, although hard feelings and even blows frequently resulted from transgression" (1911:150). By 1900, big game had returned which enlarged the territory exploited by groups.

Skinner's data confirms the earlier existence of hunting territories for the Ojibwa of Lac Seul, Osnaburgh, and Fort Hope:

Every adult male Northern Saulteaux has a certain well-known range over which he has the exclusive right of trapping and hunting known as 'Tzikewin', a word corresponding to home . . . The rules regarding the punishment for violation of the law against hunting on another man's lands are said to have been very strict at one time (1911:150).

Mention of trespass in the records becomes increasingly rare by the 1850's and it can only be hypothesized that sanctions

218

were being enforced more stringently and boundaries were better defined (cf. Hallowell 1942). It was only during the late nineteenth century when large game hunting permitted greater mobility and when a population increase and competition in the fur trade encouraged Indians to overtrap their territories and trespass on neighbouring ones, that sanctions against poaching grew weaker.

The Ojibwa winter camps near Osnaburgh House appear to have been comparatively large throughout the nineteenth century and it seems that the members moved about within the area with a certain amount of freedom, although individual hunters, or partners may have returned to the same general location each year. Most hunters handled their own accounts at the post and goods traded were likely the exclusive property of the purchaser as were the furs. Even the accounts of spouses were kept separate suggesting personal ownership. For instance, R. C. Wilson remarked in 1899, that "Big Head's wife came yesterday with 12 MB from her husband & 11½ MB from herself"[91].

Conservation practices which were attempted during the 1830's and '40's only became effective after trespass was eliminated in the 1850's. So long as trespass remained a threat, it simply did not pay to conserve beaver. Although conservation of resources was more important to Indians nearer Rainy Lake since there was more pressure on resources due to the greater population density there, such practices also developed in some areas further north. Since it is evident that during the mid-nineteenth century Osnaburgh Indians frequently had difficulties in obtaining sufficient peltry to satisfy store needs, leaving sectors fallow would guarantee that there would be furs another year. Even if such foresight was lacking, certainly the instructions of traders must have influenced Indians to test such practices. Thus, between about 1850 and 1885, individual family trapping territories with game conservation and adequately enforced sanctions against trespass were present in the Osnaburgh House region. These developed despite the interference of subsistence activities with trapping pursuits and perhaps even because of it. Nevertheless, the extreme individualization of resource ownership portrayed by Cooper for the Tête de Boule (1939) and by Landes for the Emo Ojibwa (1961:87-89) seems never to have existed at Osnaburgh. This was because the Osnaburgh House population density was lower providing more territory per trapper and less pressure on resources. Where individual families (or perhaps slightly larger units) near Rainy Lake remained alone on their territories for most of the winter, a necessary practice which intensified individualism, the trappers of Osnaburgh radiated out in twos and threes from centrally-located bush camps numbering from perhaps 10 to 30 persons. The winter bush camp then was the focal point for Indians who would disperse when food became scarce, or when on trapping expeditions. During years when hare or caribou were plentiful, several families might reside together for two or three months. This, however, does not deny the existence of family trapping territories during the last half of the nineteenth century. It does, nevertheless, demonstrate that store foods which became available after the 1860's, while allowing Indians to devote more time to trapping, were not a necessary prerequisite for the family hunting territory.

Recapitulation

The discussion so far has dealt with the contemporary Ojibwa and their nineteenth-century forerunners, as well as with intermediate phases of culture change and contact. During the nineteenth century, Ojibwa were scattered throughout northwestern Ontario in small groups which focused on Osnaburgh or other posts to trade their furs and receive their supplies. Subsistence practices and trade policies involved a good deal of mobility. Subsistence was precarious and influenced both the quantity and kind of fur bearers taken. Because trade goods had become essential for survival, subsistence came to be balanced between trapping on one hand and hunting for food on the other. In 1850 the fur trade dominated Indian life. Hudson's Bay Company post employees were the main agents of contact with Indians at large. This situation, then, was in marked contrast to that which exists today: the members of the Osnaburgh community live in a semi-permanent village, or near main transportation lines. Although the living conditions of present-day Indians are substandard in comparison with the resident White population, cases of starvation and exposure are comparatively rare. Within the past two decades, government subsidies and services have been mainly responsible for these technical improvements. Prior to 1900, Euro-Canadian materials were restricted for the most part to supplies necessary for survival in the bush and included such items as: guns, twine, leather, cloth, *capots*, axes, files, knives, pots and pans, and small quantities of food and matches later in the nineteenth century. Today the materials available to Osnaburgh Indians are only restricted by an individual's purchasing power gauged now in dollars. Items such as radios, record players, even typewriters, tape recorders and automobiles, are possessed. In 1850 virtually all food was obtained from the bush; today most food comes from the store.

During the nineteenth century the mode of adaptation had as we have seen, a profound effect upon demography and land tenure. The availability of food and furs determined to a large degree the population distribution in the region and the relationship of the people to the resources. One hundred years ago trapping was the most important means of obtaining those things necessary for survival. At present other sources of income (commercial fishing, wage labour, and—most important—government subsidies) have largely replaced trapping as a primary subsistence activity. These sources along with day school maintain a relatively permanent village population. This has had the effect of reducing the significance of trapping territories for the society and its economy. Prior to 1900, Indians resided in bush settlements most of the year exploiting discrete, bounded, family tracts of land. Today Indians spend no more than a few weeks a year in the bush and many trapping territories once used are no longer utilized. As trapping has dwindled in importance, rules against taking furs on another's territory have become relaxed.

The improved living conditions have had a marked effect on the Indian population. In 1850 there were only 200-300 people affiliated with the Osnaburgh House post; today there are over 800 Indians belonging to the Osnaburgh Band.

During the mid-nineteenth century winter settlements, the co-residential units, consisting of perhaps two to five households, averaged about 30 individuals. Membership was often based on patrilateral filiation, although both affines and consanguines were present. These settlements were not descent groups and there was no rigid postmarital residence rule. However, the settlements tended to be exogamous. Frequently Indians obtained their wives

221

from groups affiliated with other trading posts. This contrasts strongly with the situation today. The cooperative bonds uniting what once were large co-residential groups have weakened as bush life has become less important and as government subsidies have led to increased dependence of the household on outside sources of help. Again, residence within the new village has operated to separate members of winter settlements. Although the co-residential units still tend to be exogamous, marriage is generally restricted to members of groups belonging to the same community. Indeed, endogamy within the community is positively sanctioned. Sororal polygyny disappeared by the early twentieth century. With the decline in trapping and the eradication of many indigenous religious practices by missionaries, and the usurpation of control in many spheres of life by government agents, leadership has weakened.

Cross-cousin marriage still occurs and the distinction between kin and non-kin is still important in regulating marriage. However, village life and the increased population have provided a wider range of marriage partners who are more distant cousins. The kinship terminology itself is in a state of flux and appears to be emerging as a *lineal* system. During the nineteenth century the system was probably of the *bifurcate collateral* type with Iroquois cousin terminology.

In 1850, the co-residential groups bore names which appear to have been those of clans, even though members were often of mixed clan affiliation. Usually the groups were named after the clan affiliation of the leader who inherited his position through primogeniture. Marriage was regulated by clan affiliation. Until the 1840's, mourning ceremonies also were under the supervision of the clan. At present, there are many young people who do not know their clan. Although clan exogamy is still important to the older people, there are now several marriages between members of the same "clan".

The social and economic life of the nineteenth-century Ojibwa has often been described as "aboriginal" (cf. Landes 1937; Hallowell 1955; Rogers 1962). However, by 1850, the Northern Ojibwa had experienced over 200 years of contact. As we have seen and shall see further, there were drastic changes brought about through a variety of historical and ecological factors.

222

Footnotes

1. HBC Arch B155/a/42.

2. George McPherson (HBC Arch B155/a/61).

3. T. A. Rae (HBC Arch B155/a/78).

4. HBC Arch B155/a/79.

5. Letter: Thomas Corcoran chief factor at Fort Albany to George McPherson, the Osnaburgh House manager (HBC Arch B155/a/59).

6. Venison in this case refers to caribou meat. Often, however, the term was extended to apply to moose meat prior to the 1820's. Alexander Collie (HBC Arch B155/a/41).

7. Edward Mowat (HBC Arch B155/a/42).

8. HBC Arch B155/a/78.

9. HBC Arch B155/a/83.

10. HBC Arch B107/a/28.

11. HBC Arch B107/a/21.

12. James Robertson. Ontario: Department of Crown Lands 1901.

13. Charles McKenzie (HBC Arch B107/a/29).

14. HBC Arch B107/a/25.

15. HBC Arch B107/a/12.

16. HBC Arch B107/a/20.

17. HBC Arch B155/a/86.

18. HBC Arch B107/a/18.

19. 1851. HBC Arch B107/a/30.

20. Charles McKenzie, 1828 (HBC Arch B107/a/6).

21. HBC Arch B107/a/25.

22. HBC Arch B107/a/27.

23. HBC Arch B107/a/6.

24. Letter to Fort Albany, 1852 (HBC Arch B107/z/2).

25. 1851. HBC Arch B107/a/29.

26. HBC Arch B107/z/2.

27. HBC Arch B155/d/11.

28. HBC Arch B107/a/21.

29. HBC Arch B107/a/22; B107/a/31.

30. HBC Arch B155/d/9.

31. HBC Arch B155/d/12.

32. HBC Arch D/26/16.

33. Charles McKenzie, 1838 (HBC Arch B107/a/16).

34. HBC Arch B155/a/53.

35. John Vincent (HBC Arch B155/a/45).

36. HBC Arch B107/a/12.

37. HBC Arch B107/a/16.

38. HBC Arch B107/a/7.

39. HBC Arch B107/a/5.

40. HBC Arch B107/a/7.

41. William Linklater, Osnaburgh manager, 1858 (HBC Arch B155/a/70).

42. Alexander Collie (HBC Arch B155/a/41).

43. HBC Arch B107/a/8.

44. HBC Arch B107/a/10.

45. Charles McKenzie (HBC Arch B107/a/22).

46. HBC Arch B107/a/10.

47. HBC Arch B107/a/22.

48. Charles McKenzie (HBC Arch B107/a/18).

49. Charles McKenzie (HBC Arch B107/a/16).

50. Charles McKenzie (HBC Arch B107/a/14).

51. Charles McKenzie (HBC Arch B107/a/14).

52. Charles McKenzie (HBC Arch B107/a/16).

53. Charles McKenzie, 1845 (HBC Arch B107/a/24).

54. Charles McKenzie, 1843 (HBC Arch B107/a/21).

55. HBC Arch B107/a/7.

56. HBC Arch B155/a/36; B155/a/38; B155/e/12; B155/z/1.

57. HBC Arch B155/a/73.

58. HBC Arch B3/z/4; B155/a/51; B155/z/1.

59. HBC Arch B107/d/2; B107/z/2; B155/a/51; B155/z/1.

60. HBC Arch B107/a/18.

61. HBC Arch B155/a/55. There are several other examples: At Lac Seul in 1846, one man "did not kill a Rat since his wife and Child died—nor would he do anything this winter"(HBC Arch B107/a/25). In 1875, when two Indians arrived at the Osnaburgh House post with poor hunts, Alexander Harvey reported: "It is generally the case as their father died in February" (HBC Arch B155/a/82).

62. HBC Arch D4/92.

63. Charles McKenzie (HBC Arch B107/a/16).

64. HBC Arch B231/e/6.

65. In 1824, at Nipigon, the number of people was "too many for that part of the Country & for the furs about it" (HBC Arch B231/e/3). At Lac La Pluie where there was a total of 563 Indians in 1830 (HBC Arch B105/e/9), there is definite evidence that the population was too great for the resources (cf. Hickerson 1967a:59). Charles McKenzie of Lac Seul, 90 miles north of Lac La Pluie, stated that in 1838, the population there had increased greatly since 1821 and "that there is not furs in the Country to Enable them to Clothe themselves at the present Standard of European goods" (HBC Arch B107/a/16). Again, in 1853, when some Lac Seul Indians deserted for Lac La Pluie, McKenzie commented: "Let them remain where they were willing to go—we have more Indians than the Country can Support" (HBC Arch B107/a/31).

66. HBC Arch B124/e/2.

67. HBC Arch B124/e/6.

68. HBC Arch B105/e/9.

69. Peter Grant, the Northwest Company trader at Lac La Pluie, wrote in 1804: "It is customary with them, in the beginning of winter, to separate in single families, a precaution which seems necessary to their very existence, and of which they are so sensible that when one of them has chosen a particular district for his hunting ground, no other person will encroach upon it without a special invitation, and whoever discovers a beaver lodge and marks its situation may consider it his undoubted property, and no other person will attempt to

destroy it without his permission. In case of famine, however, any one may abandon his district and seek a better hunt on his neighbour's land without incurring the least ill will or reproach: they say: 'the lands were made for the use of man, therefore every one has an equal right to partake of the produce' " (Masson 1890 2:326).

70. HBC Arch B107/a/8.

71. HBC Arch B107/a/12.

72. HBC Arch B107/a/21.

73. HBC Arch B107/a/7. This Trout Lake located about 80 miles northwest of Lac Seul shouldn't be confused with the Trout Lake 200 miles north of Osnaburgh House. The former is called "Little Trout Lake" and the latter "Big Trout Lake".

74. HBC Arch B107/a/10. It appears that "Windy Lake" is actually Windigo Lake located about 130 miles northwest of Osnaburgh and 150 miles north of Lac Seul.

75. HBC Arch B107/a/13.

76. When in 1836, a Lac Seul Indian was murdered, he and his relatives "had 9 Beaver Houses to take when he was killed" (HBC Arch B107/a/14). Debts given to Lac Seul Indians in 1830 were so low that " 'tis only there attachment to their own lands" which prevented them from taking advantage of situations at other posts (HBC Arch B107/z/2). When, in 1845, an Indian lad from Albany was left at Lac Seul, McKenzie hired him for the winter "as he has neither friends nor lands" (HBC Arch B107/a/24). There is less evidence from the Osnaburgh journals, nevertheless, George McPherson, in 1852, wrote that Big Sturgeon's and Long Back's sons had no hare "on their lands" whereas two other Indians "have Rabbits upon their lands" (HBC Arch B155/a/64). In 1870, "Sugar Head goes back to his hunting grounds again" (HBC Arch B155/a/79). And, in 1874, Alexander Harvey remarked: "Wakeham & family left for his old Lands this A.M.—it would have been much Better if the old "Gentleman"—Had remained on his own lands throughout the winter, however he would not take my advice last Autumn, But go with his Son-in-law "Missabbie" " (HBC Arch B155/a/82).

77. HBC Arch B107/a/9.

78. HBC Arch B107/a/16.

79. HBC Arch B107/a/23.

80. HBC Arch B107/a/16.

81. HBC Arch B107/a/23.

82. Thomas Corcoran (HBC Arch B123/a/32).

83. HBC Arch B123/e/12.

84. HBC Arch B123/e/14.

85. HBC Arch B107/e/5.

86. HBC Arch B107/a/12.

87. The Indian, Stump, in 1834: "complains of the Osnaburgh & Sturgeon Lake Indians that they destroyed his Beaver this winter" (HBC Arch B107/a/12). Again, in 1835, an Osnaburgh Indian "Hunted the whole year on the Lac Seul ground & the Indians are not well pleased at him, for he killed the Beaver they had marked as their own (HBC Arch B107/a/13). In 1837, Two Hearts and Richard Crow brought few furs to Lac Seul, "the Osnaburgh Indians having destroyed the Beaver House they had marked last Summer." (HBC Arch B107/a/15).

88. HBC Arch B107/a/18.

89. HBC Arch B107/a/23.

90. HBC Arch B107/a/25.

91. HBC Arch B155/a/92.

Chapter Seven
Competition and Trade: 1780-1829

Introduction

The era between 1780 and 1829 is divisible into two periods. The first, from 1780 to 1820, found the Northern Ojibwa in an area rich in furs and game where competition among Northwest Company and Hudson's Bay Company traders ensured a cheap abundant supply of trade goods. The second period, from 1821 to 1829, was transitional and led to changes already discussed in previous chapters. In 1821 the Northwest Company merged with the Hudson's Bay Company. This provided scope for the Bay Company to test new trade policies. Fur animals, particularly the beaver, had grown scarce near Osnaburgh by the late 1810's.

The history of the interior region lying north and west of Lake Nipigon cannot be separated from the history of the fur trade. Trade stimulated expansion into the area, first by small groups of Ojibwa exploiting new fur and food sources, and later by competing traders who vied for the Indians' furs. By 1786 when Osnaburgh House was established, expansion had virtually reached its maximum extent. With the settling of interior posts, mass migrations ceased, although competition among traders fostered mobility among Ojibwa groups. During this period of intensive competition the area about Osnaburgh was rarely without traders. After 1770, the Ojibwa no longer had to make long treks to the posts on James Bay and Hudson Bay as they had been doing for perhaps 60 or 70 years. Supplies were made available in their very encampments.

The establishment of Osnaburgh House was a product of competition for furs. Situated at the east end of Lake St. Joseph near the head of the Albany River it occupied a strategic position in regard to the flow of trade[1].

Competition in the fur trade during the period 1780-1821 was the predominant theme, particularly during the first twenty years of Osnaburgh's history when rivalry was most intense. It moulded trade policy and affected the Indian-trader relationship. In the early years competition among Northwest Company and Hudson's Bay Company traders resulted in lavish distributions of trade goods which were so plentiful and easily obtained that the Indians considered their dissemination a foregone conclusion (cf. Masson 1960 2:296). Food was in such abundance as to support traders and Indians alike. Indeed, the traders were more dependent on the Indians for goods and services than the Indians were on them. Even prior to the establishment of Osnaburgh, the Ojibwa, according to the Northwester, Duncan Cameron, considered the Northwest traders in the area:

> as poor, pitiful creatures who could neither supply themselves nor the Indians. They would take their goods on credit, pay what they pleased with the worst of their furs and carry all their fine and prime furs at Hudson's Bay, so that the trade had become a loosing business, although the country was rich, and fortunes might have been made in it (Masson 1960 2:243).

Cameron stated that it was not long after Osnaburgh was established that the Indians began considering the Hudson's Bay traders as "pitiful" as their Northwest Company predecessors.

The relationship between Indian and trader was actually based on mutual support. A variety of services and material goods including food was necessary to maintain post employees. The post in turn, issued trade goods now needed by Indians for hunting and trapping.

One of the most important services furnished by Indians was to act as guides to traders. In a vast country dotted with lakes and rivers that all look much alike, the very lives of traders depended upon the skill of their guides. For instance, in 1789, two traders returned to Osnaburgh from Cat Lake with an Indian:

> they having lost their way, and would inevitably have

starved going back to Catt Lake, not having any Provisions and not above 30 miles from this House, they had to go back 18 miles for this Indian and then without a promise of Brandy and Tobacco the Indian would not have come with them . . .[2].

Not only did the traders' lives depend upon guides, but the fur trade was affected by the availability of individuals who knew the country. In 1793, the Osnaburgh factor Robert Goodwin remarked:

there is not a Man here that can go to Catt Lake or knows the way. I applied to the Indians if they would go with my Men they did not seem to wish to go as it was out of their road, however by Promises and Gifts . . . they consented which was a very fortunate Circumstance for me, as the Men must otherwise have returned to Albany and Cat Lake gone unsupplied[3].

The Ojibwa, aware of their advantageous position, were reluctant to perform services for traders unless reimbursed with trade goods. If the rewards were not great enough they simply refused and the traders were left to fend for themselves. For example in 1797, the Lac La Pluie, (Rainy Lake) post had to be evacuated since nobody at Osnaburgh knew the way there[4]. The inadequate knowledge of the country by traders placed Indians in a privileged position under conditions of intensive competition between the two companies, since they were often able to influence the location of outposts. In 1815, William Thomas of Gloucester House asked John Davis of Osnaburgh for more geographical information since,

we have received no sketches of the Geography of the Country and we have no idea of the position of many places mentioned in the Journals. A Sketch such as every Indian is capable of drawing however rude and inaccurate would always be better than no information at all[5].

Another Indian service to traders involved assisting the boats to and from Albany each summer. Every spring the boats would travel up the Albany River laden with trade goods for the interior posts, and late in the summer would return to Fort Albany with fur packs. Indians were hired as labourers to convey the vessels across portages and lakes, and to help load supplies. Sometimes Ojibwa were sent to meet the craft to bring down goods in their canoes in advance of them, especially if local resources had become depleted. Often at this time groups of Indians lingered about the post awaiting trade supplies. In order to prevent them from decamping to trade at nearby Northwest Company stations, canoes would be sent ahead to acquire a few things to reassure expectant Indians that more goods were on the way[6].

Frequently when traders first arrived in a region they were unfamiliar with the best fishing and hare snaring grounds. In the early years the setting of nets and snaring of hare were primary occupations of traders, since the bulk of their food was provided from local resources. Indians familiar with the country could contribute this information[7]. When land was cleared for buildings and gardens, Indians assisted in removing stumps and hauling logs[8]. Once gardens became established at Osnaburgh House after 1788 one of the annual services provided by the Indians was taking up the potatoes, the major crop grown. This was done especially by the women and children who were inclined to stuff themselves until they became sick.

By far the most vital commodity bartered by Indians to traders at interior posts was food, principally venison. In March 1792 at Osnaburgh, Robert Goodwin "sett of all the Indians to hunt more Privisions or else we must starve"[9]. In the winter of 1796-97, fishing by Hudson's Bay employees proved so unfavourable that John Best remarked, "If Inds. does not bring us Venison God knows what one are to do ... "[10]. By February 1797, Best had served the last of the flour to his men who were living almost solely on meat procured by the Indians.

The traders of Osnaburgh House, during the post's early history, were in a more precarious position with regard to food than in later years when potato gardens and fall fisheries were instituted, since they were bound to the immediate vicinity about the establishment. Also, those Hudson's Bay servants who hunted for the post often ate a considerable portion of their catch. John

McKay, in 1799, remarked that two Hudson's Bay employees could,

> eat 28 rabbits at their tent per week besides 8 lbs of Pork 12 lbs of flour & sometimes 40 Rabbits . . . I thought 2 rabbits a day was enough for any man but now I find 4 is too little[11].

Except in later years when larger gardens were cultivated, and fishing was conducted on a greater scale, starvation in the interior was always imminent.

The meat of the large cervines, caribou and moose, either fresh, dried, or pounded, constituted the primary source of food traded by Ojibwa. Other bartered foods listed in the Osnaburgh House Archival documents included bear, hare, porcupine, lynx, beaver, sturgeon, partridge, geese, ducks, and loons. Vegetable products comprised berries and wild rice, the latter being an important trade food in the more southerly trading posts. At Lac Seul, corn grown by the Eagle Lake Indians was exchanged for trade goods[12].

Although food in the northern interior was never as abundant as it was on the Plains, or in the Southeast, the quantities were sufficient to support both Indians and traders during the first two decades of the post's history. The amount of food traded by Ojibwa during the late eighteenth and early nineteenth centuries is indicative that starvation was not a problem to the Indians in the Osnaburgh area provided that climatic or social conditions did not interfere with hunting operations. Indians were usually willing and able to exchange surplus game, often vital to the survival of traders, for supplies. Indeed, James Sutherland, while exploring Lac Seul with the assistance of a group of Indians in 1786, wrote:

> Indians feasting all day from Tent to Tent: are remarkable kind to us we being always invited the same as themselves, and gives us a large share[13].

In addition to foods, Indians provided a number of material commodities needed by traders. One such article was snowshoes.

232

The means of travel during winter months both for Indian and trader was by snowshoe. Without these, it was impossible to travel any distance when snow was deep. In 1786, John Best requested

> Indians to bring in their families and to knit snow shoes for us but they tell me they are a far way off and cannot conveniently come in so I do not know what we shall do for snow shoes as the snow is no growing deep and cannot travel without them to look for anything[14].

Any person familiar with the north understands how pertinent this statement is. Although, in later years traders learned to manufacture their own snowshoes, Indians often provided them ready-made, or were paid to make new frames, or to renet old ones.

In summer, when travel was by water, Indians were employed to construct both freight and fishing canoes, including the necessary paddles.

Other wares received from the Ojibwa for local use included sleds; the hides of cervines for tents, shoes, and fur pack wrappers; fat for candles, and sturgeon oil for lamps; goose and duck feathers for mattresses and blankets, and quills for pens; birch bark for house shingles; and spruce pitch to seal roof cracks, and to patch canoes. Indian women, frequently traders' wives, were paid "for netting snowshoes, making & mending the appointees clothes and washing for them ..."[15], and also to make nets from twine. Table 34 gives a list of expenses paid to Indians at Osnaburgh House for the year 1795-96[16].

The services rendered not only show the interdependence of trader and Indian, but also indicate that the Indians were pre-occupied with pursuits other than merely trapping fur bearers. Competition guaranteed the distribution of inexpensive trade supplies fostering mobility from post to post. It also allowed Indians to devote more time to subsistence activities since they could satisfy material needs with comparatively small bundles of furs.

In order to hunt for both food and furs, Ojibwa had to be properly outfitted. Files, hatchets, twine, and guns were absolute necessities. So long as big game was available, by far the most

Table 34   Duties Performed by Osnaburgh Indians: 1795-96

Goods or Services	Value in Beaver
900 lbs of venison	60
15 gallons of rice	10
Deer's fat & sturgeon oil for lamp	12
1 large canoe	70
3 small canoes (10 beaver each)	30
Part payment to 6 Indians for bringing goods from Albany	60
Odd summer jobs by Indians	25
Shoe leather and snowshoes	40
Preparation of gun powder for Indians	10
Total	317

important of these was the gun and accessories. In August 1790, Robert Goodwin "gave the Indians some Powder and Shot to enable them to pay their debts and traded one of them 16 Beaver to keep them from starving"[17].

In addition, Ojibwa required a variety of other items. John McKay reported in 1799, that the Osnaburgh Indians "often wanted Powder and Shot in the summer and sometimes a hatchet or file, these is articles they cannot do without..."[18]. In 1791 Goodwin noted a scarcity of blankets, powder, knives, hatchets and tobacco at Osnaburgh:

> The Indians says how can they kill Beaver when they cannot get the things necessary for their winter Hunt which is very true for it is well known that the Inds can do but very little without a Hatchet in the winter time[19].

There seems to have been only a partial dependence on European-made clothes during this period. Post employees would make cloth coats to exchange for pelts and beaver coats[20]. Clothing appears to have been made from caribou or moose hide; whereas outer winter garments were made from beaver pelts. For example, in 1787, John Best reported "the Indians of the 3rd trading their Beaver coats and some deer skins"[21].

Another item issued to Indians on occasion was food. Food donations were less frequent during the first 25 years after the post was built than in the succeeding years. Indians who arrived at the post in the winter starving would be fed either fish, potatoes, or flour depending upon what was available at the time. As cervines became scarce after 1815, cases of starvation became more numerous and food contributions from the post grew larger. By this time, however, Osnaburgh House was growing more self-sufficient supported by the fall fisheries and potato crop. Thomas Vincent reported that between 200 and 300 bushels of potatoes were cultivated annually by 1814[22]. Usually from 4,000 to 5,000 fish were taken in the fall for winter use by Bay employees.

Although traders on occasion supplied starving Indians with food to tide them over harsh periods, it cannot be said that the Ojibwa of this period were by any means dependent upon the post for food. Indeed, as we have seen, the post employees were often more dependent upon the Indians for food than the other way around. The mutual interdependence of merchant and producer was to the benefit of both. Food bartered by Indians guaranteed the continuance of the post and represented "a kind of insurance system for the Indians, a system which also assured their continuing adherence to the trader with whom they first had dealings" (Hickerson 1967a:52). In turn, it was to the trader's benefit to provide for the welfare of hungry Indians. Hunters suffering from starvation were unable and often unwilling to pursue fur bearers especially if there was a chance of procuring larger denizens. This became increasingly true as the larger animals grew scarce since more time had to be spent pursuing them. So long as competition existed, Indians could almost always obtain enough ammunition and twine to supply their needs provided that game was available to hunt. Thus, tiding Indians over harsh periods with gratuities of food tended to ensure that they would be willing and capable to hunt furred animals in more favourable times. The trader became a middleman in the distribution of surplus.

General Effects of Competition

The Ojibwa let it be known that they would trade where goods were cheapest and traders had almost no control over their actions. Indians could often even command the location of outposts. For instance, a Captain, Shewequenap, arrived at Osnaburgh in September, 1790, and asked for a post 90 miles from Osnaburgh, "so the Indians would then come in Winter and not be forced to trade with Tupa" the Northwest trader[23]. The term "captain" was applied to trade chiefs who were also in most cases band leaders. Since these men often had much influence over their fellow band members, it was not expedient to ignore their requests or threats.

In 1796, an Indian's request for an outpost was granted. However, requests for outposts were not always admitted; from the traders' point of view an abundance of trading locales merely provided more supply depots for Indians who would waste their time travelling from post to post to get extra debts. Competition, nevertheless, did force the construction of numerous tiny supply stations. In April, 1791, during the most favourable period for spring trapping, Robert Goodwin, feared a poor trade at Osnaburgh since "the Indians are doing little or nothing so many different Settlements takes their Attention from hunting"[24]. When in 1798, the Hudson's Bay Company was forced to place outposts on Moose Lake (perhaps Lake Savant) and Crow Nest Lake[25] to compete with Northwest traders in those areas, John McKay, the Osnaburgh factor, commented:

> I wish the Devil might carry off Moose Lake Canadians and all. Moose Lake and Crow Nest Lake is two wicked Brothers, who for the sake of ruining their Parents will ruin themselves.

Trading Posts near Osnaburgh House

The number and exact location of Northwest Company posts in the Osnaburgh area is very difficult to determine. Northwest outposts were usually small and temporary and their locations were shifted from year to year to take advantage of as many trading localities as possible (cf. Masson 1960 2:245). There were generally from four to six each year within a 200-mile radius of Osnaburgh. In contrast, Hudson's Bay Company posts, fewer in number in the early years appear to have been larger and better stocked. The Cat Lake post, the first post established beyond

Table 35   Northwest Company Trading Posts near
            Osnaburgh: 1786-1801

Location of Posts	Dates Established
Lake St. Joseph	1787-88, 1792-95, 1797-98
Cat Lake	1787-91, 1792-97, 1798-1801
Sturgeon Lake	1787-92, 1795-98
Lake Seul	1789-92, 1798-99, 1800-01
Lake Nipigon	1786-87, 1789-95, 1796-1800
Red Lake	1789-92, 1793-97, 1799-1801
Crow Nest Lake	1786-87, 1799-1801
Eagle Lake	1794-97
Moose Lake	1798-99
Trout Lake	1800-01
Sandy Lake	1793-94, 1798-1800
Great Lake	1794-95
Manatague Lake	1786-87, 1791-92, 1796-97, 1799-1800
Saunders Lake	1797-98
Skunk Head Lake	1793-94
Horse Lake	1796-97
Fly Lake	1796-99
Mouth of the Winnipeg River	1792-93
One on the Crane's land	1800-01
One on the Tinpot's land (Sandy Lake?)	1800-01

Osnaburgh, was erected in 1788 (see Map 1). In 1790, outposts
were built at Red Lake and Lac Seul, and the following year saw
the founding of the Lac La Pluie (Rainy Lake) post by traders
from Osnaburgh. The first Hudson's Bay post on Lake Nipigon
was built in 1792, by traders arriving from Fort Albany. By 1794,
a trading centre was established at Martin's Falls 200 miles down
the Albany River from Osnaburgh which eventually replaced
Gloucester House upstream and Henley House further downstream. Gloucester House had been established in 1777, on Washi
Lake about 160 miles east of Osnaburgh, while Henley House had
been first built in 1743, at the forks of the Kenogami and Albany

Rivers 300 miles to the east. Between 1794 and 1797, outposts were sustained at Sturgeon Lake south of Osnaburgh and at lakes Saunders[26], Savant and Crow Nest. A small Hudson's Bay outpost of Osnaburgh was operated at Lac Seul in 1803 but may not have seen continuous use until after 1821. In 1807, a Hudson's Bay post was founded by traders from Fort Severn at Trout Lake at the source of the Fawn River, a tributary of the Severn. The Berens River post was established at the mouth of the Berens River on Lake Winnipeg in 1814 (cf. Hallowell 1955:112-13). A number of these posts were abandoned and reestablished according to the competitive situation of the moment. After the coalition of the two companies in 1821, some of these posts were deserted.

The majority of posts listed in Table 35 were small and temporary. The most important Northwest Company posts were located at Lake Nipigon and Sturgeon Lake. It is possible that there are some omissions in the table since information was obtained from comments made in the Hudson's Bay Company post journals. Data recorded after 1801 in the journals are less detailed, but it appears that there was a definite decline in the number of Northwest posts, especially after 1810 as furs grew scarce.

Posts operated by Montreal merchants had grown numerous in the Osnaburgh area by the late 1770's. In 1778 there were no less than seven houses inland from Gloucester House[27]. Two years before the Montreal traders united to form the Northwest Company in 1782, George Sutherland of the Hudson's Bay Company from his tiny outpost on Sturgeon Lake, listed no less than 17 outposts northwest of Lake Superior, operated by these traders[28]. It was the establishment of these numerous trading locales which led the Hudson's Bay Company to build Osnaburgh House in 1786 and other interior posts thereafter.

The major supply route to the interior for the Hudson's Bay Company was the Albany River. Northwest goods entered via Lake Superior.

Trade Goods and Competition

The numerous outposts not only provided additional locations

238

for Indians to get debts, but their existence also resulted in the depletion of trade supplies at the central post, Osnaburgh. Indeed, one of the problems that traders faced at interior posts during these early years was maintaining a sufficient quantity and variety of goods. The existence of numerous posts also had the effect of producing a scattered but highly mobile Indian population. In 1790, John Best wrote Robert Goodwin of Osnaburgh from Cat Lake, 120 miles to the northwest, that "there will be but a poor trade from inland this year there is so many traders and every one will get a little"[29]. During these early years when numerous outposts had to be supplied the effect was to injure the trade. For example, Indians who found a lack of trade goods in 1786 at Osnaburgh agreed to go to Gloucester for needed materials while threatening to trade elsewhere if in the future such shortages should again occur. In the summers of 1788 and 1789, Ojibwa absolutely refused to go further than Osnaburgh for their debts. According to Robert Goodwin, this was because "their young men are too Lazy and they know they can be supplied in the fall of the Year from the Pedlars . . . "[30]. Goodwin wrote in May, 1790, that he expected the trade to be poor since there were so many Canadians nearby, and goods were so slow in arriving in the summer. "Last year had to stay 14 or 15 days waiting which hurts the place greatly altho' not preceivable to persons at a distance"[31]. That summer Goodwin reported that only half the Indians who had been debted in the fall brought furs during the following spring.

The quality of goods was also important in luring Indians. In 1791 Captain Shewequenap and his gang[32] told Goodwin "plainly they will not come to us when they can get better with the Canadians and I am fearful the Trade will Decrease without your Honor's send out better especially so many Pedlars in the Country"[33].

Variety in trade goods was also important. Another factor, Edward Clouston, in 1798 reported that he could not prevent the Indians from going to the Northwest posts as they had

so many different sorts of trinkets & fine Gartering which attracts the attention of the capricious natives & was I to give them all the Goods & Brandy I have in the Company's

Warehouse for nothing it would not stop them from going to the Canadians[34].

Despite the constant complaints by traders of shortages of goods there is evidence that Osnaburgh House usually received the bulk of the trade in the area each year. Both the quantity and variety of goods traded at Hudson's Bay Company posts was comparatively large[35]. For example, Table 37 lists the quantity of goods traded to four Indians and their families by the Osnaburgh factor, John McKay in 1800. In addition, they got thread, hawk bells and gartering. The total value of the materials was 140 made beaver[36].

Table 37   Goods Received by Four Indian Families

9½ gallons of brandy	12 pounds of powder
2 chief coats	1 yard of cloth in breech cloth
2 lieutenant's coats	20 pounds of shot
1 common coat	10 files
2 hats	10 awls
6 feathers	30 flints
2 ruffed shirts	4 pounds of beads
3 plain shirts	20 knives
2 handkerchiefs	24 ladles
2 pairs of shoes	6 pounds of tobacco
2 pairs of stockings	5 mirrors
6 yards of cloth in petticoats	2 combs

One of the most important trade commodities was liquor, either brandy, rum, or wine, prepared especially for the Indians and often heavily watered. The attraction of liquor was so great that a shortage of it in the spring and summer when the Indians congregated at the post often meant the difference between poor and successful trade. There are numerous accounts by traders of Indians trading only where they could get liquor. Great quantities of liquor were distributed by both companies. In 1803, Northwest posts distributed 16,299 gallons of spirits (Rich 1960 2:229). I would estimate that perhaps 5,000 gallons went into the region of the Albany and Severn drainages. Indians could obtain liquor especially in regions where competition was intense. The use of alcohol created heavy expenses for all the competing posts that were forced to distribute it.

There are numerous references in traders' reports to excessive use by the Indians of alcohol in given instances in which they visited trading posts (cf. Masson 1960 2:295). Acts of violence including accidents, even homicides, while under the influence of alcohol were frequent (cf. Hallowell 1955:142). In one instance recorded in 1787 a whole family of Indians was murdered[37]. The lives of the traders themselves were often in peril. Violence and turmoil occasioned by drunkenness became so great that in 1796, the Osnaburgh factor, James Sutherland, wrote that two Indians arriving from Sturgeon Lake refused liquor because of occasions of violence. Sutherland's account of the general situation is informative:

> The Indians went away about noon, they acquaint me of three more Indians being kill'd last fall exclusive of the two murdered by Mr. Best's Brandy . . . besides two more who I hear is dead from sunfits of liquor,... Dreadfull is the devastations now which spirituous liquors is making among the Indians, between us at one end, the N.W. Company at the Other and Cameron and Co. in the middle who vieing with each other who shall pour the spirituous poison most down their throats, and not only this but those who sur- vives the deadly draught are become more abandon'd to every vice by corruption and the evils arising from opposition from those who should have taught them better principles so that the poor natives have entirely lost that natural Innocence and simplicity of manners for which they were formerly distinguished[38].

Drinking behaviour among Indians although unrestricted was a social event. In almost every case recorded, Indians drank in groups. There are even reports in the Lac Seul journals at later dates of individuals refusing their liquor ration until other band members were present. Sharing of liquor was important. Drink- ing, ironically appears to have been a social phenomenon whose purpose was to *promote solidarity*. However, internal tensions and strife frequently became manifest in socially disruptive behaviour when alcohol was consumed in quantity.

Competition and numerous trading posts stocked with liquor and other goods fostered mobility among hunting groups and ensured that the Indians were well supplied. When supplies were in plenty, traders were forced to debt Indians even though frequently the debts were not completely repaid. In June, 1790, Goodwin reported the arrival of an Indian from the "Utchapoy Country"[39], who because of a smallpox epidemic there,

> intends to leave it and come here to trade the next year if I use him well. he wanted Cloathing. at last I complyed with it the Inds to be sure are nothing but promises. If I had not granted it and he never come it might be imputed that I did not encourage him to come again.

In almost every case the trader had to give way to the demands of the Indian or lose what was already owed[40]. Should he refuse a debt to one man he might lose the trade of the entire band. In addition, Indians soon learned a number of deceptions to maximize returns. As stated by John McKay of Osnaburgh in 1800 for instance:

> An Indian will some times pay you 30 Br at 3 different times, and every time will be as expensive except cloathing, as if he paid the whole at one time[41].

Indeed, the art of playing off one trader against another became so well developed that it may be posited that considerable prestige was accorded individuals who excelled in it. A band leader who was able to procure more goods would also be likely to have a larger following. For example, McKay complained that the Indian Shewequenap "as well as his whole Blackguard family are such expensive Indians that I am sure they never brought a skin to this house, since first settled, that ever cleared itself in England"[42]. Shewequenap and his band were frequent visitors to the post for supplies. His band appears to have been one of the largest, as shall be later documented. Numerous are the accounts of Indians being debted in several different places and taking their furs where they pleased. Indians were bribed and enticed in every way, yet often to no avail. The following account presented by Robert Goodwin in September 1793 is typical:

> Inds . . . brot me 60 Beaver in furrs and gave them plenty of Ammunition etc after which they had tied their Bundles they all went to the other Trader, he opened all his Goods to let them see what a fine Assortment he had and they all took some Debt from him. he also gave Shewequenap a full Captains Dress also Coats to three other Indians and about 5 Gallons of Brandy which kept the Indians drinking all day, he expected to get half the Spring [furs] by his giving such large presents and did not get a Skin from them when they came[43].

That summer a Northwest post had been established on Lake St. Joseph near the Bay post.

During the winter of 1794-95, the Northwest post was relocated within a few yards of Osnaburgh House. Competition became so violent that even the formerly bold Indians hesitated to approach the posts. For example, Jacob Corrigal reported that in August, 1794, the Northwest Company traders threatened to shoot the Bay men if they tried to take furs from the Indians if they were "first at them"[44]. A month earlier, Corrigal related that the "Canadians" had been "plundering" the Indians of their furs. That this hostility among traders was injurious to the trade was indicated by Corrigal on October 16: "large number of Traders surrounding the House, and also a very disagreeable neighbor, who from his practice of robbing the Indians, the few that would come is afraid"[45]. In November, the Northwest traders attempted to make a deal with the Hudson's Bay Company. Furs were to be divided in proportion to Indian debts. However, the offer was declined on the grounds that the Northwest traders gave larger debts and thus would expect more furs. In December, the Hudson's Bay employees cut a concealed hole in the palisades to allow Indians in at night to trade at the Hudson's Bay post. That this tactic was necessary is illustrated by Corrigal on January 25:

> In the evening an Indian family appeared on the Lake

comming towards the house, my neighbor no sooner saw them then he sent 2 men to take what they could and actually took two Sleds from them by force, no French Trader I ever sat beside acted in this manner before . . . to see the Indians robb'd before our face in sight of the House, is a grief.

The Indians left most of their furs, later procured by the Hudson's Bay Company, hidden in the bush. Corrigal recorded numerous other similar examples that winter. He summed up the situation in March:

How! this Trade is changed! formerly our great trouble was to keep drunken Indians out, now our trouble is in keeping them in, that they may not go to or carry anything to our neighbour the Canadians and on this account the men must watch all night[46].

Competition was not always so violent. On occasion Northwest Company and Hudson's Bay Company traders even shared the same buildings.

Treatment of Indians was not always equitable. As noted, they were frequently plundered of their furs and threatened with violence should they trade with the opposing company[47]. Indian women appear to have been taken for sexual and economic purposes by men of both companies, although ordinary informal marriages also occurred. In July 1816, two Indians who had been employed on the boats to Albany quit, according to the Osnaburgh factor William McKay because:

they were starving and that the Men did not use them well, they never got liberty to sleep in the tent not even when it was raining and they say they did not get the same allowances as what the Men had, they say they used to pick out the poorest of the geese and give it to them; if this be true I do not wonder at their leaving them at all because an Indian thinks more of what he has to eat than what he does about anything else[48].

The Ojibwa during these times were equally aggressive and on occasion traders themselves were murdered[49]. During the summer of 1788, Robert Goodwin feared that the Indians would cut the gates of the post down to plunder supplies[50]. The following January, the men were cleaning and loading pistols in case of an assault. The next fall saw the Osnaburgh traders again preparing for an attack which never materialized. Indeed, references to violence on the part of Indians, including murder, are comparatively numerous in the literature during those early years in the area about Osnaburgh. One band, known as Cranes, was particularly notorious. In 1803, they tried to pull down the stockades to steal brandy, and the next year threatened to burn the post down. Some years later, in 1816, they almost captured Osnaburgh.

Decline of the Fur Trade

Thus far, little has been said about the fur trade itself. Until 1800, or shortly thereafter, there appears to have been no shortage of fur animals. The Osnaburgh post produced 4,330 made beaver in 1787-88[51]. By 1791, the total had fallen to 3,600 made beaver, but this was still considered a good trade since outposts in the surrounding area were numerous[52]. Trade was still flourishing in 1803 when 53 bundles of furs were obtained at Osnaburgh. Nevertheless, there were signs that fur bearers were becoming depleted in some areas.

In 1804, the Northwest Company trader, Duncan Cameron, in reference to the area northwest of Lake Superior (the Nipigon Country), remarked: "that this part of the country is now very much improverished since; beaver is getting very scarce ... " (Masson 1960 2:245). Cameron accurately predicted what would happen when he said:

> even if there were no opposition at all in the country to spoil the trade, it is now getting so barren and poor that in a dozen of years hence, the returns from it will be so triffling that, even if one company had the whole, on the cheapest terms, it will be little enough to pay the expences of carrying on the business, for the hunt is declining very fast ... and I believe that our discoveries are now about at an end ... (Masson 1960 2:297).

Table 38   Osnaburgh House Fur Returns: 1787-1821

Year	Beaver			Otter	Mink	Lynx	Marten	Fisher	Fox	Bear	Muskrat	Moose	Caribou
	large or whole	half or cub	coat										
1787	480	320	158	237	43	30	306	1		12	259		1
1788*	1392	755	410½	480	44	510	668	15	15	58	350	2	4
1789*	2269	1433	506½	576	78	412	988	38	14	117	627	16	
1790*	2180	1338	679½	468	77	164	517	22		74	252	18	21
1791*	2025	1470	574½	486	73	219	834	58	3	111	589	23	
1792	1674	997	356½	236	54	197	1001	7	21	54	143	9	
1793*	1558	909	407	358	85	318	1021	26	9	39	158	67	2
1794*	1405	1008	328	336	48	73	210	9		18	552	17	10
1795*	1966	1070	355	363	148	78	683	17		25	523	30	2
1796*	2870	1517	557	509	216	98	1249	10	2	41	317	72	19
1797	1390	963	322	339	198	123	1254	12	4	25	243	93	77
1798	1380	642	216	254	196	78	693	15	1	25	142	62	21
1799	1121	820	142	262	86	72	510	12	1	23	56	12	14
1800	586	385	43	142	20	49	177	5	1	20	221	16	
1806	676	309	25	128	38	6	736	4	2	11	164	22	
1807	957	476	41½	187	80	14	573	8	5	9	357	19	
1809	892	537	56	189	70	41	612		4	14	760	68	
1810	1093	578	40	205	37	55	581			21	370	50	1
1811	1344	600	9	395		137	1127	26	7	50	1062	108	
1812	1540	693	55	485	12	92	626	20	7	68	2840	14	
1813	1376	690	70	444	32	17	455	7		60	1512		18
1814	905	608	20	400	44	16	1490	16	2	38	2400	133	50
1815	870	480	35	533	71	16	1684	9	14	30	6087	111	42
1816	758	351	15½	444	104	48	1438	19	2	100	3569	60	15
1820	125	110		211	79	16	2110		2	7	2664	70	47
1821	163	89		327	336	83	2877	1	8	22	3522	32	85

*Years when the Cat Lake and Osnaburgh House fur returns were combined.

Some of the "lesser" furs such as skunks, hare, badgers, wolverine and racoons have been omitted from the table.

After 1805, reports of beaver growing scarce became increasingly frequent. In June 1806, David Sanderson of Osnaburgh declared that the trade had decreased "greatly this year on every quarter. I have no mor than 1400 Beaver at present"[53] (see Table 38). The following year, trade was up to 2,000 made beaver, but this too was considered a deficiency[54]. By 1810, Indians in certain locales began to complain of the decline. During March and April that year, several Ojibwa arrived at the Osnaburgh post having made poor hunts "occasioned by the scarcity of Beaver in their lands"[55]. Three years later in 1813, the dearth of beaver had become widespread, except to the north of Osnaburgh where the Cranes hunted. Thomas Vincent, in the Osnaburgh district report of 1814, confirms the decline:

> The Canadians have long been established in this quarter and formerly used to carry out a great many packs of good Furs but the Country thereabouts now is nearly exhausted and few Beaver are to be procured. The trade they now carry out are small and principally consist of Martins Otters, Bears Musquash and parchment[56].

By the fall of 1815, according to John Davis, both beaver and moose had been exterminated in the vicinity of Osnaburgh. Red Lake was "the only place on this quarter that there is any moose and Beaver to be found and the most of the Indians is to winter on that Quarter"[57]. As the years passed, fur bearers grew increasingly scarce as Indians searched out and destroyed the remaining pockets without regard to conservation practices.

Fur returns are available for most years from 1787 until the end of competition in 1821 (Table 38)[58]. The decline of beaver after the early 1800's is statistically confirmed. The figures for beaver in 1810-13, while higher than for previous years, can be explained in terms of the withdrawal of many outposts belonging to both companies about this time as maintenance costs and decreasing productivity did not merit their continuation. The increase in certain furs such as mink, marten and muskrat in the returns does not mean that these animals were becoming more numerous. Rather beaver, until the 1810's the *sine qua non* of the fur trade, had diminished to the point where Indians were forced to concentrate on other species to pay their debts.

There was a variety of other reasons why fur returns changed after 1810. One, of course, was due to increasing cases of starvation among Ojibwa. Indians who had to devote all their efforts to procuring food were neither able nor willing to trap. This was particularly true as long as their main support was large game animals, as shall be discussed. Beaver did supply them with some food, but not in bulk as did the larger animals. More important was the fact that Indians were overhunting fur and game resources with no concern for conservation. Under such conditions it was only a matter of time before the supply became depleted.

Even when fur bearers were numerous the conditions of competition affected the quantity of furs procured at Osnaburgh. The availability of trade supplies and the proximity of Northwest posts were important factors. The loss of Indian trade to other posts often meant a marked difference in the fur returns. For instance, the Trout Lake post attracted the Cranes who hunted approximately halfway between Osnaburgh and the latter during the 1810's. Their loss was seriously felt since they were the chief beaver hunters who annually had brought nearly 1,000 made beaver in furs to Osnaburgh before 1807[59].

Also, cultural factors were of some importance (as has been mentioned before). Should an Indian die, his relatives and band members would not hunt furs for a year. Indeed, in early years furs were destroyed. For example, in 1803, Jacob Corrigal reported that "the Old Moose and Brother cam in, brought nothing having burn't all their Furrs, one of their Wives being dead"[60]. In later times, furs became too precious to destroy. I could find no examples of the use of sorcery in the Osnaburgh documents relating to this period of the kind described by Hallowell (1938) at a later time. It might be conjectured that physical violence during this period was a more important means of exhibiting hostility than was sorcery. As we shall see, it would appear that a stable land tenure system involving families did not exist at this time and hunting groups remained large and cohesive throughout the year. Thus, open feuds may have had a more profound effect on fur returns than the more individualistic practice of sorcery.

Climatic factors and cycles in animal population could also alter the picture. These factors became more important in later times when the economic basis of the Ojibwa was more precariously balanced as has been shown. For example, Charles McKenzie, in his 1828 annual report for Lac Suel even noted a slight increase in the number of beaver:

We have 291—The cause of this increase is that several Indians went towards the Red & Trout Lake quarters where there was no Trading Post for these 8 years past—these found Beaver & some Moose & Deer & are going there again this summer[61].

Although cyclical fluctuations and the discovery of a few isolated pockets of beaver accounted for slight increases in the fur returns, the scarcity of beaver had become widespread by the early 1820's. The region to the north of Osnaburgh where the Cranes hunted was the last one that possessed beaver in any quantity. By 1820 this area too had been scoured of its beaver. In 1825, James Slater stated that the Cranes, consisting of 18 hunters, brought only 160 made beaver to the post that year; and that their hunt for the previous three years had been negligible[62]. At this time, the Cranes were still attempting to live on caribou which had grown very scarce everywhere; while other groups of Ojibwa had switched to smaller game.

Policy Changes After 1821

The coalition of the Northwest Company and Hudson's Bay Company meant that the latter was in control of the fur trade throughout most of northwestern Ontario. The termination of competition allowed the Hudson's Bay Company to implement new policies in a country drastically reduced in fur and game resources. The ready barter system, discussed in Chapter 4, was one such policy first tested at Osnaburgh in 1824. The reduction of the beaver trade induced the Hudson's Bay Company to encourage conservation policies; summer furs, for example, were no longer accepted in trade. The value of trade supplies rose. Many outposts and posts of importance under conditions of competition when furs had been plentiful were abandoned. The apathetic attitude of Indians, many of whom owed immense debts which had accumulated over a decade, led the Hudson's Bay Company to abolish these debts in 1824 to encourage them to hunt.

Indians who had accumulated large debts during the competitive era became despondent and unwilling to hunt. If traders advanced them debts, according to Charles McKenzie in 1823:

they shall not pay the one half & should they not be

advanced they shall die with cold. The most of them too are so much loaded with old Debts—that they have lost heart knowing that what they do kill will be taken for ther old score[63].

McKenzie recommended that their old debts should be abolished; at least they should be provided with ammunition so they could hunt furs and survive. John Davis of Osnaburgh, in his report for 1825, stated that Indians without old debts made better fur hunts, whereas those heavily in arrears were "Entirely Carless whether they hunt anything or not"[64]. Davis prescribed that the Indians be debted to the amount of two-thirds of their previous year's hunt, since Indians who were naked in the early winter "cannot be expected to make any hunt". The year previous Davis advised that an experienced and intelligent trader reside at Osnaburgh or Lac Seul or both, and that changes in the attitudes of the Ojibwa should be induced gradually[65]. Some of the prescribed policy changes are recorded by John Davis of Lac Seul in December, 1823:

Goods will in future be Bartered with the Indians you will perceive they will be supplied much cheaper than heretofore. but it is not intended they will be allowed advances in Debt at this rate but only in Trading their Hunts. No presents is allowed except a few pipes of Tobacco when they come in with Furs and 3/8 Gns mixed rum for every 10 Made Beaver they bring. I have already informed you verbally Debts and gratuity must be done away as soon as possible—after this winter nothing should be given in Debt but actual necessaries to enable them to Hunt[66].

After the coalition the value of materials appears to have risen slightly. In addition, goods formerly obtained gratis such as liquor and tobacco had to be purchased. Guns rose in value from eight to twelve made beaver, while blankets increased from three to seven made beaver. There were other policy modifications which were not beneficial to the Ojibwa. A proclamation was issued in the summer of 1824, that beaver were not to be taken in trade that year if possible in order to allow them to increase. Summer furs which had often provided Indians with the necessary means of acquiring ammunition, nets, etc. were no longer accepted. It appears that the meat from these animals was important in supporting Ojibwa in the summer. During the late summer of 1824, five Indians arrived at the post with 400 summer rats which the Osnaburgh factor, James Slater, refused. He recorded their reaction:

> They said of you were Starving the same as we are you would be glad to kill anything you see & if you will not take them give them to us & we will eat them. they wanted Debts as usual and I told them that no debts were now to be given to any Ind only a little ammunition etc to which they replied you should want to kill the Inds it is hard to day and it shall not be us alone that Shall diy[67].

To encourage the Ojibwa to hunt marten en lieu of beaver, in 1824, either two large or small pelts were priced at one made Beaver[68]. Three pints of rum that year were worth an equal amount. Liquor was not to be issued to Indians while taking debt after 1824[69]. Additional twine was to be issued to Indians in summer to prevent them from stealing nets.

After 1821 many posts and outposts were abandoned. The original purpose of numerous posts, to acquire furs from Indians trapping in certain locales and to discourage them from trading with the opposition tended to tie Ojibwa bands more firmly to certain regions. However, Indians who had become accustomed to trading at posts later deserted found themselves cut off from a convenient supply of goods.

Edward Mowat in 1824, wrote from Cat Lake that Indians to the northward perished for want of trade items since the post they formerly habituated was deserted. The nearest posts beyond Cat Lake were located at Trout Lake and Island Lake[70]. Relatives of these same Indians were forced to trade at Osnaburgh that fall since the Cat Lake post itself was vacated[71]. Cat Lake Indians were "allowed advances in necessaries to a greater amount than those hunting near Osnaburgh post"[72]. Those Ojibwa who hunted in the vicinity of Cat Lake were reported by the Osnaburgh factor, James Slater in March 1825, to have been "very Disatisfied . . . as no people were Sent to their Land Last Fall as the Distance is too far for them to Come to this place"[73]. Slater indicated that abandoning Cat Lake would hurt the trade in future. His prediction had already proved to be correct. For instance, in February 1825, a Cat Lake Indian had arrived at Osnaburgh:

In great want as well as his family 8 of them in number he says that he brock the Lock of his Gun in the first part of the winter which caused him to Starve so much. this is the best hunting Indian that belongs to Cat Lake and he is now reduced to nothing, he is cut up some Rat and Cat Skins together with 2 Beaver Skins for Clothing[74].

The Cat Lake post was reestablished from Osnaburgh in the fall of 1825. However, fur returns in the spring of 1826 were meagre, since the Indians had suffered from starvation. Thus, Slater wrote, "When I consider the Trade from this Post and the expense incurred in maintaining it, I would scarcely recommend to send People there the ensuing Season"[75]. It was once again abandoned that spring.

The Cat Lake Indians produced even fewer pelts the following spring, and they lacked many trade items necessary for hunting, especially ammunition. The Osnaburgh factor, Nicol Finlayson, expressed his anxiety that "2/3 of Inds will go to Windy Lake if don't get ammunition"[76]. The post at "Windy Lake", or Windigo Lake, as it eventually became known, was established as an outpost of Fort Severn during the mid-1820's after Merry's House was vacated (Rich 1961 3:474). This post attracted those Indians who hunted to the north of Osnaburgh, especially the Cranes. When the post at Windy Lake was deserted in February 1833, the Cat Lake Indians along with some Cranes returned to trade at Osnaburgh[77]. During its short existence, the Windy Lake post was a thorn in the side of Osnaburgh and Lac Seul. According to the Lac Seul manager, Charles McKenzie, the Windy Lake factor, McKay, attracted

Indians who never were at any other post—save this place & Osnaburgh for these 25 years that I knew them 'tis also repeated that he traded with the *Cat Lake* Indians every winter—some of our Indians of Red Lake sent furs to trade by the Windy Lake Inds this last winter—which answers for the poor hunts these made & there not paying their debts here[78].

To the south of Osnaburgh lay Sturgeon Lake where the earliest inland Hudson's Bay post beyond Gloucester House was established in 1779[79]. It had long been a focal point in the interior for Northwest traders. After the coalition, a Hudson's Bay post was operated there as an outpost of Fort William in the Lake Superior District. The route from Lake Superior was difficult for supply boats, and it was, according to the Fort William factor, John Haldane, "rather a hard place to live at"[80]. There thus appears to have been some attempt to induce the Sturgeon Lake Indians to trade at either Nipigon or Osnaburgh during the early 1820's in hopes that the post could be abandoned without loss of trade. After the coalition it was only a winter post, being vacated during the summer. Although the Sturgeon Lake Indians were supposed to trade within the Lake Superior District at either Nipigon or Fort William, it seems they often frequented the Lac La Pluie (Rainy Lake) post, and also Osnaburgh and Lac Seul.

In the summer of 1828, due to difficulties in transporting supplies from Fort William, and to the Indians' apparent reluctance to have the place deserted, Sturgeon Lake post was transferred to the Albany District. It became an outpost of Lac Seul from which it was supplied under the direction of Charles McKenzie[81]. The policy of vacating the post in summer was continued, only Sturgeon Lake Indians now received their supplies during this period at Lac Seul.

A false report was spread in the summer of 1827 that Sturgeon Lake was to be abandoned. The result, according to Charles McKenzie, was that the Sturgeon Lake Indians were

scattered between five different Posts—viz—Fort William, Lac La Pluie, Lac Nipigon, Osnaburgh & Sturgeon Lake— They cannot blame the Indians—They told them that nobody were to winter on their lands—& broke down the crazy old house for nails & hinges[82].

Endeavours to retrieve the Sturgeon Lake Indians were made

with partial success. Some Indians continued to trade at Nipigon, while others were lured to the Lac La Pluie post and American posts with different trade policies, and where prices were cheaper. They also were reported to have trespassed on the lands of the Rainy Lake Indians where they destroyed many of the beaver lodges[83].

The Hudson's Bay post at Red Lake had been established from Osnaburgh to offset Northwest competition. When this ended, it was abandoned. However, when the Red Lake area became the last region where beaver and large game animals could be found, an outpost was again established from Lac Seul in the winter of 1828-29. By the spring of 1829, these animals had become depleted and the post was once more vacated. The Red Lake Indians subsequently traded at Lac Seul.

Finally, the Trout Lake post originally established in 1807 from Fort Severn was deserted in 1828, owing to the paucity of furs in the Severn District.

The termination of competition in 1821 in conjunction with the decline in furs and game operated to increase the dependence of Indians on the trading post. Their mobility was restricted as a result of the change to reliance on small game and the reduced number of trading locales.

Evidence that the traders now had the upper hand is apparent from a reading of the journals relating to the period immediately following the amalgamation of the companies. In 1822, for example, the Grand Coquin arrived at the Lac Seul post. Charles McKenzie's statement is eloquent:

I was well aware of his old Shams which have lost their wonted efficacy that nothing but a good hunt would answer now—that I told him so when I gave him debt— that I am neither a Crook or a Lyier as he used to call his former traders[84].

There can be no question that the Northern Ojibwa after 1821 were tied to the trading post under the altered conditions following the coalescence of the trading companies.

254

Although Ojibwa depended upon the post for certain necessities prior to 1821, they had not passed the critical point leading to total dependence. As I have shown, traders also relied heavily upon Indians for goods and services. Competition between the two companies provided an abundant distribution of trade items, some of which had become important to Ojibwa economy. However, it was not the trade goods alone that led to the subjection of the people, as has so often been stated (cf. Steward and Murphy 1956:336). As we have seen, the Indians of the following period received smaller quantities of trade goods, and even did without certain articles they had received formerly. Actually, it was the cheaply obtained materials *in combination* with an ample food supply consisting primarily of venison which maintained the self-respect and independence of the Osnaburgh Ojibwa throughout this period. It was only when the value of goods rose after the coalescence of the two companies and food resources became depleted, that the culmination point may be said to have been reached making Indians completely reliant on the trading post.

As the fur trade waned after 1810, Indians found it more and more difficult to procure the trade goods upon which they had come to depend. Augmenting the reliance of Indians on the post was the termination of competition with the Northwest Company in 1821 resulting in several policy changes: 1) the price of trade goods rose; 3) conservation policies were tested; 3) the ready barter system was introduced; and 4) outposts with little volume of trade were abandoned. Concomitant with the fur decline was a marked decrease in the food supply, in particular large game. Fish and hare proved inadequate to support large cohesive groups during the harsh northern winters, and tended to restrict Indians to regions where such game could be found. More time had to be devoted to food production at the expense of trapping. Although hare pelts provided a warm substitute for cervine hides, the troughs in the cycle of hare provenience often prevented Indians from obtaining enough to support their needs. They then had to rely on the post for such items as blankets, capots, twine, leather, guns and ammunition.

These changes are reflected in Ojibwa subsistence practices and social organization. In the following chapter we shall discuss the way in which historical and ecological factors operated to produce cultural changes in these relatively early times leading to subsequent conditions already discussed.

Footnotes

1. That its position was not accidental is indicated by the first factor, John Best, who in attempting to locate the spot for construction commented:

   > I intend to stop here untill I see if any Indians comes this way or not that can inform me if this is the right place or not . . . I am dubious of trying in case we should go out of the Indian track . . . (HBC Arch B155/a/1).

   Before the post was completed in October 1786, several groups of Ojibwa on their way to Gloucester House located 160 miles down the Albany River stopped and traded with Best.

2. HBC Arch B155/a/3. Again, in 1791, traders returned from Red Lake and Lac Seul nearly starved. They would never have survived had Indians not guided them back (HBC Arch B155/a/6).

3. HBC Arch B155/a/9.

4. HBC Arch B155/a/13.

5. Letter: from William Thomas, manager of Gloucester House to John Davis, manager of Osnaburgh House dated October, 1815 (HBC Arch B155/a/28).

6. HBC Arch B155/a/3.

7. HBC Arch B155/a/1.

8. HBC Arch B155/a/11.

9. HBC Arch B155/a/6.

10. HBC Arch B155/a/12.

11. HBC Arch B155/a/14.

12. HBC Arch B107/a/26.

13. HBC Arch B78/a/14. Robert Goodwin, manager of Osnaburgh wrote in 1792 that the Indian, Shewequenap, "made a

Feast of Geese and invited Mr. Clouston & Self to partake"
(HBC Arch B155/a/6). At Nipigon House in 1798, Jacob
Corrigal reported that an Indian brought a "whole moose and
divided amongst the three houses—Hudson's Bay Company,
Northwest Company, and XY Company" (HBC Arch
B149/a/7). The XY Company was a splinter group of the
Northwest Company which separated from the former about
1798 and rejoined it in November, 1804 (Innis 1962:245).

14. HBC Arch B155/a/1.

15. HBC Arch B107/a/5.

16. HBC Arch B155/a/11.

17. HBC Arch B155/a/5.

18. HBC Arch B155/a/14.

19. HBC Arch B155/a/6. The Martin's Falls manager, John
    Hodgson, reported a depletion of files and twine at the post
    in 1800: "the Inds told me they could not live without those
    articles and they must go to the Canadians or their family's
    would starve" (HBC Arch B123/a/3).

20. HBC Arch B155/a/1.

21. HBC Arch B155/a/1. References to these beaver coats are
    numerous in the early literature relating to the post. Nicol
    Finlayson, factor of Lac Seul in 1826, reported that the
    Indians arrived at the Cedar Lake outpost "clothed in beaver
    skins" (HBC Arch B10/a/3). This was at the time when most
    Indians had turned to other types of apparel.

22. HBC Arch B155/e/1.

23. HBC Arch B155/a/5.

24. HBC Arch B155/a/5.

25. HBC Arch B155/a/14. I have not been able to identify the
    location of this lake. However, it appears to have been some-
    where in the vicinity of Cat Lake (cf. James Sutherland's map
    HBC Arch B78/a/14).

26. Location unknown.

27. HBC Arch B78/a/13.

28. HBC Arch B211/a/1.

29. HBC Arch B155/a/3.

30. HBC Arch B155/a/3. Hudson's Bay Company traders fre-

quently referred to Northwest Company employees as "Pedlars", "Canadians", or "French Traders".

31. HBC Arch B155/a/4. Again, in the spring of 1791 many Indians who had been debted in the fall failed to appear when they heard the post lacked goods.

32. The term "gang" is used to refer to large groups of Indians who appeared together at the post. The organization of these groups is discussed in the next chapter.

33. HBC Arch B155/a/5.

34. HBC Arch B155/a/13. In 1794, Indians traded with the Northwesters for camp kettles lacking at Osnaburgh (HBC Arch B155/a/8).

35. Table 36 provides a list of items in stock at the Cat Lake post for the year 1790-91 made by John Best the factor there (HBC Arch B30/a/3). Since Cat Lake was supplied from Osnaburgh the inventory is probably typical for the area. Not only was there a wide variety of goods, but the quantity distributed to Indians was also large.

Table 36   Cat Lake Trade Supply Inventory: 1790

Bayonets	flints	razors
beads—several sizes	gartering	rings
blankets—3 types	glasses—2 types	shirts—4 types
boxes	gunpowder	shoes—3 types
bracelets	guns—3 sizes	shot—2 types
brandy	handkerchiefs	spoons
buttons	hatchets	stockings
chisels	hats	thread
cloth—8 types	kettles—7 sizes	tobacco
combs—3 types	knives—4 types	trap steel
duffle	lace—2 types	trunks
feathers	needles—3 types	twine—5 types
files	powder	vermillion
flannel	powder horns	waters red

36. HBC Arch B155/a/15.

37. HBC Arch B155/a/1. Also, (HBC Arch B155/a/9).

38. HBC Arch B155/a/11.

258

39. Although the exact location of the "Utchepoy Country" is not given, Goodwin may have been referring to the area to the southeast near Sault Ste. Marie (HBC Arch B155/a/4).

40. A band of Indians arrived in August 1890 who hadn't paid their debt according to Goodwin, but "There is no dealing with them and if I refuse them Powder & Shot they must go some where for a supply . . . " (HBC Arch B155/a/5).

41. HBC Arch B155/a/15.

42. HBC Arch B155/a/15.

43. HBC Arch B155/a/9.

44. HBC Arch B155/a/10.

45. HBC Arch B155/a/10.

46. HBC Arch B155/a/10.

47. In 1797, John Best related that one Hudson's Bay employee struck an Indian on the head with a knife when the latter was merely reaching for a piece of bread in the store. Had Best not treated him, he might have bled to death. In addition, the same employee broke the Indian's gun which Best replaced (HBC Arch B155/a/12). An Indian arrived from Lac Seul in June 1799 informing John MacKay of Osnaburgh that the Canadians had "robbed all his relations and stabed his old Brother . . . " (HBC Arch B155/a/14).

    In 1809, an incident occurred at Eagle Lake 40 miles south of Lac Seul which received attention at the time. Rich has described it:

    > There the Northwester Agneas Macdonell forcibly seized furs from Indians who came to trade at the Hudson's Bay post, and set to work to terrify the Indians and to show them they could hope for no protection from the Hudson's Bay men. He finally descended on the Hudson's Bay post with pistols and with drawn sabre and ran amuck there, severely wounding one or two men and chasing others into the river and into the woods, until John Mowat turned and shot him dead (Rich 1960 2:274).

48. HBC Arch B155/a/29.

49. HBC Arch B155/a/1.

50. HBC Arch B155/a/2.

51. HBC Arch B155/a/2.

52. HBC Arch B155/a/5.

53. HBC Arch B155/a/20.

54. HBC Arch B155/a/21.

55. HBC Arch B155/a/22.

56. HBC Arch B155/e/1.

57. HBC Arch B155/a/28.

58. HBC Arch B3/d/96-122; B155/d/1-6; B155/e/8 & 9.

59. HBC Arch B155/a/22.

60. HBC Arch B155/a/18.

61. HBC Arch B107/a/6.

62. HBC Arch B155/e/11.

63. HBC Arch B107/a/2.

64. HBC Arch B155/e/11.

65. HBC Arch B107/e/1.

66. Letter: John Davis to James Slater, manager of Osnaburgh House (HBC Arch B155/a/35).

67. HBC Arch B155/a/36.

68. HBC Arch B107/a/4.

69. HBC Arch B155/e/10.

70. HBC Arch B155/a/35.

71. HBC Arch B155/e/11.

72. HBC Arch B155/a/36.

73. HBC Arch B155/a/36.

74. HBC Arch B155/e/11.

75. HBC Arch B155/a/37.

76. HBC Arch B155/a/37.

77. HBC Arch B155/a/45.

78. HBC Arch B107/a/10.

79. HBC Arch B211/a/1.

80. HBC Arch B231/e/1.

81. HBC Arch B107/a/6.

82. HBC Arch B107/a/6.

83. According to J. D. Cameron of Lac La Pluie:

> the Indians of Sturgeon Lake in order to spare their own Lands in conformity with the advice given them comes and hunts on the hunting grounds belonging to L.L.P. [Rainy Lake] Indians and already have destroyed most of the Lodges left by our Indians for increas. Of this the L.L.P. Indians complained very bitterly this Spring . . . These Indians of Sturgeon Lake gives us more trouble and anxiety than our LLP. Indians as we are always labouring under the fear of some of them alipping accross the Line [International Boundary] and as there are many outlets into the Lake it is impossible to guard all. However as yet no one has escaped us (HBC Arch B105/a/7).

84. HBC Arch B107/a/2. James Slater of Osnaburgh wrote Edward Mowat of Cat Lake in 1823 telling him to debt only those Indians who deserved it (HBC Arch B155/a/34). The following year, John Davis of Lac Seul lectured Indians "on their indolence and furnished them only with a small quantity of ammunition to enable them to pay more debts" (HBC Arch B107/a/3).

Chapter Eight
Economy and Social Organization: 1780-1829

Introduction

The first part of this chapter is concerned with the social and economic arrangements of Ojibwa society under conditions of intense competition among traders (1780-1821) outlined in the previous chapter. More specifically it is concerned with how the quest for trade materials, food, and furs influenced group structure and property concepts. Also, I shall attempt to demonstrate that Ojibwa mobility under competitive conditions was more an effect of than a determinant for Northern Ojibwa organization rooted in an even earlier patrilineal clan organization (cf. Hickerson 1962a:76-80).

By the 1770's, there was large-scale trade in northwestern Ontario. Although a major centre of trade was Osnaburgh House after 1786, there were numerous other posts and outposts operated by the Hudson's Bay Company and the Northwest Company in the region. As we have seen, competition among traders fostered mobility among the Ojibwa who roved from post to post to take advantage of trade conditions. The abundance of game and furs also promoted mobility. However, it has been shown that as the fur trade waned after 1810, the Ojibwa found it more and more difficult to procure enough pelts to fulfil their needs at the Osnaburgh post. With the coalition of the Northwest Company and the Hudson's Bay Company, Indians found themselves indebted to a single company in an area drastically depleted of furs and game. It is to these changes in subsistence and social organization that I next turn. The importance of the change in the mode of subsistence from previous times cannot be underestimated as a primary factor producing dependence upon the trading post and individualism in social relations.

Finally, I shall discuss property concepts, particularly in regard to land tenure, as an indicator of the degree of collectivism/individualism present and the changes between 1780 and 1829.

Although the journals indicate that the basis of subsistence was large animals prior to the late 1810's, the Ojibwa relied upon a great variety of game depending upon the season of the year and climatic conditions.

In the summer Ojibwa would congregate at the post in sizable numbers, but the duration of their stay depended upon the availability of food. Often they starved in awaiting the crafts laden with trade goods[1]. After receiving supplies, groups would resort to lakeside fishing spots[2]. Women usually would set nets and preserve fish by smoking and drying the flesh over a slow fire. When venison was difficult to obtain, in some cases even men turned to setting nets although it must have hurt their pride. In a dialogue recorded between an Osnaburgh chief and the Northwest trader, Duncan Cameron, the Indian replied:

'The English always give me two nets every spring, but you never give your chiefs any. 'I replied that I would be sorry to despise my chiefs so much as to use them like old women in giving them nets to live on when they were such good hunters and could always maintain themselves like men with their guns. Therefore, instead of nets, I always gave them ammunition, which was a much dearer article, He answered that he got ammunition as well as them but was glad to eat fish now and then, moreover, the best hunters could not find animals to kill (Masson 1960 2:281).

Large game animals were sought in the fall, and also beaver and otter, both for meat and pelts. Once the snow grew deep, moose and caribou were hunted according to the trader Peter Grant, by making a circuit to the leeward of the trail until the hunter was in front of the animal (Masson 1960 2:341-42; Rogers 1962 C42). Women and children procured smaller animals such as hare, partridge and fish to supplement the larger game.

When the weather moderated in April, Indians would usually "hunt Beaver until the Geese fly"[3]. Large game animals were sought at this time also. Once small openings in the ice appeared at the mouths of creeks, ducks and geese were taken. During

May, Osnaburgh Indians resorted to the nearby sturgeon fisheries in the Albany River.

Although variety in the diet was important, the basis of subsistence during most of the year was large game. The Northwest trader at Lac La Pluie, Peter Grant, commented in 1804 that the meat of the moose "and that of the reindeer and bear constituted the greater part of their food" (Masson 1960 2:330). Grant later adds that the moose "may, indeed, be reckoned their staff of life, and a scarcity of moose in the winter season is sure to cause a very severe famine" (1960 2:341). In addition, moose and caribou hides were manufactured into clothing and thong for snowshoes, and probably also into snares and nets.

Large animals were also an important food source at the trading post. For example, William Thomas, factor of Osnaburgh in 1813, instructed George Budge at Moose Lake (perhaps Lake Savant),

If your Indians should hunt Moose and Deer in the spring as they usually do you will endeavour to procure as much dry meat as possible to bring here[4].

So long as large game was present hunting took precedence over trapping. For instance, in February 1797, John Best commented that the Indians about Osnaburgh "I believe is doing nothing but killing Deer"[5] instead of trapping.

Although it is commonly stated that moose only moved into the interior regions of Ontario in the late nineteenth century (cf. Rogers 1966a:112), documentary evidence indicates that they were present throughout the entire area. For example, at Martin's Falls in 1811, the factor Jacob Corrigal commented that it was a good winter for venison "the Indians having killed plenty both of Moose and Deer"[6]. Evidence from the journals relating to Trout Lake, Island Lake, Berens River, Red Lake, Cat Lake, Gloucester House and Henley House substantiates the importance of caribou and moose to Indian economy.

After 1815, reports of starvation in the Osnaburgh area grew frequent as big game became scarce. Prior to 1800, cases of starvation among Ojibwa were relatively rare and food shortages seem to have been due more to physical inabilities of hunters, or to climatic factors preventing hunting than to lack of animals. During the winter of 1789, the Cat Lake Indians were reported by John Best to be starving since "so much Snow fell in the fall that they cannot take their Beaver houses there's not one that has been in yet that could make themselves a Beaver Coat to keep them warm"[7]. Too much snow also prevented Indians from hunting caribou[8]. Starvation also occurred when Indians loitered about the Hudson's Bay post in the summer awaiting the arrival of trade materials[9]. Nevertheless, there appears to have been some cases of starvation among competent hunters during favourable climatic periods. One reason for this seems to have been due to the relatively large size of the winter hunting groups at this time. In April, 1790, Robert Goodwin stated that he was supporting a young lad, his wife, mother and two sisters, and a brother-in-law who belonged to a sick Indian's group: "being so numerous they separated. the young man is not able to maintain them all". There are numerous other references to these large families or *gangs* as they were sometimes called during this period[10].

When starving Indians did appear at the post, they were often given small quantities of flour, fish, or potatoes by the traders. In January 1805, Robert Goodwin reported that part of the Indian Tinnawabino's band "carried away and eat as much fish as would serve 20 men 10 days & only 3 Inds"[11]. In some cases starving Indians seem to have been encouraged by traders to fish with hooks and line through the ice, or to snare hare during the lean winter months[12]. On occasion, Indian hunters would leave older relatives, wives, or children at the post to be fed while they hunted[13].

When large animals became difficult to procure, either due to scarcity in later years or to unfavourable hunting conditions, hare became primary objects. In 1816, when hare pelts appear to have been traded at Osnaburgh, one woman brought 800 skins to the post[14]. Nevertheless, although small animals and fish often supplemented the larger ones and produced variety in the diet, they were always a poor substitute for the latter[15]. Until necessity forced men to set hare snares and fish nets during the 1820's or earlier, these activities were performed by women.

In summary, the primary source of food throughout most of the year for the Ojibwa during this period was big game, moose and caribou. It may be conjectured that a fairly widespread big game hunting pattern existed throughout the eastern Subarctic region shortly after the introduction of the fur trade, and other factors led to a permanency of the Ojibwa population in interior regions following the withdrawal of Cree westward. Leacock's point (1954:3-4) that large animals may have provided the basis of subsistence in the early contact period in Labrador seems to be congruent with the general pattern in the interior Ontario north-land prior to the 1820's. In that part of Ontario occupied by Ojibwa, big game provided the basis of group solidarity and relative independence. The continuous maintenance of large groups of Indians was contingent upon the availability of these animals, the pursuit of which required much mobility over large tracts of land.

Social Organization: 1780-1815

The early decades after the interior was settled by traders was characterized by great mobility occasioned by the food quest, traffic of European goods, and to a lesser extent the search for furs. These factors tended to maintain large cohesive and independent groups of Ojibwa whose structure was based, in part, upon an earlier more formally structured organization (cf. Hickerson 1962a:76-81). This seems to have been the case despite a rather small population density. As we shall see, there appear to have been fewer hunting groups which exploited large tracts of land communally.

Early demographic materials relating to the Osnaburgh post are scarce. The comparatively great amount of mobility of the hunters who had the option of trading at Northwest posts as well as Hudson's Bay posts tended to prevent the gathering of accurate census data. In his district report for 1814, Thomas Vincent said that there were about 70 Indians who had taken debt at Osnaburgh but many of these, "do not belong properly to the place and seldom if ever give all their hunts to one house"[16]. The Lac Seul trader, John Davis stated that there were 37 and 43 hunters trading at Osnaburgh in 1814 and 1815 respectively[17]. Davis, in his report for 1824 recorded that there were 38 hunters at Osnaburgh, 25 at Lac Seul, and 20 at Cat Lake, but a little later he said that Lac Seul and Osnaburgh combined had a total of 102 hunting Indians[18]. Hence, the population in the Osnaburgh-Lac Seul region seems to have remained fairly constant between 1814 and 1824. One reason for this seems to have been a serious measles epidemic in the area in 1819 which, according to Charles McKenzie, "carried off 76 Seuls from this post [Lac Seul] alone—and left us Seven Hunters"[19].

By far the most crucial factor in determining group size in northern Ontario was the availability of plentiful food. This fact seems to be of universal importance in maintaining populations. The Montagnais, for instance, with whom the Jesuit Father Le Jeune wintered in 1633-34, were reported to have moved camp over twenty times in search of large game during the season, and the group splintered and reunited several times according to the facility with which moose were obtained[20]. Speck and Eiseley (1942:219) have noted the importance of large game animals in maintaining group size; and Dunning, for the Pekangikum Ojibwa, has stressed the importance of ecological factors in determining the size and territorial extent of the cooperating unit (1959a:48). Referring to the contemporary Mistassini Cree, Rogers states that

the caribou, is migratory and gregarious, but the presence of this type of game significantly influences group structure. Although caribou herds are small, effective hunting requires the utilization of all available manpower. A single hunter or a two-man team would be relatively ineffective in exploiting these animals. A tendency to increase group size is therefore encouraged (1963b:80).

Thus, according to Rogers (pers. comm.), the number of cervines taken per capita among the contemporary Round Lake Ojibwa increases with the number of men who hunt together. That is, where four or five men hunt together, the average number of moose taken per hunter is greater than when only two men hunt together. Maximum efficiency is attained when about six or seven men are involved. Beyond this number the per capita kill declines[21].

The actual size of hunting groups during the late eighteenth century is difficult to determine although there is little doubt that they were large, probably numbering between 20 and 35 persons. Robert Goodwin remarked in 1788 upon the arrival of the Indian, Tinnawabino and gang at Osnaburgh: "a numberous family indeed. three wives and 17 children"[22]. In 1796, the Osnaburgh factor, James Sutherland reported the arrival of "Capt. Utchechagu and but part of his numerous family 15 in number"[23]. As mentioned, this Indian had 23 children (see footnote 10). One of the largest groups that frequented Osnaburgh during the late eighteenth century was headed by an Indian named Captain Shewequenap, himself the son of a former leader, Nonosecash[24]. Between 1780 and 1805, he appeared annually at the trading post (Gloucester House and later Osnaburgh) with from twelve to fourteen canoes[25]. Assuming that his entire hunting group arrived at the post, and that each canoe held three persons, it would mean that his band averaged about 35 persons. The band over which Shewequenap was treated as leader seems to have altered little numerically over a 25-year period.

The region about Sturgeon Lake appears to have been occupied by a Captain Caucaukes and band who was reported to have had a great deal of influence among traders and, according to John Kipling in 1782 "had his Clothing sent yearly from the Commander at Machillimakinac"[26]. Between Sturgeon Lake and Lac Seul hunted another large band headed by the Indian, Metweash[27]. Captains Metweash and Caucaukes frequently arrived together with their bands from the Sturgeon Lake area suggesting that the two groups were closely linked through ties of kinship.

The location of these hunting groups or "tribes" as they were called by traders is given by Thomas Vincent in the Osnaburgh district report for 1814:

The Cranes and the Suckers hunt to the Northward of Osnaburgh House between that and Trout Lake where there is a settlement from Severn . . . The Loons hunt to the Eward toward Lake St. Anns, the Moose and Sturgeons to the S.W. and the Kingfishers and Pelicans toward Lake Winnipeg to the NW of Osnaburgh[28].

It is likely that these groups were the remnants of clans or lineage segments of clans, although the actual organization of the groups is difficult to discern. All the groups are given clan names with the exception of the Cranes. The group symbol of the Cranes does not seem to have been the Crane but rather the Sucker. The title Crane was derived from the name of the leader, an old Indian called Crane. During the late eighteenth century the Suckers were headed by the Indian Tinnawabino, or the Tinpot as he was sometimes called. John McKay stated in 1799 that the Tinpots and Cranes were "real Brothers, and their lands whether they are called Tinpots or Cranes are all the same"[29]. In March the following year, the band was reported to have had a pitched battle with some Martin's Falls or Severn Indians:

> The Crane told me that his Brother Tinnewabano & Gang is gone to Sandy Lake, on account of the murder he committed last fall; & the Crane himself is under the greatest apprehensions for his own safety as he is well assured that the injured party, will make no distinctions between Tinpot & any of his relations[30].

In summary, it appears that traders were giving clan designations to hunting groups except in the case of the Cranes. Although it appears that most males belonging to these clan-named groups were of the clan symbolizing them, evidence indicates that some groups contained males of other clans as well. It is also evident that some groups were named after the leader. In order to analyse group organization it is necessary to refer to Table 39 which is a summary of the clan affiliation of hunters trading at Osnaburgh compiled by John Davis in his district reports for 1815 and 1816[31].

The terms "tribe", "gang", "hunting group", and "band" need some explanation. They appear to have been applied to the same unit of social structure—those persons who continually resided together throughout the year. During the late eighteenth century, these groups numbered from about 20 to 35 persons. The traders' use of the title "tribe", while sometimes being synonymous with hunting group, had additional connotations. A tribe might consist of more than one hunting group. For instance, the Crane band belonged to the Sucker tribe which appears to have been com-

Table 39   Number of Hunters per Winter Settlement: 1815-16

Tribe	Number of Male Hunters	
	1815	1816
Eagle	3	5
Sucker	2	11 and sons
Crane	10 and sons	Included with Suckers
Sturgeon	5	4
Deer	3	9
Loon	9	9
Moose	2 and sons	2 and sons
Pelican	3	2
Fisher	—	1
	37	43

posed of several bands occupying the territory from just west of Martin's Falls northwestward to Sandy Lake, a distance of nearly 400 miles.

The animal names of these tribes suggest that they had a clan origin although some scholars might argue that they were simply animal-named groups. There are, however, several clues to suggest that the former interpretation is correct. For one thing, all the names of groups in the Osnaburgh area, in 1800, are totemic patrilineal designations in the twentieth century. There are other clues as we shall see.

The above-mentioned Cranes may pose a problem to the issue of clan organization. Rogers, who conducted extensive field research among the Round Lake Indians who are the descendants of the Cranes of 1800, was able to find no evidence of clans and stated that they always lacked them (1962:B4). Although the term "Sucker" (the tribal name for several groups one of which was the Cranes) may merely have been an appellation without several of the attributes usually associated with clans, the evidence is not at all clear. Rogers reports from Indian testimony that formerly the Round Lake Indians formed several groupings called *nintipe.ncike.win* each headed by a leader (1962:B82). The kinship structure of a group was determined by a number of principles:

> The first is that of patrilineal descent. A man will be leader of his male descendents, but this is limited to three generations. A second principle involves the solidarity of brothers. An older brother is responsible for his younger full brothers and their descendents. . . . A third principle involves the dependency of women.

Rogers adds that sometime in the past, the *nintipe.ncike.win* was equivalent to the band with political, economic and religious functions. Finally, these groups were said to have been exogamous (1962:B85). In sum, they certainly appear to have functioned very much like lineages only without the totemic connotations.

Viewing Rogers' data in terms of the historical reports of 1800, it seems that the Cranes formed a single band during these early times. In turn, the Cranes along with Tinnewabano's band and perhaps two or three others constituted the Sucker Tribe. If the "tribe" was then the exogamous unit, as it may well have been, then other "tribes" such as the Deers and Loons were likely exogamous also. If these assumptions are correct, then it is strong support for an even earlier corporate clan organization among the Ojibwa as Hickerson has argued.

It would appear that the majority of the males belonging to the Crane group were Suckers. As noted, the leader was an old man named Crane. All the remaining males in the group appear to have been sons of this old man. For example, the Osnaburgh factor, Jacob Corrigal, in March, 1804, feared an attack on the post.

> The old Crane and 14 of his Sons being within 30 miles of the House ever since last January[32].

In September, 1803, eight of the sons threatened to pull down the stockades and steal the brandy. Evidence that the Cranes were a unified band at least until 1810 is indicated in the post journals where the names of the same individuals consistently reappear together. John Davis, in his district report for 1815, listed the

Osnaburgh Indians and added comments after the name of each Indian hunter. Concerning a father and son, he commented: "They and all the Cranes hunt to the Northward"[33].

In 1815, the three men listed as Eagles consisted of a father and two sons who hunted with the Cranes. The same three men are listed as Eagles in 1816. The two additional men recorded as Eagles for that year, being brothers, were listed as the two Suckers in 1815. They hunted together between Osnaburgh and Gloucester. In 1784, James Sutherland came upon a grave about 30 miles east of Lake St. Joseph with a British flag over it and evidently the clan symbol: "he is of the Eagle Tribe"[34]. Duncan Cameron also discusses (Masson 1960 2:246-47) clan symbols left on travel routes and on graves. In the 1817 district report, the members of the Eagle group were called Snakes. One of the Indians was called Keenapick, apparently the leader[35]. The term *kee-na-pik* means snake in Ojibwa.

Male membership in the Sturgeon group in 1815 consisted of two sets of brothers who were recorded as being related. Possibly they were brothers-in-law. One brother was listed as belonging to the Deer tribe the following year, while the other remained in the Sturgeon group. Should the two sets of brothers have been linked through marriage, this in itself is strong evidence for the bilaterality of the group. Also, the tribal designation, Sturgeon, would then merely have been a convenient term to describe the group whose core members consisted mainly of males belonging to the Sturgeon clan. In the 1817 report, the Sturgeons were called Crows. They were probably the descendants of Caucaukes since *kakakay* means raven in Ojibwa. As noted, the Sturgeon band hunted to the south and southwest of Osnaburgh toward Lac Seul.

The Deer band was reported as being composed of three brothers in 1815 who hunted to the southeast of Osnaburgh. Five of the six additional members in 1816 were not recorded the previous year because they traded at the Northwest post on Sturgeon Lake. They were the Indian Metweash and his four sons who hunted together between Sturgeon Lake, Moose Lake (Lake Savant) and Lac Seul. In the 1817 report, one man was listed as being a Deer who in the 1815 and 1816 lists appeared as a Loon.

Although the majority of the members of the Pelican clan

hunted to the northwest of Osnaburgh probably in the Berens River-Lake Pekangikum region, there was one Indian of the Pelican clan named Moose who headed a hunting group in the Lake Savant (then called Moose Lake) area 60 miles to the south of the post. In 1815 the group was reported to have been large. The core members included Moose, his son, and his son's sons. In 1800, the Osnaburgh factor stated that this group consisting of "the Young Loon, two Mooses Wives, Mothers, Sisters and Children arrived here to camp, they formed 8 Canoes"[36]. Although not stated, it seems the Young Loon may have been married to one or more of Moose's daughters. The Young Loon was killed in 1802 by a son of Moose[37].

Membership in the Loon tribe which hunted to the southeast of Osnaburgh remained the same in 1815 and 1816. No relationships were given.

The Moose tribe from 1815 to 1817 was made up of a man, his three sons and a fifth individual. They were also known as Macimmies and their hunting grounds lay halfway between Lac Seul and Osnaburgh.

Whether affines were permanent members, or merely men fulfilling bride service obligations is impossible to determine. Although it is assumed that patrilocal residence was the ideal, a retention of the pre-contact form, others (Rogers 1963a) have argued that bilateral groups existed in aboriginal times and residence is considered to have been more a function of expediency than rigid rules of prescription. I am arguing here, in contrast, that mobility in the quest of furs, food and trade goods in a new environmental setting within the Boreal Forest was operating (and had been for nearly a century) to produce bilateral bands. My interpretation of the processes and the results is predicated upon the assumption that the early contact Ojibwa groups were patrilineal descent groups (cf. Hickerson 1962a, 1970); and that the evidence from the late eighteenth and early nineteenth centuries, when construed in terms of the processes of change, supports this view. It is suggested, then, that while there was a gradual dispersal of clan members among different groups, the corporateness of the clan segments was exhibited through the Feast of the Dead ceremonies upon a leader's death; the practice of hereditary leadership whereby the eldest son inherited his father's position; the communal sharing patterns among group members; and the unified aggressiveness of groups toward traders and also other Indian groups. Again, until after 1810, most (in some cases all) males of each group belonged to the same clan.

While the criteria which I list as evidence for clan corporateness might merely reflect group identity patterns (Richard Preston, pers. comm.), the contemporary ethnographic evidence combined with the historic materials extending over three centuries of contact is strong support for the view that these animal-named groups of the early nineteenth century were clan remnants in the process of change. Although Eggan has suggested (1955:527) that the Ojibwa clan system may be recent, since late nineteenth century clans lacked clearly defined functions and corporate possessions, the historical evidence already presented discussing the harsh conditions of the last century could certainly account for this. In contrast, the data from the seventeenth and eighteenth centuries can and do fit the view that corporate patrilineal clans are pre-contact. Smith and Rogers, however, argue (1973) that since Ojibwa clans have limited corporate functions, they are "best viewed as a patrilateral extension of bilateral kinship resulting from the dispersal of the original Ojibwa nations or regional named bands following the impact of the Iroquois, the introduction of the fur trade, and expansion". Since, they supply no supportive historical evidence, this interpretation is both conjectural and not congruent with the existing historical data presented here and elsewhere (cf. Hickerson 1962a, 1970). If clans did develop in postcontact times, it must be asked why the Cree, who also shifted westward, lacked them. Indeed, Lewis H. Morgan (White 1959:111-13, 120) could not detect any evidence of clans among the Upper Red River Cree (which seems to have worried him), yet had no difficulty in collecting data on Ojibwa clans in the same region. If one argues that this was because the Cree had a different history, then one must explain what these differences were. If, however, one argues from an ecological vantage point, then the origin of late eighteenth century patrilineality must be sought in the earlier records (as it shall be). In conclusion, although the question of clans is still open for further debate, the evidence, at present, suggests an earlier descent group organization which was retained in modified form into the early nineteenth century and even into the twentieth century in a very attenuated manner.

274

During the early nineteenth century, it would appear that the manner of naming groups was also in a state of flux. Just as the Eagle band came to be called after the name of its leader, Snake, and one band of the Suckers after the leader, Crane, so a number of other hunting groups took on new names. For example, one Osnaburgh captain was named Cotton Shirt and traders referred to his group as the Cotton Shirt's band (Masson 1960 2:227).

Although primogeniture characterized the inheritance of leadership, and as we shall see, may have been related to the distribution of exploitive endeavours by other clan members within territorially delimited regions, the same principle may have been operative in the dispersal of clan members, since leaders had little authority over their group. Cases where members of the same group would trade at two separate posts are frequent. For example, the Moose and his sons traded at different posts. In 1799, John McKay commented that "it is somewhat extraordinary that I cannot Draw the young Moose from the other House"[38]. The purpose of trading at two different houses may have been to compare prices. Duncan Cameron, in 1804 stated that a trade chief had influence over his band only so long as he could secure goods from the traders. One chief even had his nose bitten off by a son-in-law (Masson 1960 2:278). Thomas Vincent, chief factor for the Albany District, in his report for Osnaburgh in 1814 stated:

The Indians in this District have no Chiefs or Leaders nor do they pay any respect to one more than another; those who make good hunts are generally noticed by the Traders in order to excite the rest to be more industrious[39].

The Indian Shewequenap, nevertheless, was reported in 1781 by John Kipling of Gloucester House, to have had "great influence with his Country Men"[40]. Twenty-four years later in 1805, Robert Goodwin was still able to state that Shewequenap was "the chief Captain at Osnaburgh"[41]. During the period of intensive competition these trade chiefs had a good deal of influence over traders and could often determine where outposts were to be established. In 1787, Goodwin reported that Shewequenap "says this Lake is his & we must not affront him he being so near the

Pedlars"[42]. Indeed, there are frequent references to his absconding to the Northwest posts with his furs after having received debt from the Hudson's Bay Company.

A leader who was a good hunter and who was proficient in exploiting traders probably possessed superior supernatural powers. The source of this power resided with one's guardian spirit attained through the vision quest. The efficacy of the spirit helper was demonstrated by the success of the leader. Such individuals were polygynists whose authority was based partly on fear (cf. Dunning 1959a:180-82). For example, Charles McKenzie of Lac Seul reported in 1828 that the Indian Baptist Vincent formerly had eight wives and more children than he could remember[43]. Another Indian, the Grand Coquin, arrived at the Lac Seul post in September 1823 followed by a large band of women and children[44]. The last two Indians mentioned were described as the principal leaders at Lac Seul, and they had a mutual dislike for each other. The Grand Coquin, who died in 1829, was described by McKenzie as a sensible man, and a great hunter, yet he was more dreaded than esteemed by other traders and Indians[45]. Individuals possessing such qualities would most likely be those who also had several wives.

Collectivism was also exhibited through aggressive behaviour toward traders and other Indian groups. The group headed by the Indian Crane was particularly notorious. In 1804, Jacob Corrigal stated that the Cranes had arrived at Martin's Falls

> to murder us or some Indians belonging to this place ...
> The Indians who arrived from below would not drink at the house on their account, but set off immediately down the river[46].

Corrigal added that the Cranes carried their guns beneath their blankets and one of them chased him with a cutlass in one hand and a bayonet in the other. The Hudson's Bay employees escaped with their lives only by threatening the band with two swivel canons. In February, 1815 the Cranes arrived at the Lake Attawapiscat outpost and began destroying the property belonging to both the Hudson's Bay Company and the Northwest Company. They stabbed the Northwest trader in the chest, removed the Hudson's Bay trader William Thomas' coat by force, and killed three dogs[47]. Thomas remarked that the Cranes "are universally detested and feared by the other Indians to that degree that many of them are afraid to go any distance to hunt"[48]. In September 1816, they descended on Osnaburgh and proceeded to hack the palisade gate down. The Hudson's Bay employees were forced to shoot at them to drive them off[49].

Aggressiveness seems to have involved whole groups of Indians rather than individuals[50]. In 1778, John Kipling of Gloucester House reported that Metweash had "been at War this Summer with the Natives on Lake St. Ann [Nipigon] . . . and have killed a great Number . . . Men Women and Children"[51]. In the summer of 1786 many Indians southwest of Lac Seul including Metweash had gone to war with the "Poat" (Dakota?) Indians who were reported to have been encroaching on their lands[52].

Changes after 1810

Before the 1810's, the basic food source for the Osnaburgh House Ojibwa had been large game, moose and caribou. The hides of large animals were also important in providing clothing and snow-shoe netting. So long as the Ojibwa were able to obtain food and clothing in abundance from subsistence activities, they could survive relatively comfortably. Also numerous cervines supported large cohesive groups of perhaps 25 to 30 people throughout the year. However, by the mid-1810's there is evidence that the large game animals were growing scarce. In 1815, the Osnaburgh trader John Davis, wrote:

> The condition of most of the Indians is comparatively good though large Famalys scarce ever escaped starvation at some time through the Winter which is owing in a great measure to the decreas of Beaver Moose and Deer. . . . The Cranes only are an exception in this respect their country is better stocked with large animals[53].

Prior to 1813, there appear to have been comparatively few deaths due to starvation. However, death and starvation became increasingly frequent after this date. This was primarily due to the decrease in large game animals which appears to have been first felt to the south of Osnaburgh. George Budge at Moose Lake (Lake Savant) that year wrote William Thomas, factor of Osnaburgh, stating he encouraged the Indians to hunt meat:

> but I have not seen any since my arrival nor do I expect any. I never seed starving Indians till this Year they are really pitiful to see[54].

That winter a father and his two children died from starvation. During succeeding years, on occasion, Indians are reported to have been forced to eat their beaver skins[55].

The earliest case of cannibalism in the Osnaburgh vicinity that I was able to discover in the records, occurred in 1816. A woman belonging to a large family ate five people including her husband and three sons[56]. A possible earlier case was mentioned in 1814[57].

As time passed after the mid-1810's, cases of starvation became increasingly frequent among the Osnaburgh Ojibwa as the large game supply dwindled. By the early 1820's even the comparatively autonomous Cranes who hunted to the north of Osnaburgh began to experience the deficiencies. The decline of this band, once the most feared and independent group in the area, was indeed dramatic and is well documented in the journals and district reports. Some of the changes are worth recording since they probably illustrate what had happened to other bands, only several years earlier.

The first attested case of cannibalism occurred in March 1824. A Crane starved so much that winter that he killed and devoured his mother and daughter[58].

In January 1826, Nicol Finlayson of Lac Seul reported that the

> Cranes, who were wont to be the best hunters, are doing nothing. they lived in a great measure on big animals, their hunting grounds are now so destitute of them that they in consequence starve and those who have been in the habit of hunting these animals can scarcely be brought to fish or go to the rabbit grounds and live ... Mr. Slater and I have

278

endeavoured to oblige them to fish by giving them nets in debt[59].

Before that winter was over no less than seven Cranes had starved to death. The previous fall three had drowned when a canoe upset. The death of ten Cranes as well as another family in the same region must have had profound effects upon group solidarity, and probably accelerated the atomization of the Crane band. It has been noted that the traders Slater and Finlayson had encouraged the Cranes to pursue fish and rabbits prior to the decimation by starvation. After such a catastrophe little encouragement was needed. Finlayson, factor of Osnaburgh in 1826-27, recorded in April 1827, that the Cranes had made much better hunts. As a Crane told Finlayson:

they are living far off he says at a fishing place all winter— he has not killed a single Deer [caribou] the whole season, tho these animals were once numerous on their grounds— they are obliged now to have recourse to rabbits and fish— the very few of them could snare one of the former animals two years ago—necessity he says taught them to *choke* rabbits as he terms it—and had they been wise last year and gone to a rabbit ground so many of them would not have starved to death[60].

The same year that the Cranes starved, the Indians to the south of Osnaburgh whose lands had become depleted of large animals several years earlier lived comparatively well on hare[61].

The change in Indian economy by 1827, then, had become widespread. Fish and hare provided the basis of subsistence, and it had become impossible for the members of large groups to remain together continuously throughout the year. Many hare were needed to sustain a family even for a short period. Charles McKenzie writing at a much later time, in 1852, reported one adult Indian "at his Tent doing nothing—that Ates 12 Rabbits daily!"[62]. Fish in the winter months also, contributed to a meagre existence. McKenzie, in the summer of 1822, stated that 60 fish were required daily to support the 12 men, 5 women, and 17 children who were residing at the Lac Seul post[63]. It is little wonder that it was the *large* game animals which were preferred!

At Round Lake, during the year 1858-59, 88 moose taken by Indians provided an estimated 35,200 pounds of meat; whereas 7,500 hare produced only 11,200 pounds (Rogers 1966a:100).

Despite the decrease in large game, they continued to be the focus of the Indians' search for subsistence, even though more and more time had to be devoted to hunting them—and this distraction was reflected in the amount of time spent trapping. Further, the search for large game was blinding some Indians to the potential small game resources which would at least keep them from starving. In the writings of such traders as Charles McKenzie, Nicol Finlayson, John Davis and others, we see a humanitarian concern expressed in their attempts to encourage the Indians to turn to fishing and the snaring of hare. An example of this is in a report by Davis at Lac Seul in 1824:

> few large animals could be killed though many of the Indians employed their whole time in going after them consequently the trade suffered particularly in Martins, want of the first necessary of life is the source of most of the miseries of the poor Indian as well as of great injury to the trade in these parts. could the Indians be brought to dwell more at one place and employ less of their time in seeking the Deer and Moose they might be induced to cultivate the soil[64].

Indeed, one Osnaburgh Indian decided to try cultivating a garden. According to James Slater in May 1825; "old Moose . . . wanted Potatoes for Seed and he got 14 gallons. he is ben a hunter this 70 years back and now is to try to be a farmer"[65].

Another effect of the diminution of large animals not mentioned previously was the rather sudden deficiency of hide used for snowshoes and clothing. As early as 1817, John Davis mentioned that two Indians arrived at Osnaburgh wanting

> leather for snow shoes and other purposes for which these two Indians cut up 15 Beaver skins and part of these 15 skins was cut in thongs in lieu of twine (of which we had none to give them in the fall) for Rabbit snares and Fish Hooks[66].

The scarcity of moose and caribou was being felt in all regions except north of Osnaburgh by this date. In 1823, McKenzie mentioned that an Indian arrived who walked "upon two pairs of boards for snowshoes & his feet wrapted up in Rabbitskins & old rags of cloth instead of shoes"[67]. This Indian had nearly starved to death for lack of leather so McKenzie gave him both shoes and snowshoes.

Indians without snowshoes and proper footwear could not travel to hunt or trap. They then were not able to pay their debts. Yet if they were forced to cut up their furs, they were in the same predicament. Thus, instead of Indians supplying traders with leather as had been the case formerly, the latter now provided the hide. By 1828, when large animals were virtually extinct the situation had become endemic. In his annual report, Charles McKenzie described the Lac Seul Indians as being so miserable that hunting furs was out of the question; self-preservation was the only consideration:

> Some of them were under the necessity of making shoes of their Cloth Capots & Capots of their Blankets in order to even hunt their Rabbit snares—Snow Shoes they had none but pieces of Boards to walk on[68].

By the 1820's, Lac Seul Indians and those south of Osnaburgh were dependent, in part, on Euro-Canadian items for clothing. Cervine hides, once of considerable importance in the manufacture of apparel, had become too rare to clothe the Indians of the region. If the Ojibwa failed to receive blankets and capots, they were often forced to cut up furs in order to survive. For example, in 1822, Charles McKenzie sent an Indian a blanket and some cloth to prevent him from making clothing of his furs[69].

The Cranes were the last group who were able to clothe themselves in cervine hides. In 1825, James Slater of Osnaburgh stated that this band

> Killed a few deer which they Cloath themselves with and could they Live without ammunition, guns, Hatchets etc they would not hunt one skin[70].

Two years later, Nicol Finlayson, then of Osnaburgh reported that these same Cranes could not clothe themselves in leather as they were wont to do—were quite dispirited and of course were indifferent about hunting [trapping] [71].

After 1816, Indians appear to have been discouraged by traders from using beaver and other pelts for clothing. Competition assured Ojibwa ample supplies of cloth, and this in combination with caribou hide provided protection against the cold. When the large animals became scarce, and the value of trade goods increased after competition ceased in 1821, traders encouraged Indians to use hare skins which were of no trade importance. In 1827, for example, Nicol Finlayson "endeavoured to explain to them the necessity they lay under to procure rabbit skins to keep them from the severity of the winter"[72]. However, Indians resisted snaring hare so long as large game was available. Until necessity forced the Ojibwa to pursue small game, it was considered beneath the dignity of a hunter to concern himself with hare. For instance, Thomas Vincent in writing about the Lac Seul Indians in 1825 said:

> their former pride and ambition to excel each other is vanished. A young man may now be seen wearing an old tattered Rabbit Skin garment that a few years ago he would have considered a degrading covering for a helpless old Woman[73].

Comparative materials would indicate that the change in dress was occurring throughout northwestern Ontario during the 1820's. For instance, Robert Cummings, factor of the Trout Lake post, asserted that if the Indians could not find any caribou "they have nothing but Rabbits Skins for Both Coats and Likewise Shoese"[74]. In summary, the rabbit skin parka, so important and characteristic of Ojibwa culture in later years seems not to have been of major importance in earlier times. It, like many other features, appears to have been a product of the fur trade.

By 1827 the large animals had been virtually exterminated everywhere in northwestern Ontario. In 1828 and in the early fall of 1829, Charles McKenzie reported that there were a few moose near Red Lake, and that many Indians had congregated there to hunt them. Within a few months the moose were gone. In October 1833, the last recorded moose was killed in the Osnaburgh-Lac Seul area. It was such a rare sight that McKenzie commented: "whence he came no one knows—Strange to see a Moose Deer in this quarter for some years past"[75].

The primary reason for the decline of large game animals appears to have been overhunting. So long as the predominant economic pursuit of male Ojibwa involved cervine hunting, such animals would disappear comparatively rapidly, especially after the gun was introduced. Duncan Cameron has already been cited to this effect while comparative data support such an explanation. One band of Mistassini Montagnais were reported by Rogers to have exhausted the game within a restricted area within two or three weeks (Rogers 1963b:78). In the Archival documents there are numerous references to traders encouraging Indians to procure both meat and parchment for the posts. Hides were used to make snowshoes and to wrap fur packs[76]. An additional factor responsible for the decimation was noted in 1825 by Charles McKenzie who wrote that a large area from the Winnipeg River to Osnaburgh was devastated by forest fires. Such an area yielded no protection either in summer or winter to animals[77].

Hence, by the late 1820's the change in subsistence patterns had been completed. Hare and fish became the primary source of livelihood and remained so for the next six decades. In 1830, Charles McKenzie summed up the situation:

> 'tis not many years past since they have taken entirely to their present way of living. Any young man would think himself disgraced even be seen setting a Net to catch fish or a Snare for a Rabbit & when recourse was had to such means in the times of scarcity, it was left entirely to the women's province, Yet both young & old men lean their assistence now, without considering it a disgrace, so strong is the call of nature over prejudice[78].

Abundant evidence to support McKenzie's statement can be found in Archival documents relating to other posts including Osnaburgh.

The increasing dependence upon European goods, although an important factor responsible for the splitting of groups into family units, for trapping purposes, was not the only one. The changes in subsistence patterns as well as the termination of competition in 1821, resulted in a marked decrease in the mobility of the Indians who were forced to live in more confined regions where smaller non-migratory animals could be found. Winter hunting groups were necessarily smaller. This seems not to have been necessarily conducive to improved trapping, however, as Leacock seems to have assumed (1954:8-9). As stated by Charles McKenzie in 1827:

> Fish and Rabbits became the Chief & only food of the natives which binds them to certain spots where these are to be found in greater abundance so that they (the natives) have destroyed all the Furred Animals within a wide range of these places. Were there large animals to enable the Indians to live & rove in the forests as formerly no doubt they collect a number of small furs such as Martins, Cats, & Otters in the season when these are of most value but the miserable state of the Country not admits of this as they cannot live where these animals abound particularly the Martins[79].

Not only did the change in subsistence lead to a reduction in mobility; it also resulted in a decline in respect relations by younger Indians for their elders. According to Nicol Finlayson, in 1828, the Indians were obliged to remain in the rabbit grounds where they were opening up their fish nets for snares. Consequently they starved in the summer as well as the winter and this was the reason why they

> fly upon everything they can catch even beavers of a span long—this can scarcely be prevented, for they are so depraved that there is no dependence to be put on anything they say, even the Father of a family is treated with contempt by the younger branches of the family[80].

With some difficulty it was possible to reconstruct the size and composition of the winter settlements under altered environmental conditions. A breakdown by settlement is presented in Table 40[81].

Table 40 Osnaburgh Winter Settlements: 1828

Settlement by "Tribal" Destination	Hunters	Women	Male Children	Female Children	Orphans	Widows	Total
Crane #1	5	6	6	10	5		32
Crane #2	7	7	6	5	3		28
Crane #3	6	3	2	5	3		19
Loon	5	5	15	12		1	38
Pelican	6	9	2	4	2		23
Deer #1	3	4	12	2		1	22
Deer #2	6	9	11	5	2		33
Moose	8	11	10	13	1		43
Sturgeon	5	6	6	13			30
Cotton Shirts (Sturgeon?)	4	10	3	7	1		25
	55	70	73	76	17	2	293

The evidence presented in Table 40 suggests several things. First, it indicates that hunting groups such as the Cranes, Deer and Sturgeon who in 1800 had formed single bands, had split into two or more winter settlements by the 1820's. This was primarily due to changes in subsistence patterns and trade conditions. Second, it would appear, although the evidence is by no means clear, that the population had increased significantly which may have been a factor which either promoted fission, or occurred as a result of it. Hare, it would seem, can actually support a larger population despite hardships in acquiring enough of them, provided families remain dispersed for given periods. Finally, as fission occurred among groups whose segments scattered and grew numerically, postmarital residence became a matter of expediency.

Where before 1810, the Cranes formed a single winter settlement, by 1828, they appear to have splintered into three separate groups. The core of the first Crane settlement consisted of five hunters, one of whom was an old man and another, a youth. One man and his son (the youth) appear to have belonged to the Pelican clan whereas the rest of the Cranes were Suckers.

The second group of Cranes consisted of seven hunters two of whom were old men "who go together till they are separated by starvation"[82]. The third group numbering only 19 people appears to have been more mobile perhaps due to the smaller size since "they were nigh the Big Fall last year in search of dear but killed none till they returned to their own lands when they were more successful"[83]. All the Cranes hunted north of Osnaburgh about halfway to Trout Lake.

In 1815 it was reported that the Loons hunted to the east of Osnaburgh. In 1828 the hunters consisted of two older men and their three adult sons. In addition there were 15 male children. It seems that all the males in the Loon group may have belonged to the Loon clan: "these Indians are loons by tribe and by nature"[84].

One of the Loons was a brother to the Indian, Whisky. During the winter, the latter's wives returned to their premarital settlement, the Pelicans, since the large number of women among the latter group made it difficult for them to hunt. When the Moose's son arrived from the settlement at Paskogagan Lake in April, Finlayson stated that it was impossible for Moose's son to hunt "having to look out for his father, mother aunt besides three of Whisky's wives, his sisters and their children who always winter with them"[85]. Actually, it may be inaccurate to designate this group "Pelicans" since the only certain members of the Pelican clan are Moose and his son, the other males seem to belong to the Loon or Deer clan. Moose is reported to have been the father-in-law of one hunter. However, in 1828, the leader and chief provider was Moose's son.

The members of the Deer clan appear to have separated into two contiguous settlements by 1828. The core of the first settlement was composed of three brothers, sons of the deceased Sturgeon Lake chief, Metweash (Mataiash). During the autumn this group hunted about halfway to Sturgeon Lake "and to the Nwd of this after the middle of the winter"[86]. The second Deer group hunted further north and east almost halfway to Martin's

Falls. Four of the hunters were also Metweash's sons, two of whom hunted with the "Heads, 1 of whose wives is their Mother". The two other sons hunted together.

It appears that all the males in the Moose settlement were members of the Moose clan since the hunters consisted of an Indian named Old Macimmy (Mackemy or Tabbitoway) his younger brother and six sons of the former, in addition to ten male children of these eight Indians. The change in subsistence affected their ability to procure furs according to Finlayson:

> Mackemy or Tabbitoway and his 7 sons did not hunt much in the winter, they formerly took their advances at Cat Lake but since the post was abandoned hunt nigher Osnaburgh—they generally lived on deer but since the decrease of these animals, they don't come up to their former exertions—they think it beneath the dignity of an Indian to live on fish and rabbits and I to enable them to support this dignity sent them away with a very cold *What chere*—they said they starved yet confided they left stages of hung fish to be eaten by Crows[87].

The Sturgeons appear also to have separated into two winter settlements in the vicinity of Cat Lake, although they frequently appeared at the Osnaburgh post together. Two of the first group of Sturgeon seem to have left for other posts in 1828, one to Lake Nipigon. The other Indian, Flint, left for Lac Seul where his brothers resided. The second settlement was headed by Cotton-shirt, who, in 1828, was an old man living with his three sons and their families, 25 persons in all.

There is little doubt that the constricted ecology was "atomizing" Ojibwa social organization. This is evident from the forced splintering of former cohesive groups, the decrease of group mobility and the changes in subsistence from large to small game. Yet, despite the difficulties, the Ojibwa of the 1820's appear to have maintained cooperative patterns, which did not give way until three decades later. The core hunters of most winter settlements belonged to the same clan, and at least one clan function, the Feast of the Dead, was still in practice although considerably diminished in scope from the seventeenth century.

Nicol Finlayson reported the arrival of Metweash's eldest son upon the death of the father in 1827.

> He did not fail to tell me that his father before his death bequeathed to him his Captains Title in preference to all his other sons—I really fancied myself during the night a spectator at the burial in one of the romantic Districts of Ireland listening to a band of Kirny with their throng at the full[88].

This was the last Feast of the Dead ceremony in which clan members united reported in the Osnaburgh journals.

Hunting group corporateness is also still evident in cooperative and aggressive behaviour toward traders. As late as 1825, Nicol Finlayson of Lac Seul wrote the chief factor at Albany, Thomas Vincent, that blockhouses were to be built at Osnaburgh to guard against an Indian attack "as the Indians have been threatening last Fall. I shall leave the place as well guarded against any suprize"[89]. The Cranes were the last people to pose any real threat to the Osnaburgh post. It appears that they were able to cooperate as a unit longer than any other group that traded at the post. In 1824, when the Osnaburgh factor, James Slater, refused the Cranes debt, owing to the ready barter system then in practice, the "Chief Metayawenennee told his Son to go in the mens house and See how many men there was"[90]. Again, in 1828, Nicol Finlayson, then of Osnaburgh, wrote:

> there is no danger to be apprehended from the Natives in the Summer except the Cranes but I never saw any harm with these tho they are not to be trusted but should any of these Indians who frequented Trout Lake come to Osnaburgh on the abandonment of that post would make the Band much bolder as they are all of one Tribe, Suckers; if the present mode of dealing with them is pursued am confident they will not attempt any thing against the place but let them be driven to desperation or insulted and I should fear the worst consequences—They still have a custom of numbering all the Men they see at the House; but they have behaved with the greatest propriety in my time[91].

The Cranes as a unit never threatened Osnaburgh again after the incident in 1824.

Aggressiveness by whole groups was one manifestation of collectivism. Another involved property concepts, particularly in regard to land tenure. Just as group aggressiveness decreased with changes in subsistence and trade policies, so also did property concepts change.

Land Tenure

As we have seen (see Chapter 6) tenure in severalty (the family hunting territory system) was operating in the Osnaburgh region during the last half of the nineteenth century. Here, I discuss the conditions surrounding the emergence of this system following the establishment of the Osnaburgh House trading post.

In 1786, the Ojibwa who tended to reside in the Osnaburgh House region were relatively new arrivals. Groups appear to have been comparatively large and well-knit as we have demonstrated. Mobility both in the food quest and in attempts to maximize trading benefits resulted in a good deal of shifting around. Then, competition in combination with a primary food source of large migratory game tended to keep large groups together. Only toward the close of this period does one get a picture of increasing stability and uniformity in residence and tenure. There is copious evidence in the journals and annual reports at this time to demonstrate that tenure in severalty, so well described by Speck (1915; 1928), Speck and Eiseley (1939; 1942), and Cooper (1939), for the twentieth century northeastern Algonkians did not exist in the Osnaburgh region during the period of competition between the trading companies (1780-1821). Indeed, the type of land proprietorship for this period is very difficult to determine, indicating perhaps that there was no set form, or at least that the traders may not have understood it.

Competition between the companies and food resources kept the Indians mobile and relatively independent. Evidence has already been presented indicating that the Ojibwa were more interested in hunting for food than for furs. Also, I have shown that there was no shortage of trade goods for Indians, since if the Osnaburgh post ran short, the Indians would merely go elsewhere.

In June 1797, John Best said that Indians were drinking and paying their debts:

> but the most part of them is not able to pay all, the Canadians being on every Quarter and it is Impossible to Keep the Inds from them particularly at present as I have neither Cloth or Blankets which is a Chief article of Trade at this place[92].

Even the lack of a single trade commodity or a poor quality item would be reason enough to drive Indians elsewhere. For instance, the Osnaburgh post lacked a desirable type of blue cloth in June 1796, yet had a cheaper red cloth which according to James Sutherland was "the refuse of the upper settlement and which is well known is detested by the Indians of this and several other posts"[93]. In December 1800, John Best declared that the post was completely depleted of cloth, blankets, shots, files, hatchets, and twine, and the remaining tobacco was mouldy. Should fresh supplies not arrive, soon, he lamented "the trade will be lost at this place for this year and perhaps for a good many years to come"[94]. By March, that year, Best had stripped his bed of blankets to supply Indians. In June 1796, Sutherland was forced to borrow trade goods from some Indians to give to others, a cooperative pattern apparently acceptable to Ojibwa culture of the times.

During the first twenty years of the post's history, mobility was considerable, although the distances travelled were not so great as during the previous period. Indians no longer had to go to the posts on Hudson Bay and James Bay, although there are occasional references to a few who still made the journey. Places listed from which Indians arrived at Osnaburgh include Lake Winnipeg, Lake of the Woods, Eagle Lake, Nipigon River, and Trout Lake. Robert Goodwin in 1790 reported the arrival of "a good many strange Inds here from the great North"[95]. The great north was the area which lay to the northwest of Lake Winnipeg.

Although trade goods often lured Indians great distances, there was no scarcity and comparatively little dependence upon particular trading posts. Traders recognizing prevalent sharing patterns, sometimes gave Indians extra large quantities of goods to be distributed among their friends who traded elsewhere to entice them to bring their furs. Indians who tended to hunt in the vicinity of the post generally received less than those who came from more remote quarters. Evidence seems to signify that there was a good deal of communalism in property. For example, James Sutherland in 1786 reported that Metweash's sons brought a large black bear to the camp at Lac Seul, the meat of which was distributed to all present: "such strangers are the Indians to frugality that they vye with each other who shall give most away"[96]. Again, in criticizing the policy of giving summer debts, John McKay, in 1800, stated:

those Summer debts is the destruction of goods and the loss of many a good Indian, the goods is merely taken by them to distribute away in presents among their relations or play away at their games[97].

So long as trade goods were abundant, Indians were not inclined to trap more than was required to obtain their few necessities. A constant complaint of traders at this time was the lack of initiative among Indians who could not be bothered to trap[98].

Until 1810, there was no shortage of fur bearers in the region. In the area north of Osnaburgh, James Sutherland reported in 1795, that:

The Beaver is in great plenty here, the Indians throwing away numbers of the half Beaver as beneath their notice, and even cuts pieces of the Whole Beaver to make them lighter carriages[99].

Under such conditions, it is difficult to see how tenure in severalty could have operated. The question is then: What type of land tenure existed under the conditions described?

It has been noted that the Indian Shewequenap referred to the land around Lake St. Joseph as belonging to him. Yet Sheweque-nap was the leader of a sizable group, and it is more probable that he trapped the area communally with other band members. It may be suggested that he even allocated sections of land to other members, although no data to support such a claim exist. Oldmixon (1741 1:548), in quoting Thomas Gorst's journal for 1670-75 at Rupert's House on James Bay has suggested the possibility of tenure by allocation, although Cooper has interpreted this statement to be insignificant and due to the trader's bias (1939:78).

Whether an allotment system or some other type existed is difficult to determine. Another possibility is what Rogers has termed the hunting range system or hunting area (Rogers 1963b:82). According to this, the hunting group returns to the same general area each year but possesses no exclusive rights to resources. Boundaries are not sharply demarcated. There is some evidence that this form existed in the Osnaburgh region. In May 1790, Robert Goodwin reported the arrival of Caucaukes and six canoes "poorly gooded he having traded a part with the Canadians on his own Lake"[100]. However, in 1796, James Sutherland stated that Caucaukes and his gang were "on their way back to their own Country"[101]. Other Indian arrivals that summer were reported to be headed back "to their hunting ground". And Robert Goodwin in 1788, "Dispatched the Indians to their winter quarters"[102]. Again in 1800, John Best in complaining about the numerous Northwest traders in the Osnaburgh region mentioned that "one gone to Tinnewabanos land one also to the Cranes land"[103]. Both Tinnawabano and the Crane were group leaders, and such a statement likely does not indicate individual land tenure. Indeed, references indicating possible individual tenure are almost nonexistent in the journals relating to this period. One questionable case occurred in 1796 noted by the Osnaburgh trader James Sutherland. An Indian from Sturgeon Lake arrived who had killed a relative there:

that Indian having first kill'd his relation and is the cause of his coming here with his furs. tho he had a large Debt from the Trader on his own land[104].

These, however, were the words of the trader, not the Indian. Such a statement cannot be taken to indicate tenure in severalty in light of the total picture. Evidence indicates that family trapping territories were not in existence at that time.

292

Indeed, the Indians of this period appear to have demonstrated a good deal of resistance to accepting the concept of individual ownership of resources. I have shown that the hunting bands who apparently resided in the same general area year after year were of a considerable size. Within a general region, movement of large bands was probably unrestricted. Cameron's statement concerning moose hunting would seem to indicate this (see footnote 21). Also, feuds seem to have occurred between whole bands and not individual Indians. Such conflicts may have resulted as groups competed for band hunting areas in a formerly unrestricted region. Even at a later date in 1817, individual tenure had not supplanted the more communal type of hunting pattern. That year, John Davis related the arrival of two Indians who complained that "they could not fall in with Beaver though they went nearly to Attawapiscat seeking them"[105]. Attawapiscat Lake is fully 150 miles from Osnaburgh. Had there been bounded areas recognized by these Indians, they would have been trespassing, yet there was no mention at all of trespass.

Davis, the previous year, mentioned the arrival of four Cranes who

> inform me on reaching the Ground they intended to make their hunt on they found it previously occupied by other Indians consequently they made poor hunts[106].

No hostility was reported which would likely have been the case had individualism in tenure existed. In truth, the other Indians invited the Cranes to take their furs to Severn with them. Perhaps, however, these other Indians invited the Cranes to go to the Severn post with them since the Cranes did show constraint; or maybe they intended to give a portion of the goods received for the furs to them in compensation.

Resistance to individualism proved so strong that even after competition ended in 1821, at a time when large game animals were virtually depleted, Indians, by then in smaller winter trapping units appear to have roamed indiscriminately. Although the Indians were marking beaver lodges by the 1820's to indicate proprietorship, the tendency was to ignore such marks. By this time Ojibwa were competing for beaver which had become scarce.

This stage appears to have been a prerequisite for that which followed characterized by the familiar family hunting territory. For instance, in December 1828, Nicol Finlayson narrated the arrival of an Indian, the Pelican, who had recently marked a beaver lodge

> on the Cranes usual track and they are afraid that these Indians will take them should they let them alone for some time; for one tribe pays no regard to the mark of another should they happen to see it at a beaver lodge especially if they are a weaker tribe then themselves. Consequently they kill the Beaver when they see them[107].

Thus, we have evidence that although band members tended to hunt in the same general region each year, resources belonged to those who came first, even when they were within the region inhabited by a different band. In Pelican's case, the factor sent other Indians to assist him to raid the house. A similar coopertive situation was described by Leacock for the Natashquan band of Montagnais (Leacock 1954:34-35). The staking of beaver houses, related to individual interests, appears to indicate the emergence at this time, albeit against resistence, of an economic pattern that eventually developed into proprietorship in severalty.

The influence of traders who preferred to deal with individuals rather than entire groups cannot be omitted as a causative factor in the formation of the family hunting ground system. Early evidence indicates that although some Indians received debts individually, often the leader procured goods on behalf of the group and the furs procured were distributed within a band to pay the debts of others. Nevertheless, the tendency to distinguish furs as a distinct type of property from food and other material possessions appears to have developed early. For example, James Sutherland wrote in 1786 that Captain Metweash

> being a Old man has left off hunting having plenty of sons and Sons in Law which maintain him and what ever any belonging to the Tent kills is laid at his feet when they come home: I do not mean furs[108].

Magnus Birsay wrote from the Osnaburgh outpost at

Wibenaban[109] in 1796, that the Indians there were behind in paying their debts and "I do not like to afront the Indians by insisting on their paying other mens Debts". Again, in his district report for 1817, John Davis remarked that "The Indians who visited the Canadians at Sturgeon Lake are already noticed individually"[110].

Individual ownership in the Osnaburgh region appears to have developed later than in the Central Great Lakes area (cf. Cooper 1939:73). Conditions during the early nineteenth century at Osnaburgh may have, in some respects, approximated those described by Jenness for the Parry Island Ojibwa (cf. Jenness 1935:5-7). In the latter case, land belonged to the entire band. Members could change their territory each season and even ally themselves with members of other bands. In former times the band chief allotted parcels of land to families seasonally. It is not unreasonable to assume that in a number of instances, hunting band leaders in the Osnaburgh vicinity during the early nineteenth century determined the locations where lesser individuals should hunt. This, however, may not have occurred until reliable food and fur resources became scarce, perhaps after 1810, when larger groups were forced out of necessity to split up during the winter. Evidence that the larger groups had already begun to break up by the above date is presented by Thomas Vincent in the Osnaburgh district report for 1814:

> The Indians in this part have no exclusive right or claim to any particular part to hunt in and it frequently happens that different families meet together, altho in winter they endeavor to avoid one another as much as possible on account of spoiling each others hunts and at the same time very probably of starving when a number of them are gathered together[111].

In summary, throughout this period land appears to have not been individually possessed. During the first few years after the establishment of the post, group and individual mobility in quest of food and trade goods seems to have been considerable. Within a few years however, the records indicate a gradual stabilization of hunting groups in certain regions around major lakes and waterways. Groups remained comparatively large throughout the year, and probably moved *en masse* within a roughly defined area. As furs and game became depleted, and hardships increased, bands fragmented into family units for part of the year to trap and hunt. Yet competition in trade and a preference for migratory food sources prevented the immediate formation of individual territories. At this time, band leaders may have, in some cases, allotted sections of family units on a seasonal basis as furs and game dwindled. Shortly after, the demarcation of beaver houses by individual hunters may have begun. Resistance to individualism was exhibited in the disregard for beaver stakes, cooperative raids on beaver houses, freedom of movement from area to area, and the "first come first served" attitude toward hunting lands with little or no remonstrance.

Summary and Conclusions

During the late eighteenth and early nineteenth centuries, there existed a widespread big game hunting pattern throughout northwestern Ontario. Nevertheless, although moose and caribou provided the basis of subsistence for the Northern Ojibwa, the utilization of a variety of resources was necessary. So long as food and trade items were plentiful, trapping remained secondary to hunting. The acquisition of large animals and trade supplies maintained large, cohesive and mobile hunting groups of perhaps 25 to 35 people throughout the year. The structure of these groups was based, in part, on an earlier patrilineal clan organization. Until about 1800, hunting groups resembled lineages. They were given clan or lineage names and most males within a group were agnates. Upon the death of a notable hunter, clan-mates would perform a Feast of the Dead ceremony although this was a diminished version of early contact performances. Leadership descended patrilineally to an eldest son. The esprit de corps of these groups was exhibited through aggressiveness toward traders and other groups. Such behaviour is not characteristic of "atomistic" people like the contemporary Ojibwa described by recent scholars. Also, property concepts during the early nineteenth century indicate communalism and sharing rather than individualism.

296

It can only be concluded from the evidence that the later atomization of Ojibwa society was a product of the increasing dependence on trade supplies, the disappearance of large game, and a diminished number of fur bearers.

The period from about 1810 to 1829 can be considered transitional for the Osnaburgh House Ojibwa. During these years their position altered from one characterized by relative mobility and freedom, to one of relative stability and dependence. The shift occurred as furred animals, particularly beaver, and cervines, moose and caribou, dwindled in number due to over-hunting. Traders desiring furs and cervine hides provided the Ojibwa with the necessary equipment and incentive to obtain them. Under the altered ecological conditions, it was only a matter of time before the resources became depleted, a fact predicted by some traders over a decade earlier. Nevertheless, change was not sudden, although it took place in a comparatively short period. Neither beaver nor cervines disappeared within a single year. Yet each year saw fewer and fewer such animals until the supply was exhausted. Even within the Osnaburgh region extinction was uneven. The area north of Osnaburgh, and to the west near Red Lake endured somewhat longer as a productive beaver and moose locale. Notwithstanding, the fate of these regions was the same as others earlier depleted.

This period was also marked by intensive reliance on the trading post. One factor increasing the dependence of the Indians was the amalgamation of the Hudson's Bay Company and Northwest Company. After this the former company controlled the fur trade throughout most of northwestern Ontario. Only near the American border was there competition with the American Fur Company which had been in existence since the conclusion of the War of 1812. Further north the Ojibwa found themselves obligated to a single company in a country drastically depleted of furs and game through previous intensive trade during the era of trading company rivalry. The end of competition meant that the Hudson's Bay Company was free to implement new policies to improve the trade.

Concomitant with the decline in game and policy changes were small but cumulative socio-economic changes. Heizer (1955:3) has written that when cultural processes are added to already

297

existing ones the result is a new "eco-cultural" development involving the resources and people "in a new web of continually adjusting relationships (ecosystem)". For the Ojibwa, adaptation involved the replacement of an older mode of subsistence by a new more expedient one under altered conditions. Not only had much of their former subsistence base been destroyed or replaced, but also their means of exploiting it. That the modifications in the socio-economic arrangements were necessary but not desirable is stated by Charles McKenzie in his Lac Seul district report for 1831:

> The Indian life is become a most miserable life . . . the procuring of the means of existence keeps the very best Indian in constant employment every day of the year & not to live as Indians were want to live 20 years ago but merely to exist[112].

I have shown that prior to the decline of game and furs, an effective socio-political organization existed among the Northern Ojibwa more elaborate and cooperative than that which followed. Yet in the 1780's the Ojibwa were fully immersed in the fur trade. What remains to us is to trace the movement of Ojibwa into the interior of northern Ontario, and to outline, albeit incompletely, the socio-economic changes which occurred.

Footnotes

1. HBC Arch B155/a/5.
2. HBC Arch B155/e/1.
3. HBC Arch B155/a/1.
4. HBC Arch B155/a/25.
5. HBC Arch B155/a/12. In 1800, John McKay of Osnaburgh remarked: "an Indian here thinks more of his Meat than an Indian at Red River thinks of his furrs" (HBC Arch B155/a/15). In later times when large animals were growing scarce, cervine hunting took up even more time which

according to traders should have been devoted to trapping. For example, in April 1825, the Lac Seul factor Nicol Finlayson remarked when the Indians brought moose and caribou meat to the post: "Indeed the Moose and deer hunters are always the worst hunters of furs" and "the Rascals will not hunt fur when they can get living on big animals" (HBC Arch B107/a/4).

6. HBC Arch B123/a/15.

7. HBC Arch B155/a/3.

8. HBC Arch B155/a/5.

9. HBC Arch B155/a/3.

10. HBC Arch B155/a/4. In March 1795, the Osnaburgh factor James Sutherland wrote that two of the Hudson's Bay clerks

> returned with Six of Captn Utchechaques Sons with all their Trade, the father being sick did not come. They are actually in a starving condition. the Snow being so little they can get no Deer to maintain this numerous family. This Indian is the father of 23 children 16 of which is Sons, first only arrived at manhood, and the youngest in the Cradel (HBC Arch B155/a/10).

11. HBC Arch B155/a/19.

12. HBC Arch B155/a/8.

13. HBC Arch B155/a/4.

14. HBC Arch B155/a/28.

15. The Lac Seul factor, Charles McKenzie, in 1843, when large animals had disappeared, remarked that the Indians "are always short of Food when they live on Rabbit alone, and the Snaring takes up the time of every individual of the family able to set a Snare" (HBC Arch B107/a/21). In 1845, he commented that "Their souls hunger for a change—continually on these insiped Rabbits—which I take to be the poorest living in this Country" (HBC Arch B107/a/24). Concerning waterfowl, McKenzie sardonically stated that "Several of this Lake ... are starving—or I should say feasting upon small white ducks" (HBC Arch B107/a/13). During the winter of 1851, McKenzie reported that there was much starvation among the Lac Seul Indians hunting at Lac La Glaise who were striving to live off fish alone, there being no other game. "I should know it—having wintered in it in

1810—and would have Starved did we depend entirely on Fish—but in those days—there were both Moose Deer & Beaver in great plenty" (HBC Arch B107/a/29).

16. HBC Arch B155/e/1.

17. HBC Arch B155/e/2; B155/e/3.

18. HBC Arch B107/e/1.

19. HBC Arch B107/a/25.

20. Thwaites 1896-1901 7:95-110.

21. The Northwester, Duncan Cameron, provides evidence that mobility in the food quest was primarily responsible for maintaining group size for the Northern Ojibwa in the late eighteenth century:

> All these Indians lead a wandering life, both winter, and summer and when they have killed or started all the moose and deer in the neighbourhood and dried or eaten up all their meat, they move to some other lake or river and look for fresh tracks (Masson 1960 2-254).

Thus, perhaps as Rogers suggests, a group of several adult males could best exploit the large game resources, and in turn, greater quantities of meat in bulk form would support larger groups.

22. HBC Arch B155/a/2.

23. HBC Arch B155/a/10. See also, Footnote 10 above.

24. The Gloucester House factor, John Kipling reported in 1780 that Shewequenap was a son of the late Nonosecash "who formerly was a Leader belonging to Albany but none of his gang has been down this 12 years past" (HBC Arch B78/a/5).

25. In May 1784, James Sutherland who was exploring the area near Lake St. Joseph met Captains Shewequenap and Cannematchie "and their adherents 15 men besides women and Children so that the place lookt like a little Fair" (HBC Arch B78/a/11). In September 1786, "Capt Shaw-e que-nap and She-she-kay came in accompanied by 14 canoes" (HBC Arch B155/a/1). Again in May 1788, "Captn Shewequenap and all his gang with other Indians came in . . . In all 13 canoes (HBC Arch B155/a/2). The size of Shewequenap's gang seems to have fluctuated somewhat. In September 1789, Shewequanap appeared with his gang of seven canoes (HBC

Arch B155/a/4). Again in September 1795, his band consisted of only six canoes. Yet the following May he arrived at the post with thirteen canoes (HBC Arch B155/a/11). Perhaps on occasion, part of his band remained behind to participate in subsistence activities. However, as late as 1805 Shewequenap arrived at Osnaburgh with his gang in thirteen canoes.

26. HBC Arch B78/a/7.

27. In May 1786, James Sutherland, who was exploring the Lac Seul region, reported that Metweash was

> "a worthy generous Indian; he has 5 Sons 6 Daughters and 7 grand Children beside brothers and other relations so that he is a man of great Power among all the Indians in this part of the Country (HBC Arch B78/a/15).

In May 1789, Captains Caukaukes and Metweash and thier lieutenants and gangs arrived at Osnaburgh in "16 Canoes from Sturgeon Lake" (HBC Arch B155/a/3). In 1787, Metweash headed a gang consisting of twelve canoes (HBC Arch B155/a/2).

28. HBC Arch B155/e/1.

29. HBC Arch B155/a/15.

30. HBC Arch B155/a/15.

31. HBC Arch B155/e/2; B155/e/3.

32. HBC Arch B155/a/18. Possibly some of the sons were classificatory ones. However, leaders often had three or four wives and it is possible that they were real sons. As noted Captain Utchecheque fathered sixteen sons and 23 children (see Footnote 10 above).

33. HBC Arch B155/e/2.

34. HBC Arch B78/a/11.

35. HBC Arch B155/e/4.

36. HBC Arch B155/a/14.

37. HBC Arch B155/a/16.

38. HBC Arch B155/a/14.

39. HBC Arch B155/e/1.

40. HBC Arch B78/a/7.

41. HBC Arch B155/a/19.

42. HBC Arch B155/a/2.
43. HBC Arch B107/a/7.
44. HBC Arch B107/a/2.
45. HBC Arch B107/a/8.
46. HBC Arch B123/a/8.
47. HBC Arch B10/a/2.
48. HBC Arch B10/e/2.
49. HBC Arch B155/a/29.
50. HBC Arch B155/a/15.
51. HBC Arch B78/a/4.
52. HBC Arch B78/a/16.
53. HBC Arch B155/e/2.
54. HBC Arch B155/a/25.
55. HBC Arch B155/a/27.
56. HBC Arch B155/a/29.
57. HBC Arch B155/a/27.
58. HBC Arch B155/a/36.
59. HBC Arch B107/a/5.
60. HBC Arch B155/a/38.
61. HBC Arch B107/a/5.
62. HBC Arch B107/a/30.
63. HBC Arch B107/a/2.
64. HBC Arch B107/e/1.
65. HBC Arch B155/a/36.
66. HBC Arch B155/a/25.
67. HBC Arch B107/a/2. Charles McKenzie of Lac Seul noted in 1823 that:

> large or land animals are getting so very scarce in this quarter that the natives cannot supply themselves with leather for their consumption—which is a drawback on their exertions when not provided with Shoes & Rackets—Consequently they have little or no meat to spare for trade (HBC Arch B107/a/2).

At Osnaburgh in 1826, Nicol Finlayson gave

> all the Home Guards leather for shoes and snowshoes which they had not for these three years back and if they killed a beaver or otter they were obliged to cut it up (HBC Arch B155/a/38).

68. HBC Arch B107/a/6.

69. HBC Arch B107/a/9.

70. HBC Arch B155/e/11.

71. HBC Arch B155/a/38.

72. HBC Arch B155/a/38.

73. HBC Arch B3/e/10. In 1828, Nicol Finlayson recorded the effects of subsistence changes on the Cranes who

> have lost a good deal of their former pride for they have learned that an Indian clothed in rabbit skins in the winter can live as comfortable as he who is clothed in cloth (HBC Arch B155/a/39).

74. HBC Arch B220/a/5.

75. HBC Arch B107/a/12.

76. HBC Arch B107/a/2.

77. HBC Arch B107/e/3.

78. HBC Arch B107/a/8.

79. HBC Arch B107/e/3.

80. HBC Arch B155/a/39.

81. HBC Arch B155/a/39. I have included Nicol Finlayson's discussion of the Osnaburgh Indians for 1828 in total in the Appendix.

82. HBC Arch B155/a/39.

83. HBC Arch B155/a/39. The Big Fall is a waterfall on the Albany River.

84. HBC Arch B155/a/39.

85. HBC Arch B155/a/39.

86. HBC Arch B155/a/39.

87. HBC Arch B155/a/39.

88. HBC Arch B155/a/39. The Feast of the Dead by this time was a mere shadow of what it had been during its peak in the mid-seventeenth century (cf. Hickerson 1960). Feasts at that time often involved 1,500 persons belonging to a number of groups. Nevertheless, there is evidence of some continuity. The Jesuit, Louis André who described a Feast held by the Amikwa in 1670 noted that the name of the deceased chief was taken by his eldest son (Thwaites 1896-1901 55:137-39).

89. HBC Arch B107/a/4.

90. HBC Arch B155/a/36.

91. HBC Arch B155/a/39.

92. HBC Arch B155/a/12.

93. HBC Arch B155/a/11.

94. HBC Arch B155/a/16.

95. HBC Arch B155/a/5.

96. HBC Arch B78/a/15.

97. HBC Arch B155/a/14.

98. cf. April 1791. (HBC Arch B155/a/5).

99. HBC Arch B155/a/10.

100. HBC Arch B155/a/4.

101. HBC Arch B155/a/11.

102. HBC Arch B155/a/2.

103. HBC Arch B155/a/15.

104. HBC Arch B155/a/11.

105. HBC Arch B155/a/29.

106. HBC Arch B155/a/28.

107. HBC Arch B155/a/39. A month later Finlayson reiterated this point when an Indian named Big Eyes appeared at the post with both large and small pelts:

> had he let them alone another would not be so scrupulous—It is very hard if not impossible to prevent the Natives from killing every little animal they see as well as the larger so long as the ground is in common among then (HBC Arch B155/a/39).

108. HBC Arch B78/a/14.

109. Exact location unkown but somewhere to the southeast of Osnaburgh House (HBC Arch B155/a/11).

110. HBC Arch B155/e/5.

111. HBC Arch B155/e/1.

112. HBC Arch B107/e/4.

Chapter Nine
Ojibwa Expansion and Settlement of the Interior

Introduction

Before tracing Ojibwa expansion into northwestern Ontario, let us summarize briefly the stages of Northern Ojibwa culture history from the late eighteenth century, particularly as they were revealed at Osnaburgh House.

Today most Indians belonging to the Osnaburgh treaty band reside semi-permanently in one of several villages; the main group being settled on Doghole Lake near the northeast end of Lake St. Joseph. The contemporary community has no overall authority structure yet endogamous marriages are positively sanctioned. Hence it can be characterized as an acephalous endo-deme. Cross-cousin marriage occurs but is usually restricted to remote cousins; while sanctions against intra-clan marriage have been relaxed. Clan affiliation is determined patrilineally. Almost all Indians are nominally Christians and most indigenous religious ceremonies have disappeared. Government subsidies and day school have been responsible for the increased proportion of time spent in the village amounting to about 9 months of the year. Subsidies provide the bulk of the community's income, followed by commercial fishing, trapping, and wage labour.

The period from about 1890 to 1945 can be considered as transitional. By the latter date many Indians were residing in log cabins in a village on Lake St. Joseph for several months each year; whereas 50 years earlier there had been no Indians' log cabins at Osnaburgh. From 1900 the processes leading to permanent village life were intensified, especially during the period following World War II. Between 1959 and 1963 the village was relocated near the road bisecting the band territory. In 1950 summer school began; and a year earlier a nursing station was completed near the Hudson's Bay Company store. After 1930 wage employment became available in the gold mines near Pickle Lake. The Osnaburgh Reserves were surveyed during the 1910's following the signing of Treaty Number 9 with the Canadian government in 1905.

Despite fewer contacts with Euro-Canadians in 1890, there is evidence of a trend toward increased sedentariness even then. For example, summer gardens were being cultivated by some families of Indians, and had been since perhaps the 1870's. The introduction of store foods after 1865, albeit in very small quantities, had made survival less precarious as had the return of large animals: moose after 1900, and caribou after 1869. At this time Indians lived for most of the year in exogamous bilateral winter settlements composed of several households and numbering about 25 to 30 people located within 100 miles of the Hudson's Bay trading post. In 1890 there were between eight and ten such co-residential groups affiliated with the Osnaburgh post. Males belonging to these settlements radiated out to exploit family-possessed tracts of land. The fur trade dominated Indian life and the Hudson's Bay manager was the most important contact agent. Prior to 1880 many native religious practices flourished although Christian missionaries entered the area by the 1840's.

The period between 1821 and 1890 was economically a most difficult one for the Northern Ojibwa. Fish and hare were the most important foods, especially the latter in winter. During years when hare were scarce, Indians had to devote all their efforts to food production to prevent starvation. At the same time they were intensively dependent upon the trading post for a variety of goods without which they would perish. Frequently when they required trade supplies most, which could only be obtained in exchange (or on credit) for furs, they had to devote all their time to hunting for food. The reliance on the trading post and the pursuit of fur bearers and small non-migratory game led to the formation of discreet tracts of land most efficiently exploited by family units. The winter settlements, although often given clan names (Moose, Loon etc.), were usually of mixed clan composition. However, leadership tended to descend from a father to an eldest son. Both the winter settlements and the clans were exogamous, forcing co-residential group members to marry more distant cross-cousins when first cousins resided within the same settlement. It was common for marriages to link co-residential groups affiliated with different posts (e.g. Osnaburgh and Lac Seul). This is in marked contrast to the situation today where communities tend to be almost totally endogamous.

The period between 1810 and 1829 was also transitional in that major socio-economic transformations occurred. Large game animals, moose and caribou, which had been the primary food source were exterminated through overhunting in the Osnaburgh region by the early 1820's. Fur bearers, particularly beaver, grew very scarce by the late 1810's since conservation practices had been nonexistent and a first-come first-served attitude existed toward all animals. Finally in 1821, the Northwest Company was absorbed by the Hudson's Bay Company ending competition and resulting in such policy changes as the withdrawal of many trading posts, conservation measures on beaver and muskrat, and an increase in the price of trade supplies. These changes occurred at approximately the same time and reduced the mobility of Indian groups which became more dependent on the trading post for such items as twine for hare snares and fish nets, and moose hide for snowshoes and mocassins. The end of competition also meant that most Indians in the Osnaburgh area were forced to trade at a single post. Small game did not provide food in bulk as did large animals and resulted in the dispersal of hunting group members for part of the year in areas where it could be found. Hunting group leaders lost much authority when they were forced to set hare snares (formerly considered women's work) and when hunters began receiving their trade supplies individually. The transferal of economic ties from within the group to outside reduced the collective significance of the clan. Indeed, the last Feast of the Dead ceremony uniting clan members upon the death of a leader was recorded at Osnaburgh during the late 1820's.

Competition among Northwest Company and Hudson's Bay Company traders prior to 1821 ensured the Indians of large quantities of cheap trade supplies. The area was dotted with numerous trading stations and resulted in much mobility of large cohesive Indian groups supported by big game animals the pursuit of which fostered this mobility. During the 1780's competition grew most intense in northwestern Ontario. Osnaburgh, itself a product of this competition, was established in 1786 along with other Hudson's Bay posts: Gloucester House (1777), Cat Lake (1788), Lac Seul (1790), Nipigon House (1792) and Trout Lake (1807). At this time fur bearers, indeed game of all sorts, were plentiful and cases of starvation were comparatively rare. Indian groups averaging perhaps 20 to 35 individuals remained united throughout the year. These groups were given clan names. Indeed, they appear to have been the remnants of clans or segments of such groups. Evidence indicates that communalism with regard to property was more important than individualism. Until 1800, at least, leaders obtained trade supplies on behalf of the group. Again, the Feast of the Dead and group aggressiveness via-à-vis other groups and also traders, was symptomatic of group collectiveness.

During the late eighteenth century the Northern Ojibwa were characterized by collective, yet mobile groupings devolving around a big game hunting economy supplemented by trade supplies. One cannot attribute the fur trade as a factor responsible for the solidarity of these hunting groups. Indeed, as we have seen, the fur trade either directly or indirectly did much to atomize Ojibwa society. The fur trade, which had extended to the Ojibwa since about 1620, had already modified the distribution and organization of Ojibwa groups. We must look for historical causes to explain the origins of Ojibwa society of the late eighteenth century in northern Ontario.

Expansion and Settlement of the Interior

The origins for the distribution of Ojibwa settlements in north-western Ontario and eastern Manitoba are to be sought in an earlier era (1660-1780). At first, Ojibwa penetrated the Boreal Forests on a seasonal basis to act as middlemen to Cree and Assiniboin to the north and west of Lake Superior; and slightly later to exploit the retreating fur and game supply beyond the Upper Great Lakes.

The details involving Ojibwa expansion and settlement are as follows. By the late seventeenth century the fur trade in the Upper Great Lake region was expanding. Following the Iroquois wars during the 1640's and 1650's the Ojibwa among other

Algonkian groups dispersed to the west[1] and were acting as middlemen to the Siouan Dakota and Assiniboin and to the Cree west of Lake Superior[2]. However, some Cree were on the north shore of Lake Superior in 1660[3]. The evidence seems to signify that the Ojibwa migrated along the northern and southern shores of Lake Superior before they expanded northwards. As early as 1660, the trader-explorer, Pierre Esprit Radisson, at a lake which has been identified as Lac Court Oreille, Wisconsin, observed a Feast of the Dead ceremony among a group of Indians[4]. After arranging a treaty with the warring Dakota and Cree slightly further to the west, Radisson returned "with a company of people of the nation of Sault [Ojibwa from Sault Ste. Marie] that came along with us, loaded with booty"[5]. At the west end of Lake Superior, he encountered a village of Ottawa, refugees from the Iroquois wars, and as he proceeded north toward Hudson Bay met with "a company of new wildmen . . . that liveth on fish"[6]. The fact that Radisson refers by name to the Cree, Ojibwa and Dakota might indicate that these last were Assiniboin who at this time were still entrenched in the region to the west of Lake Nipigon. These Indians, eager for trade goods, accompanied Radisson to Hudson Bay (if he indeed reached it).

The Saulteurs, a small group (or groups) who originally lived near the rapids at Sault Ste. Marie, may have been the first to penetrate along the south shore of Lake Superior. The purpose of this movement was not merely to escape Iroquois incursions into the area, but to take advantage of the richer fur country to the west and to reap the advantages of being middlemen to the Dakota in Wisconsin.

A group of Ottawa in 1662 followed the Saulteur settling at Chequamegon. The trader Perrot stated that:

> They searched along the lake to find whether other tribes were there, and encountered the Saulteurs who; had fled northwards. Part of the Saulteurs had gone toward Kionconan [Keweenaw] . . . that they did not all return together because they had left their people at the north; that the latter intended to dwell here, but without a fixed residence proposing to roam in all directions; and that the Nepissings and Amikouets were at Alimibegon [Nipigon][7].

Thus, the migration westward had begun by the 1660's and involved the Ottawa, the Amikwa (people of the beaver clan from the shores of Georgian Bay[8]), the Saulteur, as well as other Ojibwa groups. Upon learning of the presence of these other peoples, the Ottawas moved further north to trade with those "who gave them all their beaver robes for old knives, blunted awls, wretched nets, and kettles used until they were past service"[9]. Both Ojibwa and Ottawa continued to return to the region around Sault Ste. Marie during the summer months to hunt deer and to fish in the rapids of the St. Mary's River. After 1643 the trading post at Michilimackinac provided an outlet for their furs and it was not necessary for them to go to Quebec through country infested with Iroquois war parties. As early as 1641, Jesuit priests had met an assemblage of 2,000 Algonkians at Sault Ste. Marie[10]. With the influx of trade goods during the late seventeenth century then, Sault Ste. Marie became the locus for group gatherings supported by bountiful fisheries (Hickerson 1962a:82).

During the middle of the seventeenth century Cree appear to have moved south from original centres north of Lake Superior and east of Lake Winnipeg, arriving in the Assiniboin country near Rainy Lake and Lake of the Woods.

Until the 1670's, both the Cree and Assiniboin were forced to trade through Ottawa and Ojibwa middlemen, while the latter did little or no trapping. However, this monopoly was broken after the newly-founded Hudson's Bay Company (1670) began supplying Cree and Assiniboin on a large scale at settlements on James Bay and Hudson Bay[11]. By 1673, some Ottawa and Ojibwa were under the necessity of hunting furs themselves in order to procure trade goods. In 1673, the Jesuit, Father Henri Nouvel, at Sault Ste. Marie wrote, "les anglais ont des-jas fait une grande diversion des sauvages des terres qui parrissoient au lac Superieur"[12]. The Cree, north of Lake Superior in the Shield region, released from the necessity of trading through middlemen were able to acquire many new trade items including guns at the Bay posts. Others remained in the area west of Lake Superior and traded at the French posts at Michilimackinac and Lake Nipigon. After the establishment of Fort Nelson in 1682, at the mouth of the Nelson River on Hudson Bay and Fort Albany at the mouth of the Albany River a few years earlier, the fur trade expanded to

310

include all the Indians between Lake Superior and Hudson Bay. By 1690, the Hudson's Bay Company had added York Factory and Fort Severn.

Meanwhile, to thwart these Indian excursions to the Bay, and to consolidate their trade, the French established the Compagnie du Nord in 1676. Two years later, Charles de la Tourette, brother of Daniel Greysolon, Sieur Duluth, built Fort Camanistogoyan at the mouth of the Kaministiquia River (present Thunder Bay, Ontario). This was followed by Fort La Maune on the northeast shore of Lake Nipigon in 1684[13]. Its purpose is indicated by the statement, "Poste du Sr Duluth pour empêcher less Assiniboels et autres sauvages de decendre a la Baye de Hudson"[14]. In 1685, the French built Fort de Francais near the forks of the Albany and Kenogami Rivers[15]. Finally, after 1686, the French were able to capture and hold several Hudson's Bay Company posts until they were returned to the English following the Treaty of Utrecht in 1713.

It was likely at this time that the infiltration of Ojibwa into the northern interior began as small roving bands were lured to Hudson Bay and James Bay to capitalize on the cheaper and better quality supplies distributed by the English[16]. The importance of these posts in attracting Indians is indicated by the Hudson's Bay trader James Knight, who in 1716 at York Factory, reported that the area about the post had been cleared of deer (caribou) for 100 miles around, and, "that it goes very hard with our home Indians"[17]. That same summer there were more than 1,000 Indians at the post awaiting the arrival of the ship laden with trade supplies. Prior to the arrival, Knight in expressing his anxiety indicated the great distances traversed by Indians: "the Indians will not come 1000 or 1200 Mile to give away their goods for to have little for it for here has been Indians this Year as will not gett into their Own Country again till Octobr"[18]. Evidence indicates that some were Assiniboin, while others were Cree. Although positive proof that some were Ojibwa would require a more intensive scrutiny of the documents, it is not unreasonable to assume a few Ojibwa were trading at Hudson Bay posts by the 1710's. However, the Ojibwa do not seem to have become firmly entrenched in the area north and west of Lake Superior until the 1730's.

By 1716, the French were reported to have built a post seven days paddle up the southwest river (Kenogami) which was attracting Cree who normally traded at Fort Albany. That spring, a "french" Indian travelled to Fort Albany to report that there were 30 more canoes "coming to Destroy us being Encourag'd by y french with a promise of 40 Beavr for Evry Scalp of y English they bring to them"[19]. The French, who had built another post on the Kaministiquia River in 1717, were also inciting the Dakota. In 1718, some Cree informed the Fort Albany manager, Thomas MacLish, that "A Nation of Indians called Poats has Destroyed a great number of their Country men that Frequents this place"[20]. Sometimes even the Assiniboin fought the Cree. In 1723, the "sinepoils" were reported to have killed nearly 100 Cree, leading Joseph Myatt of Fort Albany to remark:

> The Kannaday wood runers doe all they can to intercept our trade and set the Inds at variance on wth another that comes to trade with us[21].

The above report could also have been a rumour spread by Indians as an excuse not to go to the English posts to repay their debts. Nevertheless, there is no denying intertribal hostilities.

Frequently mentioned in the journals are "French" Indians who were those who either habitually traded with the French, or who came from territories controlled by French coureurs de bois. Although these French Indians could have been Cree, Assiniboin and Ojibwa, it seems more likely that they were either the latter group, or perhaps Ottawa. They are clearly distinguished by English traders from the "Christeens" (Cree Proper of the Shield north of Lake Superior) during the 1710's and 20's.

After 1720, it would seem that a few Ojibwa had moved north of Lake Superior. Nevertheless, the Cree still occupied most of northern Ontario while the Assiniboin continued to reside in their aboriginal homeland along the International Border west of Lake Superior. Another group of Cree, the Sturgeon Indians, occupied the region west of Lake Nipigon and traded mainly with the French. It is possible that the Sturgeon Indians were the same people as the Monsoni since the English traders never used the latter term—or at least the two may have been from the same general area, and hence culturally similar.

There is also a hint that the Cree of the Shield were shifting to the west by the 1720's. Several bands were reported to have gone to Port Nelson to trade rather than Fort Albany as in the past. By 1726, Fort Albany was losing the trade of many of the western Indians who were too involved in warfare with the Dakota to make the trip, or who preferred to trade at nearby French posts. Another reason for the loss was that the Ojibwa, who by this time were occupying portions of the upper Albany drainage area, were threatening to kill any Cree who tried to travel to Fort Albany. An Indian told Joseph Myatt that the Flag Merchant's band of Cree didn't come because

> ye Echeepoes [Ojibwa] threatned to kill them if they came here and there was a great many of ye Kaneday wood runners got amongst them and they traided with ye Ind better then they used to doe[22].

Some angry Cree, loyal to the English, offered to purchase poison to give to the Wood Runners. Christeens continued to trade at Fort Albany until 1732, when they reported that there were two French posts up the river and a third under construction only four days paddle away[23]. One of these posts may actually have been Fort Saint Pierre built on Rainy Lake in 1731, or Fort St. Charles established on Lake of the Woods in 1732, by the explorer-trader Pierre Gaultier de Varennes de la Vérendrye[24]. It may be, however, that the traders were referring to other French settlements nearer Fort Albany. Whatever, these posts were luring Indians away from the Bay.

During the 1730's, there are specific references to "Oachiapoia" trading at Fort Albany. This may have been due to a temporary truce with the Dakota. For a brief period before 1736, the Ojibwa from Chequamegon had allied themselves with the Dakota against the Cree (Hickerson 1962a:66-69). That year, a breach in the Dakota-Ojibwa alliance occurred and the Ojibwa joined the Cree and Assiniboin in their raids against the Dakota after the latter massacred 21 French at Lake of the Woods. The French expansion west had destroyed the advantageous position of the Ojibwa who had acted as middlemen to the Dakota and the French massacre gave the former the excuse to penetrate west into richer game and fur regions (cf. Hickerson 1962a:70-72). By 1736, a group of Ojibwa had settled at Vermillon River near Rainy Lake (Hickerson 1967a:45), while there were 60 Auwause warriors at the mouth of the Kaministiquia River[25]. At Lake Nipigon in 1736, there were 40 "Oskemanettigons" (perhaps Nipissings) and 200 Monsonis along the Nipigon River. Near Lake Nipigon there were 60 "Christinaux" and 150 Assiniboin[26]. It would only be a matter of a few years before such a large number of Indians would exterminate the fur animals in the vicinity and hence be forced to push further inland or to the west.

There can be no question that by the 1730's, the Cree Proper were moving westward while Ojibwa were shifting into former Cree territories. After 1740, very few Cree Proper travelled to Fort Albany. When two canoes of "our farthest off Indians" (probably Ojibwa) came to Fort Albany in 1741, Joseph Isbister remarked:

These Indians borders one ye Clisteens & ye Leading Indiane of ye 2 Cannoes told me he was acquainted with Some of ye Leading Clisteen Indians: So I Gave him a Litle Tobaco To Smoke with ye Clisteens when he mette with them ... for its a 11 Years Since any Clisteen hath ben Downe. Never Since Mr. Moyats Time[27].

Although Ojibwa had penetrated north into the upper reaches of the Albany, the inland area seems to have been rather sparsely populated. One reason for this was that warfare between the Dakota and Cree and Sturgeon Indians was "Depopulating their Country"[28]. Thus, it would seem that there were relatively vast tracts of land north of Lake Superior occupied by only a few bands of Indians.

In the spring of 1743, the French established camp trade inland 60 miles up the Albany River and were intercepting all the Indians on their way to Fort Albany including the homeguard Cree[29]. The Ojibwa told Joseph Isbister that if the English didn't settle inland, the French would capture the entire trade. Isbister instructed the Ojibwa to stop going to war. He recognized the difficulties they had in reaching the post and therefore sent men "on a Just Cause To build a house in order to Secure & preserve

314

This Trade". The new inland post, called Henley House, was erected at the forks of the Kenogami and Albany Rivers. Its construction proved a success since the French vacated the area and the HBC was able to recapture much of the Ojibwa trade. When the Ojibwa arrived in 1744, there was "Not one French Coat a mongst them all"[30]. The French, however, were able to prevent the Cree to the northwest from going to Albany by spreading a rumour that the "Nattawees" (Mohawks) were coming to destroy them. Nevertheless, 41 canoes of Sturgeon Indians traded at Albany where only two canoes had come the previous year. According to Captain Coats: "The Pike Indians, Owashoes, and Eagle Eyes, do all go down to Albany"[31]. The Pike Indians and Owashoes (Wasses) were Ojibwa, while the Eagle Eyes were a band of Assiniboin.

The competition with the French posts at Nipigon and Michilimackinac was so fierce that in 1744, Governor Beauharnois wrote to Count Maurepas that Henley was to be destroyed if possible. During the 1740's, from 30 to 100 canoes passed Henley House for Fort Albany annually[32].

By 1746, the French were again intercepting the trade having built a settlement 150 miles above Henley House on the Albany. However, the French again vacated their post during the winter of 1746-47 but continued to control the trade in the Lake Nipigon area where the lure of French goods was preventing the "Atimpaig" (Nipigon) Indians from coming to Albany. Joseph Isbister also reported that the "French Coureurs de Bois has gote among our Catt Indians who live on ye Sturgeon Lake"[33]. Nevertheless, "Ouchipoua" north of Lake Nipigon continued to trade at Albany. In 1749, numerous bands from the west including Sturgeon Indians, "Shishique" Indians and "Keeshkeman" Indians were once more reaching the HBC Albany post. By this date only an occasional "Clisteen" Indian bothered to make the journey. It would appear that only a few pockets of Cree Proper remained east of Lake Winnipeg. Most Cree living in northern Ontario were Swampy Cree who occupied the lowland area nearer James Bay and Hudson Bay.

The Henley House post while attracting Ojibwa during the initial years after its construction, was operated more as a way station where Indians could get tobacco, brandy and oatmeal. Their furs, however, were to be traded at Fort Albany. Thus, by the 1750's, Indians were complaining about the long journey which could be shortened if they were allowed to trade their pelts at Henley House. In 1754, the five traders at Henley were massacred by some Indians due either to French encouragement or to difficulties in interpersonal relations since the Henley men had taken two Indian women as concubines. Indian threats—no doubt encouraged by the French—prevented the re-establishment of Henley until the summer of 1759, when it was again attacked by twenty warriors. The manager was shot down while the remaining post employees fled for their lives on foot for Fort Albany. Henley was not rebuilt until 1766, due to the hardships of living inland combined with a justified fear on the part of the Fort Albany post employees.

During the late 1750's, competition between the English and French declined until Canada was ceded to the British. Thereafter, for a few years, more detailed information on the interior Indians is available, since they now began to trade annually at the permanent posts on the Bay. Great fleets of upland Ojibwa travelled to Fort Albany. During the early 1760's, from twelve to fifteen captains and their gangs are mentioned annually. One of these captains was Nonosecash, father of Shewequenap, who became the "chief captain" at Osnaburgh House some 30 years later. Another important Indian was "lieutenant Tinnewabano" first mentioned in 1761. This Indian was elder brother of the Crane who quite likely accompanied him to Fort Albany[34].

During the 1760's, the trade brought by the Ojibwa was considerable and constituted the better part of that at Fort Albany. However, by the mid-1760's, the "pedlars", now including English and Scots as well as French from Montreal, were again making inroads on the Bay trade. Nevertheless, for a while the Ojibwa remained loyal to the English at the Bay. In 1764, Captain Mekiss and his gang killed three English and four French traders from Montreal. When they arrived at Fort Albany, Humphrey Marten said they were:

> continualy dancing and Singing the Warr and beging Songs and are so impudent in their demands that I know not what to do, the green Scalps of the unhappy wretches they murder'd, are presented as a trophy of their valour to every

Person they come near at the same time they demand a reward for killing those they call our Enemys[35].

Captain Mekiss' gang killed several more pedlars the next year telling Marten that they "will not suffer their Country to be stole from them"[36]. Despite these instances of violence, the Montreal traders were growing numerous up country by 1766. In 1767, Tinnewabano informed Marten "that he was Obliged to trade part of his Goods with them" (the pedlars) and that the pedlars were telling the Indians that they no longer had to make the long voyage to Fort Albany since they could supply them with the same goods and as cheaply as the HBC[37]. Henley House continued to operate as a resting station only, which greatly displeased the Indians. Many Indians refused to travel to Fort Albany after 1767, which marked the last year that Assiniboin made the journey[38]. That fall, the Ojibwa, incited by the French, threatened to capture Henley House. Fortunately, the manager at Henley collected the men and fired the guns driving the Indians away. According to Humphrey Marten.

had the English been fools enough to open the Gates the Tommahawks and long knives would have sent our Countrymen to the Other world long before morning[39].

Captain Nonosecash later that year informed Marten that the French would again try to take Henley. Marten feared that the post would "once more be Destroy'd by these cursed Indians"[40]. Although these threats never materialized, the trade at Fort Albany steadily fell off as more Ojibwa began trading at the Montreal posts. The Fort Albany trade fell from 21,556 made beaver in 1761-62[41] to a mere 5,940 made beaver in 1768-69[42]. The year 1771 marked the end of the inland trade for Fort Albany since the traders from Montreal were by then well established at inland camps and were trading the furs at a moderate standard as the Indians trapped them.

In 1759, the Fort Severn post was re-established from York Fort having been abandoned since the turn of the century. Soon after, Ojibwa began trading there. However, by the late 1760's, the Severn trade was also declining due to competition with

Montreal traders. To regain the trade, William Tomison was sent inland to the east shore of Lake Winnipeg in 1767. Tomison reported meeting large numbers of traders on their way to Basquea (The Pas)[43]. During the winter he met many Indians but couldn't persuade them to go to Severn since they were trading with the Montreal men on the Misquagamaw River (The Bloodvein River). Despite this competition, Fort Severn continued to attract a few Ojibwa or Bungee, as they were called, throughout the 1770's. One reason for this was that groups of Ojibwa during the 1750's and 60's had expanded as far north as Big Trout Lake locating them closer to Fort Severn than to either Fort Albany or the Montreal traders whose settlements lay primarily to the south. Another reason why some Ojibwa preferred to travel to Fort Severn seems to have been the attraction of the caribou herds which annually crossed the Severn River[44]. These herds, numbering several thousand animals provided a food source unavailable on the Albany River.

The Hudson's Bay Company trade at Fort Albany remained low for almost another decade. The English on the Bay, unlike their French counterparts, were unaccustomed to the hardships of bush life and were reluctant to settle inland if it could be avoided. However, the decline in the fur trade and resultant criticisms from abroad forced them to change their tactics. Thus, in 1777, Gloucester House was built on Washi Lake some 300 miles up the Albany River and that same year George Sutherland surveyed the situation further inland when he wintered with a family of Ojibwa near Lake Winnipeg. Gloucester House, while attracting some Ojibwa, was not sufficient to regain the trade. For instance, although Tinnewabano was reported to have been only a short distance further inland from Gloucester, "he would not come down this year. But he sent his grand Pipe to Smoke with us"[45]. In 1779, George Sutherland made a second trip inland wintering near a pedler's post on Sturgeon Lake. He listed no less than seventeen trading camps operated by Montreal men and underscored the cheapness of their goods

...it is no wonder the trade is fallen off at Albany and who can raise it, one might strive till Eternity give them presents and indulge them as much as he chuses and never be abit the better for it. It does not signify taking about Indians for they will not come down give them what you plase, and it is very plain to be seen that the pedlars are in Every hole and cornr where there are any Indians to be found, besides as far as I can learn the pedlars give away more to the Indians than what we doo when we give them most[46].

The intensive competition between the French traders and the Hudson's Bay Company resulted in lavish and extravagant distributions of trade goods at extremely low prices. The standard of currency from 1694 on became the beaver and all trade items and furs were gauged in terms of this animal. The value of goods varied from post to post depending upon the intensity of the competition. Where competition was keen, the value of trade goods remained low, whereas if there was little competition and the Indians had no alternative trading post, values increased. The following articles were listed by Sutherland as given away free by Montreal traders: rum, powder, shot, tobacco, mirrors, paint, knives, beads, ribbons, flints, steels, combs, awls, needles, gunworms, rings, ear-rings, bracelets, armbands, hair plates and ruffed shirts[47]. By the 1770's, it may be said that such items as the gun, hatchet and twine spool had become requirements in the cultural accoutrements of the Northern Ojibwa.

Evidence that there was not an Indian in the north that had not been contacted is recounted by Sutherland in the following incident involving a Montreal trader and his servant:

Mr. Solomon asked him very foolishly if he had any Indians that had never seen White people yet, the man assured him very prettily—o yes Says he I did indeed Sir, Lord Says Solomon can't we get among them, to be shour you can what is to hinder you, well done me lade, I will double you your wages for this lucky jaunt of yours. Oh Sir I am afeard you will not because those Indians that I saw never killed anything in their Lives. What the divel kind of Indians are they says Solomon. why says he I never saw any but two small Children and I thought they had never seen white people because they seemed to be afraid of me—is this the

wisdom of Solomon to imagine that there was Indians
wethin three or four hundred miles of hudsons bay that had
never seen white people. Oh thou foolish blockhead change
thy name[48].

The quantity of goods received from the Montreal trader at
Sturgeon Lake for the year 1779-80 is indicated in Table 41 and
the fur returns for the same post are given in Table 42.

Table 41   Quantity and Value of Items Traded at Sturgeon
Lake: 1779-80

Item	Value in Beaver
20 pieces of cloth (20 yards each)	880
70 blankets....................................	420
350 lbs of gun powder	233
672 lbs of shot................................	134
100 gallons of rum............................	400
Total...........................	2067

Table 42   Quantity and Value of Furs Traded at Sturgeon
Lake: 1779-80

Species	Quantity	Value in Beaver
Beaver	700	700
Marten	300	100
Otter	200	200
Lynx	100	200
Bears & others		100
	Total . . .	1300

As indicated in Tables 41 and 42 nearby competing posts
often gave away more than they took in, the result being the
distribution of prodigious quantities of commodities.
From 1780 to 1782 a severe smallpox epidemic swept through
the country greatly injuring the fur trade and drastically reducing
the population in the area. In June, 1782, Indians arrived at

Gloucester House from Rainy Lake informing John Kipling, the factor, that "there is a great Mortality among the Indians and that most of the Indians in and Near the Raney Lake is dead and that the Assineybois Country is almost Depopulated"[49]. That year it was "raging among the poor Pungee Deer Hunters of whom almost every one that has been seized with it have died"[50]. The smallpox epidemic, plus the increased tempo of trade and competition in the interior led to the union of the Montreal merchants who formed the Northwest Company in 1782.

After 1780, the English trade began to recover as inland posts were built. It also marked a turning point for the Ojibwa who no longer had to travel long distances for their trade supplies. Patterns of mobility, as we have seen, became closely linked with trade competition as well as the food and fur quest.

By the 1770's, the Ojibwa had expanded into northern Ontario and eastern Manitoba to approximately their present limits. This expansion, as we have noted, was intimately linked to the fur trade. Although the exact steps in this migration are difficult to trace since there are no on-the-spot reports documenting it, there are, however, several good statements at a slightly later time. For example, Andrew Graham during the late eighteenth century remarked that the Nakawawuck Nation extended as far northwest as the Nelson River:

> They are the most northern tribes of the Chipeways. It is our opinion that they have drawn up to the northward gradually as the Keiskatchewans receded from it[51].

These Keiskatchewan Indians (Cree) at the time of contact with the Hudson's Bay Company, "inhabited the country from the sea-coast up to the Lakes". However, they moved west to the buffalo country in search of furs or new food resources[52]. A fuller understanding of these population movements requires a more intensive examination of historical and cultural relationships among Ojibwa and Cree.

Relations with the Cree

Although the details of Indian migrations are difficult to pinpoint, it is nevertheless possible to determine the relations among Ojibwa and Cree groups in the interior. The affects of this relationship along with other historical and ecological factors have led some scholars to state that cultural and linguistic differences were never very great. Rogers states, for example, that adequate evidence for Ojibwa expansion during the past 200 years has not been established (1963b:65) and that "the distinction between Cree and Ojibwa, in this area (Round Lake) at least, is one based on such minute linguistic details that early travellers and later residents would not have been able consistently to distinguish between the two groups (Jean Rogers 1963)" (Rogers 1963b:66). Nor, according to Rogers, can cultural variations be used to distinguish them.

The evidence presented would indicate that the population shifts in northern Ontario were by no means minimal. Regarding linguistic and cultural variations it remains to be shown that there were differences between the early historical Cree and Ojibwa who under similar historical and ecological conditions later came to resemble each other. What is the evidence?

During the 1760's, Alexander Henry reached Lake Winnipeg at the mouth of the Winnipeg River and came upon a large village of Cree. He commented:

Lake Winipegon is sometimes called the Lake of the Killistinons or Cristinaux. The dress and other exterior appearances of the Cristinaux are very distinguishable from those of the Chippeways and the Wood Indians[53].

Henry's observations are particularly relevant since he lived with the Ojibwa for a year (1763-64) and dressed like them (cf. Quimby 1962:220). Hence, during the middle of the eighteenth century despite extensive trade in European commodities including apparel, the Cree differed at least externally from the Ojibwa. There were differences in social organization as well. As previously noted, there is no evidence that the Cree possessed clans or totemic descent groups. Differences in social organization are explainable in terms of ecological and historical factors. The aboriginal Ojibwa who resided near their more sedentary linguistic cousins, the Potawatomi, developed patrilineal descent group organization. The more mobile Cree hunting bands to the north seem never to have stressed descent.

Although it is difficult to determine exactly when the cultural distinctiveness began to break down, there is strong evidence that by the early nineteenth century the process of convergence was well on the way. The Northwest Company trader, Duncan Cameron, writing on the Nipigon Country in 1804, made the following comment:

> This part of the Country has been peopled about one hundred and fifty years ago, partly from Lake Superior and partly from Hudson's Bay, as it would evidently appear from the languages of the Natives, which is a mixture of the Ojiboiay, or Chippeway as some call it, spoken at Lake Superior and the Cree or Masquigon spoken at Hudson's Bay.
>
> Every old man with whom I conversed, and from whom I made some enquiry on this subject, told me his father or grand father was from either of these two places, and that the reason they came so far back could be accounted for in no other way then in the following: Population was then on the increase both in Hudson's Bay and on the shores of Lake Superior, and as Indians, who are obliged to rove from place to place for a good hunting ground, are equally at home in any place where they can find their living, they took to the interior of the country where they found innumerable rivers and lakes, swarming with a vast quantity of fish, beaver and others. When one place was exhausted, they would retire farther and farther back till these two people, who are undoubtedly of the same origin . . . began to meet one another in the interior and to intermarry by which they at length became one people[54].

Not all the Cree retreated from the north shore of Lake Superior during the eighteenth century. For example, at Michipicoten, George Keith, the factor in 1829, was still able to identify the Cree: "The Natives of this District are a mixed race deriving their origin from the Maskigon Crees and Ojhibway Tribes"[55]; and a year later: "There does not exists a doubt that the majority derive their origin from the Ojhibeway or Saulteau Tribe, altho a number of them are decended from the Maskigon or Swampy Cree Tribe"[56]. Almost 70 years earlier when Alexander Henry visited Michipicoten he met a group of people he called "Gens de Terre" who were scattered throughout the area between Lake Superior and Hudson Bay. Henry stated that their language was "a mixture of those of its neighbours, the Ojibwa and Christinaux"[57]. Henry also called them Opimittish Ininiwac or Têtes de Boule or Wood Indians.

There is a good deal of evidence to support the view that there was a rather sharp distinction between the Cree and Ojibwa languages in the early contact period. For example, the Hudson's Bay trader, George Sutherland, located at Sturgeon Lake in 1780, remarked: "there is not a man on the Albany Establishment that is capable of trading with these Indians, as they differ far in their language from our Indians at hudson's bay"[58]. Aeneas McDonnell, the Northwest trader at Lac Seul in 1807, mentioned a band he thought were Mississaugas, "At least their language and manners much rememble each other and seem to be a mixture of the Sauteux and Maskigon" Cree[59]. Although it appears that the Cree and Ojibwa dialects had diverged during the prehistoric period so that mutual intelligibility had become difficult, enough similarity remained that in the marginal areas the two could "fuse" to produce a fully-blown intermediate dialect[60]. The statement by the fur trader, McDonnell, appears to support this view. The Hudson's Bay factor at Martin's Falls, George Barnston, also commented on the fusion of language and culture in marginal areas in 1839.

The Greater number of the families belong to that tribe of Sauteux denominated the Suckers—a Band of the Great Chippewa Divisions which appear to have pushed farthest to the northward at least in this quarter ... They are known at York Factory and Severn as Bungees, a name I imagine given to them from their use of the Sauteaux word Pungee—a little. To the northward they keep up an intercourse with the Severn Indians, to the eastward with those of Albany mixing and intermarrying which connections I may say have already produced a Half Cree, Half Sauteux

Breed affecting the Language and Character in no slight degree. On the southside again we have relationship with the pure Chippewa of Long Lake[61].

Barnston, then, has provided additional evidence of this fusion. He nevertheless seems to have been misinformed concerning the alleged "purity" of the Long Lake Indians. The Long Lake factor wrote concerning the Indians of that post, in 1833:

> They are a mixed race of Saulteauxs and Masquegongue Tribes. Their language is a mixture of both the latter tongues, but in many instances varies much, for a pure Soulteaux speaker requires to be for some time with the Indians of this Post before he can understand them perfectly[62].

Although the Ojibwa and Cree mingled at trading posts and interior lakes and formed marriage and trade alliances during the eighteenth and nineteenth centuries, there is considerable data to indicate that hostilities were also frequent. We have already mentioned the conflicts of the mid-eighteenth century when the Ojibwa, encouraged by the French, threatened the Cree who tried to reach the English posts. Captain W. Coats of the Hudson's Bay Company in commenting on the progress of the French couriers de bois during the 1740's in the area north of Lake Superior remarked concerning the Indians:

> some of the branches on the eastern side, and those to westward, of [Lake Superior] seem always to have been strangers to them, perhaps owing to the intestine warrs and divisions amongst those different tribes[63].

At Osnaburgh House in 1787, an Ojibwa family was murdered by a Cree from Fort Severn[64]. Such incidents are common in the Archival records dating to this period. However, skirmishes between Indians in the interior never existed on a tribal level; warfare involved families and extended kinship groups at most. Conflicts arose when two groups found themselves to be in the same area competing over local fur resources, or when drunk on trade rum at the posts. Whether the cause was intertribal animosity, the expansion of the fur trade westward, or game and fur depletions, the Cree were largely replaced by Ojibwa east of Lake Winnipeg by the 1770's. A picture of this expansion is presented by Donald Sutherland, the factor of Berens River post, in 1815:

> The Indians who inhabit this part of the country belong to the extensive class of Southward or Kristeneaux Indians ... it is probable that these tribes were formerly confined to the East side of Lake Winnipic, but from the diminution of animals, there appears to have been a general migration to the westward, one tribe displacing or rather driving back other tribes 'till at length a great part of the Indians once living on the east side of the Lake are now found to the westwards of it whilst the original inhabitants of the westward are driven still further into the interior[65].

The animosity among the Cree and Ojibwa continued into the nineteenth century. For example, in 1827, the Hudson's Bay factor at God's Lake—a post marginal to Cree and Ojibwa—commented on the relationship among the two tribes:

> would not the Indians of Oxford and Manitou Lake be fitted out from the same establishment. I am afraid not—they are not only distinct tribes but the Same Algonquins have but an indifferent opinion of the Swampy Crees of Oxford—while the latter possess an untolerable aversion to the hostile disposition of the Former which in my opinion is a pretty strong proof against an immediate union of these two tribes[66].

The above-mentioned Oxford was the Oxford House post located 120 miles northeast of Lake Winnipeg, while Manitou Lake was the God's Lake post 60 miles to the east of Oxford House and 300 miles northwest of Osnaburgh House.

In summary, there is evidence for both fusion and aggression among contiguous groups of Cree and Ojibwa who, despite animosities, were undergoing processes leading to cultural convergence in marginal areas. An indication of this convergence is the statement by Barnston that these Algonkians were half Chippewa-half Cree. Hence, it would be erroneous to categorize the contemporary Algonkians of such marginal trading centres as Ogoki (Martin's Falls), Round Lake, Big Trout Lake and God's Lake as either *Ojibwa* or *Cree*. The similar historical and ecological experiences of all interior Algonkians—whether of Cree or Ojibwa ancestry—has led to convergence in cultural type which has no doubt been augmented by borrowing in marginal regions. Rogers' term *Cree-Ojibwa* (1963b) seems most appropriate for marginal interior groups but for different reasons than he has indicated, i.e., that the overall similarity has always characterized contemporary interior Algonkians. As I have demonstrated on the basis of documentary evidence, the interior was not inhabited permanently by the Ojibwa until the 1730's. After 1770, when trading posts were established in the interior, the Algonkians who were trapping in the area, began to trade at these centres. The majority of them were Ojibwa.

Northern Ojibwa Culture during the Mid-Eighteenth Century

Ojibwa social and economic organization was definitely in a state of flux during the eighteenth century. As we have seen, groups of Ojibwa began residing permanently in the interior region north of Lake Superior by the late 1720's. The movement of French coureurs de bois laden with trade goods into the area lessened their need to linger nearer the posts to the southeast, although groups continued to travel to Michilimackinac until the 1760's. Charles McKenzie, in reporting the death of a very old woman (over 90) in 1845, gives evidence of this:

> The oldest woman in all this part of the Country died here this morning—She must have been very old indeed—She remembered being twice to "Mackna" When the Indians went yearly there to Trade their Furs—there being no Traders then on this side of Lake Superior[67].

Another attraction of the Sault Ste. Marie area was the fisheries. According to the explorer-trader, Alexander Henry, a skillful fisherman could catch 500 fish in two hours in the rapids of the St. Mary's River during the autumn run[68]. Nevertheless, the expanding fur trade and the lure of both Ojibwa and Cree to the wars with the Dakota in Minnesota were making trips back to the east less necessary and less practical. This warfare, as we have seen, was also preventing the Ojibwa from travelling to the Hudson's Bay Company posts. For example, Humphrey Marten of Fort Albany remarked in 1768

> The Principal cause of the decrease we firmly believe & hope will prove tempory, as all the Indians Declare that it is principally occation'd by very many of Our Leaders and their Young Men being at War, their Enemys are called Poets and Whychepo Indians whose Country they say abounds with Beaver, which they kill not, nor will suffer others to Kill, this with their own Country being greatly exhausted are the reasons they Give for going to War, they say they have got PoSseSsion of the Heart of the Enemys Country . . . [69]

The Poets and Whychepo were the Dakota and Assiniboin and the country referred to was the parkland belt of Minnesota and Manitoba.

Although there are few specific references to the subsistence practices of the emergent Northern Ojibwa, there was very likely a heavy emphasis on moose and caribou. No doubt Indians exploited a variety of other foods including fish, beaver and wild rice during the seasons when these foods were available. Whatever, food was relatively easy to acquire and was in such quantity that large bands of Ojibwa were able to maintain continual residence throughout the year. Food problems only arose when Indians made the long trip to Fort Albany, or when the men deserted the women and children to go to war.

The picture of Ojibwa social organization during the mid-eighteenth century is blurred by fragmentary reports of traders writing at a distance. The very dynamics of the situation, however, are reflected in these data. Although relatively few bands of Ojibwa came to reside on the Shield northwest of Lake Superior these were large in size. Since they often numbered over 80 persons, it might be suggested that they were in fact lineages.

There are several references to the size of Ojibwa bands. At Rainy Lake, Jonathan Carver, in 1767, reported "a considerable band of Chipeways" while to the east were several smaller ones[70]. Alexander Henry, in 1775, mentioned an encampment of fifty lodges at Rainy Lake[71] and another at Lake of the Woods composed of 100 persons. Another trader, John Long, in 1777, at Pays Plat on the north shore of Lake Superior traded with 150 Indians "most of them were of the Chippeway tribes; the rest were the nation of the Wasses"[72]. On his trip north of the Lake, he reported that near Lake Nipigon hunted about 300 Ojibwa[73] while at Sturgeon Lake lived the Musquash tribe[74]. While at his trading camp at Lac La Mort (just north of Lake Nipigon) a band of "eighty, men, women, and children" arrived in February to trade with "dried meats, oats, bears' grease, and eight packs of beaver"[75]. A short time later another "large band of Chippeways arrived"[76].

Although groups south of the Albany River drainage appear to have been large, those to the north and west toward Lake Winnipeg were considerably smaller. This was because groups near the east side of Lake Winnipeg had expanded into the area from the Border Lakes area via the south shore of Lake Superior. They differ in dialect from the Ojibwa to the east in the Albany and Severn River drainage areas. In 1777, George Sutherland of the Hudson's Bay Company was sent inland from Fort Albany to lure down the more distant bands. In travelling from Henley House to Lake Winnipeg he met few Indians but remarked that warfare had depopulated the country[77]. Somewhere near Cat Lake, he met a family of 27 (eight men, twelve women, and seven children) and a short distance further, perhaps around Lake Pekangikum since he gives the latitude as $52°26'$, he met another family of 31 (seven men, nine women and fifteen children). He wintered with a family of six just inland from Lake Winnipeg (which he reached at $52°31'$). Once winter set in, they met few Indians. On December 21, they met a family of seven, and on January 23, a family of fifteen. The small size of groups and low population density reflect the relatively late replacement of Cree by Ojibwa in this region rather than a poverty of resources. Between October 23 and May 22, the seven persons killed six moose, seven caribou, twenty-three beaver, and fifty-one lynx. All the fish consumed, amounting to thirty-one, were caught by Sutherland[78]. Although there was plenty of food for all, Sutherland complained that the Ojibwa gorged themselves after a kill until the meat was consumed after which they would have nothing to eat for several days. According to Sutherland:

> we are all obliged to Eat up what we get before we sleep let it be Ever so much according to the Indians mennar hang them—for I find my self now as bad with Eating too much as I was Leatly with Eatting nothing. Each of the Moose is Larger then any bullock I ever saw at Albany—for all That they will not Last us above 7 Days at farthest the way that they go to work. and if they ware to Live modrally yesterdays hunt might serve us two months . . . [79].

As reported by Duncan Cameron three decades later, the Ojibwa shifted camp every few days but never moved great distances. In May, 1778, Sutherland summed up his travels:

> I am sertain we Did not go one hundred and fifty miles niether the one or the other Durring the whole winter—for Ever since we Left our Canoes in the fall—we Generaly Traveled about 8 or 10 miles at a time that is when we repitcht[80].

On the day camp was to be moved, the men would set off early in the morning with their sleds which they would leave about eight or ten miles away. The women and children were left to take down the wigwams and pack the goods. The men, meanwhile, would spend the day hunting after which they would return to the new camping spot where the tents had already been put up again by the women. Although Sutherland spent his time hunting with the men, he was compelled to turn over the fur pelts he obtained to the Indians whom he otherwise feared would abandon him.

The picture presented by Sutherland suggests that the Northern Ojibwa had adjusted to a trapping and hunting economy.

330

After 1765, most Indians residing north of Lake Superior ceased making their summer treks to the southwest to fight the Dakota who by then were being pushed westward. Although large bands of 50 or more Ojibwa were reported south of the Albany River during the 1760's and '70's, it would seem that by the 1780's, these groups had segmented into smaller units of from 20 to 35 persons. This process of segmentation also was related to an evident population growth during the eighteenth century despite disease and warfare as mentioned by Duncan Cameron. Clan or lineage segments finding themselves in a vast region with bountiful resources grew in size and in the process segmented into more viable winter bands. Thus, it seems that the eight or ten groups that originally pushed north and west of Lake Superior during the 1720's and '30's had increased to perhaps thirty groups by the 1780's. Indeed, the Ojibwa population northwest of Lake Superior probably doubled during this fifty year span. As these groups came to more fully exploit the game resources, they became localized in certain regions—especially after interior posts were built during the 1770's and '80's. Segmentation, as we have seen, continued into the nineteenth century so that the descendants of the original migrant bands became scattered over a wide region. The few clan or lineage functions that had been present in the late eighteenth century had atrophied by the mid-nineteenth century except for totem exogamy and a rather weak concept of hereditary leadership within bands. In sum, the migration of Ojibwa northwest of Lake Superior along with the growing importance of the fur trade during the eighteenth century spelled the doom of the clan as a functionally viable form of social organization.

Recapitulation

The movement of Ojibwa has been traced first to the west along the shores of Lake Superior, thence into the interior at the expense of the Cree. Originally, the Ojibwa lived in a rather confined region near the upper Great Lakes. The fur trade and the attraction of trade goods led to a gradual dispersal, at first on a seasonal basis. It has been noted that complete expansion did not

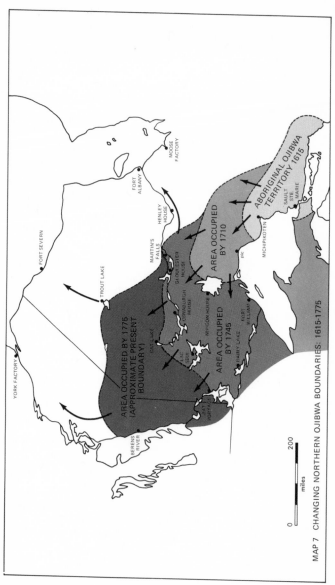

MAP 7 CHANGING NORTHERN OJIBWA BOUNDARIES: 1615-1775

ABORIGINAL OJIBWA TERRITORY 1615

AREA OCCUPIED BY 1710

AREA OCCUPIED BY 1745

AREA OCCUPIED BY 1775 (APPROXIMATE PRESENT BOUNDARY)

MOOSE FACTORY

FORT ALBANY

HENLEY HOUSE

MARTIN'S FALLS

GLOUCESTER HOUSE

OSNABURGH HOUSE

NIPIGON HOUSE

FORT WILLIAM

RAINY LAKE

LAC SEUL

CAT LAKE

FORT SEVERN

TROUT LAKE

YORK FACTORY

BERENS RIVER

RAT PORTAGE

SAULT STE. MARIE

MICHIPIKOTEN

PIC

0   200

miles

MAP 8 EARLY HISTORICAL MAP 1699

333

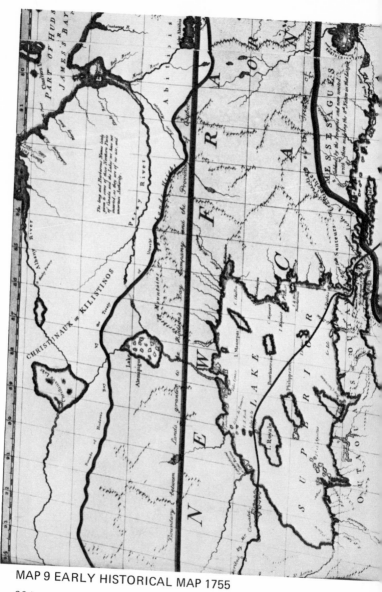

MAP 9 EARLY HISTORICAL MAP 1755

occur until competition over furs drew traders into the interior nearer to where the Indians were trapping, thus permitting the Indians to remain in the country throughout the year. The catalyst for the shift inland by French traders was, first, the depletion of furs in the area adjacent to Lake Superior, and second, the competition with well-stocked Hudson's Bay posts to the north. By the 1770's all the Indians throughout the north were being supplied by vast quantities of goods at the expense of the competing traders. The well-equipped Ojibwa who traded mainly with the French and later the Northwest Company were able to penetrate deep into territory formerly inhabited by Cree groups. Although skirmishes with the Cree were frequent in newly disputed fur regions, intermarriages and friendships developed resulting in a fusion of the two cultures in marginal regions at an early date. Ojibwa groups, supported by large game animals appear to have remained for a while large and cohesive. Finally late in the eighteenth century the Hudson's Bay Company established Osnaburgh House on Lake St. Joseph, which by that time was being frequented by Ojibwa hunting bands, as a counterpoise to the numerous Northwest traders in the region.

The occupation of the interior Boreal Forest region also had repercussions for social and economic organization. As the original groups adapted to the new fur trade conditions and ecology, both the overall population and the number of groups increased which in the process inhibited clan functions—especially economic and political ones.

Footnotes

1. Innis 1962:37.
2. Innis 1962:43-48.
3. Scull 1943:149ff., 193, 219.
4. Adams 1961:129.
5. Adams 1961:133.
6. Adams 1961:144.
7. Blair 1911 1:173-74.
8. Thwaites 1896-1901 18:229-31.
9. Blair 1911 1:174. cf. also NYCD 1853-87 9:160-61.
10. Begg 1894 1:150.
11. HBC Arch B239/a/1-3. Innis 1962:47-49.
12. Rich 1945 1:xlii.
13. Voorhis 1930:128.
14. Voorhis 1930:98.
15. Innis 1962:49.
16. Innis 1962:78.
17. HBC Arch B239/a/3.
18. HBC Arch B239/a/3.
19. HBC Arch B3/a/9.
20. HBC Arch B3/a/9.
21. HBC Arch B3/a/12.
22. HBC Arch B3/a/14.
23. HBC Arch B3/a/20.
24. Innis 1962:91.
25. NYCD 1853-87 9:1054.
26. NYCD 1853-87 9:1053-54.
27. HBC Arch B3/a/30.
28. HBC Arch B3/a/33.
29. HBC Arch B3/a/34.
30. HBC Arch B3/a/35.
31. Barrow 1852:41.
32. HBC Arch B86/a/1-7.
33. HBC Arch B3/a/38.

34. HBC Arch B3/a/57. For instance, in 1765, "Tinnewabano, Tabatakesaca and Eackekeshick" (the Crane?) traded at Fort Albany (HBC Arch B3/a/57). Again, in 1766, "Captain Nonosecash & Lieut. Tinnewabinos Brothers came in to take trust" (HBC Arch B3/a/59). No doubt the Crane was among them.

35. HBC Arch B3/a/57.

36. HBC Arch B3/a/57.

37. HBC Arch B3/a/59.

38. HBC Arch B86/a/13.

39. HBC Arch B3/a/60.

40. HBC Arch B3/a/60.

41. HBC Arch B198/a/4.

42. HBC Arch B198/a/12.

43. HBC Arch B198/a/10.

44. HBC Arch B198/a/17.

45. HBC Arch B78/a/3.

46. HBC Arch B211/a/1.

47. HBC Arch B211/a/1.

48. HBC Arch B211/a/1.

49. HBC Arch B78/a/7.

50. HBC Arch B3/b/20.

51. Williams 1969:204.

52. Williams 1969:191.

53. Henry 1901:246.

54. Masson 1969 2:241-42. The fur trader at Rainy Lake, Peter Grant, in 1804, made a similar remark:

> They [Ojibwa] assert as an undoubted fact that, formerly, the Sciews /Sioux/ possessed the greatest part of the country, but, in course of time, as population increased, they emigrated to the westward in search of subsistence, where finding a vast unihabited country, of milder climate and abundance of game, they remained and took possession of it, leaving behind only a few tribes, more attached to their native land. In this state they say their ancestors found the country when, for similar reasons, they emigrated from their ancient pos-

sessions to the eastward (Masson 1960 2:346).

55. HBC Arch B129/e/6.

56. HBC Arch B129/e/7.

57. Henry 1901:62.

58. HBC Arch B211/a/1.

59. Douglas 1929:37.

60. Both Drs. Gordon Day and George L. Trager have confirmed this possibility. Personal communication.

61. HBC Arch B123/a/14.

62. HBC Arch B117/e/5. Skinner (1911:11) states that the Indians "at English River Post spoke Ojibway, but they have been in contact with the Albany Cree until they have given up their old language for that tongue, and have lost their native culture." During the nineteenth century most of the English River Indians traded at Martin's Falls. Thus, Skinner and George Barnston are in mutual agreement.

63. Barrow 1852:41.

64. HBC Arch B155/a/1.

65. HBC Arch B16/e/1. See also Hallowell's remarks (1955:114-15). Skinner adds additional evidence (1911:11): "the Ojibway, who originally dwelt inland along the north shore of Lake Superior, have worked northward to the headwaters of the Attawapiscat River in pursuit of furs, since the advent of the Hudson's Bay Company, forming a northern wedge, as it were, projecting into Cree domains."

66. HBC Arch B283/e/1.

67. HBC Arch B107/a/24.

68. Henry 1901:62

69. HBC Arch A/1/3.

70. Carver 1956:115.

71. Henry 1901:240.

72. Long 1791:45.

73. Long 1791:51.

74. Long 1791:62.

75. Long 1791:85.

76. Long 1791:86.

77. HBC Arch B3/a/73.

78. HBC Arch B3/a/73.
79. HBC Arch B3/a/73.
80. HBC Arch B3/a/73.

Chapter Ten
Summary and Conclusions

This study has attempted to reconstruct the cultural history of the Northern Ojibwa in the upper Albany River drainage area.

In sum, it is impossible to view Ojibwa socioeconomics organization as something that was static or unchanging. It is true that many customs and beliefs continued, and still exist even today, from earlier times. It may be suggested that these cultural elements are less strongly tied to subsistence and economic activities (cf. Steward 1955: 37). These are what have given Ojibwa culture its continuity through time. By viewing Ojibwa culture from this perspective, it is fruitful, as I hope this study has demonstrated, to consider such factors as kinship, settlement pattern, land use and demography in relation "to one another and to the environment" (Steward 1955: 42). As Steward has so aptly put it:

> Land use by means of a given technology permits a certain population density. The clustering of this population will depend partly upon where resources occur and upon transportation devices. The composition of their size, of the nature of subsistence activities, and of cultural-historical factors. The ownership of land or resources will reflect subsistence activities on the one hand and the composition of the group on the other (1955: 42).

We would only add to this that the interaction among these variables must also be viewed historically. It is impossible to understand the exact relationships between environment, social organization and economy except through their dynamics. When the dynamics of cultural ecological processes are to be understood over an extended period of time, the ethnohistorical method is the best one. Guesswork and memory ethnography, while helpful, are insufficient. Indeed, historical reconstructions based on these latter techniques have led to faulty conclusions and much sterile debate which, in many instances, could have been avoided.

This study, which has combined both archival and field data, has, I believe, provided answers to some problems with which scholars have grappled. I have offered a number of tentative answers to others. Before summarizing Northern Ojibwa culture history, I now turn to the crucial issue of Ojibwa clans.

The issue is indeed crucial since this study began with the assumption that late prehistoric and early contact Ojibwa social organization was founded upon a patrilineal clan basis, and that changes after contact would reflect the organizational shifts which would be expected given alterations in trade and ecological conditions. The historical data relating to the entire historical period conforms to and supports this basic assumption. A more detailed discussion of Ojibwa clans will give additional meaning to the data presented in this study.

The Question of Ojibwa Clans

Prior to 1960, scholars suggested that Ojibwa totem groups were either borrowed from peoples to the south, or were indigenous but non-elaborated because of the harsh conditions prohibiting their development. One scholar, even suggested that they emerged within the historical period. Without a knowledge of the history of the Ojibwa in relation to changing conditions of contact and ecology, there was no way to resolve this question of totem group origin. Beginning in 1960, Harold Hickerson, having carefully evaluated the historical literature pertaining to the early contact Ojibwa and their descendants who migrated to Wisconsin and Minnesota, concluded that the proto-historic Ojibwa were "divided into autonomous territorial patrilineal totemic groups" (1962a: 88). These corporate patrilineal descent groups, as Hickerson argued, resided near clan-possessed fisheries which permitted settled village life for extended periods of the year and the functioning of the clan system. The different clan-villages were linked through ties of marriage and ceremonial activities (The Feast of the Dead). This argument has met with skepticism because data were not available to "prove" that the animal-named groups of the seventeenth century were indeed clans. The richness of the supporting resource base, especially the fisheries, has also been questioned. While there is no need to re-hash Hickerson's data since they are presented fully elsewhere (Hickerson 1962a: 76-86; 1970: 42-50), several points need re-stressing.

The first relates to the geographical location of the early historic Ojibwa. At contact they were confined to the area immediately north of Lake Huron and eastern Lake Superior. This region is not within the true Boreal Forest zone and has a richer and more varied resource base than the former. Indeed, the early historic literature indicates that food was quite plentiful, as does the archaeological data. A site on Bois Blanc Island in the Straits of Mackinac dating to late prehistoric times produced great quantities of fish bones (McPherron 1967: 281-84). Fish combined with other foods allowed Indians to reside continually at the site from early spring until late autumn. There is also evidence of the Feast of the Dead with one ossuary containing thirty-five individuals (1967: 289-93). Thus, the ecological basis necessary to the maintenance of a clan organization was present.

The early contact Ojibwa lived in an area adjacent to other Central Great Lakes Algonkians to the south where there is reasonably good evidence for clan villages. For instance, according to the explorer-trader, Nicolas Perrot[1] writing about the late seventeenth-century Algonkians (including Ojibwa):

> Accordingly, some of the savages derive their origin from a bear, others from a moose, and others similarly from various kinds of animals ... You will hear them say that their villages each bear the name of the animal which has given its people their being—as that of the crane, or the bear or other animals.

The Ojibwa were the most northerly of the Central Great Lakes Algonkians to possess a patrilineal clan system.

Finally, there is the additional source of information from more recent ethnographic reports. Most of the present-day totem designations appear to coincide remarkably closely to the names given to early contact groupings. The actual tracing of names and groups, however, is rendered difficult by gaps in this historical record. This is further complicated by the emergence of sub-groups of parent clans and even new totem groups as autonomous entities within the historic period concomitant with geographical expansion and perhaps contact with Siouan-speakers. Yet infer-ences based upon the totality of evidence permit historical re-construction. In such reconstruction, it is necessary to examine alternative possibilities. Since the literature is nebulous, it is possible to assume that early contact groups had some sort of bilateral organization. Indeed, many of the behavioral norms associated with bilateral organization such as cross-cousin mar-riage also exist in societies with descent groups. Descent, of course, is not one thing but many, and involves a variety of forms of belief and behaviour. The basic attributes, however, are descent from a common mythical ancestor and exogamy, pro-ducing a corporate group of consanguinal same-sexed kin and their spouses and children. Such a group regulates marriage alli-ances and resource exploitation, distribution and ownership. Compared to bilateral forms, descent group organization is rela-tively inflexible, and thus can only function (apart from regulat-ing marriage) given a relatively stable, productive and localized resource base. With respect to the Ojibwa, studies in the past tended to stress a poverty of resources, social atomism and so forth—conditions which, while true for some groups during the nineteenth century, bore no relation to the situation some two centuries earlier when the environment was considerably richer. If it is argued that Ojibwa groups at contact were not based on unilineal descent, there exists the difficulty of explaining the emergence of patrilineal exogamous totemism. In contrast, we argue here that it is more parsimonious to view aboriginal Ojibwa social structure as being founded upon a corporate clan-village organization. This model is able to account for changes within the historical period as well as present forms. It is also based upon the

343

totality of evidence: environmental, locational, historical, ethnographic, and linguistic. Those who wish to dispute the model must do so in terms of essentially the same source materials.

All that remains is a summary of Northern Ojibwa culture history.

Outline of Northern Ojibwa Culture History

Hickerson (1962a: 88-89) has distinguished seven eras of culture history for the Southwestern Chippewa, four of which occur prior to 1780. I believe that it is possible to discern eight eras for the Northern Ojibwa, the first two being identical with those described by Hickerson. The latter six eras are relevant only to the Northern Ojibwa. The eras are as follows:

1. Late Prehistoric-Earliest Contact Era (? to 1660's).
2. The Era of Population Concentration (1640 to 1680).
3. The Era of Dispersal and Relocation (1680 to 1730).
4. The Era of Permanent Interior Settlement (1730 to 1780).
5. The Era of Large Game Hunting Under Conditions of Competition Among Traders (1780 to 1821).
6. The Era of Small Game Hunting and Dependency Upon the Trading Post (1821 to 1890).
7. The Era of Early Government Influence (1890 to 1845).
8. The Present Era of Village Ojibwa (1945 to 1967).

During the time of earliest contacts with Europeans, the Ojibwa lived semi-permanently in a series of villages which formed patrilineal clan groups along or near the north shore of Georgian Bay and at the east end of Lake Superior. These groups were united through ties of kinship and a common culture and language.

The influx of European trade goods and Europeans themselves during the mid-seventeenth century produced a centripetal movement of Ojibwa and other Algonkian-speakers who were eager to exchange these new wares. For awhile social life was actually intensified and the Feast of the Dead ceremony grew in significance and fostered economic and social alliances among many Algonkian groups. Nevertheless, Ojibwa clans did not surrender their identity since they continued to hunt and fish in their traditional territories much as in the prehistoric period. However, with the expansion of the fur trade west of the Great Lakes during the 1680's, some Ojibwa began pushing westward both along the north and south shores of Lake Superior in an attempt to retain their lucrative middleman position with tribes to the west. South of Lake Superior, Ojibwa congregated in large villages which tended to weaken the functional significance of the clan organization. The Midewiwin ceremony replaced the Feast of the Dead as the primary integrating ceremonial during the early eighteenth century. To the north of Lake Superior, the Ojibwa gradually replaced the westward moving Cree as bands of Ojibwa began to permanently occupy the rich as yet unexploited fur regions of the Shield. These groups appear to have been lineages, clans or clan remnants which continued to retain their separate identities. By the 1770's, these groups had expanded to their present-day parameters. Thoroughly immersed in the competitive fur trade, their subsistence was now based both on trapping and hunting big game.

As Northwest Company and Hudson's Bay Company trading posts were located in the newly occupied area, the Northern Ojibwa became attached to certain posts even though they were able to take advantage of the competition among the traders. Hunting groups gradually became stabilized in certain areas. By 1800, these winter hunting groups had dwindled to about thirty persons although there were more of them. The population density seems to have doubled between 1740 and 1810. After 1810 the Northern Ojibwa began experiencing hardships as the large game and beaver supply declined, because of overhunting. When trade competition ended, Indians became totally dependent upon the Hudson's Bay Company for many basic requirements in a drastically altered environment.

Despite extreme conditions of stress and deprivation, the Ojibwa were able to survive by eking out a meagre existence on hare and fish, and by developing more individualistic patterns of proprietorship. The largest effective, socio-economic unit was the co-residential group which at Osnaburgh House numbered about thirty persons. There were about six such groups within 100 miles of the post during the mid-nineteenth century. Although this

345

group somewhat resembled the hunting band or "lineage" of the eighteenth century, it had become strictly bilateral as a result of environmental and trade pressures. As clan mates became dispersed, clan functions, apart from regulating marriage, had totally atrophied by the middle of the last century. Even co-residential group members could not remain together permanently since family units had to disperse for trapping purposes and to maximize subsistence requirements during the harsh winter months. Despite the hardships the Ojibwa population actually increased during the nineteenth century.

By the early twentieth century, the Northern Ojibwa were experiencing new changes. Missionaries had already converted (albeit superficially) many people, while treaties with the Canadian government guaranteed new rights and privileges. Ojibwa economy was strengthened by improved trade conditions and by new items including store foods which became more readily available. Toward the end of the last century, moose and caribou again penetrated Indian hunting territories.

Contact with the outside world has accelerated, especially since World War II, so that today the Ojibwa live semi-permanently in a number of lakeside villages scattered throughout northwestern Ontario. The focus of this study has been on those people who came to form the Osnaburgh House village.

The present economy of the Northern Ojibwa is significantly different than it was only three decades ago. Families now live in government-built welfare houses, while a great variety of new material items such as radios, outboard motors, and automobiles are on hand. Almost half the total band income is derived from unearned sources while trapping is growing increasingly residual.

Socially, the Osnaburgh House community can be character-ized as an acephalous endo-deme. The money economy is strengthening the independence of the household at the expense of the hunting group. The very arrangement of the village into streets has led to the residential separation of co-residential group members. The kinship terminology is presently in a state of flux and will likely emerge as a lineal system within a generation—a type congruent with the increased self-sufficiency of the house-hold and the widening of social relationships within a growing permanent village. Today community endogamy is preferred,

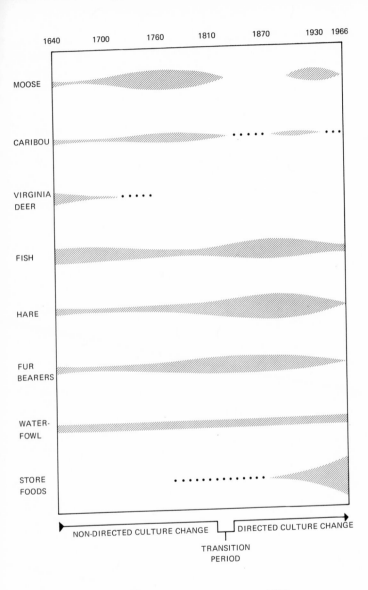

Figure 5: Changes in Food Consumption Patterns: 1640-1966.

while sanctions against intra-clan marriage have weakened. Distant cross-cousin marriages still occur and usually involve people belonging to separate bush settlements. Nominal leadership is vested in the band chief and eight councillors who act mainly as liaison officers with Euro-Canadian agencies.

Although the rate of culture change over the past 350 years has varied, modifications have been cumulative. For most of the historic period change has been inaugurated largely through the influence of a single type of contact agent, the fur trader. As Dunning has noted at Pekangikum (1959a: 208), the effective contact until recently has been economic and indirect: i.e., "acculturation at a distance". Yet, there have been major shifts in the social and economic arrangements of Ojibwa culture. For example there have been major changes in food consumption patterns (see Figure 5). In 1640, fish was probably the most important food. By the late eighteenth century, this was replaced by cervines until their decimation when Indians turned to hare and fish. Since 1945, most food has come from the store.

According to Spicer's model (1961:520-21) of directed and non-directed culture change, the Osnaburgh House Ojibwa moved into the orbit of directed change about 1821 (within a variant of five years either way). After this time they were subject to the sanctions of traders and their superiors which the Indians could no longer ignore, since they had become utterly dependent upon the trading post. Too many indigenous materials had been replaced by Euro-Canadian ones, and the economy of a clan-based type society had been destroyed with 1) the move into the interior away from bountilful territorially-based fisheries, and with 2) the decimation of large game animals at a later date.

Northern Ojibwa winter co-residential groups of the nineteenth century were intermediate in size between the household units of more southerly Ojibwa groups, as for example at Emo (Landis 1937), and the regional or composite bands of the western Subarctic (Slobodin 1962; Helm 1965). All three types were bilateral, flexible and highly mobile. The type and quantity of food was an important factor in determining the size of hunting groups throughout the Subarctic. The exact nature of their social organization, however, is another question. Ojibwa social groups of the nineteenth century were the product of multiple historical and ecological factors. A more flexible social organization had developed which was congruent with the altered environment and economic involvement in the fur trade. I would suggest that similar patterns of adjustment may have occurred elsewhere in the Subarctic and that the organization of Athabaskan groups described for the mid-nineteenth century merely represent a stage midway in the acculturative process. There is even some evidence to suggest that peoples of the western Subarctic were characterized by a former matrilineal organization (Osgood 1936, 1937; Slobodin 1962; McKennan 1965), although more research is needed to unravel specific acculturative stages there. Whatever may have occurred, there seems to be little doubt that the breakdown of unilineal systems can occur quickly and under a variety of conditions: migration, environmental change, involvement in the European market system, decimation by disease or warfare, and numerous other changes.

There is some variation in cultural and linguistic patterning within the area presently occupied by the Northern Ojibwa. The communities located in the western portion of the region nearer Lake Winnipeg speak a different dialect from those of the east. Included within the western area are the Indians of Berens River, Pekangikum, Deer Lake, and Sandy Lake. The Indians at those places are frequently referred to as Saulteaux and often refer to themselves by this name. To the east at Cat Lake, Osnaburgh House, Nipigon House, Fort Hope, and Landsdowne House the Indians are called Ojibwa. Does this distinction between Indians in the eastern and western portions mean that the groups were derived from a different origin place, and/or followed different migration routes into various parts of the interior? Or have separate dialects arisen merely through isolation of Indian groups in an extensive Boreal Forest region? The evidence suggests that the Ojibwa of the western portion on and contiguous to the Lake Winnipeg drainage represented the van of Saulteaux expansion south of Lake Superior which spilled north and west of the lake toward the end of the seventeenth century. Significantly the Midewiwin ceremony which was a product of dynamic sociopolitical factors associated with tribal village life within the historic period is more highly developed among groups nearer Lake Winnipeg and Lake of the Woods.[2] Indeed, Jenness (1935:

69) states that the Midewiwin was not practiced by the Parry Island Ojibwa until it was introduced there by the Potawatomi from Michigan during the early nineteenth century. In contrast, it would seem that the Indians in the eastern portion, which includes the Osnaburgh area, arrived in the region having first skirted the north shore of Lake Superior. Needless to say, much more research in all branches of anthropology needs to be undertaken to provide more detailed information.

At the recent end of the historic continuum, Northern Ojibwa social organization will within a generation, approximate that of Euro-Canadians in the surrounding areas as English becomes the dominant language, and as households grow more self-sufficient. At present the community is beginning to resemble one similar to that of "poor Whites" (cf. James 1961). Yet a community identity remains and there are many features that distinguish it as "Indian" and "Ojibwa", although these are not necessarily aboriginal. Economic success in the future is dependent upon employment opportunities and adequate training, neither of which exist today. As long as welfare plays such a vital role in maintaining the community, it will obstruct the development of leadership and village cohesion. Within the past decade, chronic drinking, juvenile delinquency and a general apathetic attitude have prevailed concomitant with the rise of welfare. There is no question that at present the people could not survive without substantial economic aid. However, training and employment in occupations near home are needed badly. Perhaps community co-operatives would alleviate some problems. Some communities in the north have established villate co-operatives (cf. Vallee 1966: 43) which have become a thriving success in overcoming social, psychological and economic attitudes of dependency on Euro-Canadians. The Northern Ojibwa are in a difficult period of transition and their future is still uncertain.

Footnotes

1. Blair 1911 1:37.

2. Edward S. Rogers states that the Indians of Sandy Lake have a ceremony which resembles the Midewiwin in several respects. Sandy Lake is one of the most northerly Ojibwa communities and some of the Indians there call themselves Saulteaux. Personal communication.

Table 43: Changes in Social Organization: 1640-1966

	?-1660's	±1640-1680	1680-1730	1730-1780	1780-1821	1821-1890	1890-1945	1945-1966
UNIT OF SOCIAL ORGANIZATION	Corporate patrilineal descent groups (clans)	Multi-clan settlements in summer. Winter settlements much the same as before	Clan segments	Clan segments fragmenting with a trend toward bilaterality	Clan-named lineage segments with a continuing trend toward bilaterality	Bilateral winter settlements from which families radiate out to exploit game and furs	Bilateral winter settlements at base camps from which families and extended families exploit game and furs	Merging of winter groups into a semi-permanent village and breakdown of co-residential families; residential group autonomy
SIZE OF GROUPS	100-300	1,000+ (in summer)	40-300	20-80	20-35 with splintering into family units at end of era in winter	25-30 In summer and when food is available. Family trapping groups in winter	20-25 In summer some extended groups gain separate co-residential group status	230± (Osnaburgh village in 1966)
POPULATION TRENDS IN THE OSNABURGH	—	—	?	150? (1770)	200 (1810)	±200 (1820's) ±300 (1890's)	300 (1890's) 450 (1940's)	800± (Total band population 1966— includes Cat Lake people)

Bibliography

Adams, Arthur T., ed.

1961 *The Explorations of Pierre Esprit Radisson.* From the original manuscript in the Bodleian Library and the British Museum. Minneapolis. Ross and Haines Inc.

Baker, Jocelyn.

1936 "Ojibwa of the Lake of the Woods." *Canadian Geographical Journal.* January pp. 47-54.

Barnouw, Victor.

1950 "Acculturation and Personality among the Wisconsin Chippewa." *American Anthropological Association Memoir,* 72.

1961 "Chippewa Social Atomism." *American Anthropologist* 63:1006-13.

1963 *Culture and Personality.* Illinois: The Dorsey Press.

Barrow, John, ed.

1852 *The Geography of Hudson's Bay: Being the Remarks of Captain W. Coats, in many Voyages to that Locality, between the years 1727 and 1751.* New York: Burt Franklin, published for The Hakluyt Society.

Bartleman, Factor J.

1929 "Superior-Huron Trading Posts." *The Beaver.* Outfit 260, June. pp. 218-19.

Begg, Alexander.

1894 *History of the North-West.* 3 vols. Toronto: Hunter, Rose & Co.

Bell, Robert.

1870 *Report of Progress from 1866 to 1869: On Lake Superior and Nipigon.* Ottawa: Geological Survey of Canada.

1887 Report on an Exploration of Portions of the At-ta-wa-pish-kat and Albany Rivers, Lonely Lake to James Bay. Geological and Natural History Survey of Canada, Annual Report, Part G, Geological and Natural History Survey of Canada, Ottawa.

Bishop, Charles A.

1970 "The Emergence of Hunting Territories Among the Northern Ojibwa." *Ethnology* 9:1-15.

1972 "Demography, Ecology and Trade Among the Northern Ojibwa and Swampy Cree." *Western Canadian Journal of Anthropology,* 3:58-71.

Bishop, Charles A., and Ray, Arthur J.
1972 "The Early Culture History of Northern Ontario and Manitoba: Some Problems of Interpretation." Paper presented at the American Anthropological Association Meetings: Toronto.

Black, Mary B.
1972 "Evidence for Linguistic Diversity in a Small Northern Ojibwa Community." Paper presented at the American Anthropological Association Meetings: Toronto.

Blair, E. H., trans. and ed.
1911 *The Indian Tribes of the Upper Mississippi Valley and the Region of the Great Lakes.* 2 vols. Cleveland: Arthur H. Clark Co.

Bloomfield, Leonard.
1957 *Eastern Ojibwa: Grammatical Sketch, Texts, and Word List.* Ann Arbor: University of Michigan Press.

Bohannan, Paul
1963 *Social Anthropology.* New York: Holt, Rinehart & Winston Inc.

Bovey, Martin K.
1936 "Albany River Adventure." *The Beaver.* Outfit 266, March, pp. 40-45.

Burgesse, J. A.
1945 "Property Concepts of the Lac-St.-Jean Montagnais." *Primitive Man* 18:1-25.

Burpee, L. J., ed.
1927 "Journals and Letters of Pierre Gaultier de Varennes de la Vérendrye and his Sons." Toronto: The Champlain Society.

Callender, Charles
1962 "Social Organization of the Central Algonkian Indians." *Milwaukee Public Museum Publications in Anthropology:* Number 7.

Cameron, Duncan
1890 "The Nipigon Country." *In* L. R. Masson, *Les Bourgeois de la Compagnie du Nord-Ouest.* 2:231-65. Quebec: Impr. Générale A. Coté et Compagnie.

Camsell, Charles
1906 "Country around the Headwaters of the Severn River." *Geological Survey of Canada, Summary Report on the Operations of the Geological Survey for the Year 1904.* Annual Report, Vol. XVL, A, Ottawa.

Canada
1858 Report of the Special Commission Appointed on the 8th of September 1856 to Investigate Indian Affairs in Canada. Toronto.

1905 Indian Treaties and Surrenders from 1680 to 1890. 2 vols. Ottawa.

1906 *Sessional Paper No. 27, Annual Report of the Department of Indian Affairs for the Year Ended June 30, 1906.* Ottawa.

1910 *Sessional Paper No. 27, Annual Report of the Department of Indian Affairs for the Year Ended March 31, 1910.* Ottawa.

1912 *Indian Treaties and Surrenders.* Vol. 3. Ottawa.

1913 Schedule of Indian Reserves in the Dominion: Supplement to the Annual Report of the Department of Indian Affairs for the Year Ended March 31, 1913. Ottawa.

1929 Annual Report of the Department of Indian Affairs for the Year Ended March 31, 1929. Ottawa.

1931 Annual Report of the Department of Indian Affairs for the Year Ended March 31, 1930. Ottawa.

1957 The James Bay Treaty No. 9 (Made in 1905) and Adhesions Made in 1929 and 1930. Ottawa.

n.d.   Letters: Pertaining to the Osnaburgh House and Cat Lake Indians. Indian Agency Headquarters, Sioux Lookout. Ontario.

n.d.   Letters: Survey of Osnaburgh House Indians Reserves. Ottawa: Public Archives of Canada.

n.d.   Letters: Treaty No. 9 Negotiations and Adhesions. Ottawa: Public Archives of Canada.

Canada, Department of Citizenship and Immigration
1959 Census of Indians in Canada. Ottawa.

1964 Big Trout Lake: A Pilot Study of an Indian Community in Relation to Its Resource Base. Report 1G-3. Ottawa.

Canada, Department of the Interior
1926 Northwestern Ontario Natural Resources and Development. Ottawa.

Canada, Department of Transport
1956 Climatic Summaries for Selected Meteorological Stations in Canada. Vol. III Frost Data. Toronto.

Canadian Mining Journal
1931 Pickle Lake Report. 52:455.

1935 Discovering a Mine: The Diary of John MacFarlane, Joint Discoverer with H. H. Howell, on September Tenth, in the Year 1928, of the Pickle Crow Gold Mine in Northwestern Ontario. 56:562-66.

Carruthers, Janet
1952 "Land of the Ojibway." *The Beaver.* Outfit 282. March pp. 42-46.

Carver, Jonathan
1956 *Travels Through the Interior Parts of North America in the Years 1766, 1767, and 1768.* Minneapolis: Ross & Haines, Inc.

Collins, W. H.
1906 On Surveys along the National Transcontinental Railway Location between Lake Nipigon and Lac Seul. Sessional Paper No. 26. Summary Report of the Geological Survey Department of Canada for the Calendar Year 1906. Ottawa.

Cooper, John N.
1939 "Is the Algonquian Family Hunting Ground System Pre-Columbian?" *American Anthropologist* 41:66-90.

1944 "The Shaking Tent Rite Among Plains and Forest Algonquians." *Primitive Man* 17:60-67.

Cross, E. C.
1937 "The Mammals of the Quetico Provincial Park of Ontario." *Journal of Mammals* 18:12-13.

Crouse, Nellis M.
1956 *La Verendrye: Fur Trader and Explorer.* Ithaca: Cornell University Press.

Dailey, Robert C.
1968 "The Role of Alcohol Among North American Indian Tribes as Reported in the Jesuit Relations". *Anthropologica*, 9:45-59.

Davidson, D. S.
1928 "Family Hunting Territories of the Waswanipi Indians." *Indian Notes*, Museum of the American Indian. Hehe Foundation. New York 5:42-59.

DeBlois, A. D., ed.
1967 "Contributions to Anthropology: Linguistics I." *National Museum of Canada Bulletin 214.* Ottawa.

Delanglez, Jean
1948 *Life and Voyages of Louis Jolliet (1945-1700).* Chicago: Institute of Jesuit History.

Dewdney, Selwyn and Kidd, Kenneth
1967 *Indian Rock Paintings of the Great Lakes.* Toronto: University of Toronto Press.

Douglas, R.
1929 *Nipigon to Winnipeg: A Canoe Voyage through Western Ontario by Edward Umfreville in 1784.* Ottawa: Commercial Printing.

Driver, Harold E.
1961 *Indians of North America.* Chicago: University of Chicago Press.

Dunning, Robert W.
1959a *Social and Economic Change among the Northern Ojibwa.* Toronto: University of Toronto Press.

1959b "Rules of Residence and Ecology among the Northern Ojibwa." *American Anthropologist* 61:806-16.

1959c "Ethnic Relations and the Marginal Man in Canada." *Human Organization* 18:117-22.

Eggan, Fred
1955 *Social Anthropologoy of North American Tribes.* Chicago: University of Chicago Press.

1966 *The American Indian: Perspectives for the Study of Social Change.* Chicago: Aldine Publishing Company.

Eiseley, Loren
1947 "Land Tenure in the Northeast: A note on the History of a Concept." *American Anthropologist* 49:680-81.

Emerson, J. N.
1959 "The Puckasaw Pit Culture: A Pilot Study." *Ontario History,* Vol. 51, No. 1. Toronto.

Evans, Edward G.
1961 "Prehistoric Blackduck—Historic Assiniboine: A reassessment". *Plains Anthropologist,* 6:271-275.

Feit, Harvey A.
1969 *Mistassini Hunters of the Boreal Forest: Ecosystem Dynamics and Multiple Subsistence Patterns.* M. A. thesis, McGill University.

Fenton, William N.
1949 "Collecting Materials for a Political History of the Six Nations." *Proceedings of the American Philosophical Society,* 93:233-38.

Flannery, Regina
1938 "Cross-Cousin Marriage among the Cree and Montagnais of James Bay." *Primitive Man* 11:28-33.

1939 "The Shaking-Tent Rite among the Montagnais of James Bay." *Primitive Man* 12:11-16.

Friedl, E.
1956 "Persistence in Chippewa Culture and Personality." *American Anthropologist* 58:814-25.

Garigue, Philip
1957 "The Social Organization of the Montagnais-Naskapi." *Anthropologica* No. 4 pp. 107-35.

Gibb, June
1961 We're Bushed and We Love It. Chatelaine, March.

Godsell, Philip H.
1932 "The Ojibwa Indian." *Canadian Geographical Journal.* January, pp. 51-66.

1934 *Arctic Trader.* New York: G. P. Putnam's Sons.

1952 "The Pleasant Speaking People." *Canadian Cattleman.* December pp. 18-27.

Grant, Peter
1890 "The Sauteux Indians." *In L. R. Masson, Les Bourgeois de la Compagnie du Nord-Ouest* 2:305-66. Quebec: Impr. Générale A. Coté et Compagnie.

Greenberg, Adolph M., and Kovac, Karen D.
1972 "Acculturation and Cultural Ecology: A Reconsideration of Ojibwa Ethnography." Paper presented at the Central States Anthropological Society Meetings, Cleveland.

Hall, Frank
1960 "Medicine on the Rocks—The Strange Tale of the Ojibwa Mosaics." *In The Bison.* Official Publication of the Manitoba Government Employees. June, pp. 14-16.

Hallowell, A. I.
1928 Was Cross-Cousin Marriage Practised by the North-Central Algonkian? Proceedings, Twenty-third International Congress of Americanists.

1934 "Some Empirical Aspects of Northern Saulteaux Religion." *American Anthropologist* 36:389-404.

1936 "The Passing of the Midewiwin in the Lake Winnipeg Region." *American Anthropologist* 38:32-51.

1937 Cross-Cousin Marriage in the Lake Winnipeg Area. in *Publications of the Philadelphia Antrhopological Society,* ed. D. S. Davidson, Vol. I pp. 95-110. Philadelphia.

1938 "The Incidence, Character and Decline of Polygamy among the Lake Winnipeg Cree and Saulteaux." *American Anthropologist* 40:235-56.

1942 The Role of Conjuring in Seaulteaux Society. Philadelphia.

1949 "The Size of Algonkian Hunting Territories: A Function of Ecological Adjustment." *American Anthropologist* 51:35-45.

1955 *Culture and Experience.* Philadelphia: University of Pennsylvania Press.

Hamilton, Raphael N., S.J.
1970 *Marquette's Explorations: The Narratives Reexamined.* Madison: The University of Wisconsin Press.

Harmon, Daniel
1929 Daniel Harmon's Journal 1907-08. In R. Douglas. *Nipigon to Winnipeg: A Canoe Voyage through Western Ontario by Edward Umfreville in 1784.* Ottawa: Commercial Printing.

HBC (Hudson's Bay Company)
n.d. Hudson's Bay Company Archives. Public Archives of Canada. (microfilm) Ottawa, and manuscripts, London.

Heizer, Robert

1955 "Primitive Man as an Ecologic Factor." *Kroeber Anthropological Society Papers* 13:1-31. Berkeley.

Helm, June

1961 "The Lynx Point People: The Dynamics of a Northern Athapaskan Band." *National Museum of Canada Bulletin 176.* Ottawa.

1965 "Bilaterality in the Socio-Territorial Organization of the Arctic Drainage Dene." *Ethnology* 4:361-85.

Helm, June, and Leacock, Eleanor Burke

1971 "The Hunting Tribes of Subarctic Canada" pp. 343-74 *in North American Indians in Historical Perspective.* eds. Eleanor Burke Leacock and Nancy Oestreich Lurie. New York: Random House.

Henry, Alexander

1901 *Travels and Adventures in Canada and the Indian Territories between the Years 1760 and 1776 by Alexander Henry.* ed. James Bain, Toronto.

Hickerson, Harold

1956 "The Genesis of a Trading Post Band: The Pembina Chippewa." *Ethnohistory* 3:289-343.

1960 "The Feast of the Dead among the Seventeenth Century Algonkians of the Upper Great Lakes." *American Anthropologist* 62:81-107.

1962a "The Southwestern Chippewa: An Ethnohistorical Study." *American Anthropological Association Memoir 92.*

1962b "Notes on the Post-Contact Origin of the Midewiwin." *Ethnohistory* 9:404-23.

1963 "The Sociohistorical Significance of Two Chippewa Ceremonials." *American Anthropologist* 65:67-85.

1965a "The Virginia Deer and Intertribal Buffer Zones in the Upper Mississippi Valley." *In* Man, Culture, and Animals: The Role of Animals in Human Ecological Adjustments. eds. Anthony Leeds and Andrew Vayda. Publication No. 78, *American Association for the Advancement of Science;* Washington, D.C.

1965b "William T. Boutwell of the American Board and the Pillager Chippewa: The History of a Failure." *Ethnohistory* 12:1-29.

1966 "The Genesis of Bilaterality among Two Divisions of Chippewa." *American Anthropologist* 68:1-26.

1967a "Land Tenure of the Rainy Lake Chippewa at the Beginning of the 19th Century." *Smithsonian Contributions to Anthropology* 2:37-63.

1967b Some Implications of the Theory of Particularity, or 'Atomism', of Northern Algonkians." *Current Anthropology.* 8:313-343.

1967c "A Note of Inquiry on Hockett's Reconstruction of PCA." *American Anthropologist* 69:362-63.

1970 The Chippewa and Their Neighbors: A *Study in Ethnohistory.* New York: Holt, Rinehart and Winston, Inc.

1971 "The Chippewa of the Upper Great Lakes: A Study in Socio-political Change" pp. 169-199 *in* North American Indians in Historical Perspective. eds. Eleanor Burke Leacock and Nancy Oestreich Lurie. New York: Random House.

Hickerson, Harold, ed.
1959 "Journal of Charles Jean Baptiste Chaboillez, 1797-1798." *Ethnohistory* 6:265-316; 363-427.

Hlady, Walter M.
1964 "Indian Migrations in Manitoba and the West". *Historical and Scientific Society of Manitoba.* Series III, No. 17, pp. 24-53, Winnipeg.

1970 "Manitoba—the Northern Woodlands" pp. 93-121 *in* Ten Thousand Years: Archaeology in Manitoba ed. Walter M. Hlady. *Manitoba Archaeological Society.* Altona, Manitoba: D. W. Friesen & Sons Ltd.

Hlady, Walter M., ed.
1970 "Ten Thousand Years: Archaeology in Manitoba." *Manitoba Archaeological Society.* Altona, Manitoba: D.W. Friesen & Sons Ltd.

Hockett, Charles
1942 "The Position of Potawatomi in Central Algonkian." Papers of the Michigan Academy of Science, Arts and Letters 28:537-42.

1964 "The Proto-Central Algonquian Kinship System." *In Explorations in Cultural Anthropology: Essays in Honor of George Peter Murdock.* Ward H. Goodenough, ed. pp. 239-68. New York: McGraw-Hill.

Hodge, F. W., ed.
1907-10 Handbook of the American Indians. 2 parts Bureau of American Ethnology Bulletin 30. Washington.

Honigmann, John J.
1962 Foodways in a Muskeg Community. Northern Co-ordination and Research Centre, Dept. of Northern Affairs and National Resources, NCRC-61-1, Ottawa.

Howard, James H.
1965 The Plains Ojibwa or Bungi, Hunters and Warriors of the Northern Prairies, with Special Reference to the Turtle Mountain Band. Anthropological Papers, Dakota Museum, No. I.

Hudson, Charles
1966 "Folk History and Ethnohistory." *Ethnohistory* 13:52-70.

Hunt, George T.
1960 *The Wars of the Iroquois: A Study in Intertribal Relations.* Madison: the University of Wisconsin Press.

Innis, H. A.
1962 *The Fur Trade in Canada.* New Haven: Yale University Press.

James, Bernard
1954 "Some Critical Observations Concerning Analysis of Chippewa 'Atomism' and Chippewa Personality." *American Anthropologist* 56:283-86.

1961 "Socio-psychological Dimensions of Ojibwa Acculturation." *American Anthropologist* 63:721-46.

1970 "Continuity and Emergence in Indian Poverty Culture" *Current Anthropology.* 11:435-52.

Jenness, Diamond
1935 The Ojibwa Indians of Parry Island, Their Social and Religious Life. National Museum of Canada Bulletin 78. Ottawa.

1963 The Indians of Canada (6th edition). National Museum of Canada Bulletin 65. Ottawa.

Jones, Culver
1936 Gentlemen Adventurers. The Toronto Star Weekly. February 22.

Keating, W. H., ed.
1824 Narrative of an Expedition to the Source of St. Peter's River, Lake Winnepeek, Lake of the Woods etc. Preformed in the Year 1823, by Order of the Hon. J. C. Calhoun, Secretary of War Under the Command of S. H. Long. U.S.T.E. 2 vols. London.

Kennedy, M. S., ed.
1961 *The Assiniboines: From the Accounts of the Old Ones Told to First Boy* (James Larpenteur Long). Norman: University of Oklahoma Press.

Kenyon, Walter
1960 Rainy River Project—1959. Ontario History 42 Toronto.

1961 The Swan Lake Site. Royal Ontario Museum, Art and Archaeology Division, Occasional Paper 3. Toronto.

Kinietz, W. V.
1965 *The Indians of the Western Great Lakes 1615-1760.* Ann Arbor: The University of Michigan Press.

Knight, Rolf
1965 "A Re-examination of Hunting, Trapping, and Territoriality Among the Northeastern Algonkian Indians" *in* Man, Culture and Animals: The Role of Animals in Human Ecological Adjustments. eds. Anthony Leeds and Andrew Vayda. Publication No. 78, American Association for the Advancement of Science: Washington, D.C.

Kohl, J. G.
1860 *Kitchi-Gami: Wanderings around Lake Superior.* London: Chapman and Hall.

Kroeber, Alfred L.
1939 "Cultural and Natural Areas of Native North America." *University of California Publications in Anthropology and Ethnology.* 38.

Landes, Ruth
1937 "Ojibwa Sociology." Columbia University Contributions to Anthropology, Vol. 29. New York, Columbia University Press.
1961 "The Ojibwa of Canada." *in Cooperation and Competition among Primitive Peoples.* Margaret Mead, ed. Boston: Beacon Press.

Lane, K. S.
1952 "The Montagnais Indians 1600-1640." *Kroeber Anthropological Society Papers* 7:1-62. Berkeley.

Leacock, Eleanor
1954 "The Montagnais 'Hunting Territory' and the Fur Trade." *American Anthropological Association Memoir 78.*
1955 "Matrilocality in a Simple Hunting Economy." *Southwestern Journal of Anthropology* 11:31-47.

Leacock, Eleanor Burke, and Lurie, Nancy Oestreich eds.
1971 *North American Indians in Historical Perspective.* New York: Random House.

LeBeurdais, D. M.
1957 *Metals and Men: The Story of Canadian Mining.* Toronto: McClelland and Stewart Ltd.

Levin, M. G., and Potapov, L. P., eds.
1964 *The Peoples of Siberia.* (translated by S. P. Dunn). Chicago: University of Chicago Press.

Levi-Strauss, Claude
1963 *Structural Anthropology.* New York: Basic Books, Inc.

Lips, Julius E.
1937 "Public Opinion and Mutual Assistance Among the Montagnais-Naskapi." *American Anthropologist* 39:222-28.
1947 "Naskapi Law." Transactions of the American Philosophical Society. Philadelphia 37:379-492.

Long, John

1791 Voyages and Travels of an Indian Interpreter and Trader. London.

Low, A. P.

1887 Preliminary Report on an Exploration of Country between Lake Winnipeg and Hudson Bay. Geological and Natural History Survey of Canada. Annual Report. Part F. Ottawa.

Mackenzie, Charles

1890 "The Mississouri Indians: A Narrative of Four Trading Expeditions to the Mississouri 1804, 1805, 1806." *In* L. R. Masson, *Les Bourgeois de la Compagnie du Nord-Ouest* 1:315-93, Quebec: Impr. Générale A. Coté et Compagnie.

Mackenzie, John D.

1935 Letter to the Hudson's Bay Company, Winnipeg, dated September 7, 1935. Hudson's Bay Company Library, Winnipeg.

MacNeish, Richard S.

1958 An Introduction to the Archaeology of Southeast Manitoba. National Museum of Canada Bulletin 157. Ottawa.

Mandelbaum, David G.

1940 "The Plains Cree." *Anthropological Papers of the American Museum of Natural History* 37:155-316. New York.

Manitoba Free Press

1910 "A Plea for the Indian." October 26. Manitoba.

Masson, L. R., ed.

1890 *Les Bourgeois de la Compagnie du Nord-Ouest, Récits de Voyages, Lettres et Rapports Inédits Relatifs au Nord-Ouest Canadien.* 2 vols. Quebec: Impr. Générale A. Coté et Compagnie.

Mayer-Oakes, William J. ed.

1970 *Life, Land and Water.* Winnipeg: University of Manitoba Press.

McFeat, T. F. S.

1962 Museum Ethnology and the Algonkian Project. Anthropological Papers 2, National Museum of Canada, Ottawa.

McGee, John

1961 *Cultural Stability and Change among the Montagnais Indians of the Lake Melville Region of Labrador.* Washington, D.C.: The Catholic University of America Press.

McInnis, William

1905 The Upper Parts of the Winisk and Attawapiskat Rivers. Geological Survey of Canada. Annual Reports, Vol. XVI, Ottawa.

1906 The Winisk River, Keewatin District. Geological Survey of Canada. Annual Report 1902-03. Vol. XV. Ottawa.

1909 Report on a Part of the Northwest Territories of Canada Drained by the Winisk and Upper Attawapiskat Rivers. Department of Mines, Geological Survey Branch, Ottawa.

McKee, Russell
1966 *Great Lakes Country.* New York: T. Y. Crowell Company.

McKennan, Robert
1965 The Chandalar Kutchin. Arctic Institute of North America. Technical Paper No. 17.

McPherron, Alan
1967 "The Juntunen Site and the Late Woodland Prehistory of the Upper Great Lakes Area," *Anthropological Paper No. 30,* Ann Arbor: Museum of Anthropology, University of Michigan.

Michelson, Truman
1935 "Phonetic Shifts in Algonquian Languages." *Int. Journal of American Linguistics* 8:131-71.

Morgan, Lewis H.
1870 "Systems of Consanguinity and Affinity of the Human Family." *Smithsonian Contributions to Knowledge,* XVIII.

Murdock, George Peter
1949 *Social Structure* New York: The MacMillan Company.

1965 "Algonkian Social Organization." *In Context and Meaning in Cultural Anthropology.* ed. Melford Spiro pp. 24-35. New York: The Free Press.

Murphy, Robert F.
1967 Cultural Change. *In* Biennial Review of Anthropology. eds. Bernard J. Siegel and Alan R. Beals, pp. 1-34. Stanford, California: Stanford University Press.

Murphy, R. F., and Steward, J. H.
1956 "Tappers and Trappers: Parallel Process in Acculturation." *Economic Development and Cultural Change* 4:335-355. Chicago.

NYCD (New York Colonial Documents)
1853-57 Documents Relating to the Colonial History of New York. 15 Vols. Albany.

Oldmixen, John
1741 *The British Empire in America.* 2 Vols. London.

O'Meara, Walter
1966 *The Grand Portage.* Toronto: Bantom.

Ontario
1879 North-Western Ontario: Its Boundaries, Resources and Communication. Prepared under Instruction from the Ontario Gov't. Toronto.

Ontario: Department of Crown Lands
1901 Report of the Survey and Exploration of Northern Ontario by H. B. Proudfoot, James Robertson, Daniel McPhee, and I. E. Davison. Ontario.

Ontario: Department of Lands and Forests
1949-66 Sioux Lookout District Annual Fish and Wildlife Management Reports.

1965-66 Summary of the Ontario Regulation which Apply to Trapping and Fur-Dealing.

Osgood, Cornelius
1936 "Contributions to the Ethnography of the Kutchin." *Yale University Publications in Anthropology.* No. 16 New Haven.

Owen, Roger C., Deetz, James J. F., and Fisher, Anthony D. eds.
1967 *The North American Indians: A Sourcebook.* New York: The MacMillan Company.

Patterson, E. Palmer
1972 *The Canadian Indian: A History Since 1500.* Don Mills: Collier-Macmillan Canada, Ltd.

Perrot, Nicolas
1911 "Memoir on the Manners, Customs, and Religion of the Savages of North America," *In* E. H. Blair trans and ed., *The Indian Tribes of the Upper Mississippi Valley and the Region of the Great Lakes* 1:31-272. Cleveland: Arthur H. Clark Co.

Peterson, Randolph L.
1955 *North American Moose.* Toronto: University of Toronto Press.

1957 "Changes in the Mammalian Fauna of Ontario." *In Changes in the Fauna of Ontario* ed., by F. A. Urquhart pp. 43-58. Toronto: Royal Ontario Museum.

Phillips, Paul C.
1961 *The Fur Trade.* 2 vols. Norman: University of Oklahoma Press.

Quimby, George I.
1952 "The Archaeology of the Upper Great Lakes Area." *In Archaeology of the Eastern United States,* ed., J. B. Griffin. Chicago: University of Chicago Press.

1960 *Indian Life in the Upper Great Lakes 11,000 B.C. to A.D. 1800.* Chicago: The University of Chicago Press.

1962 "A Year with a Chippewa Family, 1763-1764." *Ethnohistory* 9:217-39.

1966 *Indian Cultures and European Trade Goods.* Madison: The University of Wisconsin Press.

Ray, Arthur J.
1971 "Indian Exploitation of the Forest-Grassland Transition Zone in Western Canada, 1650-1860: A Geographical View of Two Centuries of Change." Ph.D. Dissertation, University of Wisconsin.

1972 "Indian Adaptations to the Forest-Grassland Boundary of Manitoba and Saskatchewan, 1650-1821: Some Implications for Interregional Migration". *Canadian Geographer* 16:103-118.

Rich, E. E.
1961 *Hudson's Bay Company 1670-1870*. 3 vols. New York: The MacMillan Company.

1967 *The Fur Trade and the Northwest to 1857*. Toronto: McClelland and Stewart Ltd.

Rich, E. E., ed.
1942 *Minutes of the Hudson's Bay Company 1671-1674* Toronto: The Publications of the Champlain Society.

1945 *Minutes of the Hudson's Bay Company 1679-1684, First Part 1679-1682*. Toronto: Publications of the Champlain Society.

1946 *Minutes of the Hudson's Bay Company, Second Part 1682-1684*. Toronto: The Publications of the Champlain Society.

1949 Isham's Observations and Notes: 1743-1749. Toronto: Publications of the Champlain Society.

Riddlough, Norman
1962 "Treaty Time at Lac Seul." *The Beaver*. Outfit 292 Summer pp. 10-13.

Rogers, Edward S.
1962 "The Round Lake Ojibwa." Ocass. Paper 5, Art and Archaeology. Division, Royal Ontario Museum, Toronto: University of Toronto.

1963a The Hunting Group—Hunting Territory Complex among the Mistassini Indians. National Museum of Canada Bulletin 195, Ottawa.

1963b "Changing Settlement Patterns of the Cree-Ojibwa of Northern Ontario." *Southwestern Journal of Anthropology* 19:64-88.

1964a The Eskimo and Indian in the Quebec-Labrador Peninsula. Le Nouveau-Quebec. Contribution a l'etude de L'occupation humaine. Ecole Pratique des Haute Etudes Sorbonne, Sixieme Section: Sciences Economiques et Socials. Biblioteque Archtique et Anartique, 2.

1964b "The Fur Trade, the Government and the Central Canadian Indian." *Arctic Anthropology* 2:37-40.

1966a Subsistence Areas of the Cree-Ojibwa of the Eastern Sub-arctic: A Preliminary Study. National Museum of Canada Bulletin 204, Contributions to Anthropology 1963-64, Pt. II. Ottawa.

1966b A Cursory Examination of the Fur Returns from Three Indian Bands of Northern Ontario." Department of Lands and Forests, Ontario.

1967 "The Material Culture of the Mistassini." National Museum of Canada Bulletin 218, Ottawa.

1972 "Ojibwa Fisheries in Northwestern Ontario. Ontario: Commercial Fish and Fur Branch Division of Fish and Wildlife, Ministry of Natural Resources.

Rogers, Edward S. and James G. E. Smith
1973 "Cultural Ecology of the Shield Sub-Arctic" IX International Congress of Anthropological and Ethnological Sciences, Chicago.

Rogers, Jean H.
1963 "Survey of Round Lake Ojibwa Phonology and Morphology." *National Museum of Canada Bulletin 194, Contributions to Anthropology, 1961-62.* Pt. II. Ottawa.

Rowe, R. C.
1934 "The District of Patricia." in *Canadian Mining Journal* 55:470-74.

Ryder, R. A., Scott, N. B., and Crossman, E. J.
1964 "Fishes of Northern Ontario North of the Albany River." Contribution #60, Royal Ontario Museum, Toronto: University of Toronto.

Sahlins, Marshall D.
1962 *Moala: Culture and Nature on a Fijian Island.* Ann Arbor: The University of Michigan Press.
1965 "On the Sociology of Primitive Exchange." in *The Relevance of Models for Social Anthropology,* ed., Michael Banton, Frederick A. Praeger, pp. 139-236. Tavistock: London.

Sandoz, Mari
1964 *The Beaver Men.* New York: Hasting House Publishers.

Scull, G. D., ed.
1943 *Voyages of Peter Esprit Radisson, Being an Account of His Travels and Experiences among the North American Indians, from 1652 to 1684.* New York: Peter Smith.

Service, Elman R.
1962 *Primitive Social Organization, An Evolutionary Perspective.* New York: Random House.
1963 *Profiles in Ethnology.* New York: Harper and Row.

Siebert, Frank T.
1967 "The Original Home of the Proto-Algonquian People." in *Contributions to Anthropology: Linguistics I.* ed., D. DeBlois. pp. 13-47. National Museum of Canada Bulletin 214. Ottawa.

Skinner, Alanson
1911 "Notes on the Eastern Cree and Northern Saulteaux." *Anthropological Papers of the American Museum of Natural History*, Vol. 9, Part 1, New York.

1914 "Political Organization, Cults, and Ceremonies of the Plains-Ojibway and Plains-Cree Indians". *Anthropological Papers of the American Museum of National History.* Vol. II, Part 6, pp. 476-541.

Slobodin, Richard
1962 "Band Organization of the Peel River Kutchin." *National Museum of Canada Bulletin 179.* Ottawa.

Snow, Dean R.
1968 "Wabanaki 'Family Hunting Territories' ". *American Anthropologist* 70:1143-51.

Speck, Frank
1915 "The Family Hunting Band as the Basis of Algonkian Social Organization." *American Anthropologist*, 17:289-305.

1918 "Kinship Terms and the Family Band among the Northeastern Algonkian." *American Anthropologist*, 20:143-61.

1923 "Mistassini Hunting Territories in the Labrador Peninsula." *American Anthropologist*, 25:452-71.

1928 Land Ownership among Hunting Peoples in Primitive America and the World's Marginal Area. Atti del XXXII Congresse Internaz. *Deigi Americanisti*, Rome, 1926 pp. 323-332.

1931 "Montagnais-Naskapi Bands and Early Eskimo Distributions in the Labrador Peninsula." *American Anthropologist*, 33:557-600.

Speck, Frank, and Eiseley, Loren C.
1939 "The Significance of the Hunting Territory Systems of the Algonkian in Social Theory." *American Anthropologist*, 41:269-80.

1942 *Montagnais-Naskapi Bands and Family Hunting Districts of the Central and Southern Labrador Peninsula.* Proceedings of the American Philosophical Society 85:215-42.

Spicer, Edward H., ed.
1961 *Perspectives in American Indian Culture Change.* Chicago: The University of Chicago Press.

Steinbring, John
1965 "An Anthropologist Takes a Look at Ojibwa Culture in Manitoba." February 6, Winnipeg Free Press.

Steward, Julian
1942 "The Direct Historical Approach to Archaeology." *American Antiquity*, 7:337-43.
1955 *Theory of Culture Change*. Urbana: University of Illinois Press.

Stock, George
1965 "Historian Outlines Early Struggle, Re-Lives Nipissing's Trading Empire." October 16, Sudbury Star.

Strong, W. D.
1929 "Cross-Cousin Marriage and the Culture of the Northeastern Algonkian." *American Anthropologist*, 31:277-88.

Sturtevant, William C.
1966 "Anthropology, History, and Ethnohistory," *Ethnohistory*, 13:1-51.

Tanner, Adrain
1971 "Sickness and Ideology Among the New Osnaburgh Indians". Unpublished Research Report II.

Taylor, Garth J.
1972 "Northern Ojibwa Communities of the Contact-Traditional Period," *Anthropologica*, 14:19-30.

Taylor, S. A.
1950 Letter to the Hudson's Bay Company, Winnipeg. Hudson's Bay Company Library, Winnipeg.
1965 "Fort Hope Post of Fifty Years Ago," *Moccasin Telegraph*, Winter pp. 40-41.
n.d. Letter to the Hudson's Bay Company, Winnipeg, Entitled: *Reminiscences of Lac Seul Post 1906*. Hudson's Bay Company Library, Winnipeg.

Thwaites, R. G., ed.
1896-1901 *The Jesuit Relations and Allied Documents: Travels and Explorations of the Jesuit Missionaries in New France, 1610-1791*. 73 vols. Cleveland: The Burrows Brothers Company.

Townsley, B. F.
1935 *Mine-Finders: The History and Romance of Canadian Mineral Discoveries*. Toronto: Saturday Night Press.

Turner, L. M.
1894 *Ethnology of the Ungava District, Hudson Bay Territory*, Bureau of American Ethnology 11th Annual Report, 1889-90.

Tyrrell, J. B. ed.
1916 *David Thompson's Narrative of His Explorations in Western America 1784-1812*. Toronto: The Champlain Society.

1931 Documents Relating to the Early History of Hudson Bay. Toronto: The Champlain Society.

Vallee, Frank
1966 "The Co-operative Movement in the North," in *People of Light and Dark*, ed., M. van Steensel pp. 43-48. Department of Indian Affairs and Northern Development. Ottawa.

Van Stone, James W.
1963 "Changing Patterns of Indian Trapping in the Canadian Sub-arctic," *Arctic*, 16:158-74.

1965 "The Changing Culture of the Snowdrift Chipewyan," *National Museum of Canada Bulletin 209*, Ottawa.

Vickers, Chris
1948a "The Historical Approach and the Headwaters Lake Aspect", *Plains Archaeological Conference Newsletter*, Vol. 1, No. 3, pp.8-11.

1948b "Cultural Affinity in the Minnesota-Manitoba Region", *Minnesota Archaeologist*, 14:38-41.

Voegelin, C. F., and E. W.
1946 "Linguistic Considerations in Northeastern North America. *in* Man in Northeastern North America," *Foundation of Archaeology*, Vol. 3.

Voorhis, Ernest
1930 *Historic Forts and Trading Posts of the French Regime and of the English Fur Trading Companies*. Dept. of the Interior, National Resources Intelligence Branch, Ottawa.

Warren, William W.
1957 *History of the Ojibway Nation*. Minneapolis: Ross and Haines.

White, Leslie A., ed.
1959 *Lewis Henry Morgan: The Indian Journals: 1958-62*. Ann Arbor: The University of Michigan Press.

White, Theodore E.
1953 "A Method of Calculating the Dietary Percentage of Various Food Animals Utilized by Aboriginal Peoples," *American Antiquity*, 18:396-98.

Wilford, Lloyd A.
1955 "A Revised Classification of the Prehistoric Cultures of Minnesota," *American Antiquity*, 21:130-42.

Willey, Gordon R.
1966 *An Introduction to American Archaeology. Vol 1. North and Middle America*. New Jersey: Prentice-Hall.

Williams, Glyndwr, ed.
1969 "Andrew Graham's Observations on Hudson's Bay 1767-91," *The Hudson's Bay Record Society*, Vol. 27. London.

Wilson, A. W. G.

1903 *A Geological Reconnaissance about the Head-Waters of the Albany River.* Summary Report on the Operations of the Geological Survey for the Calendar Year 1902. Annual Report, Vol. 15, Geological Survey of Canada, Ottawa.

1909 *Report on a Traverse through the Southern Part of the North West Territories from Lac Seul to Cat Lake in 1902.* Department of Mines: Geological Survey Branch, Ottawa.

1910 *Geology of the Nipigon Basin, Ontario.* Department of Mines: Geological Survey Branch, Ottawa.

Wright, David

n.d. *Reminiscences of Twenty-One Years Trading for the Hudson's Bay Company.* Department of Lands and Forests, Ontario.

Wright, James V.

1963 "An Archaeological Survey along the North Shore of Lake Superior," *Anthropological Papers, National Museum of Canada,* No. 3, Ottawa.

1966 "The Pic River Site," *National Museum of Canada Bulletin 206,* Contributions to Anthropology 1963-64, Part L, Ottawa.

1968a "The Application of the Direct Historical Approach to the Iroquois and the Ojibwa," *Ethnohistory,* 15:96-111.

1968b "Cree Culture History in the Southern Indian Lake Region," *National Museum of Canada Bulletin 232,* Contributions to Anthropology VII: Archaeology. Ottawa.

1968c "The Boreal Forest" *in Science, History and Hudson Bay,* Dept. of Energy, Mines and Resources. Ottawa.

1972 *Ontario Prehistory: An Eleven-Thousand-Year Archaeological Outline.* Ottawa, National Museums of Canada, National Museum of Man.

Appendix
Nicol Finlayson's Account of the Osnaburgh House Indians Presented in His Annual Report: 1828-29

Those of the Southward of the Post live pretty well in the winter now rabbits are increasing in their lands. Crow and his two sons live at or near Moose Lake. Moose and son on the same quarter never starving as they live among rabbits—they hunt pretty well except the last who is superannuated, and a good many beaver skins are got there—Bull Head likewise hunted on this quarter, did not starve made an excellent hunt tho he did not hunt the whole winter (see journal March 31).

Big blood and Soung wewatun son of the late Matwass hunt generally between Osnaburgh and Sturgeon Lake for the first part of the year and to the Nwd of this after the middle of the winter, never starve much are good hunters but the first is a proud conceited Indian and not good to please. they pay a debt of from 80 to 90 skins each—their eldest brother Puquauyae hunts generally in the vicinity of Osnaburgh starved has a large family and is a good hunter when his gods favour him is an easy Indian and good natured, hunts from 70 to 80 skins

Big Eyes and Darion, sons likewise of Mataiash hunt between the post and the Snake portage half way to Martins Falls this man is a good hunter and not hard to please, the other is but indifferent, he went to Lac Nipigon last summer got advances from the Gentleman in charge of there to amount of about 30 skins—he came to me short after with not a say of the debt upon him and of course gave him advances to amount of his last years hunt not knowing his being at any other post. his father-in-law noticed him to go there and he likewise is an OH Indian but the Indian Darion paid me his debt and I believe it was the whole amount of his hunt.

Two other sons of Mataiash, Injick and Swamplake generally hunt together with the Heads, 1 of whose wives is their Mother, are but two young lads, tho both have wives and children; hunt from 45 to 50 skins each—the last mentioned went to Martins Falls last fall and starved consequently did not hunt much. he was enticed by his wives Relations

Heads—are two good Indans and hunters their lands are pretty well stocked with Martins, beaver and Otter; the youngest is generally ailing—they hunt from about 60 to 90 fine skins and they generally come in but twice in a twelve month.

Loons—Muskass and Whisky brother—are two lazy Rascals especially the last and a notorious liar—I would not give these Indians an inch of Cloth for they have such large familys that were they to get advances to the amount of 150 skins each, it would not be an assian (sp?) to each . . . the first has a son who hunts from 15 to 20 the other has two who hunt from 20 to 30 skins—these Indians are loons by tribe and by nature

Cranes—Hookima, Pucequan, Macdonald's son and Okimaka generally go together are pretty good hunters except Mcdlds son— they were nigh the Big Fall last year in search of dear but killed none till they returned to their own lands when they were more successful . . . all these Indians paid their debts and traded a little —Trader, his 1st & 2nd Son, Shabwash, Sheweykeesheek & son, another band of Cranes who go together till they are separated by starvation, the first is an old man who hunts about 35 skins his 1st son from 35 to 40, his 2nd from 50 to 60 skins, the other, Shabwash is a sly dog and no good hunter. Sheweykeesheek is an old man, was a good hunter but had the misfortune to lose one of his hands by the accidental discharge of his gun. he still pays a debt of about 30 skins—has a son—a fine lad that hunts from 35 to 40 skins—drinks no Rum—Little Englishman, Econite, Old man and Friday another band of the Cranes who hunted pretty well last winter except the last—these Indians range over a large tract of land and are pretty comfortable now that they catch fish and rabbits. have lost a good deal of their former pride for they have learned that an Indian clothed in rabbit skins in the winter can live as comfortable as he who is clothed in cloth. these Indians come only in twice a year and never without their debts—there is no trouble with them—Shabwash and Unasash I have not seen— they were ashamed to come in as they wanted a few Skins of their debts—

Cat Lake Indians—Cotton shirts, a fine set of Indians the wicked paid their debts and traded a considerable quantity of furs—the 3 sons of the old man paid 56 each and they traded 130 skins among them, Bears Breast, Handy & sons paid likewise their debts—they always want a man or two at Cat Lake with supplies for them, but I do not think it would pay the expence of keeping people there, for am certain they hunted as much now as when the Post was established if not more.

Mackimy or Tabbitoway and his 7 sons did not hunt much in the winter, they formerly took their advances at Cat Lake but since the post was abandoned hunt nigher Osnaburgh—they gener- ally lived on dear but since the decrease of these animals, they don't come up to their former excertions—they think it beneath the dignity of an Indian to live on fish and rabbits and I to enable them to support this dignity sent them away with a very cold *What chere*—they said they starved yet confided they left stages of hung fish to be eaten by Crows—Young Mackemy—brother to the Elder—a noted Liar tho not a bad hunter when he likes—has a thriving family and is full of the habits of his Relations—Had these Indians exerted themselves like the rest of the Cat Lake Indians, the trade would be equally good with last years. the Loon, also did not come near their last year hunts—however as it is I hope it will be found in value to the last—

Hawk, this Indian took advances from Mr. Slater in 1825 and he went in 1826 to Nipigon and traded his whole hunt there, he frequented that place since but arrived last spring at Osnaburgh and paid his debt and that only—says that he will not go there again—the Gentleman in charge there (Nipigon) wishes to charge the amount of their advances to Albany when he could not Keep the Indian.

The materials in the Appendix were taken from the Osnaburgh House post journals dating to the spring of 1829 (HBC Arch B155/a/39).

Schedule of the Indian Population at Osnaburgh Trading Post
Taken in the Spring 1828

Name	Tribe	No. of Hunting Indians	No. of Women	No. of Male Children	No. of Female Children	Orphan taken within family	Widows	Total
Old Man	Crane	1	1					2
Econite	Crane	2	1	3	1	2		8
Trader	Crane	3	1		3	1		6
1st son	Crane	4	2	2				5
2nd son	Crane	5	1	1				3
Bull Head		6	2	1	2			6
Shewey Keeshick	Crane	7	2	1	2	2		8
1st son	Crane	8						1
Little Englishman	Crane	9	2	2	8			13
Macdonald's son	Crane	10						1
Pucequan	Crane	11	1		1			3
Hookima	Crane	12	1	1	1	1		5
stepson	Crane	13						1
Big Eyes	Crane	14	2	2	1	1		7
Shabwash	Crane	15	1	2				4
Unagush (a boy)		16						1
Orkeeneekee		17	1	1	3	2		8
stepson		18						1
Friday	Pelican	19	1		1			3
Pelican (brother to above)	Pelican	20	1	1		3		6
Ijuk	Deer	21	1	1	1			4
Swamp Lake	Deer	22	1	1	1	1		5
Darion	Deer	23	2	3				6
Big Blood	Deer	24	2	2				5
Saury wewatum	Deer	25	1	2	1		1	6
Puquauyae	Deer	26	1	8	1			11
Moose		27	2					3
Son		28						1

Name	Tribe	No. of Hunting Indians	No. of Women	No. of Male Children	No. of Female Children	Orphan taken within family	Widows	Total
Muskass	Loon	29	2	4	3		1	11
1st son	Loon	30						1
2nd son	Loon	31						1
Whisky	Loon	32	3	11	9			24
1st son	Loon	33						1
Old Head		34	1	3	1			6
Young Head		35	2	1	1			5
Young Mackemy or Louat	Moose	36	3	4	5	1		14
Old Mackemy	Moose	37	2	2	2			7
1st son	Moose	38	1	1	3			6
2nd son	Moose	39	1	1	1			4
3rd son	Moose	40	1	1				3
4th son	Moose	41	1	1	1			4
5th son	Moose	42	2		1			4
6th son (a boy)	Moose	43						1
Handy	Moose	44	1	4	4			10
Flint	(gone to Lac Seul)	45	1	1	1			4
Bears Breast		46	1	1	4			7
Stepson		47	2		1			4
Hawk		48	1		3			5
Crow		49	2		2	1		6
1st son		50	2	1		1		5
2nd son		51	1					2
Cotton Shirt (superannuated)		52	1					2
1st son		53	3	2	4			10
2nd son		54	3	1	1			6
3rd son		55	3		2	1		7
			70	73	76	17	2	293

375

Woman with fish prepared for drying

Beaver pelts being stretched

Woman setting
a trap for mink

Some ladies of
Osnaburgh House

377

Man with a
conjuring drum

Old style
dwelling still
in use in 1965

Members of an Osnaburgh House hunting group

Children in school, December 1965

1751A